THE SAGA OF TANYA THE EVIL

07

ORIGINAL STORY: Carlo Zen

ART: Chika Tojo

CHARACTER DESIGN: Shinobu Shinotsuki

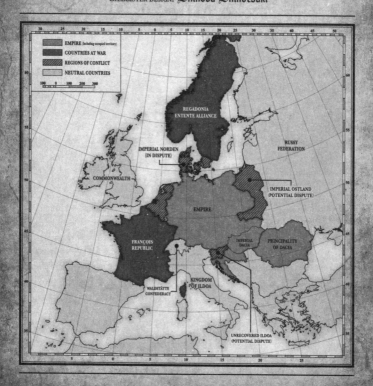

EMPIRE (Including occupied territory)
COUNTRIES AT WAR
REGIONS OF CONFLICT
NEUTRAL COUNTRIES
100 0 100 200 300
REGADONIA ENTENTE ALLIANCE
RUSSY FEDERATION
IMPERIAL NORDEN (IN DISPUTE)
COMMONWEALTH
IMPERIAL OSTLAND (POTENTIAL DISPUTE)
EMPIRE
FRANÇOIS REPUBLIC
IMPERIAL DACIA
PRINCIPALITY OF DACIA
KINGDOM OF ILDOA
WALDSTÄTTE CONFEDERACY
UNRECOVERED ILDOA (POTENTIAL DISPUTE)

Die Zeiten

DIE KRIEGSGESCHICHTE EINES KLEINEN MÄDCHEN No.007

The battle log so far...

Our protagonist, a coolheaded salaryman in contemporary Japan, dies after being pushed off a train platform by a resentful man he fired.

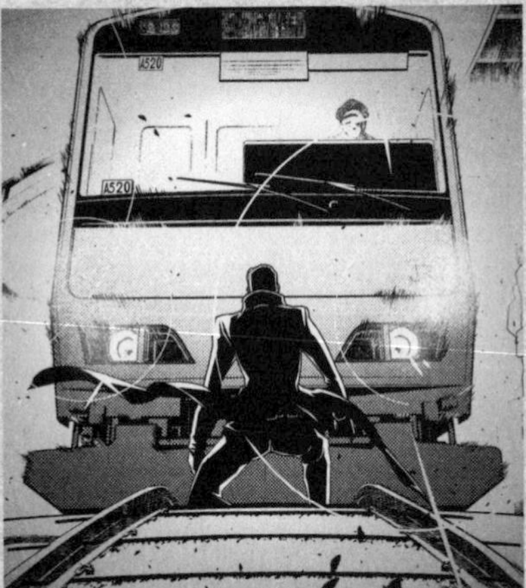
A520
A520

In the world beyond death, he encounters Being X, who claims to be the Creator. His lack of faith angers the being, and he is reborn in another world where gunfire and magic intermingle in combat. "You will be born into an unscientific world as a woman, come to know war, and be driven to your limits!"

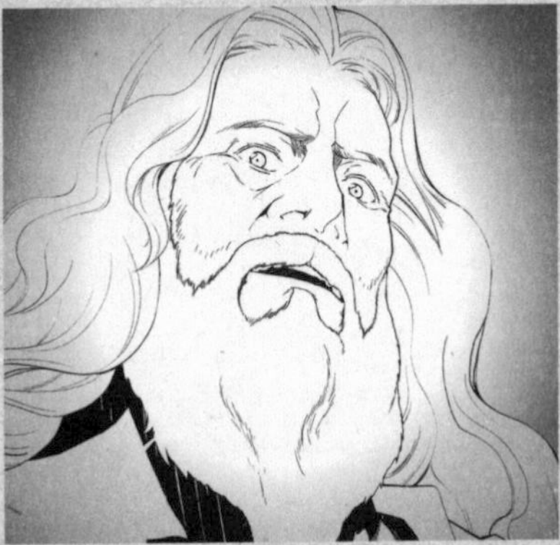

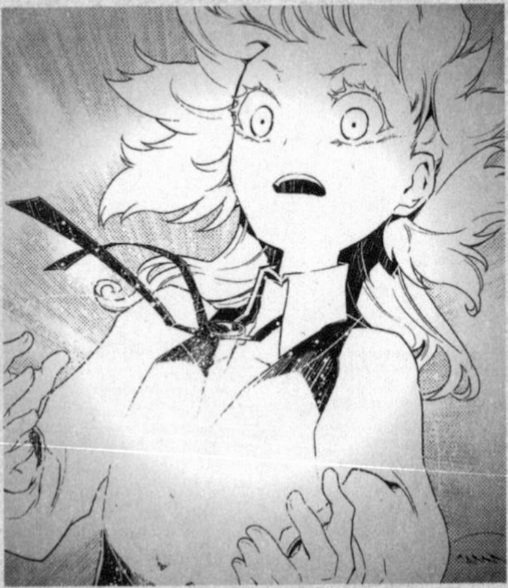

In the other world, he is reincarnated as Tanya Degurechaff. Upon recognition of her magic aptitude, she is sent to the battlefield at the age of nine.

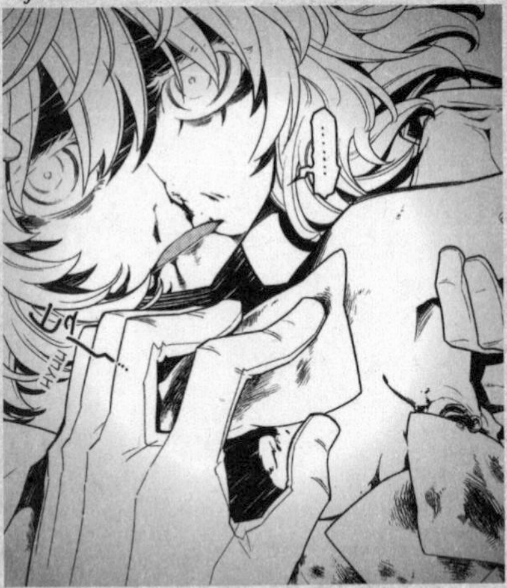
HYUU

Using the knowledge from her previous life, she climbs the ranks, aiming for a safe position in the rear, but her outstanding achievements and bravery make such a good impression on her superiors that she is, on the contrary, repeatedly sent to the front lines...

As a result, the Imperial Army achieves a crushing victory. The Regadonia Entente Alliance, as well as the François Republic and Albion Commonwealth, both of which formed a voluntary army supporting the Entente Alliance in secret, lost most of their forces and headquarters, and Regadonia is finally forced to withdraw from Norden.

Having completely taken over Norden, the Empire moves to advance into Regadonian territory but faces some issues with the imminent northern winter... namely "supply hell."

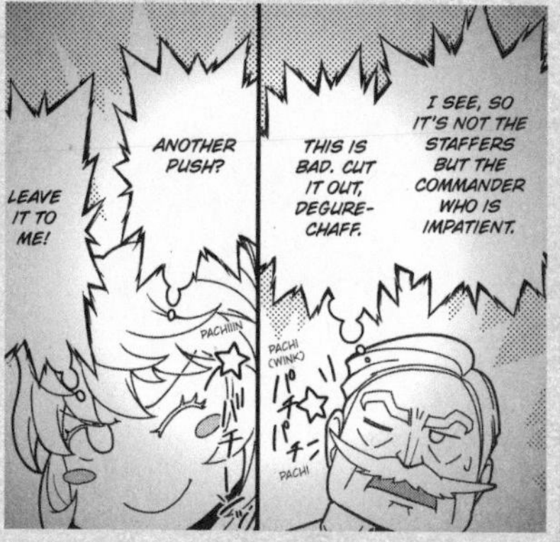
I SEE, SO IT'S NOT THE STAFFERS BUT THE COMMANDER WHO IS IMPATIENT.
THIS IS BAD. CUT IT OUT, DEGURE-CHAFF.
PACHI (WINK)
PACHI
ANOTHER PUSH?
LEAVE IT TO ME!
PACHIIIN

No matter how well-trained troops are, they can't do anything if their equipment freezes. Tanya knows how serious the "supply hell" winter can be from the world history in her previous life, so she suggests they wait until spring. However, due to a misunderstanding that unfolds before her very eyes, she ends up giving them a push to go forward with the winter offensive......

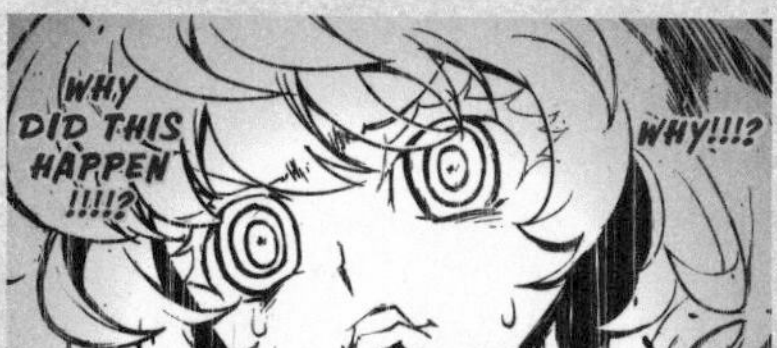
WHY!!!?
WHY DID THIS HAPPEN !!!!?

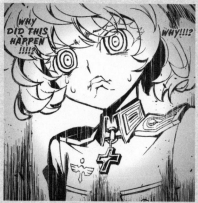

Tanya is shocked to hear that the operation will actually be put into action. To figure out what's going on, she requests a meeting with Major General von Rudersdorf......

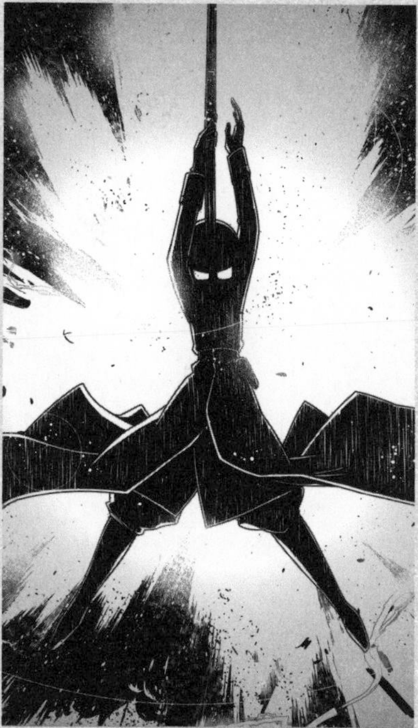

In November of Unified Year 1925, Tanya and the 203rd Aerial Mage Battalion are sent to achieve a breakthrough on the front between the Empire and the Regadonia Entente Alliance in the north.

The 203rd is so impeccably trained, it makes even people within the Imperial Army think that the battalion's performance is in such a realm of its own that it renders all the existing units obsolete. The group overwhelms enemies one after the other.

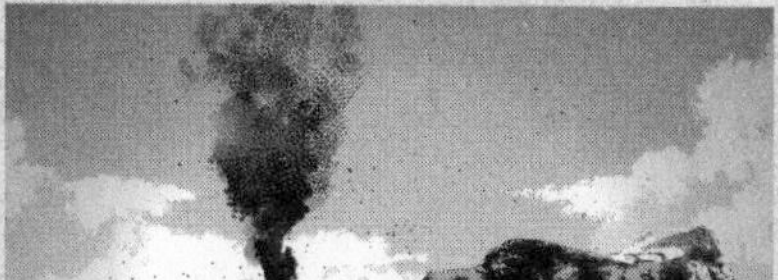

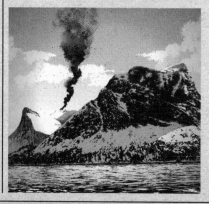

THE SAGA OF TANYA THE EVIL

Character Introductions

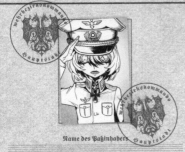

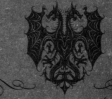

Die Kriegsgeschichte eines Kleinen Mädchen

Name des Paßinhabers

Tanya von Degurechaff

(Rufname, Familienname)

Dienstgrad	Dienststellung
MAJOR	AERIAL MAGIC OFFICER

An extremely rational little girl who was a salaryman in her previous life. Joins the army to escape life in the orphanage. Becomes a mage after her talent for magic is recognized. She couldn't care less about national defense and simply wants to live a quiet life safe in the rear. Unfortunately, misunderstanding after misunderstanding causes others to think she is a patriot full of fighting spirit.

(Angaben zur Person)

Name des Paßinhabers

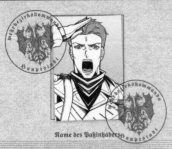

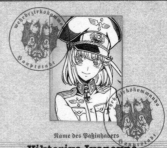

Viktoriya Ivanovna Serebryakov

(Rufname, Familienname)

Dienstgrad	Dienststellung
SECOND LIEUTENANT	AERIAL MAGIC OFFICER

A mage in the Imperial Army. After being practically forced to enlist in the cadet corps due to her magic abilities, she is stationed in a unit on the front lines. Having proven herself capable in combat, she is recommended for the officer track. She sees Major Degurechaff as a kind, peace-loving individual and respects and supports her as her outstanding adjutant.

(Angaben zur Person)

Name des Paßinhabers

Johann-Mattäus Weiss

(Rufname, Familienname)

Dienstgrad	Dienststellung
FIRST LIEUTENANT	AERIAL MAGIC OFFICER

A mage in the Imperial Army and a member of Major Degurechaff's 203rd Aerial Mage Battalion. He's an earnest, outstanding soldier, but because he doesn't have much combat experience, most of his knowledge comes from textbooks. Having made it through the hellish training, it's clear his skills and fighting spirit are impeccable. That plus his talent for unit management means the army has high expectations of him.

(Angaben zur Person)

Name des Paßinhabers

Kurt von Rudersdorf

(Rufname, Familienname)

Dienstgrad	Dienststellung
MAJOR GENERAL	**DEPUTY DIRECTOR OF OPERATIONS IN THE GENERAL STAFF**

One of the geniuses on whose shoulders the future of the Empire rests. He conducts operations throughout imperial territory with his broad perspective and is involved in the majority of orders given. Unlike his friend, Major General Zettour, the deputy director of the Service Corps, he has the hearty air of a military man—to the point where during the war college screening, he was acknowledged as "sharp and dynamic" but criticized for his "tendency to daydream."

(Angaben zur Person)

Name des Paßinhabers

Hans von Zettour

(Rufname, Familienname)

Dienstgrad	Dienststellung
MAJOR GENERAL	**DEPUTY DIRECTOR OF THE SERVICE CORPS IN THE GENERAL STAFF**

Employing his clear thinking and wealth of knowledge, he works on logistics and plans operations with his friend and colleague Major General Rudersdorf, the deputy director of Operations. He has a very high opinion of Major Degurechaff and does what he can to take her wishes into account. He's so far learned that in war college, evaluators had concerns that he was "too scholarly and thus not suited to becoming a general."

(Angaben zur Person)

Name des Paßinhabers

Being X

(Rufname, Familienname)

Dienstgrad	Dienststellung

A lofty being calling himself the Creator who is disappointed by humanity's loss of faith. Having concluded that the protagonist's impiety stems from living a comfortable life in a scientific world as a man with no experience of war, he has him reborn into the opposite circumstances. He's even willing to plunge the world into the chaos of war in order to mend the man's ways.

(Angaben zur Person)

Name des Paßinhabers

Erich von Lergen

(Rufname, Familienname)

Dienstgrad	Dienststellung
LIEUTENANT COLONEL	**SENIOR STAFF OFFICER IN THE GENERAL STAFF**

A sensible man whose hard work shows. The army expects great things from this General Staff officer; he is currently gaining experience in Personnel. Major Degurechaff makes him nervous because he can sense how abnormal and insane she is, but he's also forced to admit that she is right when it comes to the war, so his personal feelings and duty come into conflict.

(Angaben zur Person)

The Saga of Tanya the Evil

07

Original Story: Carlo Zen   Art: Chika Tojo
Character Design: Shinobu Shinotsuki

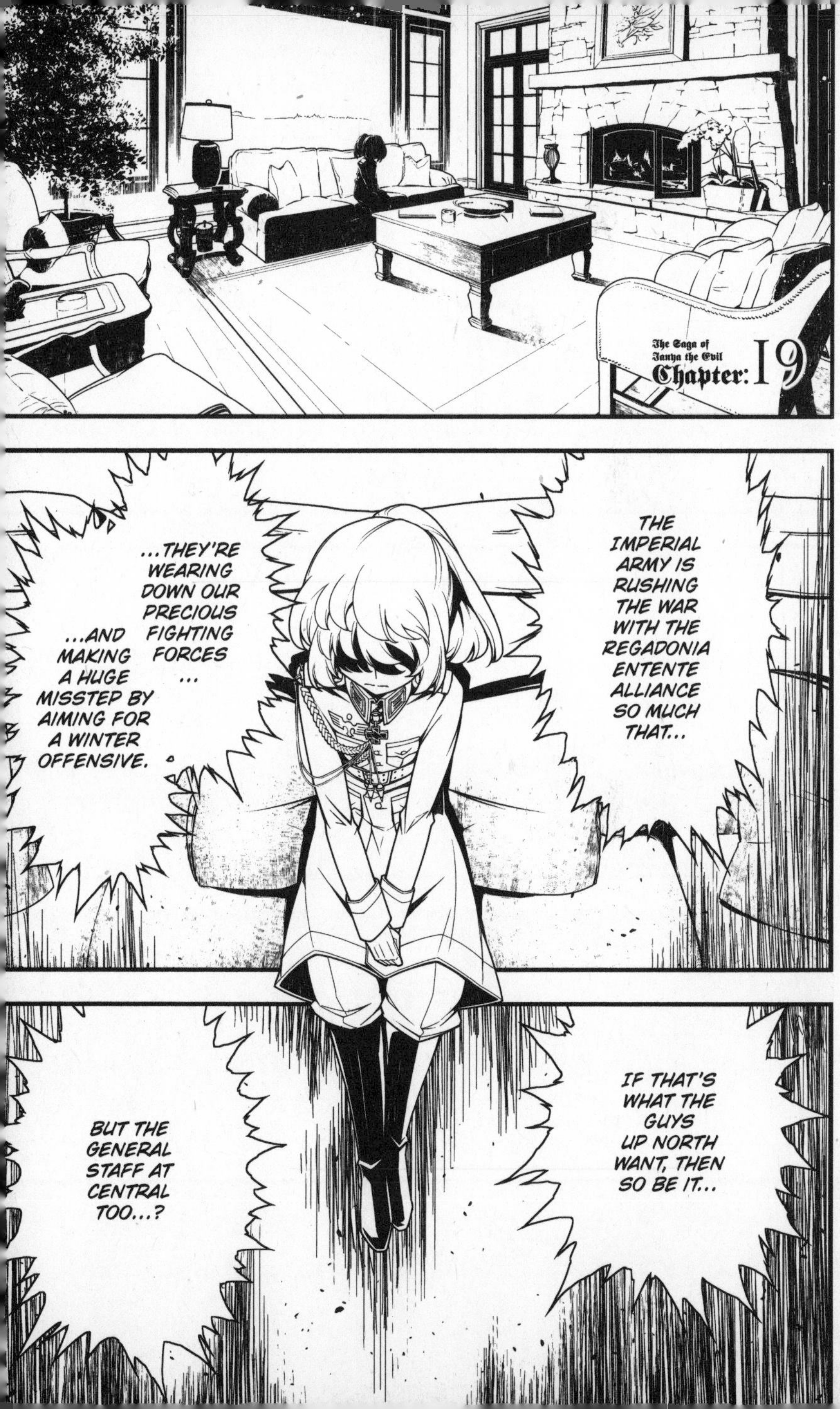
The Saga of Tanya the Evil
Chapter: 19
THE IMPERIAL ARMY IS RUSHING THE WAR WITH THE REGADONIA ENTENTE ALLIANCE SO MUCH THAT...
...THEY'RE WEARING DOWN OUR PRECIOUS FIGHTING FORCES ...
...AND MAKING A HUGE MISSTEP BY AIMING FOR A WINTER OFFENSIVE.
IF THAT'S WHAT THE GUYS UP NORTH WANT, THEN SO BE IT...
BUT THE GENERAL STAFF AT CENTRAL TOO...?

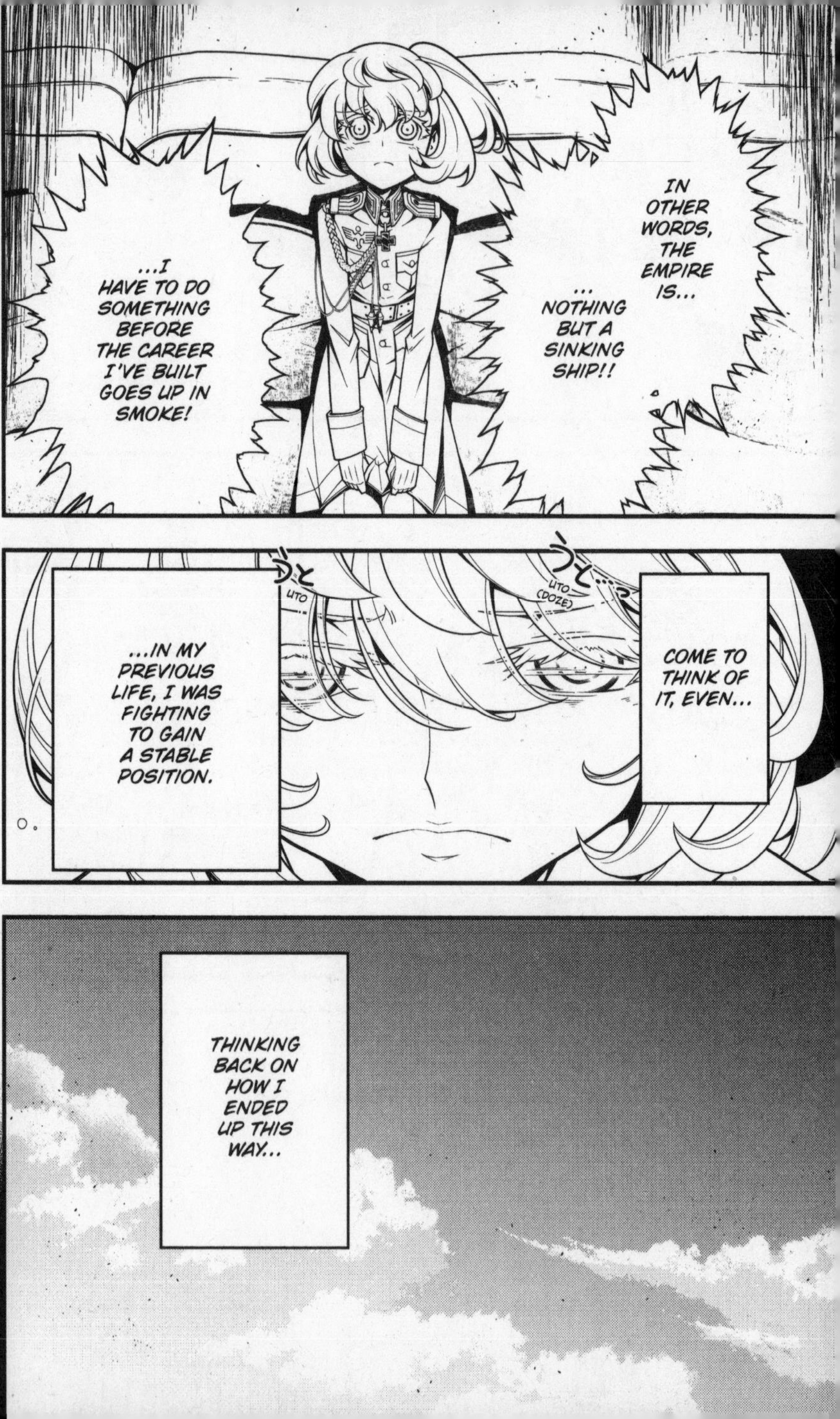

IN OTHER WORDS, THE EMPIRE IS...
...NOTHING BUT A SINKING SHIP!!
...I HAVE TO DO SOMETHING BEFORE THE CAREER I'VE BUILT GOES UP IN SMOKE!
うと…
UTO (DOZE)
COME TO THINK OF IT, EVEN...
うと
UTO
...IN MY PREVIOUS LIFE, I WAS FIGHTING TO GAIN A STABLE POSITION.
THINKING BACK ON HOW I ENDED UP THIS WAY...

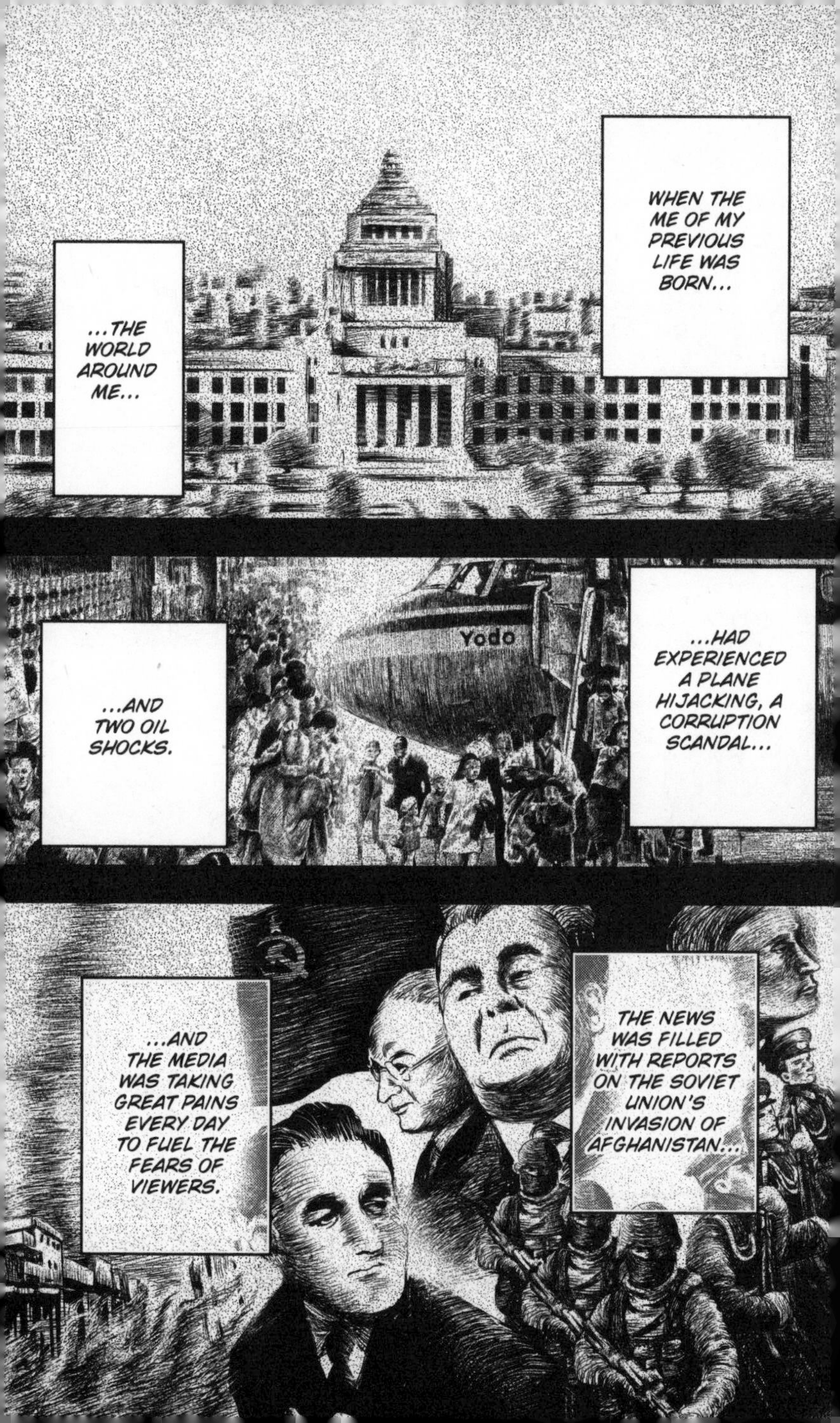
WHEN THE ME OF MY PREVIOUS LIFE WAS BORN...
...THE WORLD AROUND ME...
...HAD EXPERIENCED A PLANE HIJACKING, A CORRUPTION SCANDAL...
Yodo
...AND TWO OIL SHOCKS.
THE NEWS WAS FILLED WITH REPORTS ON THE SOVIET UNION'S INVASION OF AFGHANISTAN...
...AND THE MEDIA WAS TAKING GREAT PAINS EVERY DAY TO FUEL THE FEARS OF VIEWERS.

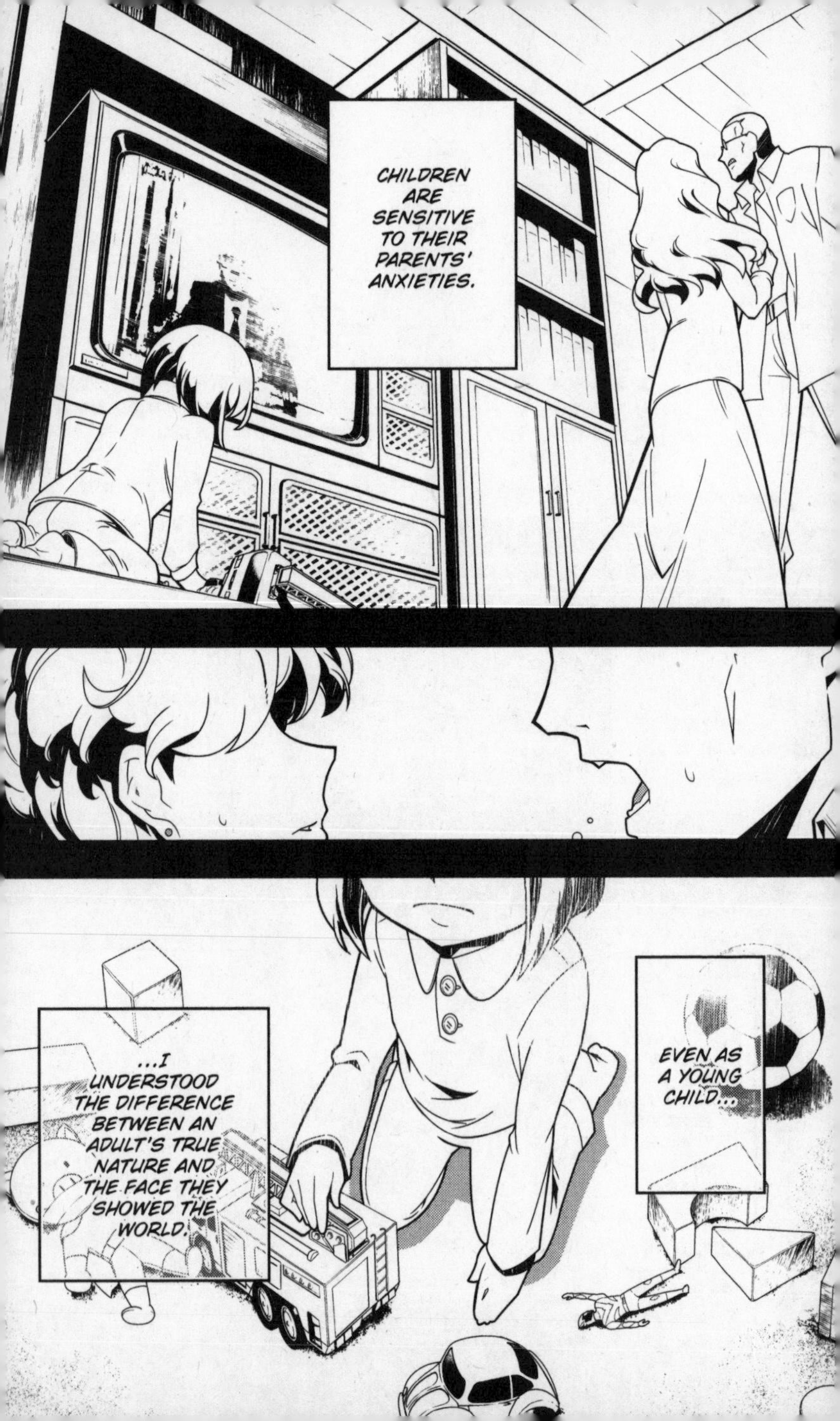
CHILDREN ARE SENSITIVE TO THEIR PARENTS' ANXIETIES.
EVEN AS A YOUNG CHILD...
...I UNDERSTOOD THE DIFFERENCE BETWEEN AN ADULT'S TRUE NATURE AND THE FACE THEY SHOWED THE WORLD.

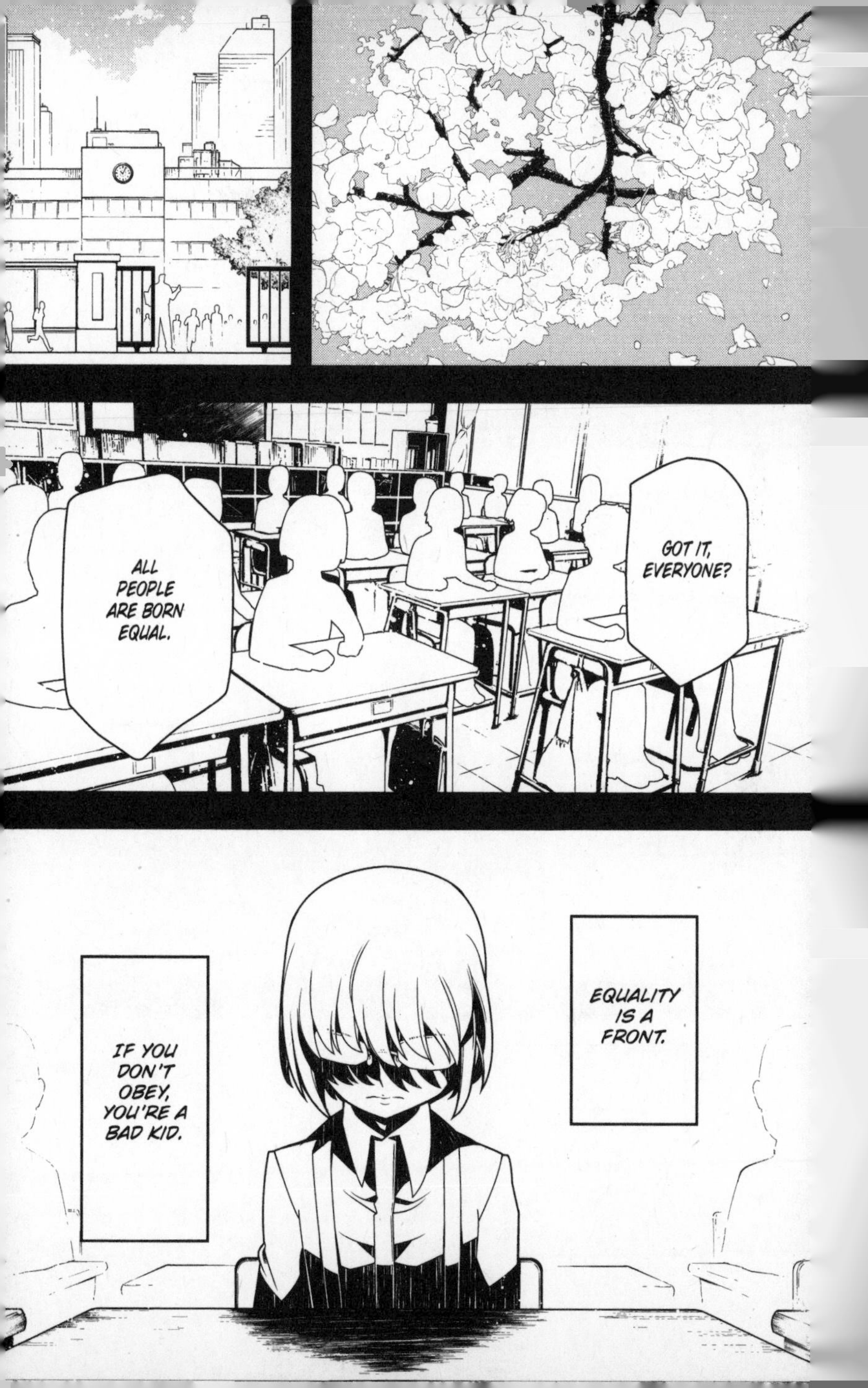
GOT IT, EVERYONE?
ALL PEOPLE ARE BORN EQUAL.
EQUALITY IS A FRONT.
IF YOU DON'T OBEY, YOU'RE A BAD KID.

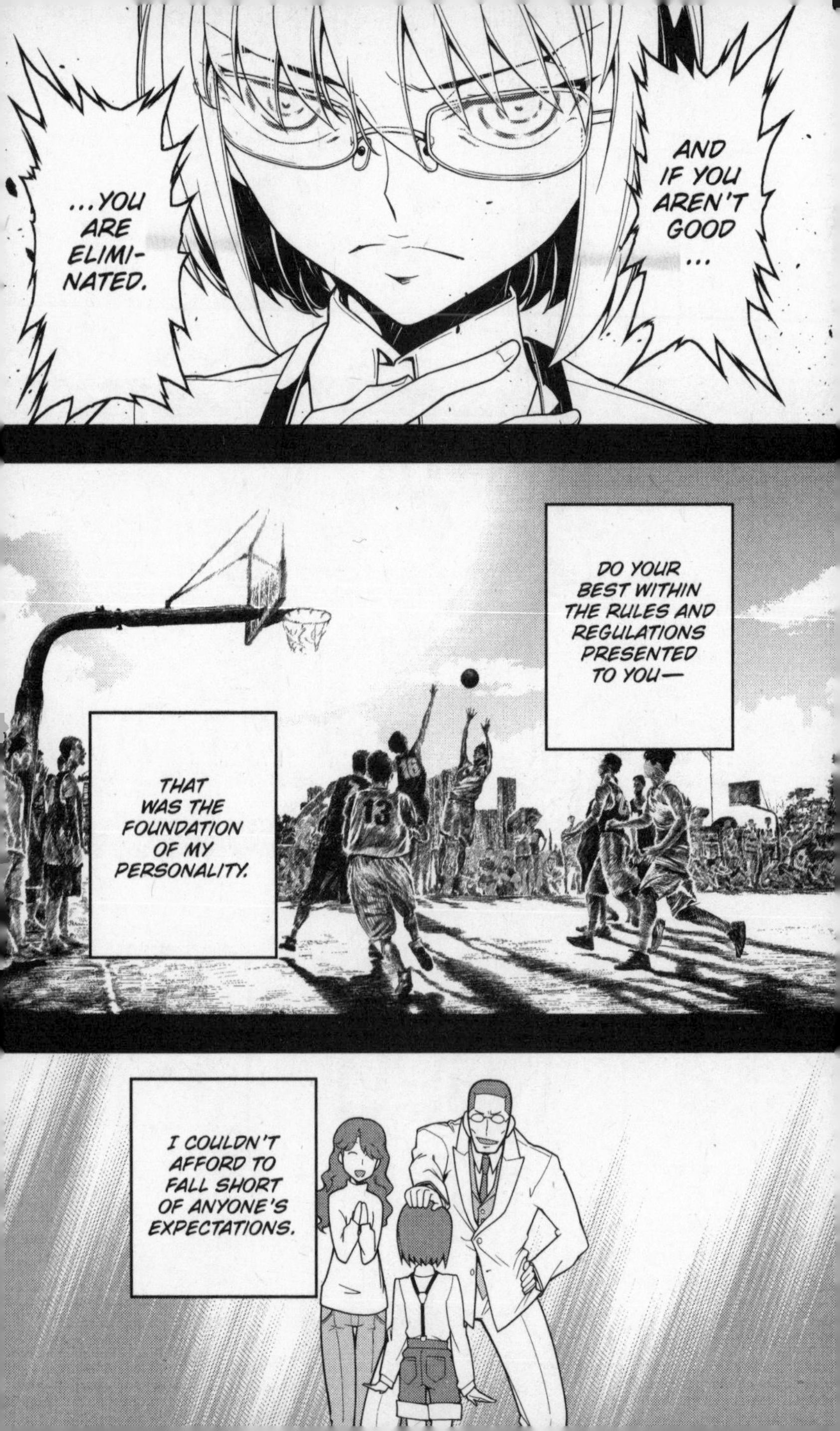
AND IF YOU AREN'T GOOD...
...YOU ARE ELIMINATED.
DO YOUR BEST WITHIN THE RULES AND REGULATIONS PRESENTED TO YOU—
THAT WAS THE FOUNDATION OF MY PERSONALITY.
I COULDN'T AFFORD TO FALL SHORT OF ANYONE'S EXPECTATIONS.

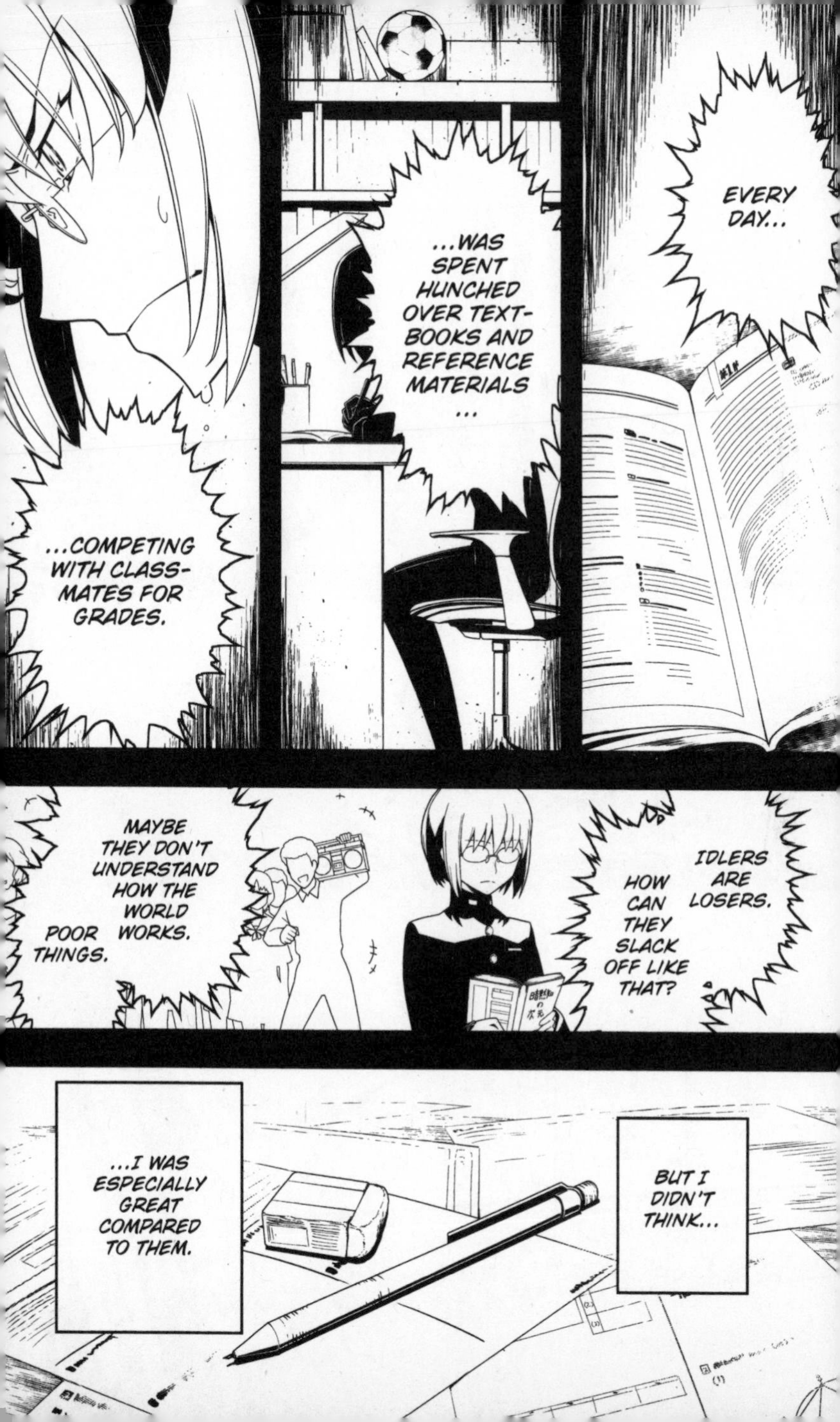
EVERY DAY...
...WAS SPENT HUNCHED OVER TEXT-BOOKS AND REFERENCE MATERIALS ...
...COMPETING WITH CLASS-MATES FOR GRADES.
IDLERS ARE LOSERS.
HOW CAN THEY SLACK OFF LIKE THAT?
MAYBE THEY DON'T UNDERSTAND HOW THE WORLD WORKS.
POOR THINGS.
BUT I DIDN'T THINK...
...I WAS ESPECIALLY GREAT COMPARED TO THEM.

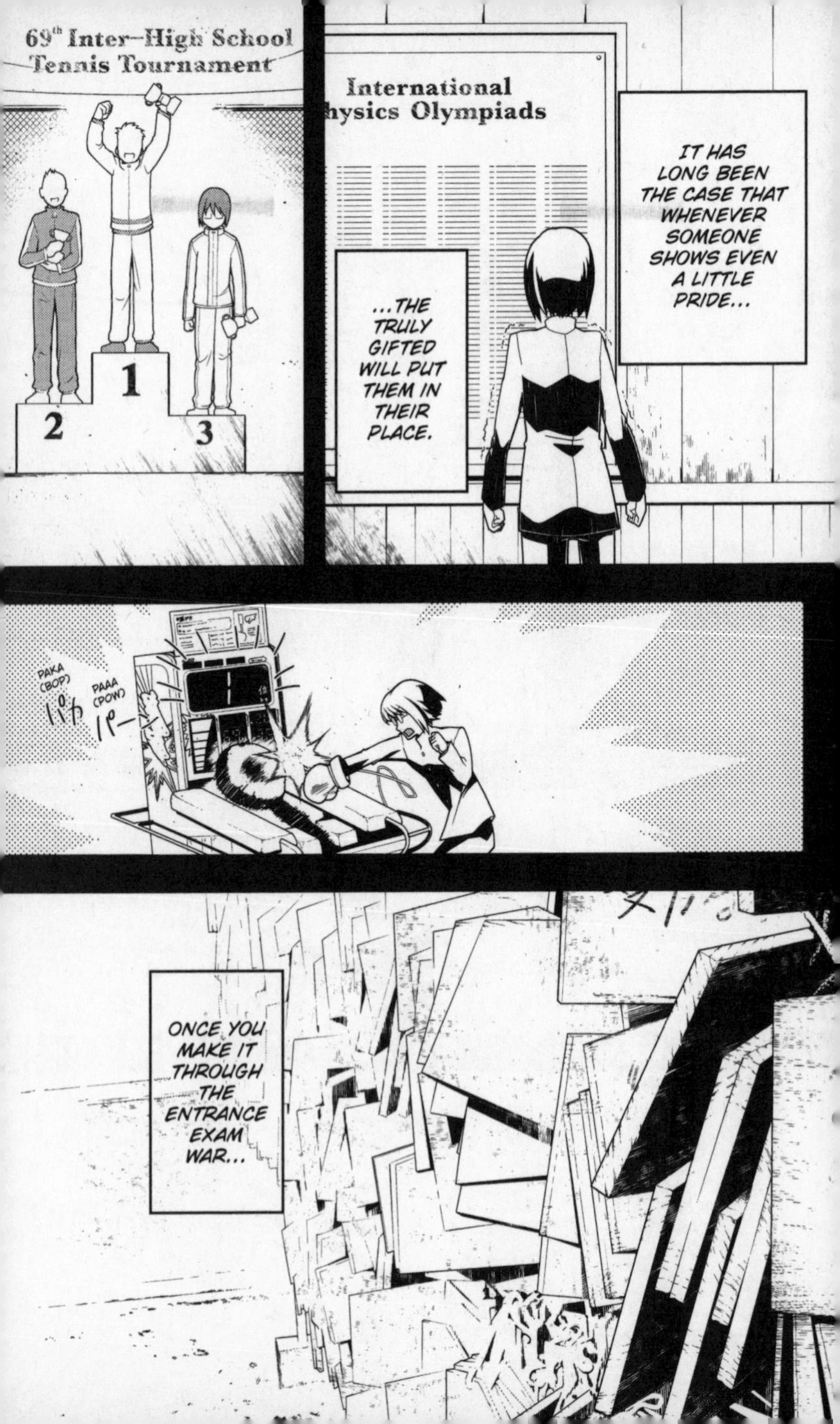
International
hysics Olympiads
IT HAS LONG BEEN THE CASE THAT WHENEVER SOMEONE SHOWS EVEN A LITTLE PRIDE...
...THE TRULY GIFTED WILL PUT THEM IN THEIR PLACE.
69th Inter-High School Tennis Tournament
1
2
3
PAAA (POW)
パー
PAKA (BOP)
パカ
ONCE YOU MAKE IT THROUGH THE ENTRANCE EXAM WAR...

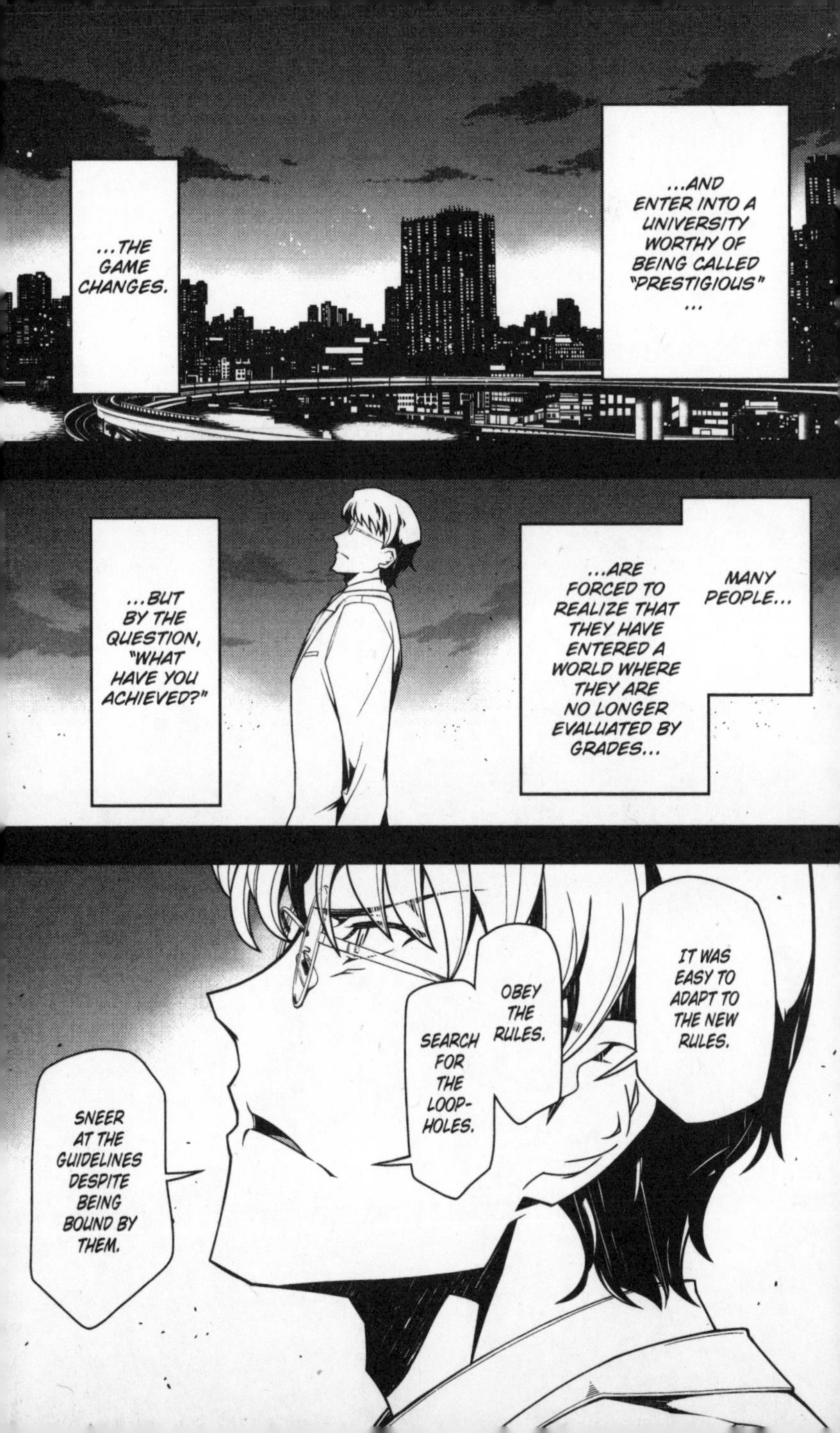
...AND ENTER INTO A UNIVERSITY WORTHY OF BEING CALLED "PRESTIGIOUS" ...
...THE GAME CHANGES.
MANY PEOPLE...
...ARE FORCED TO REALIZE THAT THEY HAVE ENTERED A WORLD WHERE THEY ARE NO LONGER EVALUATED BY GRADES...
...BUT BY THE QUESTION, "WHAT HAVE YOU ACHIEVED?"
IT WAS EASY TO ADAPT TO THE NEW RULES.
OBEY THE RULES.
SEARCH FOR THE LOOP-HOLES.
SNEER AT THE GUIDELINES DESPITE BEING BOUND BY THEM.

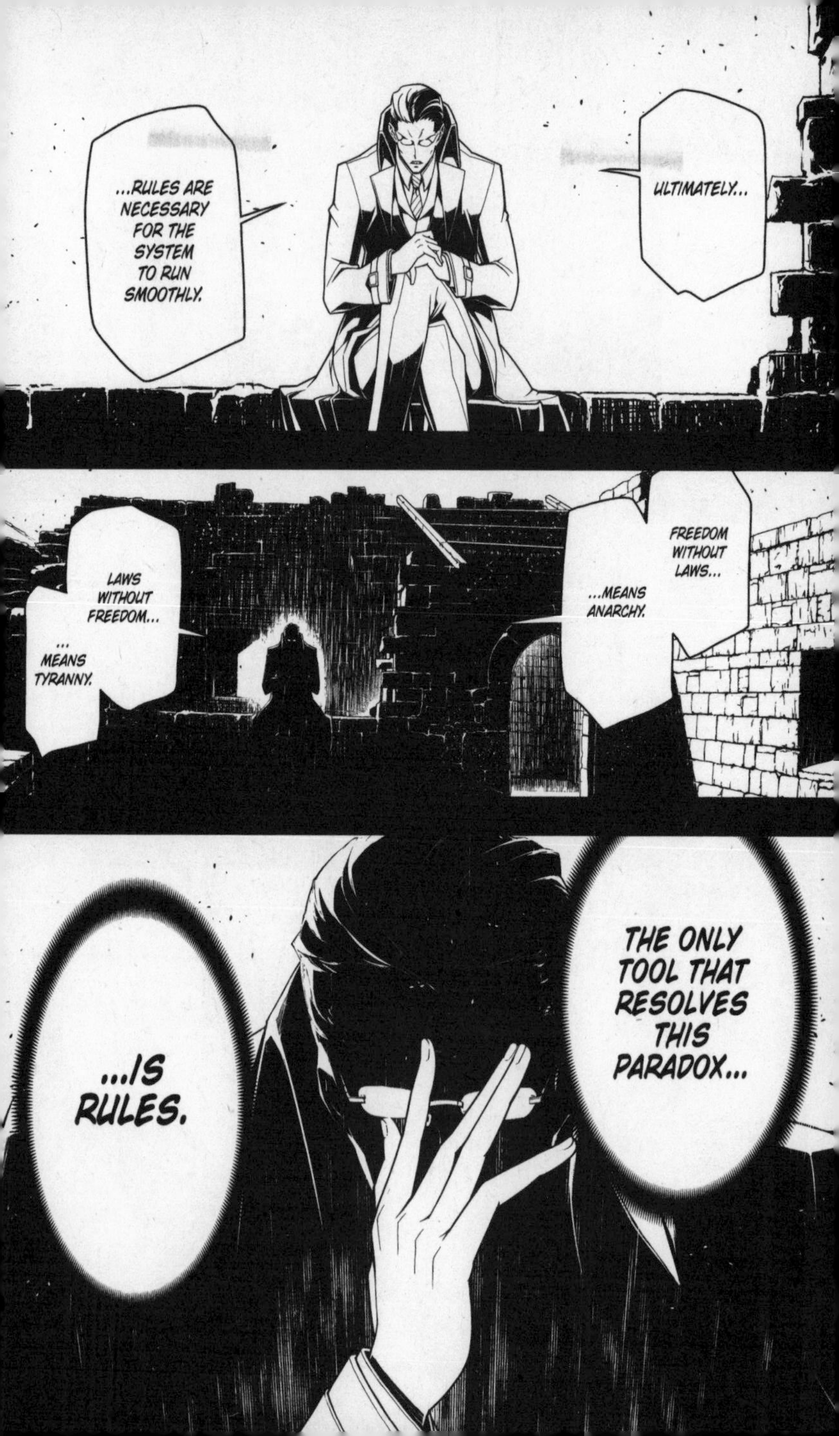
ULTIMATELY...
...RULES ARE NECESSARY FOR THE SYSTEM TO RUN SMOOTHLY.
FREEDOM WITHOUT LAWS...
...MEANS ANARCHY.
LAWS WITHOUT FREEDOM...
...MEANS TYRANNY.
THE ONLY TOOL THAT RESOLVES THIS PARADOX...
...IS RULES.

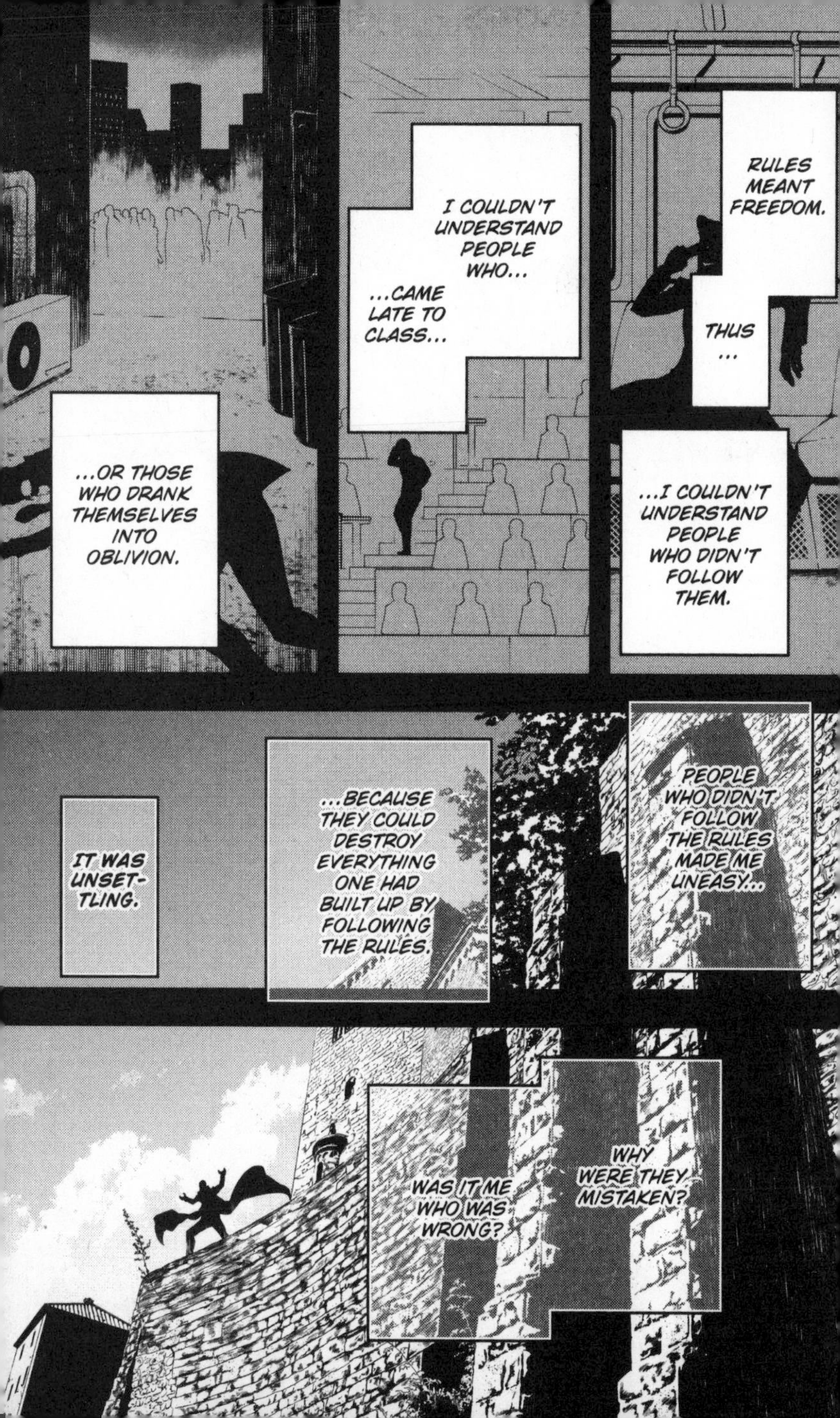
RULES MEANT FREEDOM.
THUS ...
...I COULDN'T UNDERSTAND PEOPLE WHO DIDN'T FOLLOW THEM.
I COULDN'T UNDERSTAND PEOPLE WHO...
...CAME LATE TO CLASS...
...OR THOSE WHO DRANK THEMSELVES INTO OBLIVION.
PEOPLE WHO DIDN'T FOLLOW THE RULES MADE ME UNEASY...
...BECAUSE THEY COULD DESTROY EVERYTHING ONE HAD BUILT UP BY FOLLOWING THE RULES.
IT WAS UNSET-TLING.
WHY WERE THEY MISTAKEN?
WAS IT ME WHO WAS WRONG?

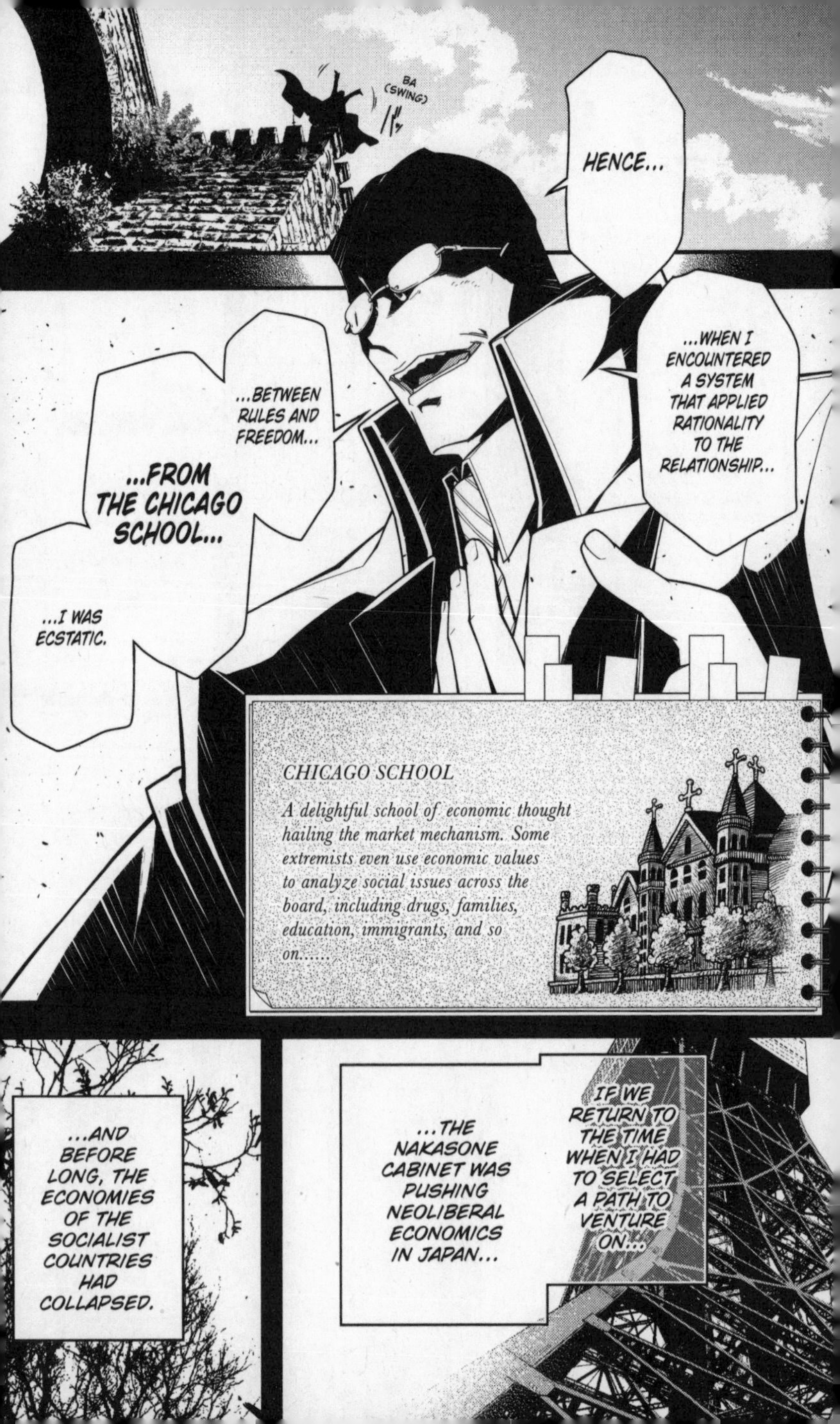
HENCE...
BA (SWING)
...WHEN I ENCOUNTERED A SYSTEM THAT APPLIED RATIONALITY TO THE RELATIONSHIP...
...BETWEEN RULES AND FREEDOM...
...FROM THE CHICAGO SCHOOL...
...I WAS ECSTATIC.
CHICAGO SCHOOL
A delightful school of economic thought hailing the market mechanism. Some extremists even use economic values to analyze social issues across the board, including drugs, families, education, immigrants, and so on......
IF WE RETURN TO THE TIME WHEN I HAD TO SELECT A PATH TO VENTURE ON...
...THE NAKASONE CABINET WAS PUSHING NEOLIBERAL ECONOMICS IN JAPAN...
...AND BEFORE LONG, THE ECONOMIES OF THE SOCIALIST COUNTRIES HAD COLLAPSED.

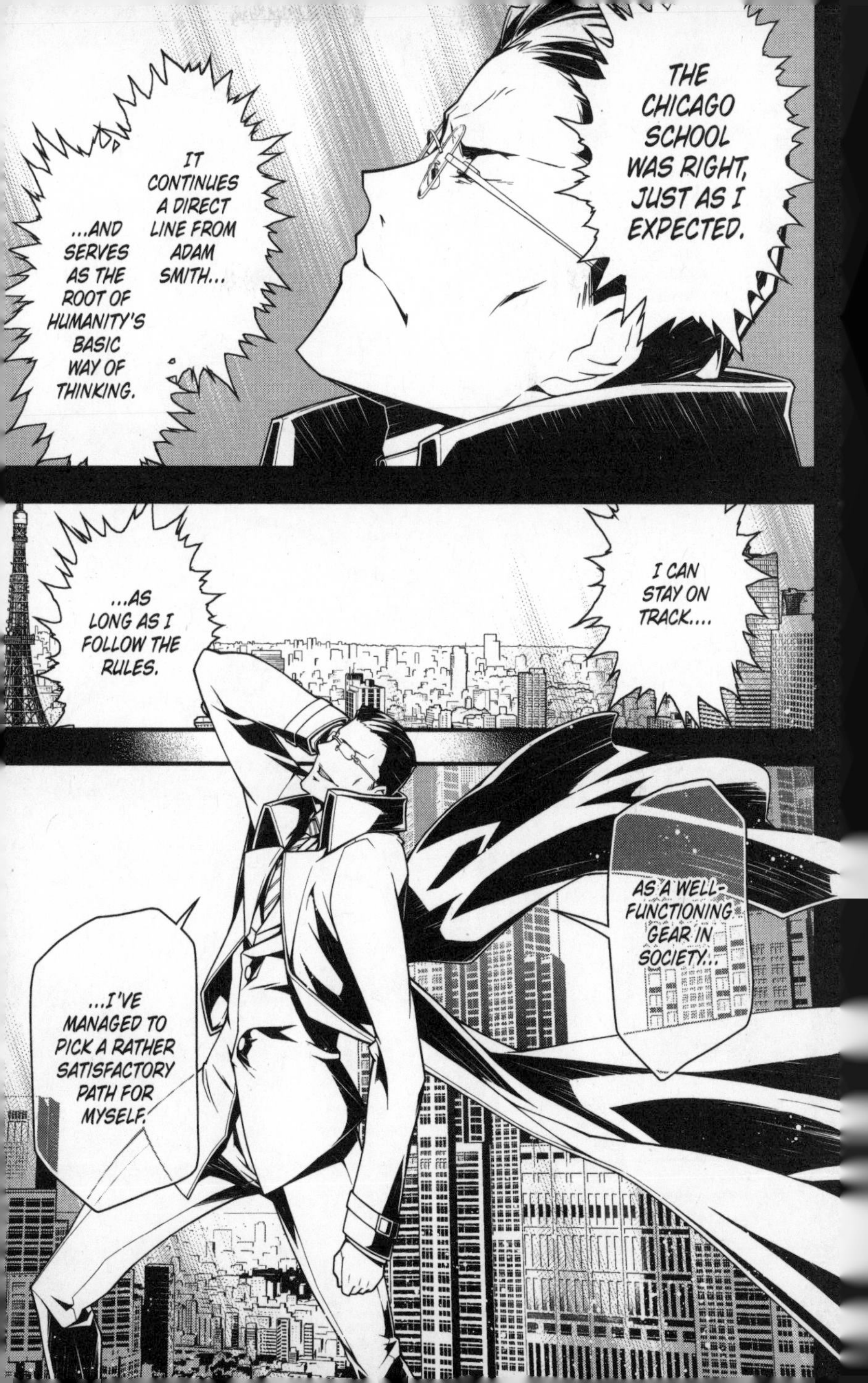
THE CHICAGO SCHOOL WAS RIGHT, JUST AS I EXPECTED.
IT CONTINUES A DIRECT LINE FROM ADAM SMITH...
...AND SERVES AS THE ROOT OF HUMANITY'S BASIC WAY OF THINKING.
I CAN STAY ON TRACK....
...AS LONG AS I FOLLOW THE RULES.
AS A WELL-FUNCTIONING GEAR IN SOCIETY...
...I'VE MANAGED TO PICK A RATHER SATISFACTORY PATH FOR MYSELF.

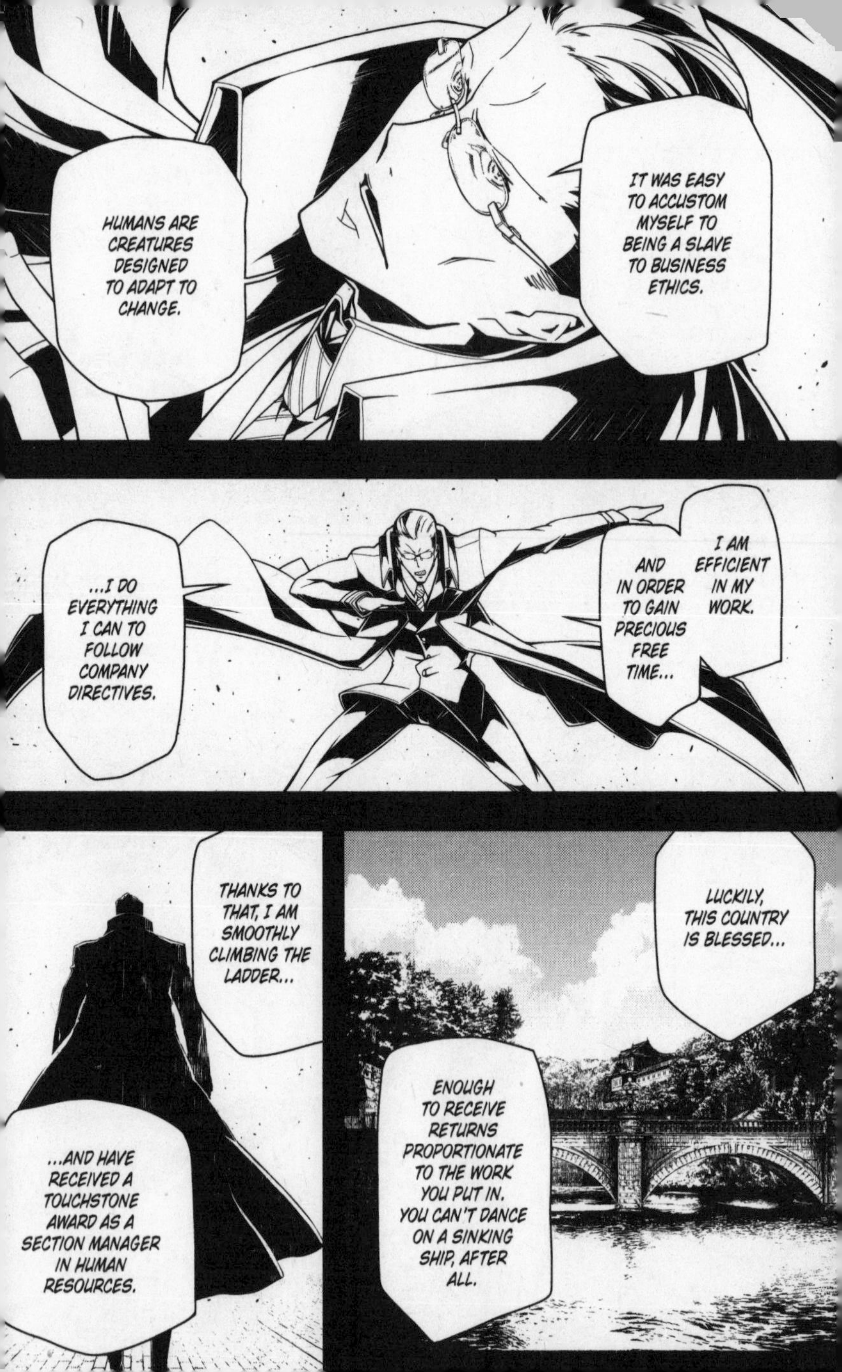
IT WAS EASY TO ACCUSTOM MYSELF TO BEING A SLAVE TO BUSINESS ETHICS.
HUMANS ARE CREATURES DESIGNED TO ADAPT TO CHANGE.
I AM EFFICIENT IN MY WORK.
AND IN ORDER TO GAIN PRECIOUS FREE TIME...
...I DO EVERYTHING I CAN TO FOLLOW COMPANY DIRECTIVES.
LUCKILY, THIS COUNTRY IS BLESSED...
ENOUGH TO RECEIVE RETURNS PROPORTIONATE TO THE WORK YOU PUT IN. YOU CAN'T DANCE ON A SINKING SHIP, AFTER ALL.
THANKS TO THAT, I AM SMOOTHLY CLIMBING THE LADDER...
...AND HAVE RECEIVED A TOUCHSTONE AWARD AS A SECTION MANAGER IN HUMAN RESOURCES.

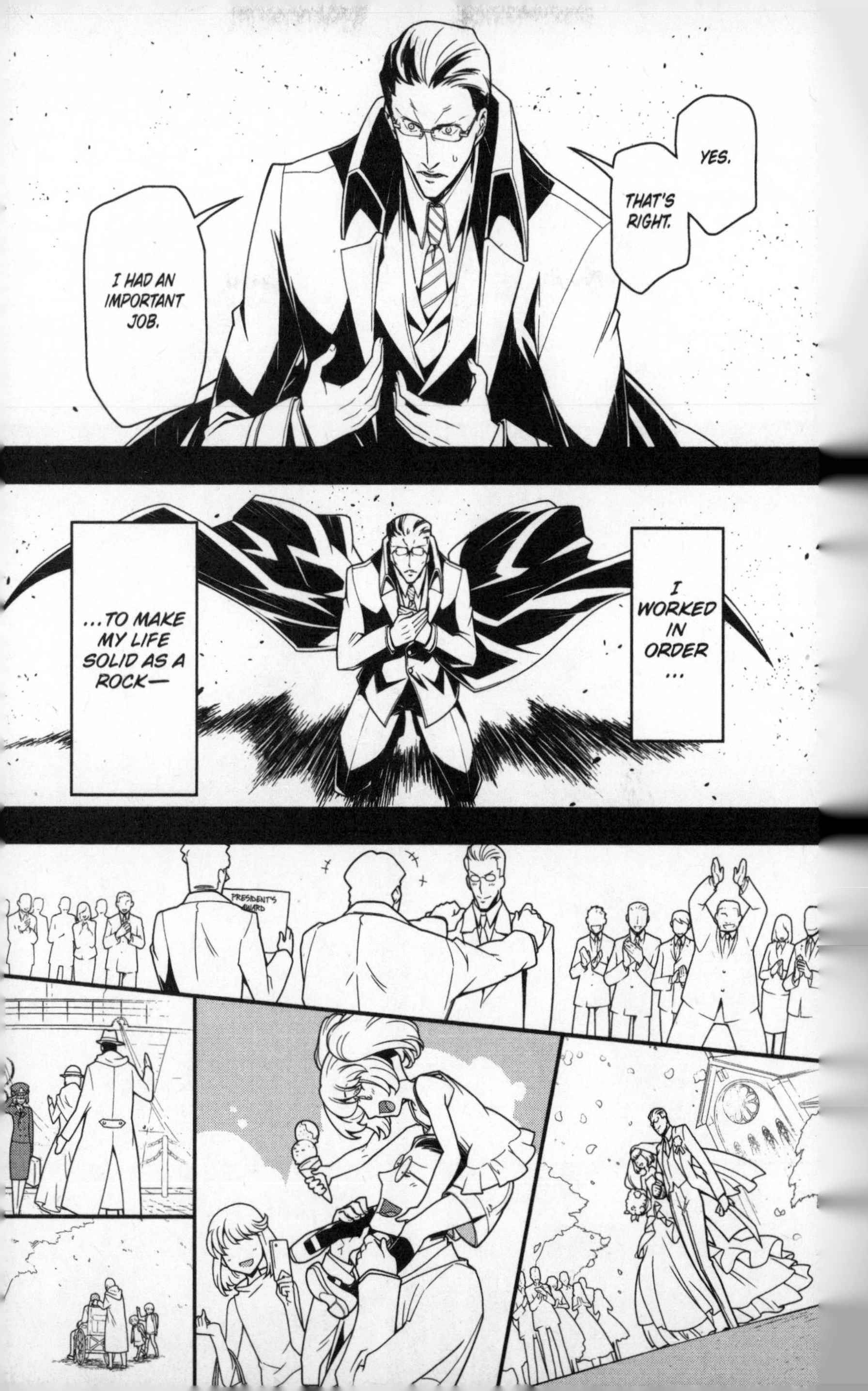
YES.
THAT'S RIGHT.
I HAD AN IMPORTANT JOB.
I WORKED IN ORDER...
...TO MAKE MY LIFE SOLID AS A ROCK—
PRESIDENT'S AWARD

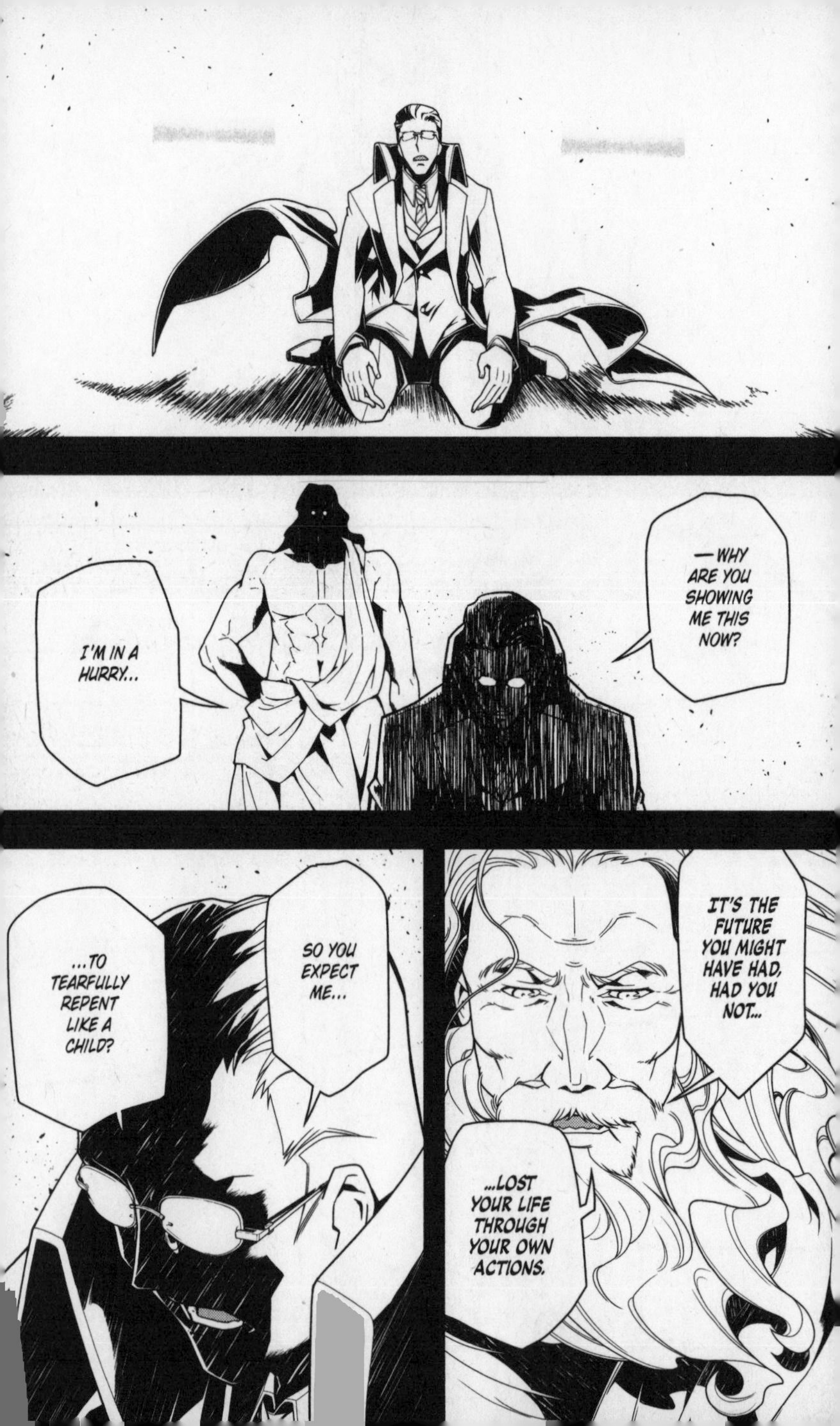
—WHY ARE YOU SHOWING ME THIS NOW?
I'M IN A HURRY...
IT'S THE FUTURE YOU MIGHT HAVE HAD, HAD YOU NOT...
...LOST YOUR LIFE THROUGH YOUR OWN ACTIONS.
SO YOU EXPECT ME...
...TO TEARFULLY REPENT LIKE A CHILD?

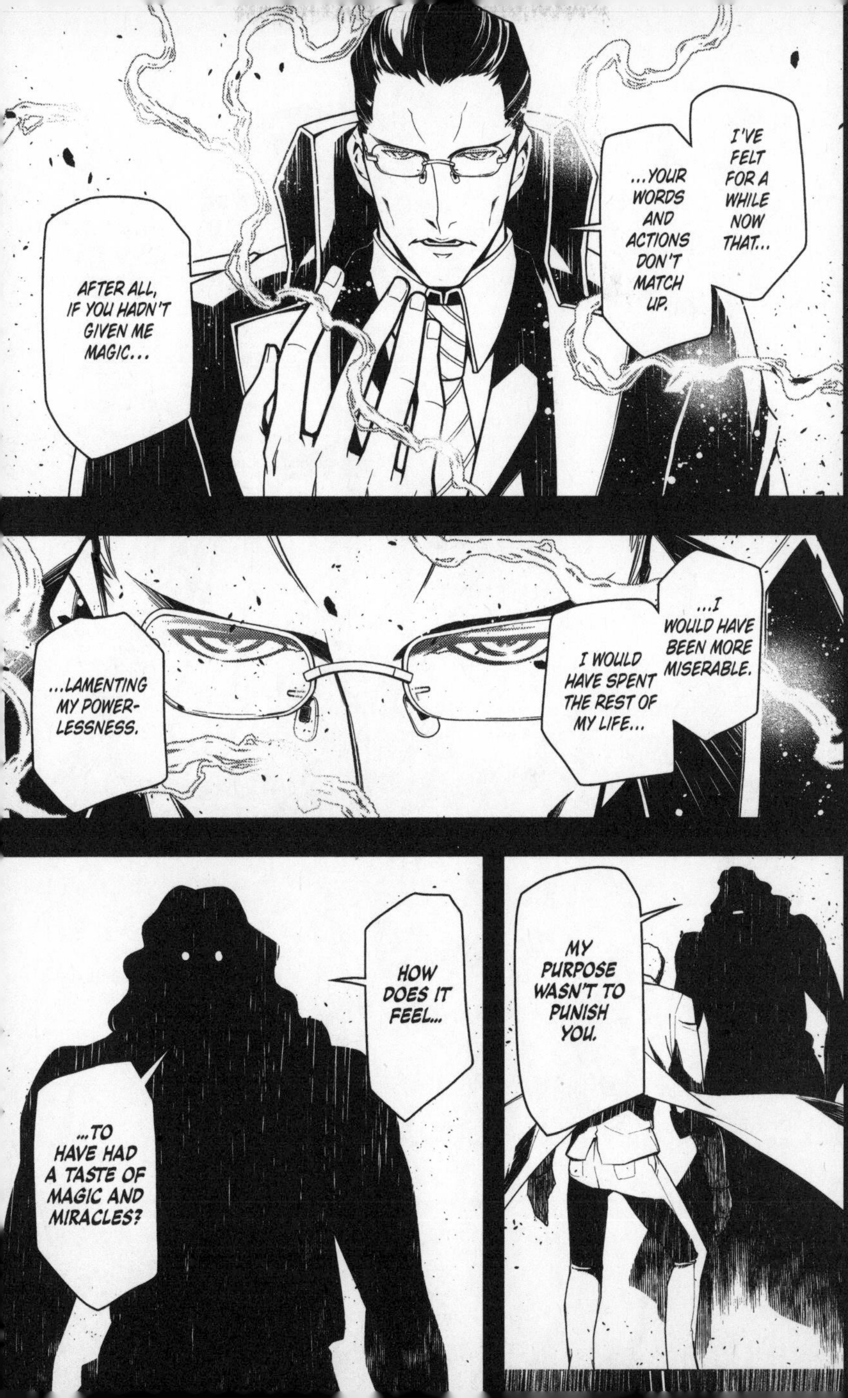
I'VE FELT FOR A WHILE NOW THAT...
...YOUR WORDS AND ACTIONS DON'T MATCH UP.
AFTER ALL, IF YOU HADN'T GIVEN ME MAGIC...
...I WOULD HAVE BEEN MORE MISERABLE.
I WOULD HAVE SPENT THE REST OF MY LIFE...
...LAMENTING MY POWER-LESSNESS.
MY PURPOSE WASN'T TO PUNISH YOU.
HOW DOES IT FEEL...
...TO HAVE HAD A TASTE OF MAGIC AND MIRACLES?

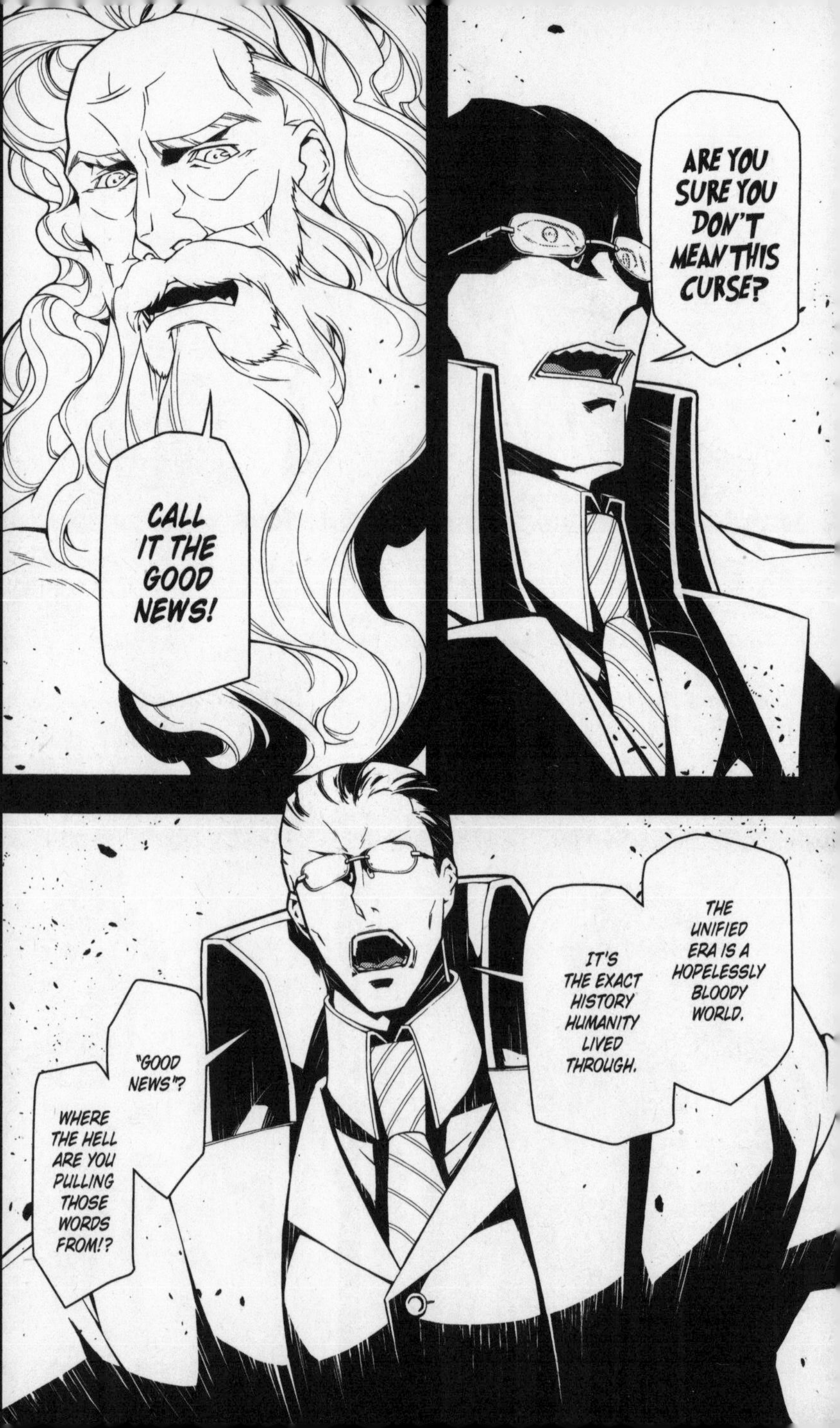
ARE YOU SURE YOU DON'T MEAN THIS CURSE?
CALL IT THE GOOD NEWS!
THE UNIFIED ERA IS A HOPELESSLY BLOODY WORLD.
IT'S THE EXACT HISTORY HUMANITY LIVED THROUGH.
"GOOD NEWS"?
WHERE THE HELL ARE YOU PULLING THOSE WORDS FROM!?

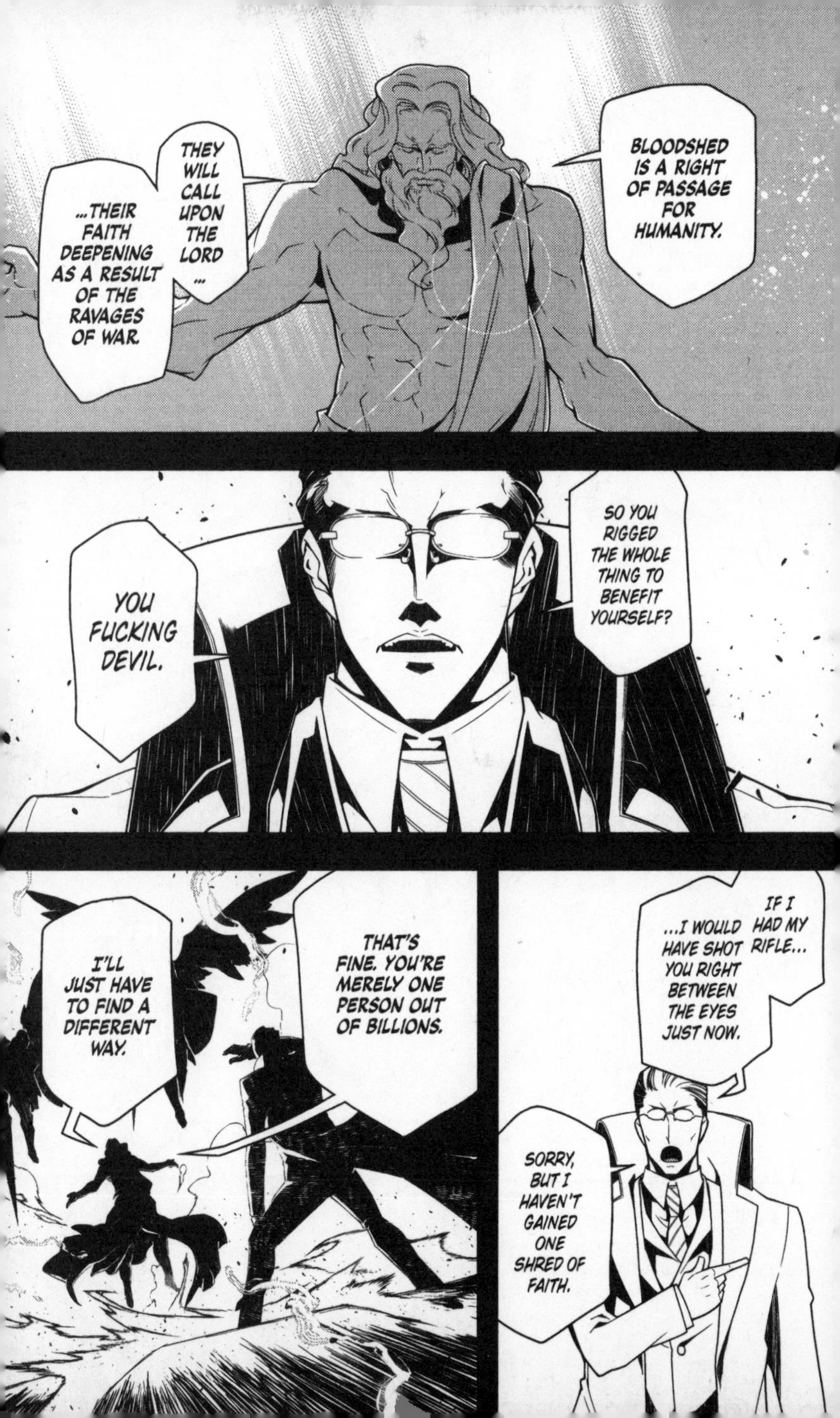
BLOODSHED IS A RIGHT OF PASSAGE FOR HUMANITY.
THEY WILL CALL UPON THE LORD ...
...THEIR FAITH DEEPENING AS A RESULT OF THE RAVAGES OF WAR.
SO YOU RIGGED THE WHOLE THING TO BENEFIT YOURSELF?
YOU FUCKING DEVIL.
IF I HAD MY RIFLE...
...I WOULD HAVE SHOT YOU RIGHT BETWEEN THE EYES JUST NOW.
SORRY, BUT I HAVEN'T GAINED ONE SHRED OF FAITH.
THAT'S FINE. YOU'RE MERELY ONE PERSON OUT OF BILLIONS.
I'LL JUST HAVE TO FIND A DIFFERENT WAY.

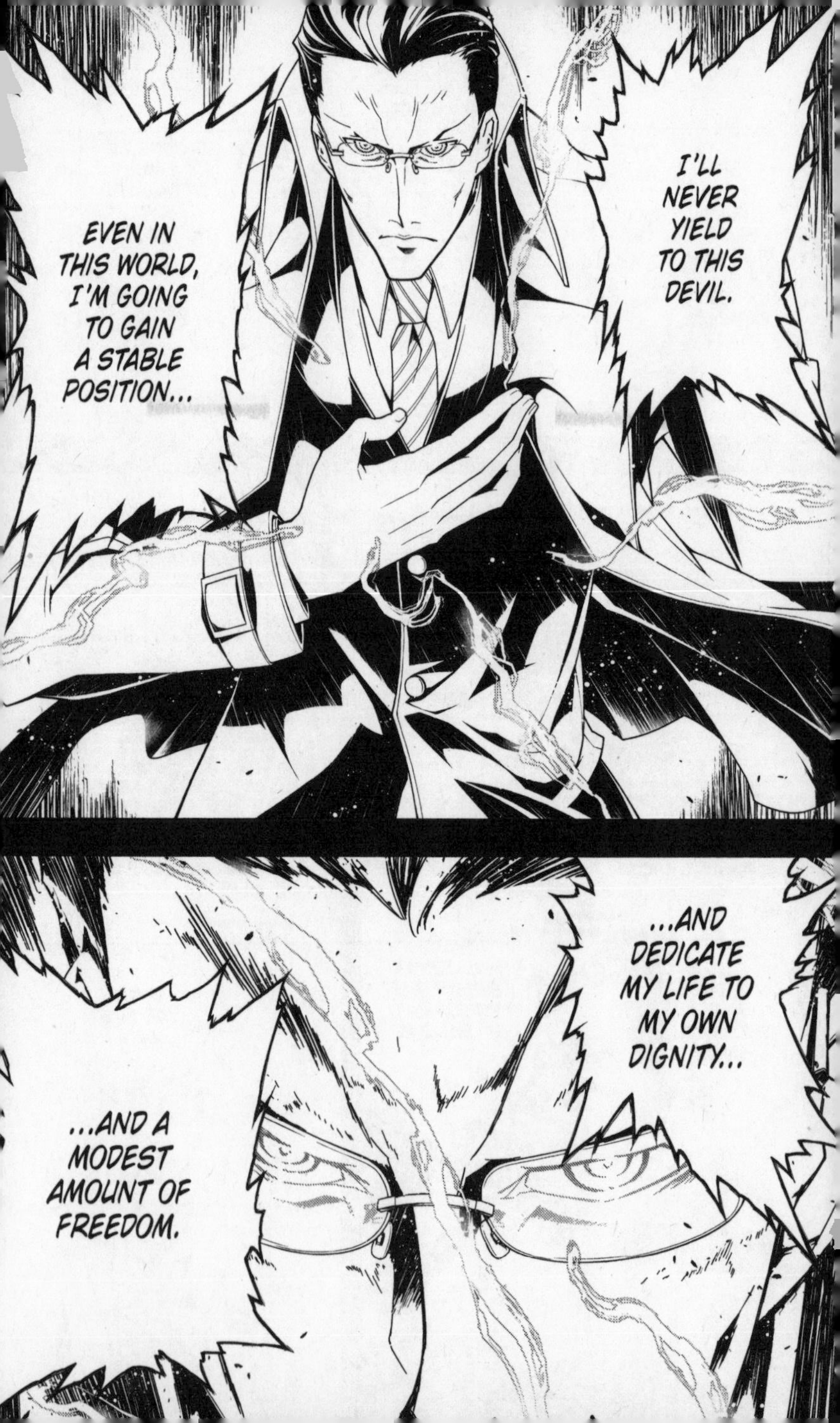
I'LL NEVER YIELD TO THIS DEVIL.
EVEN IN THIS WORLD, I'M GOING TO GAIN A STABLE POSITION...
...AND DEDICATE MY LIFE TO MY OWN DIGNITY...
...AND A MODEST AMOUNT OF FREEDOM.

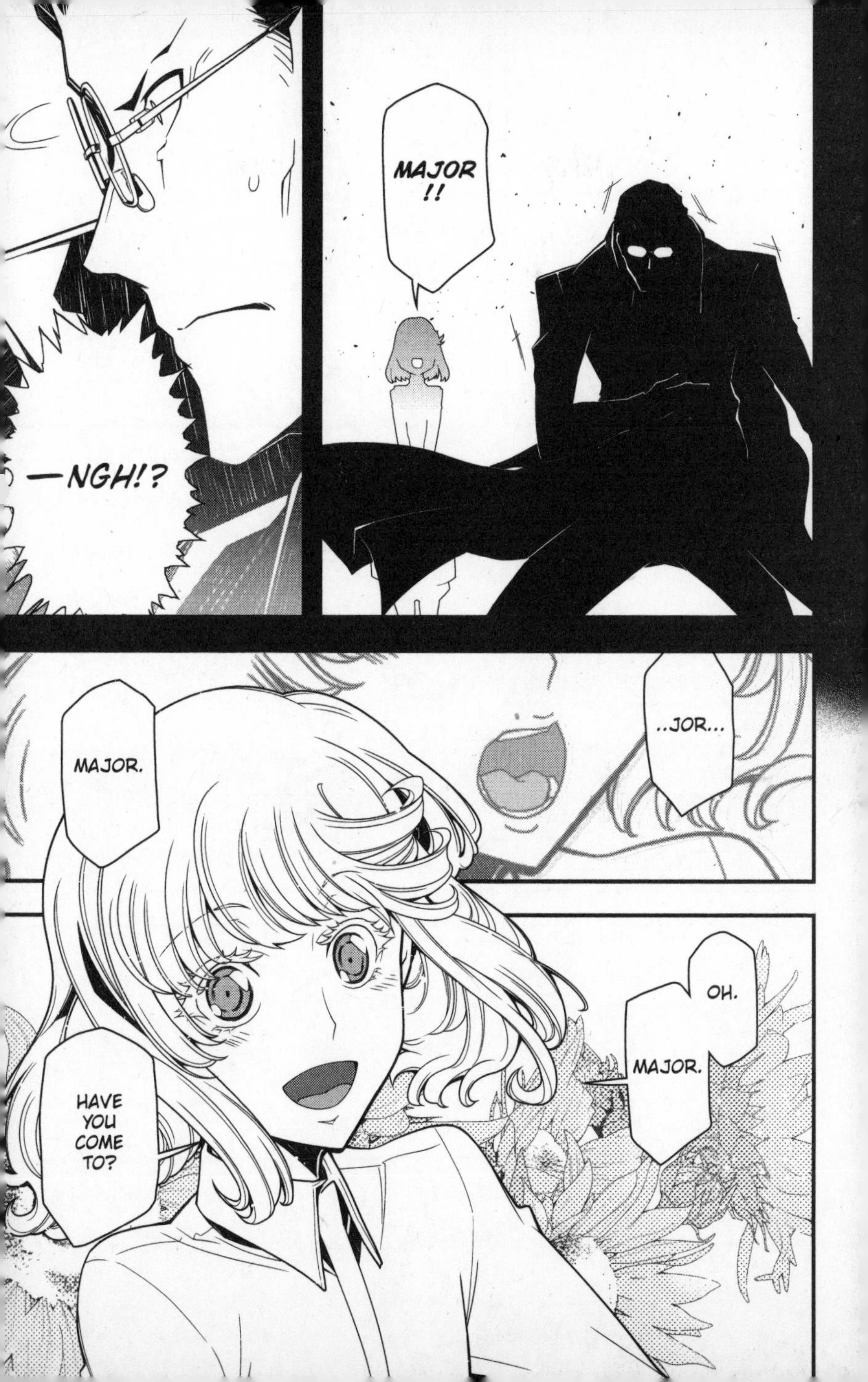
MAJOR !!
—NGH!?
..JOR...
MAJOR.
OH.
MAJOR.
HAVE YOU COME TO?

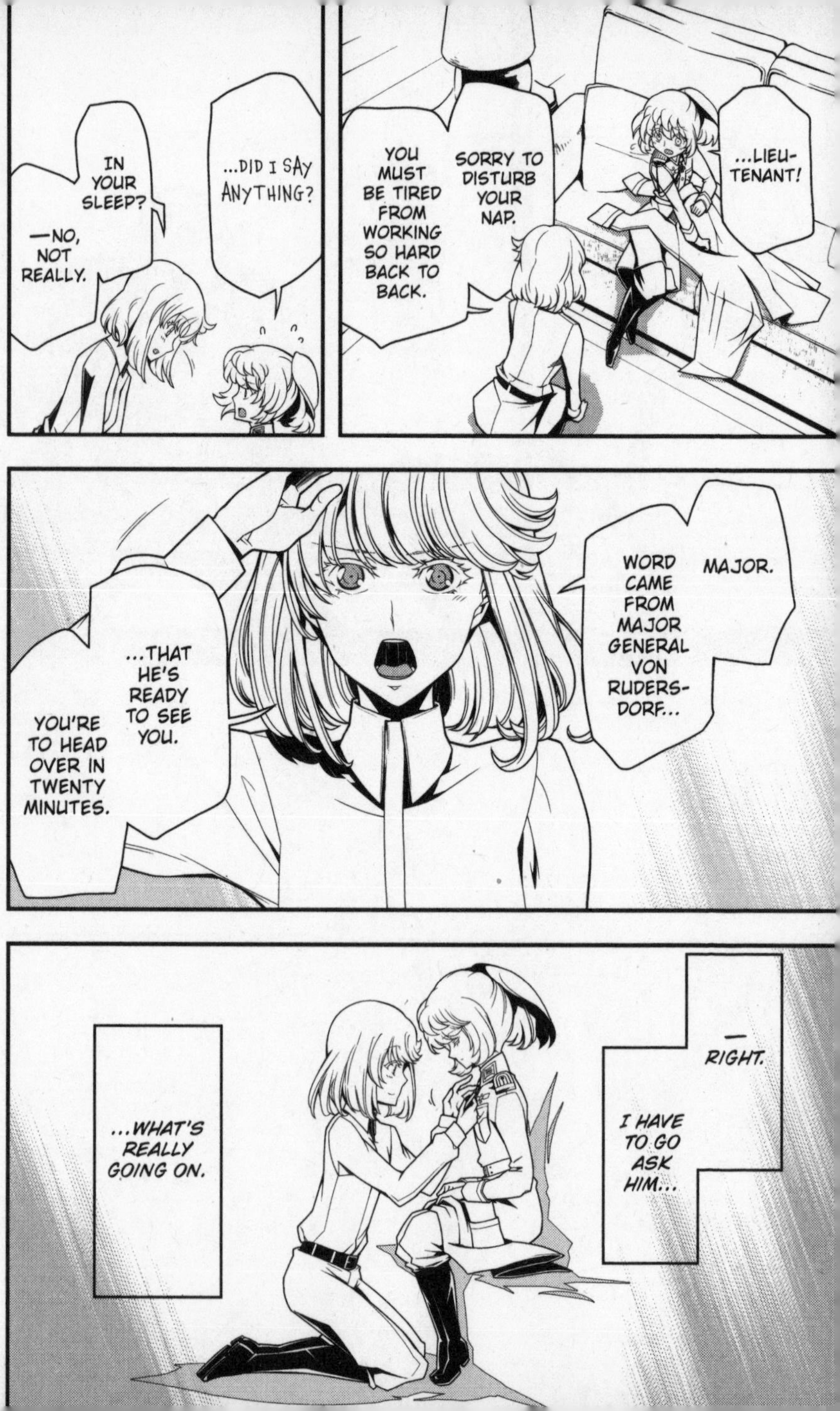
...LIEU-TENANT!
SORRY TO DISTURB YOUR NAP.
YOU MUST BE TIRED FROM WORKING SO HARD BACK TO BACK.
...DID I SAY ANYTHING?
IN YOUR SLEEP?
—NO, NOT REALLY.
MAJOR.
WORD CAME FROM MAJOR GENERAL VON RUDERS-DORF...
...THAT HE'S READY TO SEE YOU.
YOU'RE TO HEAD OVER IN TWENTY MINUTES.
—RIGHT.
I HAVE TO GO ASK HIM...
...WHAT'S REALLY GOING ON.

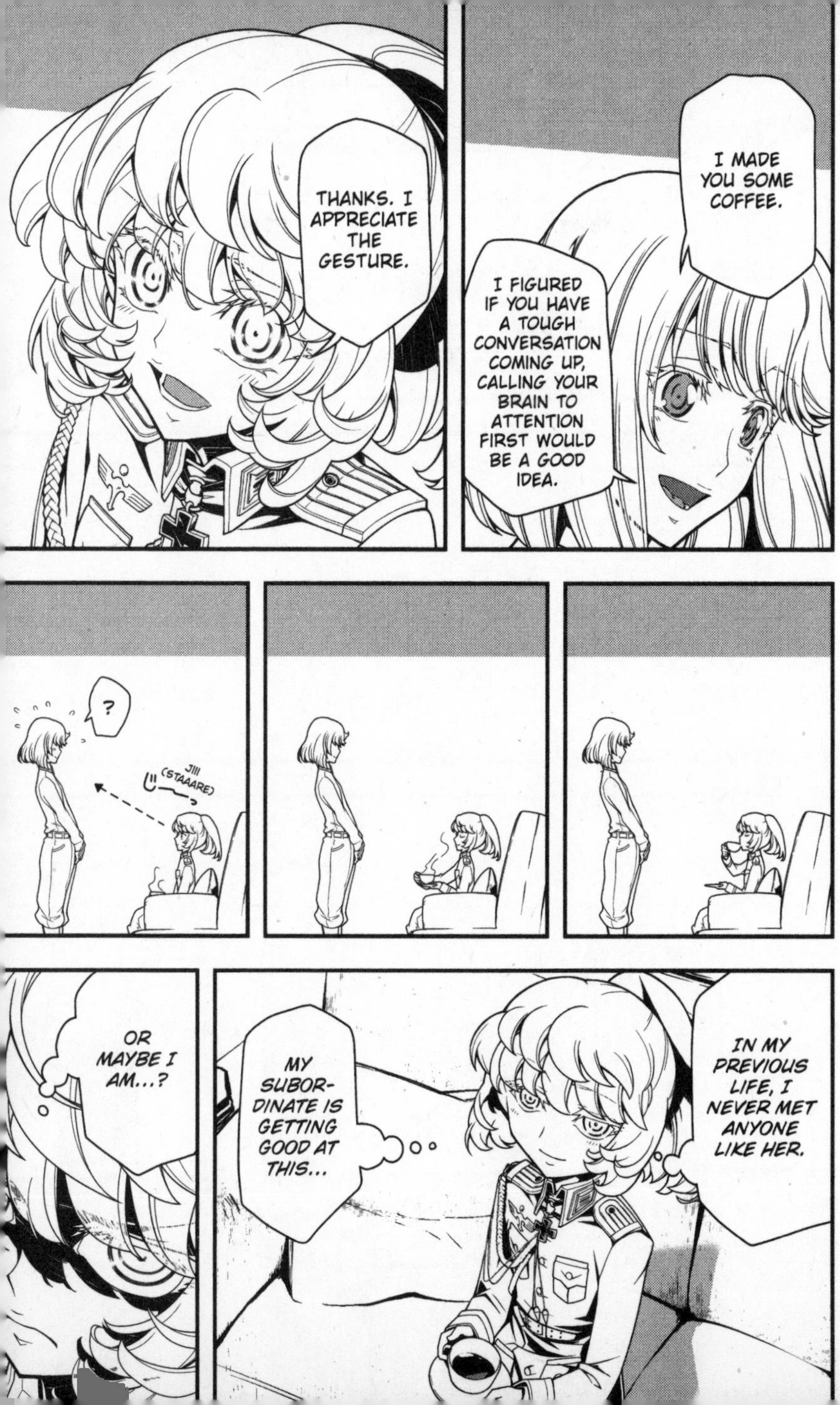
I MADE YOU SOME COFFEE.
I FIGURED IF YOU HAVE A TOUGH CONVERSATION COMING UP, CALLING YOUR BRAIN TO ATTENTION FIRST WOULD BE A GOOD IDEA.
THANKS. I APPRECIATE THE GESTURE.
?
JIII (STAAARE)
IN MY PREVIOUS LIFE, I NEVER MET ANYONE LIKE HER.
MY SUBOR-DINATE IS GETTING GOOD AT THIS...
OR MAYBE I AM...?

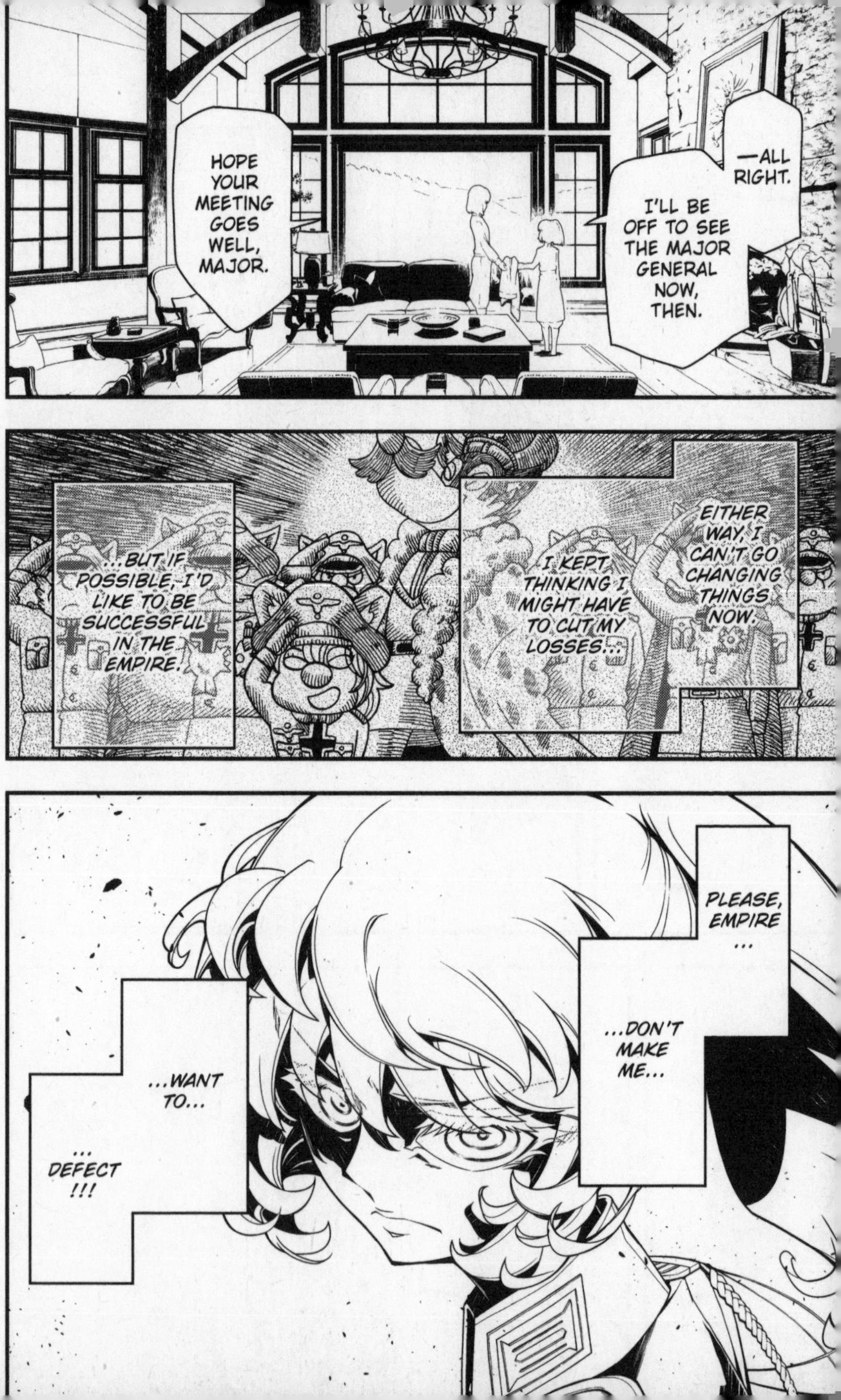
—ALL RIGHT.
I'LL BE OFF TO SEE THE MAJOR GENERAL NOW, THEN.
HOPE YOUR MEETING GOES WELL, MAJOR.
EITHER WAY, I CAN'T GO CHANGING THINGS NOW.
I KEPT THINKING I MIGHT HAVE TO CUT MY LOSSES...
...BUT IF POSSIBLE, I'D LIKE TO BE SUCCESSFUL IN THE EMPIRE.
PLEASE, EMPIRE...
...DON'T MAKE ME...
...WANT TO...
...DEFECT!!!

Chapter 19

Norden VI

The Saga of Tanya the Evil

Chapter: 19

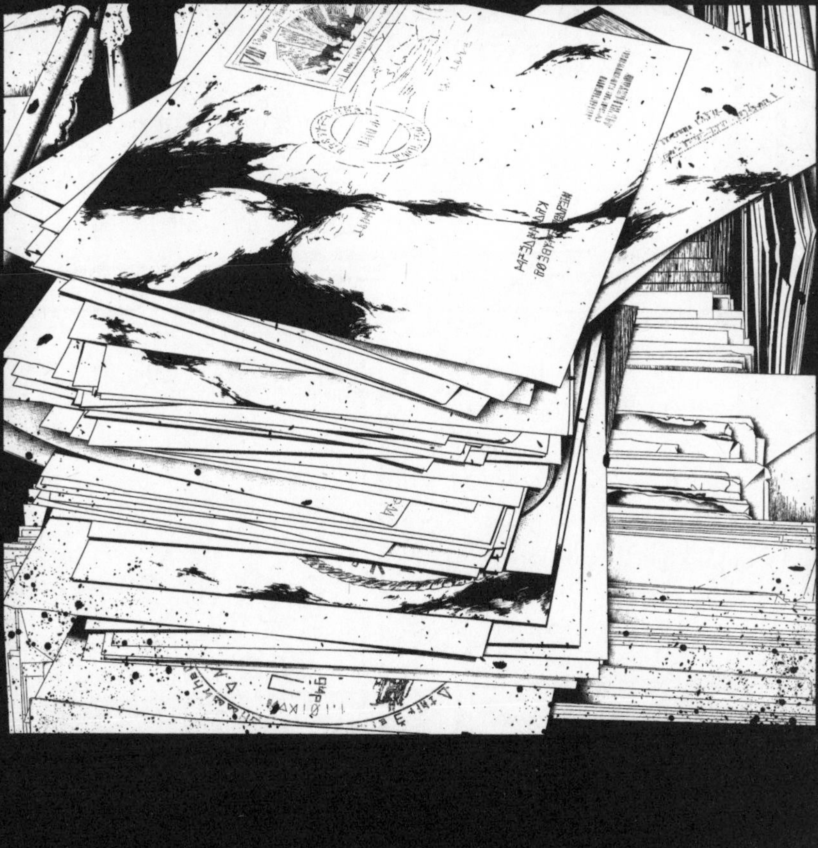

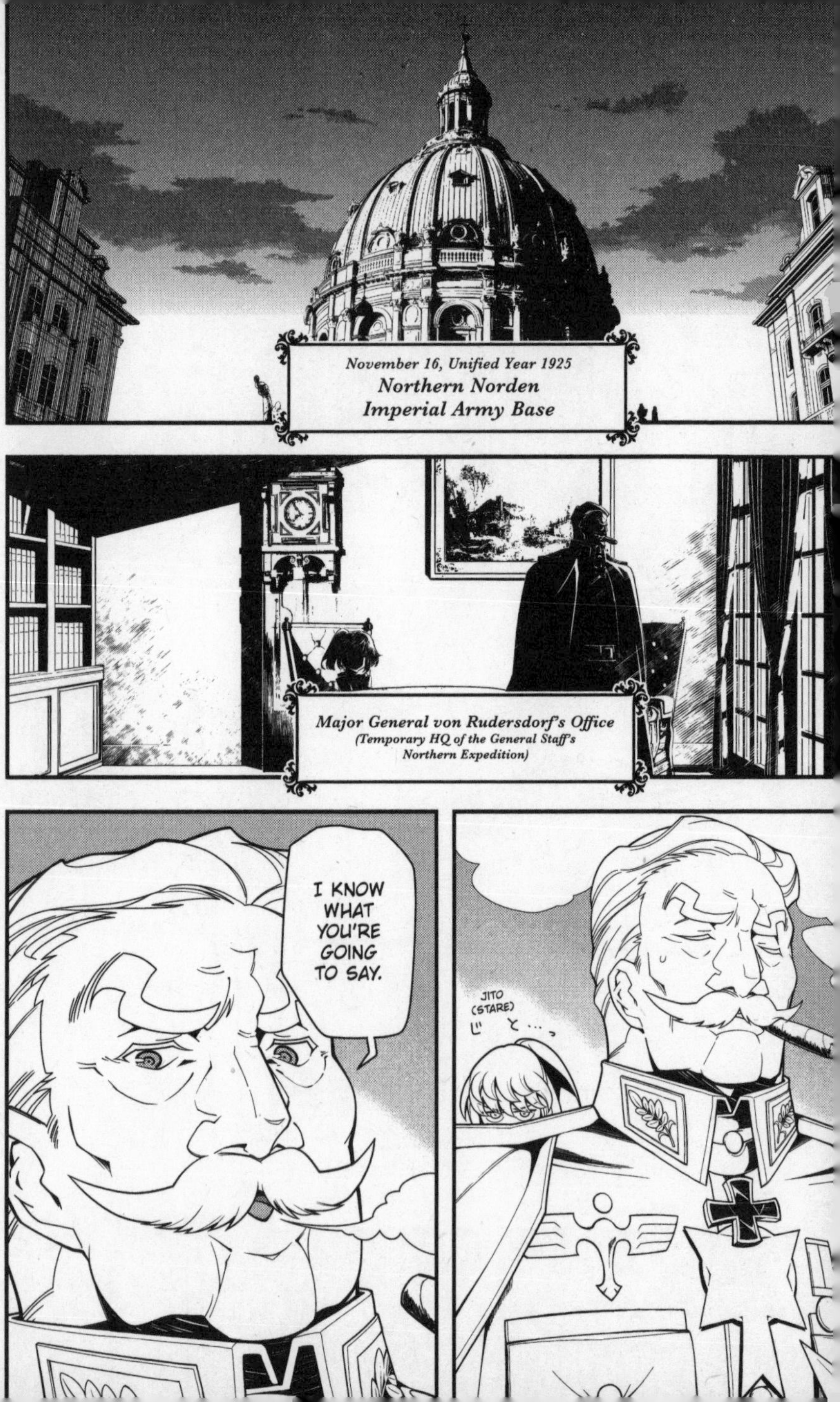
November 16, Unified Year 1925
Northern Norden
Imperial Army Base
Major General von Rudersdorf's Office
(Temporary HQ of the General Staff's
Northern Expedition)
JITO
(STARE)
じと…っ
I KNOW WHAT YOU'RE GOING TO SAY.

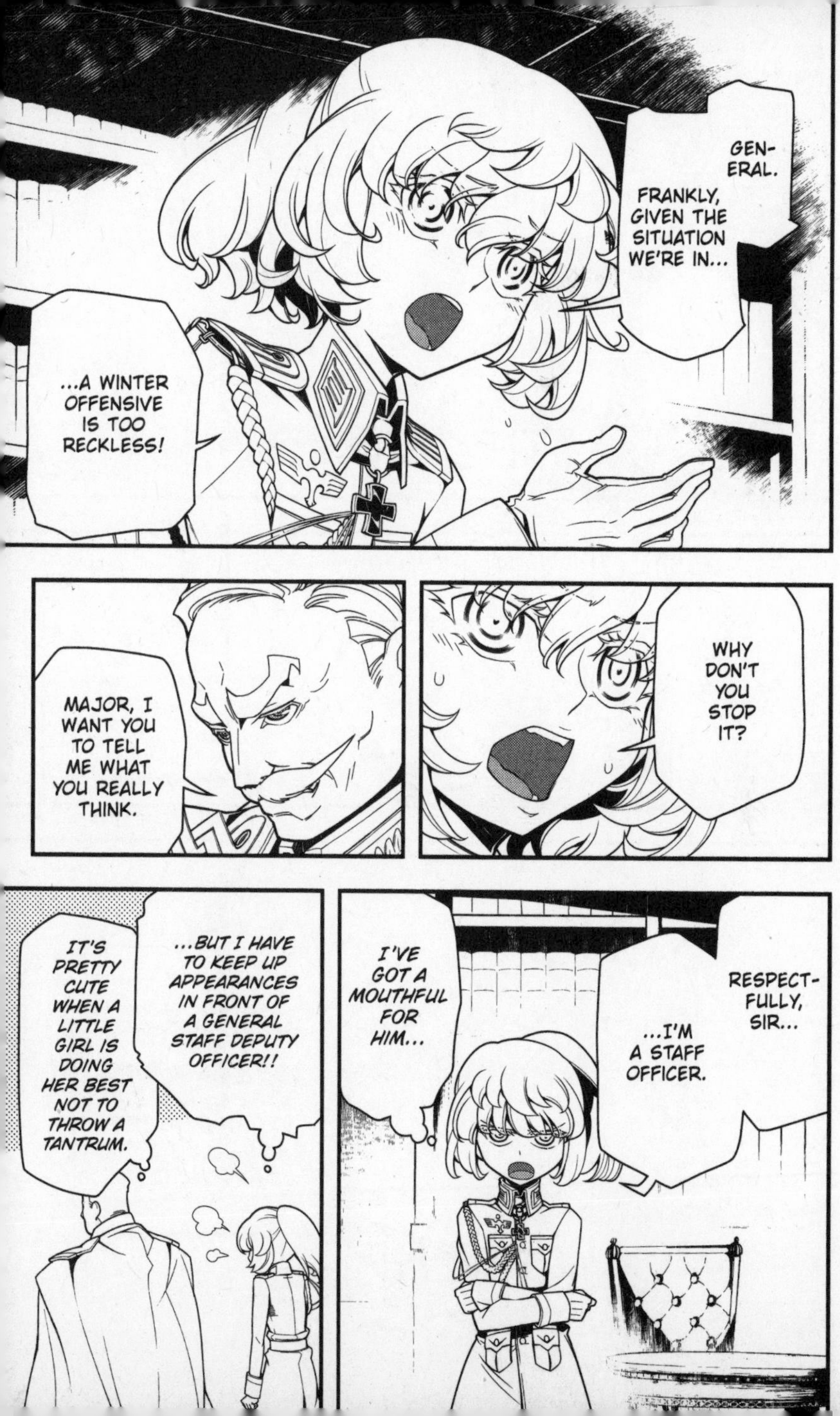
GEN-ERAL.
FRANKLY, GIVEN THE SITUATION WE'RE IN...
...A WINTER OFFENSIVE IS TOO RECKLESS!
WHY DON'T YOU STOP IT?
MAJOR, I WANT YOU TO TELL ME WHAT YOU REALLY THINK.
RESPECT-FULLY, SIR...
...I'M A STAFF OFFICER.
I'VE GOT A MOUTHFUL FOR HIM...
...BUT I HAVE TO KEEP UP APPEARANCES IN FRONT OF A GENERAL STAFF DEPUTY OFFICER!!
IT'S PRETTY CUTE WHEN A LITTLE GIRL IS DOING HER BEST NOT TO THROW A TANTRUM.

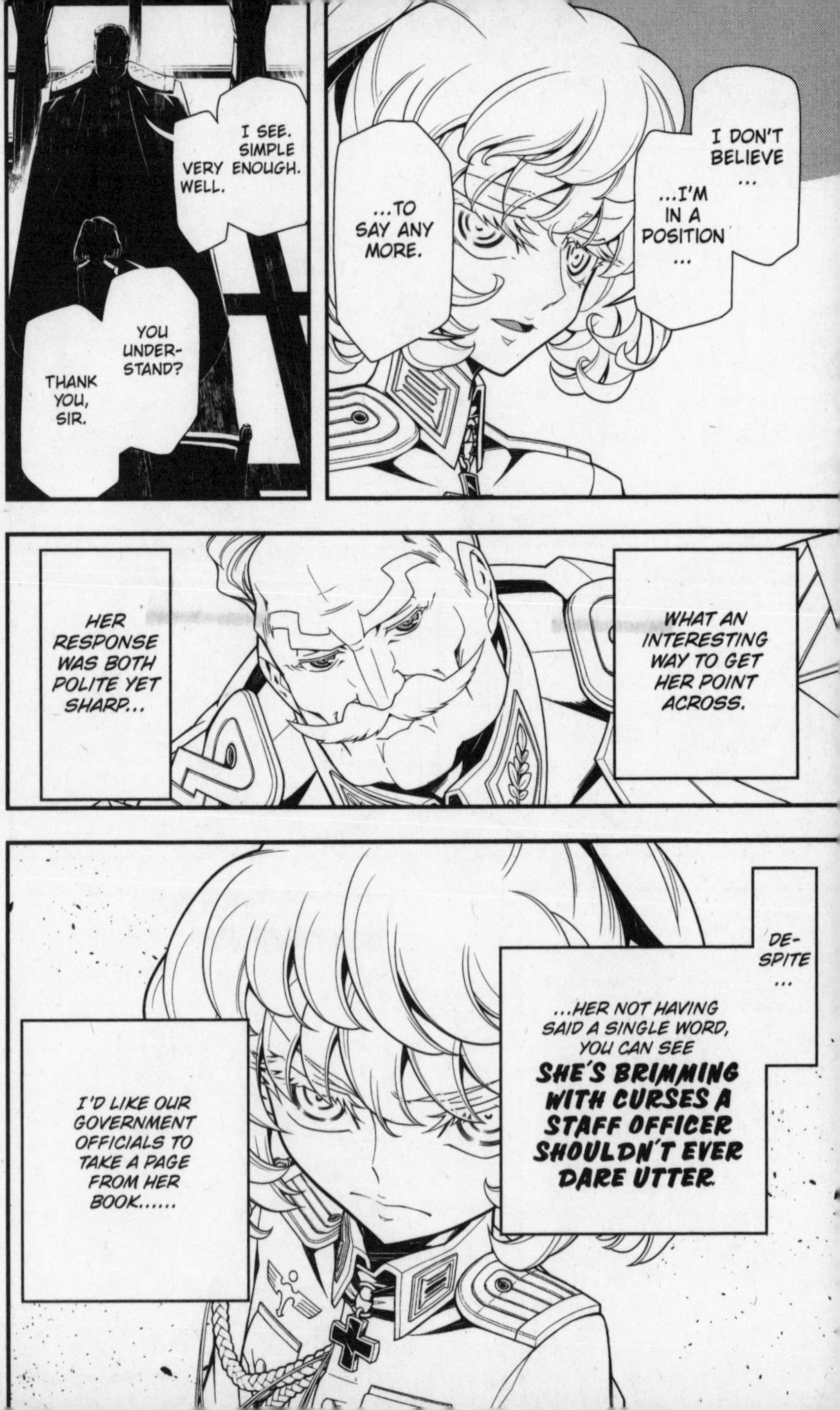
I DON'T BELIEVE...
...I'M IN A POSITION...
...TO SAY ANY MORE.
I SEE. SIMPLE ENOUGH.
VERY WELL.
YOU UNDERSTAND?
THANK YOU, SIR.
WHAT AN INTERESTING WAY TO GET HER POINT ACROSS.
HER RESPONSE WAS BOTH POLITE YET SHARP...
DE-SPITE...
...HER NOT HAVING SAID A SINGLE WORD, YOU CAN SEE SHE'S BRIMMING WITH CURSES A STAFF OFFICER SHOULDN'T EVER DARE UTTER.
I'D LIKE OUR GOVERNMENT OFFICIALS TO TAKE A PAGE FROM HER BOOK......

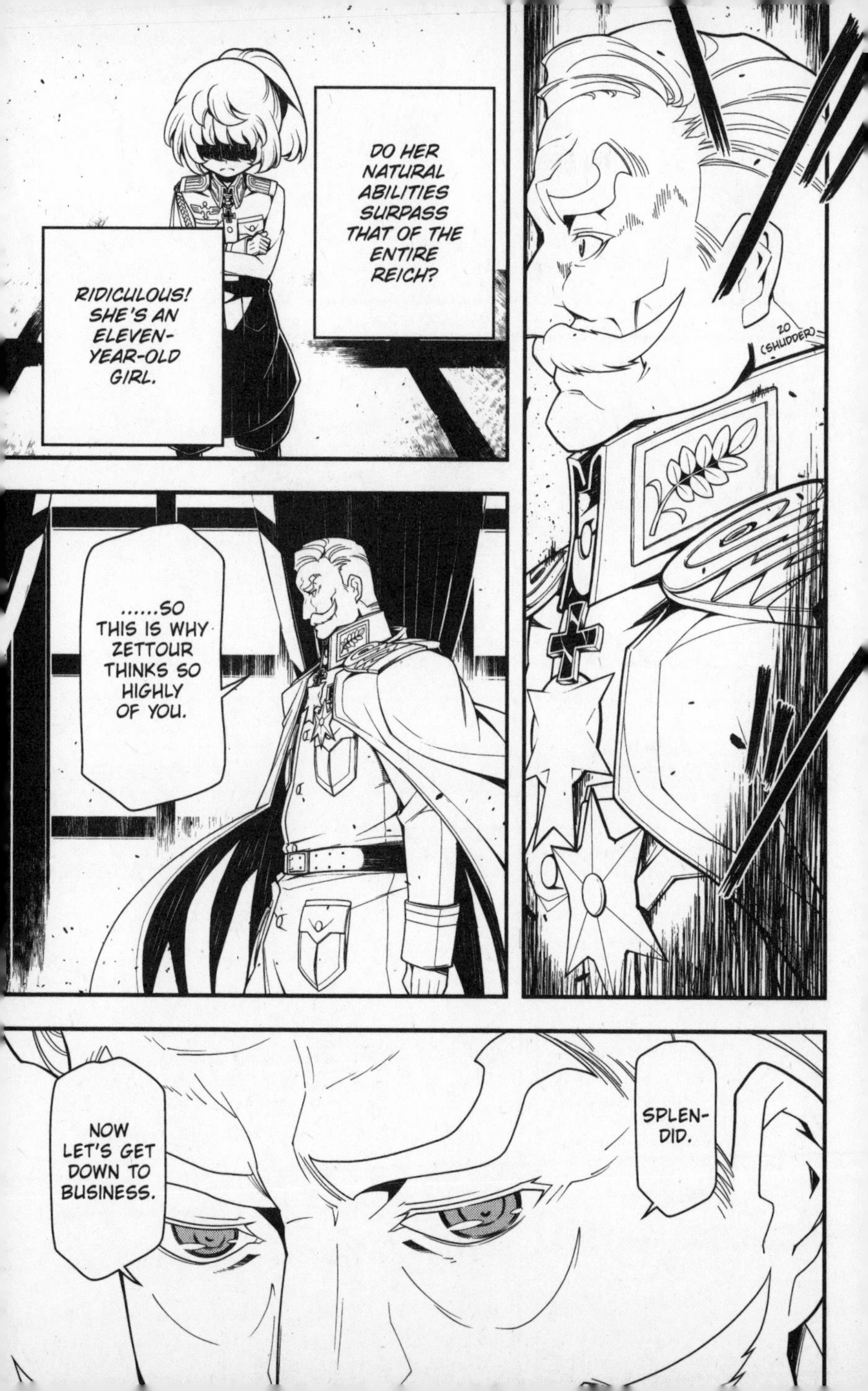
ZO (SHUDDER)
DO HER NATURAL ABILITIES SURPASS THAT OF THE ENTIRE REICH?
RIDICULOUS! SHE'S AN ELEVEN-YEAR-OLD GIRL.
......SO THIS IS WHY ZETTOUR THINKS SO HIGHLY OF YOU.
SPLEN-DID.
NOW LET'S GET DOWN TO BUSINESS.

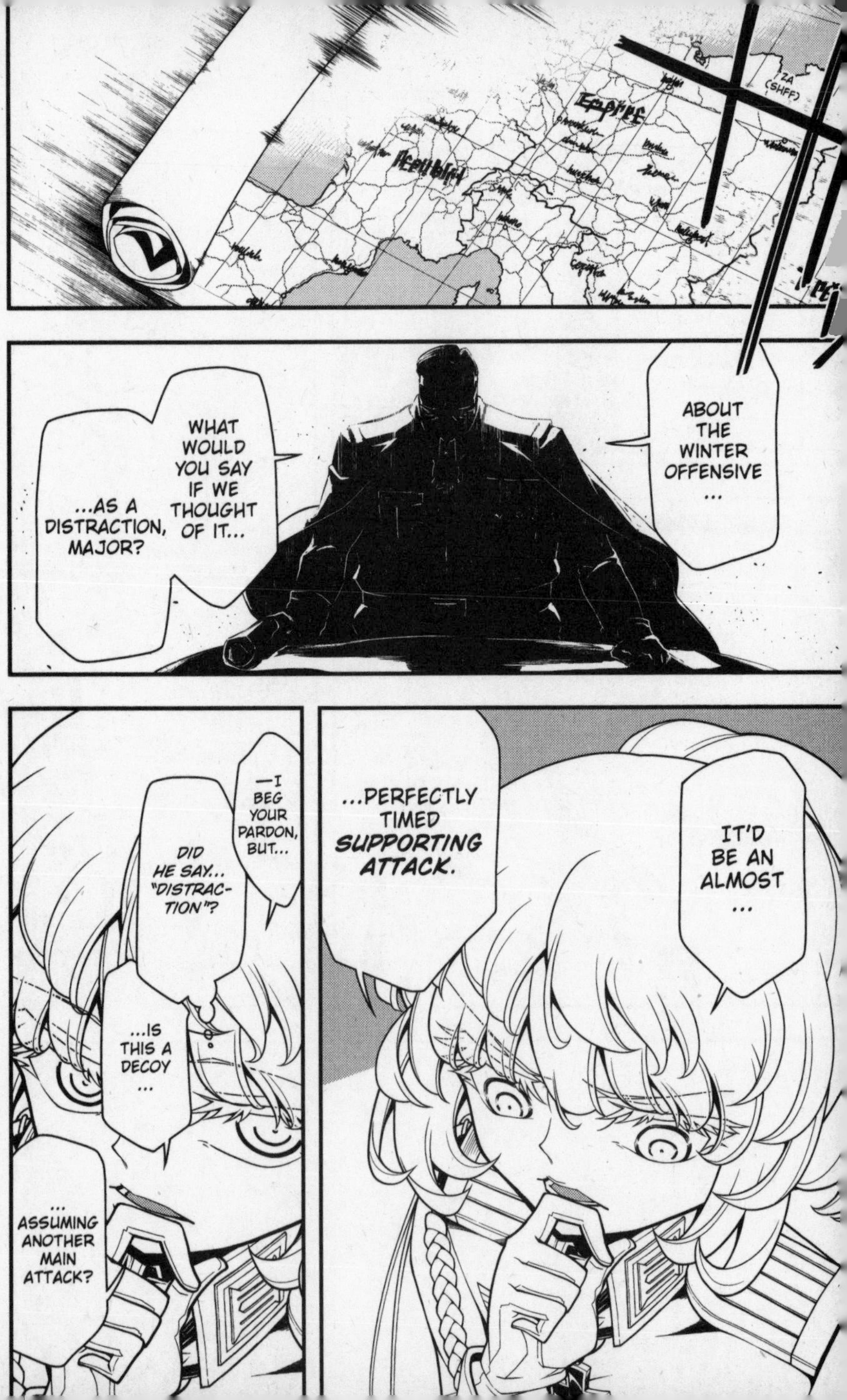
ZA (SHFF)
ABOUT THE WINTER OFFENSIVE...
WHAT WOULD YOU SAY IF WE THOUGHT OF IT...
...AS A DISTRACTION, MAJOR?
IT'D BE AN ALMOST...
...PERFECTLY TIMED SUPPORTING ATTACK.
—I BEG YOUR PARDON, BUT...
DID HE SAY... "DISTRACTION"?
...IS THIS A DECOY...
...ASSUMING ANOTHER MAIN ATTACK?

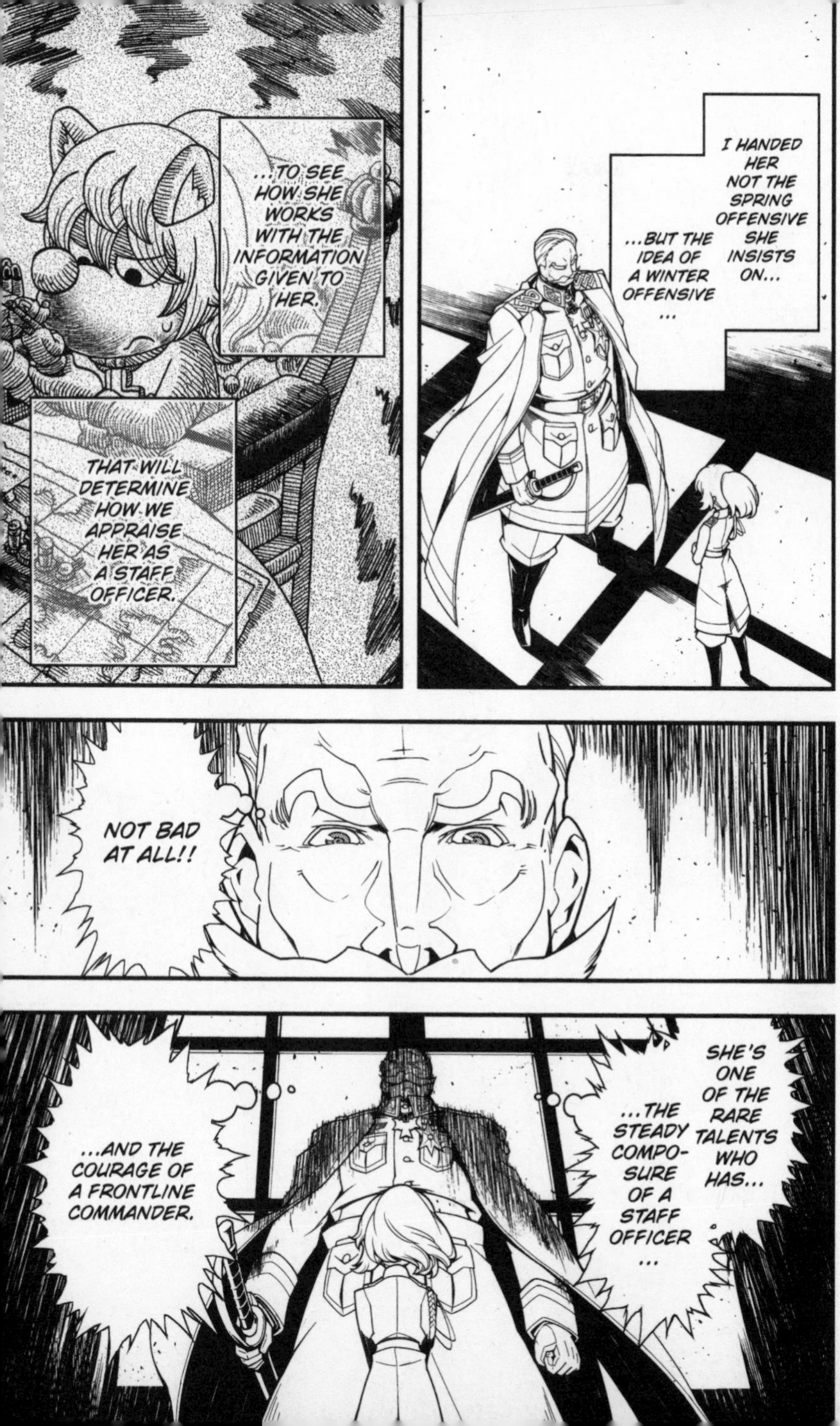
I HANDED HER NOT THE SPRING OFFENSIVE SHE INSISTS ON...
...BUT THE IDEA OF A WINTER OFFENSIVE...
...TO SEE HOW SHE WORKS WITH THE INFORMATION GIVEN TO HER.
THAT WILL DETERMINE HOW WE APPRAISE HER AS A STAFF OFFICER.
NOT BAD AT ALL!!
SHE'S ONE OF THE RARE TALENTS WHO HAS...
...THE STEADY COMPO-SURE OF A STAFF OFFICER...
...AND THE COURAGE OF A FRONTLINE COMMANDER.

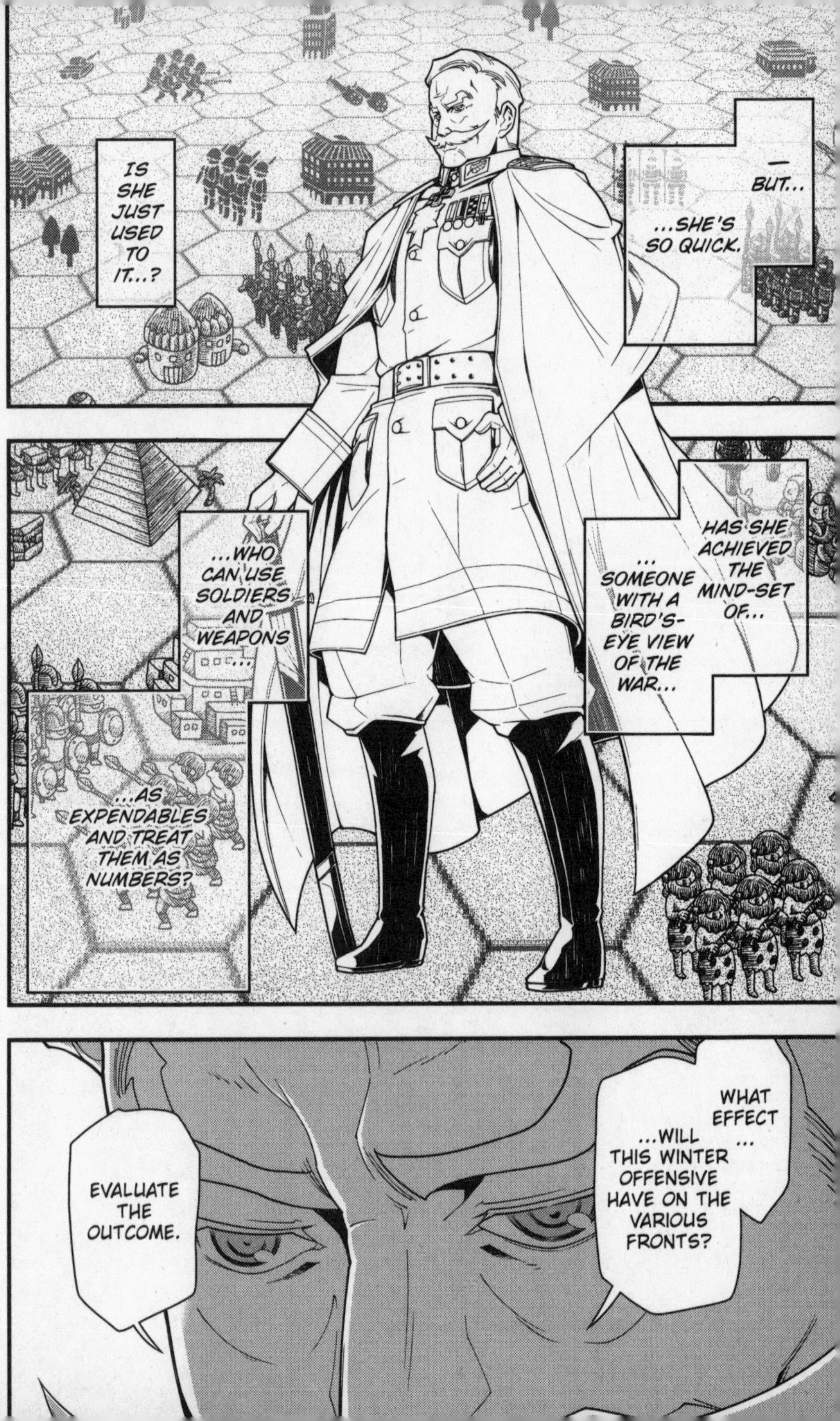
—BUT...
...SHE'S SO QUICK.
IS SHE JUST USED TO IT...?
HAS SHE ACHIEVED THE MIND-SET OF...
...SOMEONE WITH A BIRD'S-EYE VIEW OF THE WAR...
...WHO CAN USE SOLDIERS AND WEAPONS...
...AS EXPENDABLES AND TREAT THEM AS NUMBERS?
WHAT EFFECT...
...WILL THIS WINTER OFFENSIVE HAVE ON THE VARIOUS FRONTS?
EVALUATE THE OUTCOME.

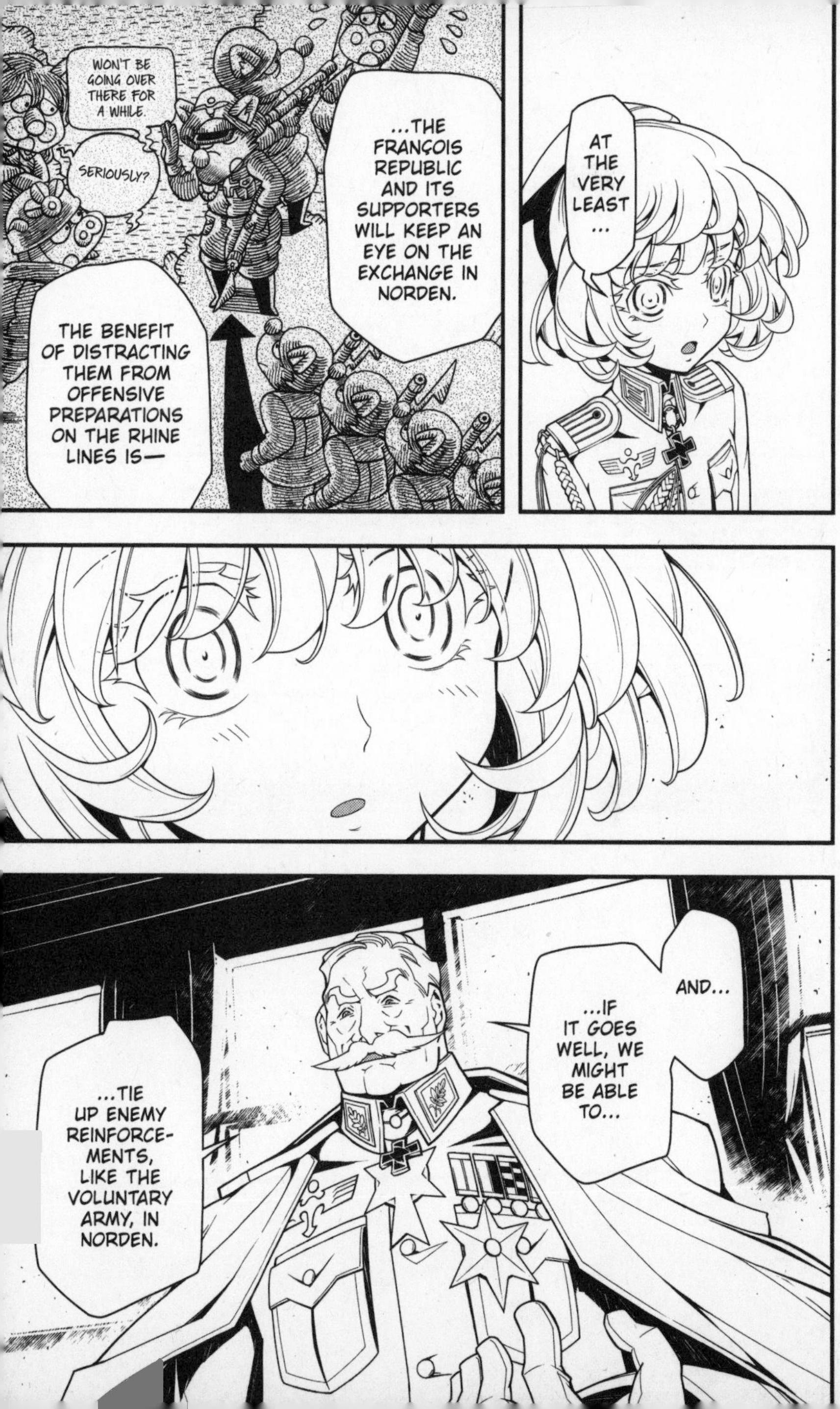
AT THE VERY LEAST...
...THE FRANÇOIS REPUBLIC AND ITS SUPPORTERS WILL KEEP AN EYE ON THE EXCHANGE IN NORDEN.
WON'T BE GOING OVER THERE FOR A WHILE.
SERIOUSLY?
THE BENEFIT OF DISTRACTING THEM FROM OFFENSIVE PREPARATIONS ON THE RHINE LINES IS—
AND...
...IF IT GOES WELL, WE MIGHT BE ABLE TO...
...TIE UP ENEMY REINFORCEMENTS, LIKE THE VOLUNTARY ARMY, IN NORDEN.

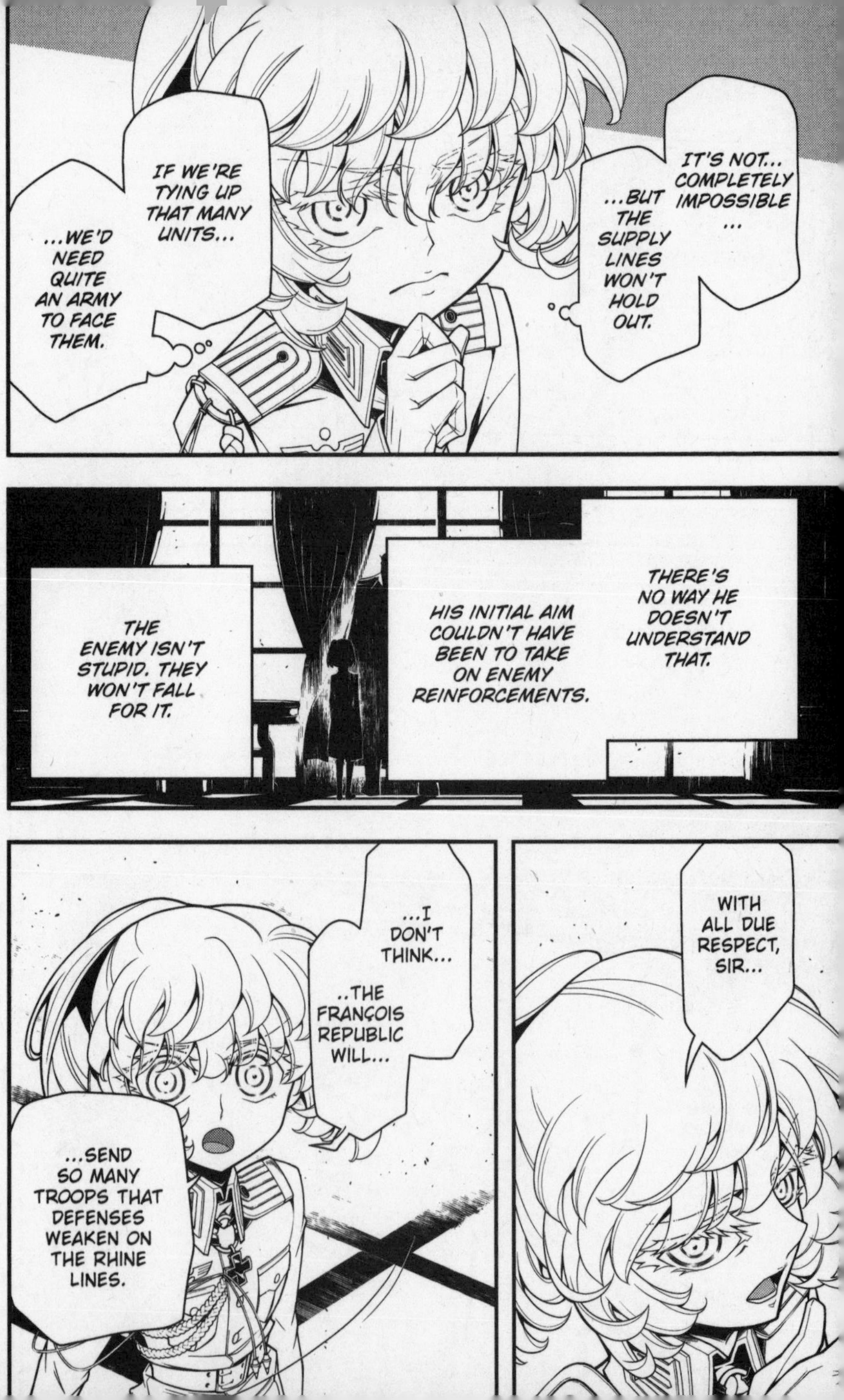
IT'S NOT... COMPLETELY IMPOSSIBLE ...
...BUT THE SUPPLY LINES WON'T HOLD OUT.
IF WE'RE TYING UP THAT MANY UNITS...
...WE'D NEED QUITE AN ARMY TO FACE THEM.
THERE'S NO WAY HE DOESN'T UNDERSTAND THAT.
HIS INITIAL AIM COULDN'T HAVE BEEN TO TAKE ON ENEMY REINFORCEMENTS.
THE ENEMY ISN'T STUPID. THEY WON'T FALL FOR IT.
WITH ALL DUE RESPECT, SIR...
...I DON'T THINK...
..THE FRANÇOIS REPUBLIC WILL...
...SEND SO MANY TROOPS THAT DEFENSES WEAKEN ON THE RHINE LINES.

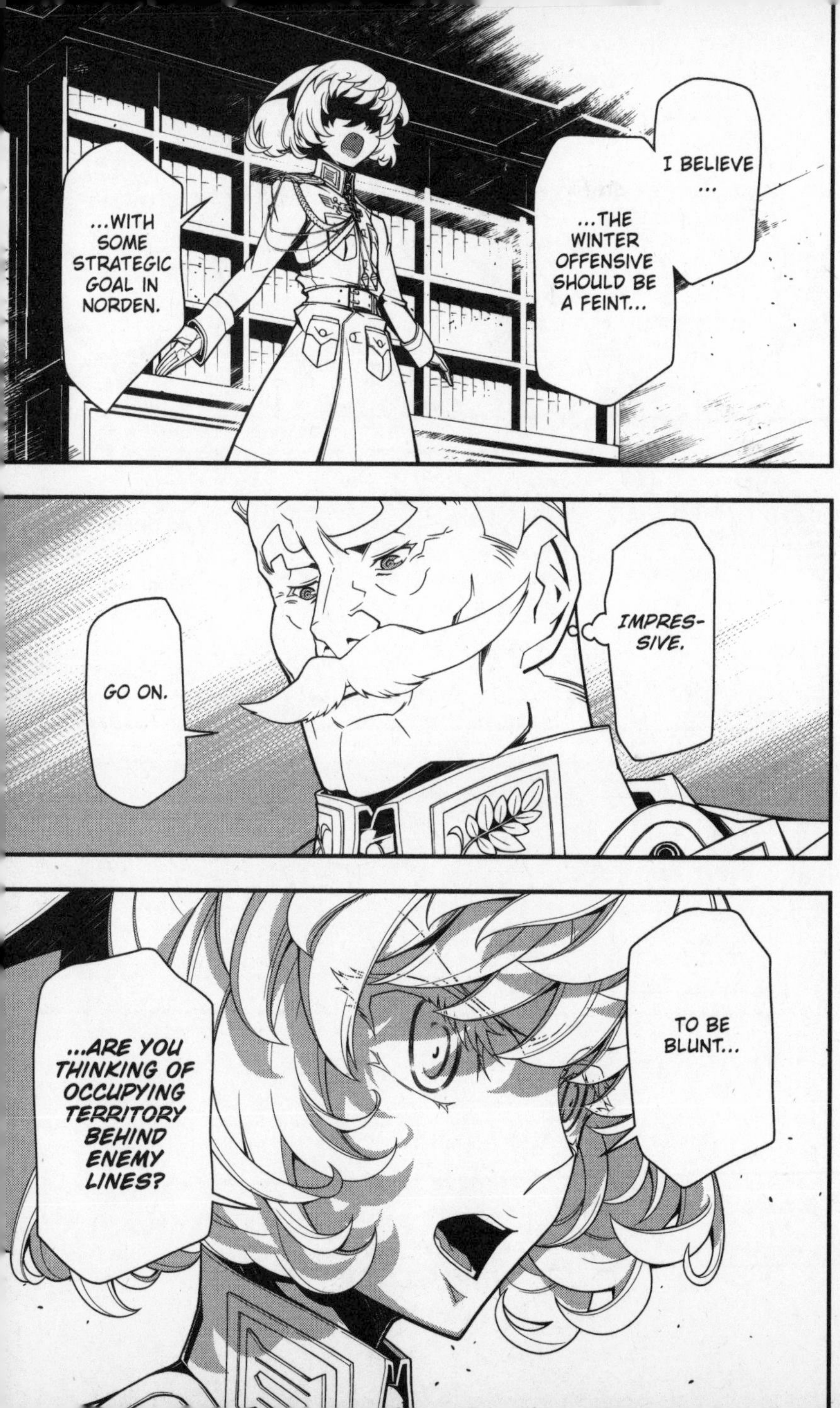
I BELIEVE ...
...THE WINTER OFFENSIVE SHOULD BE A FEINT...
...WITH SOME STRATEGIC GOAL IN NORDEN.
IMPRES-SIVE.
GO ON.
TO BE BLUNT...
...ARE YOU THINKING OF OCCUPYING TERRITORY BEHIND ENEMY LINES?

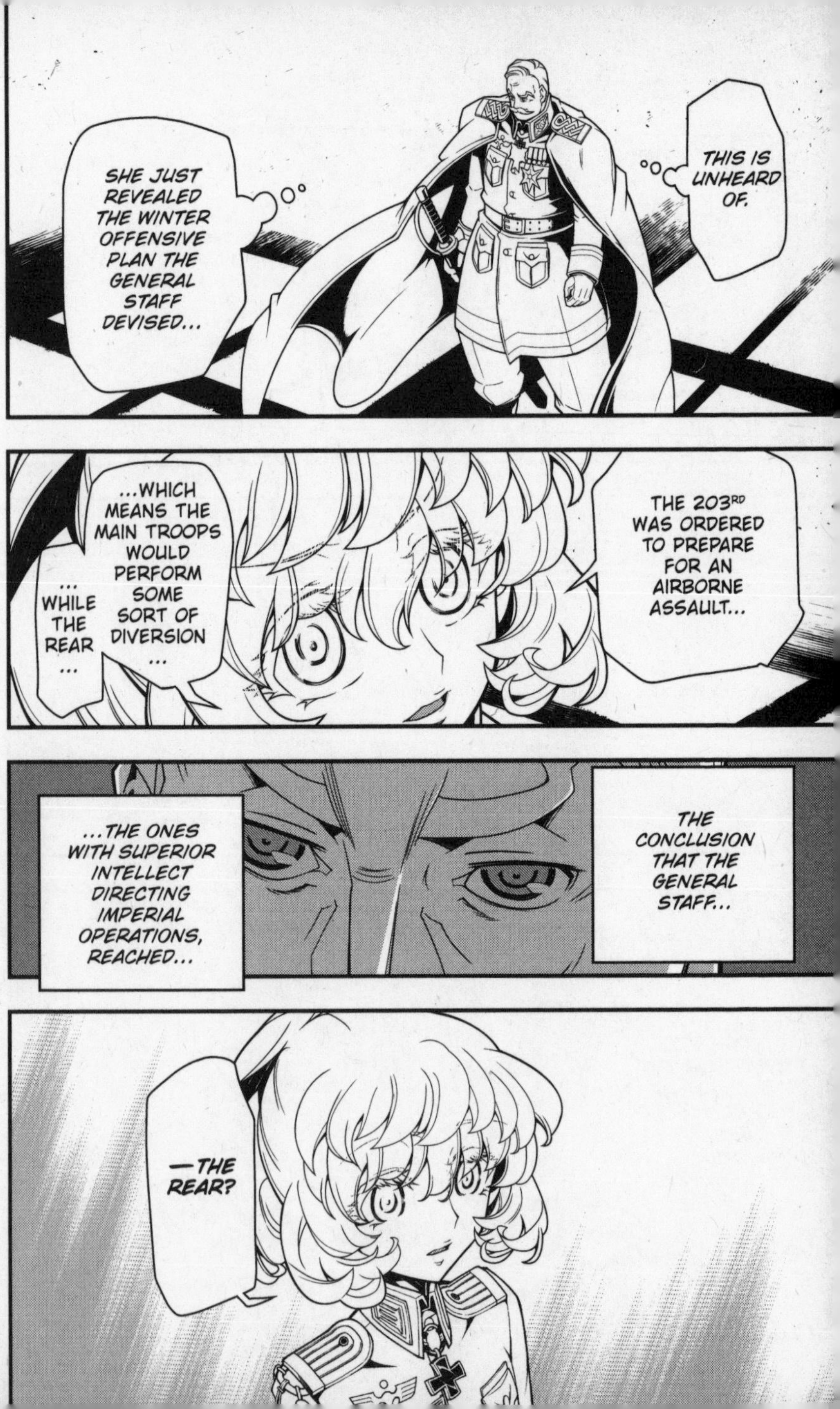
THIS IS UNHEARD OF.
SHE JUST REVEALED THE WINTER OFFENSIVE PLAN THE GENERAL STAFF DEVISED...
THE 203RD WAS ORDERED TO PREPARE FOR AN AIRBORNE ASSAULT...
...WHICH MEANS THE MAIN TROOPS WOULD PERFORM SOME SORT OF DIVERSION...
...WHILE THE REAR...
THE CONCLUSION THAT THE GENERAL STAFF...
...THE ONES WITH SUPERIOR INTELLECT DIRECTING IMPERIAL OPERATIONS, REACHED...
—THE REAR?

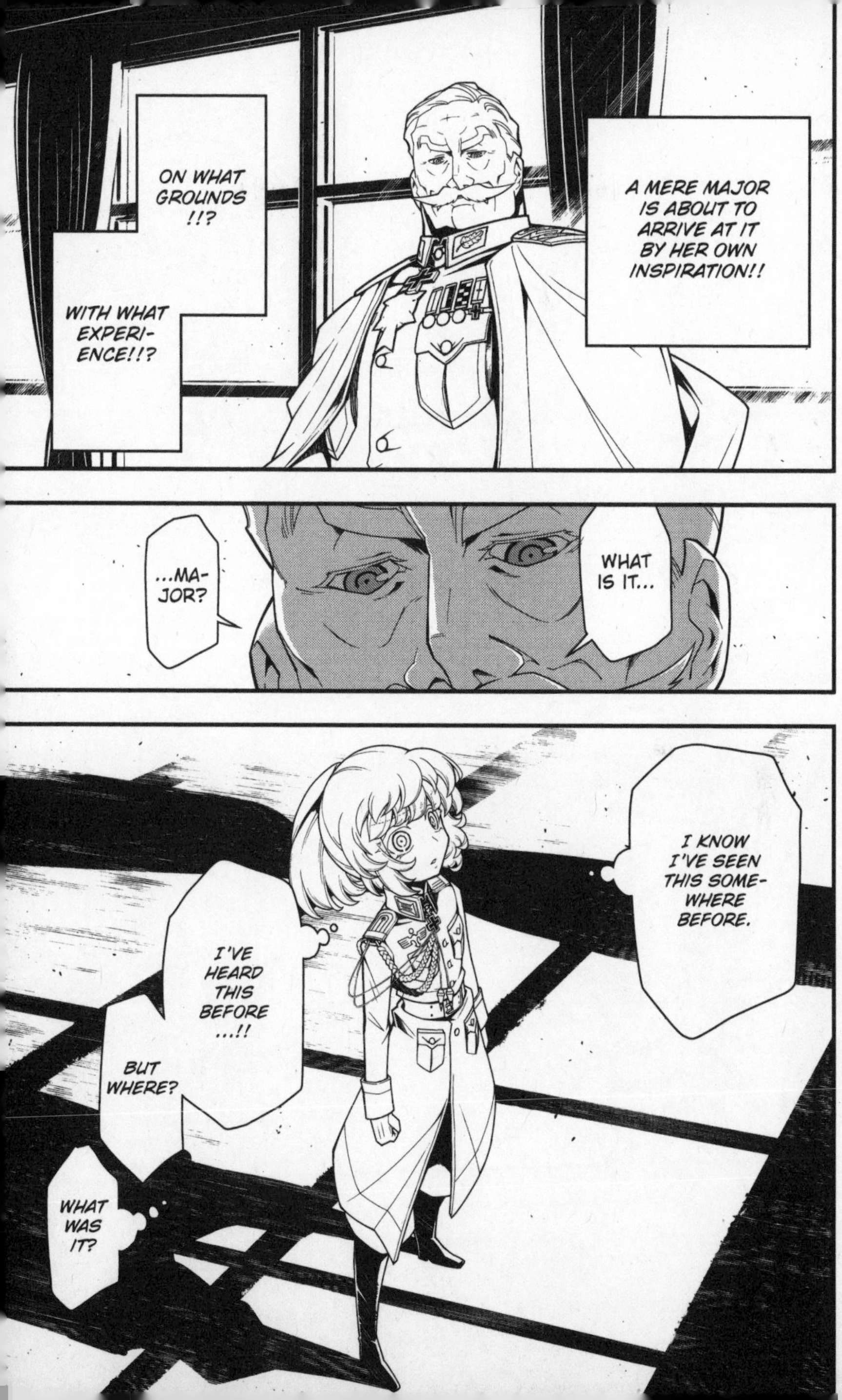
A MERE MAJOR IS ABOUT TO ARRIVE AT IT BY HER OWN INSPIRATION!!
ON WHAT GROUNDS!!?
WITH WHAT EXPERI-ENCE!!?
WHAT IS IT...
...MA-JOR?
I KNOW I'VE SEEN THIS SOME-WHERE BEFORE.
I'VE HEARD THIS BEFORE...!!
BUT WHERE?
WHAT WAS IT?

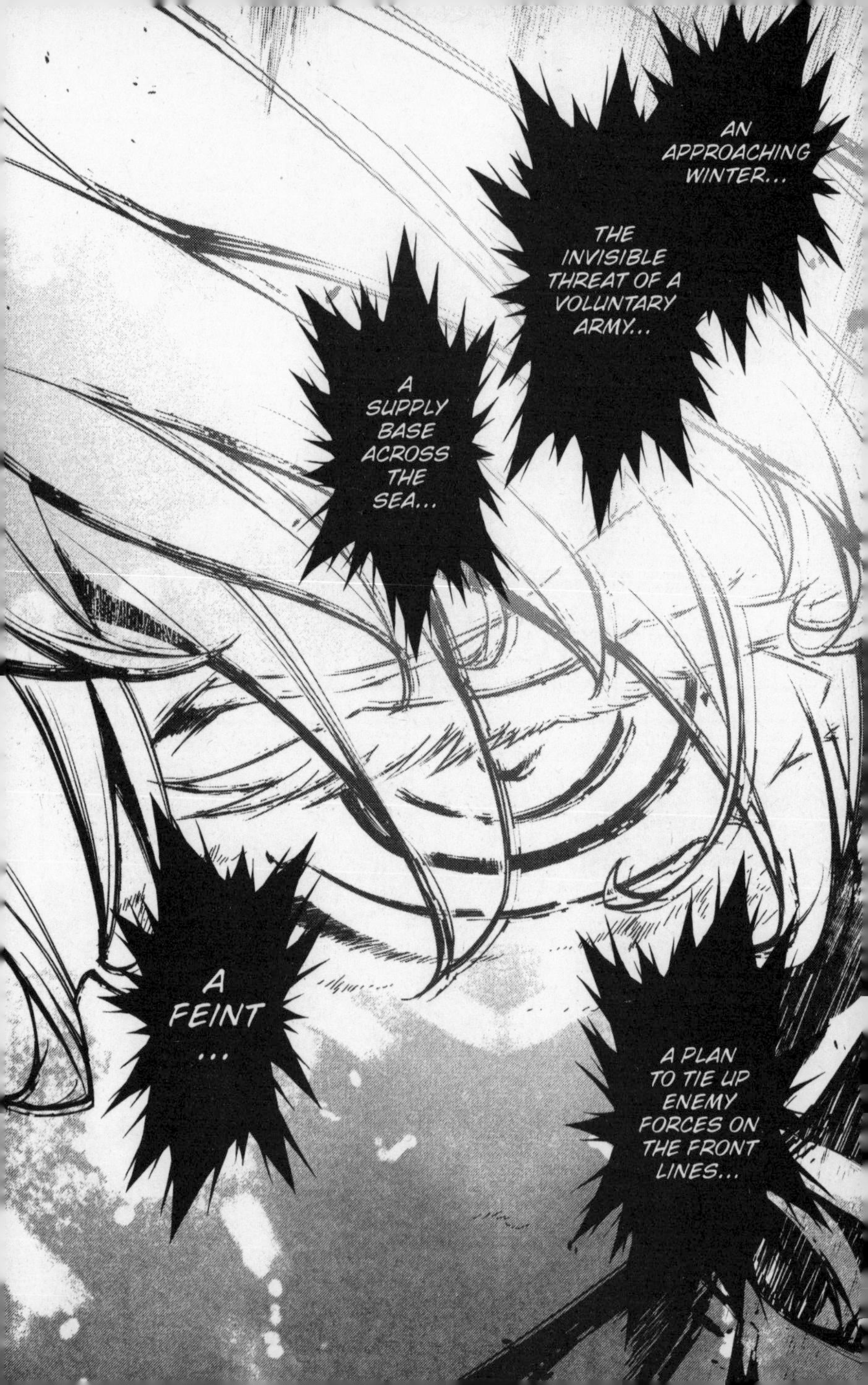
AN APPROACHING WINTER...
THE INVISIBLE THREAT OF A VOLUNTARY ARMY...
A SUPPLY BASE ACROSS THE SEA...
A PLAN TO TIE UP ENEMY FORCES ON THE FRONT LINES...
A FEINT...

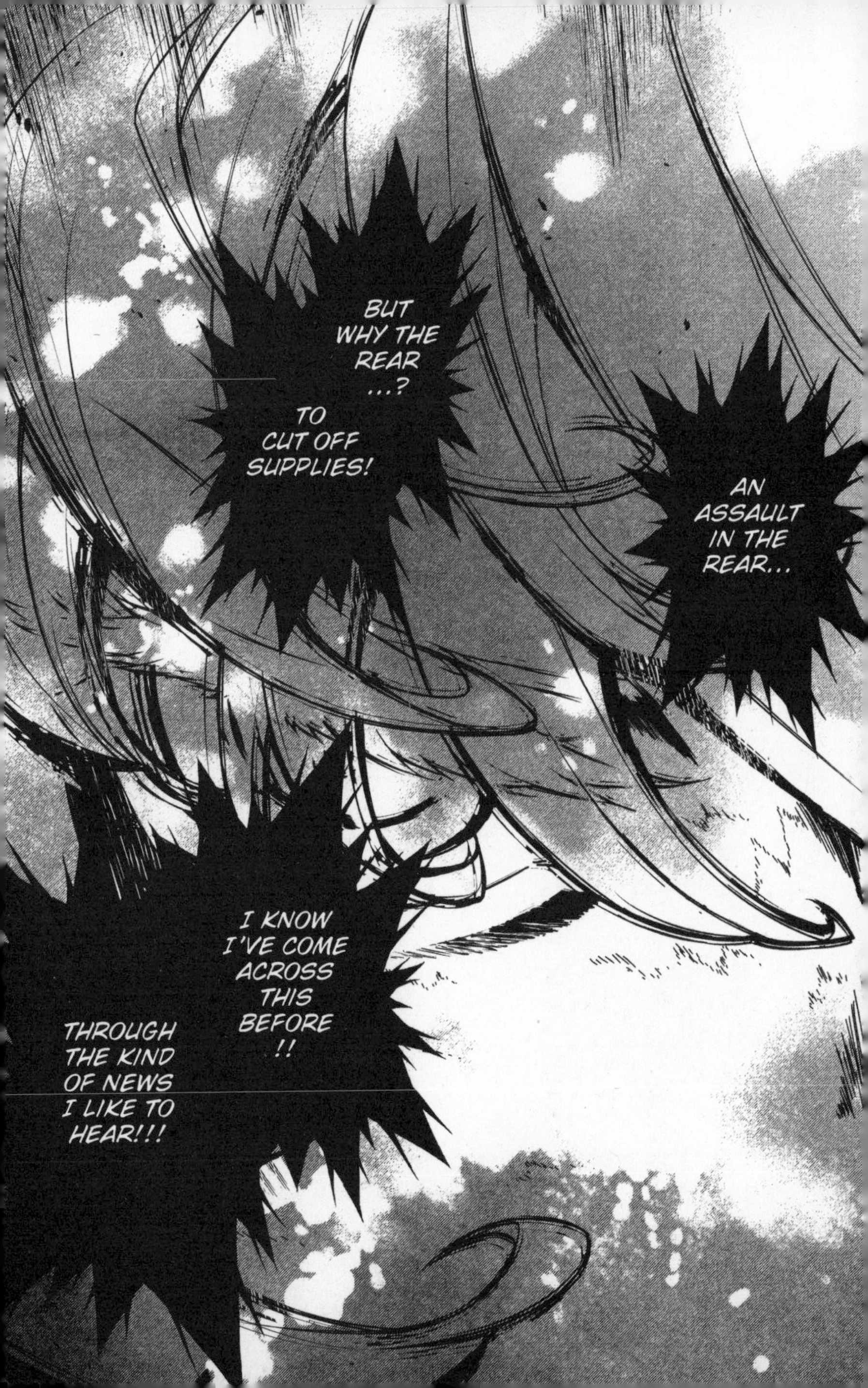
AN ASSAULT IN THE REAR...
BUT WHY THE REAR ...?
TO CUT OFF SUPPLIES!
I KNOW I'VE COME ACROSS THIS BEFORE !!
THROUGH THE KIND OF NEWS I LIKE TO HEAR!!!

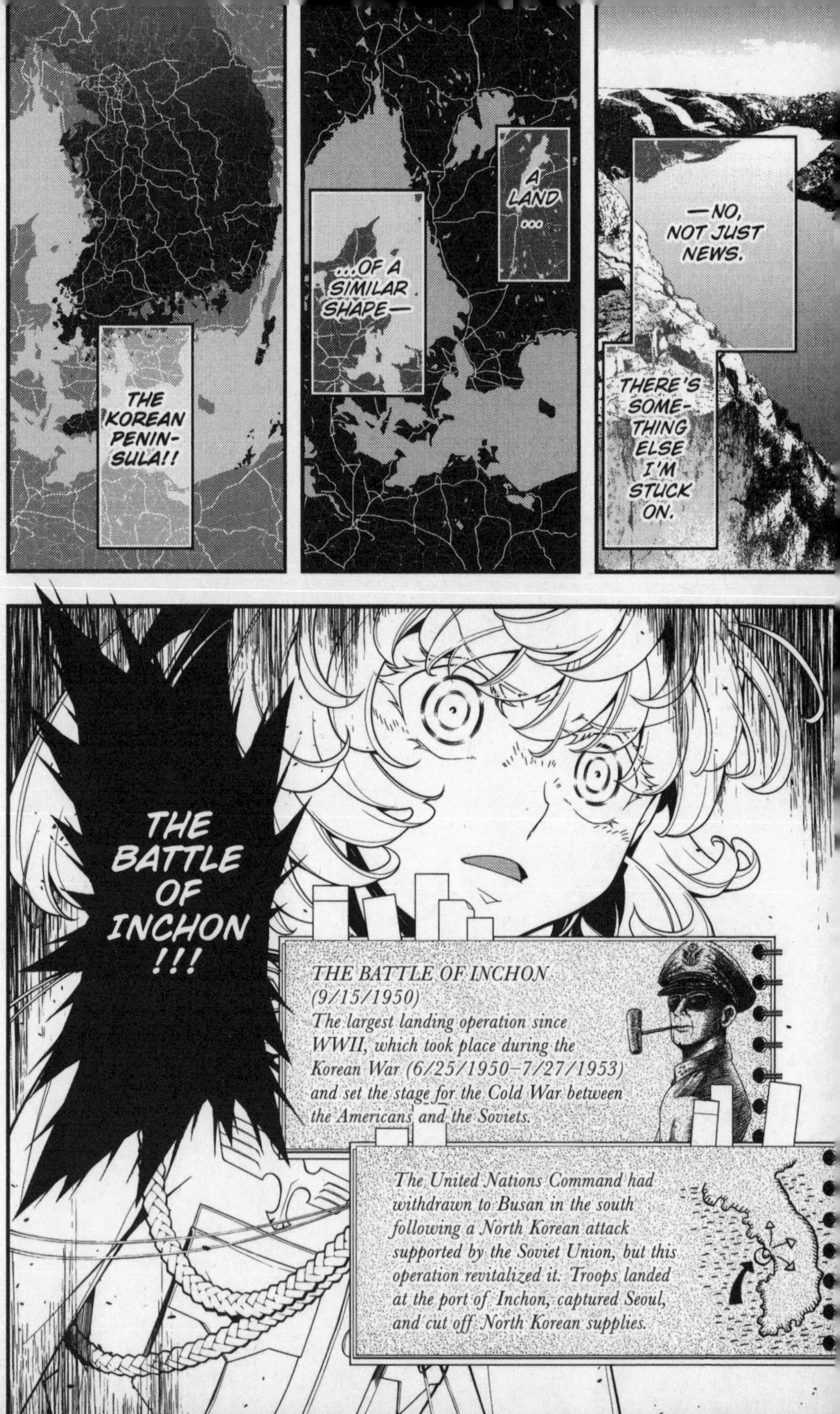
—NO, NOT JUST NEWS.
THERE'S SOME-THING ELSE I'M STUCK ON.
A LAND...
...OF A SIMILAR SHAPE—
THE KOREAN PENIN-SULA!!
THE BATTLE OF INCHON!!!
THE BATTLE OF INCHON (9/15/1950)
The largest landing operation since WWII, which took place during the Korean War (6/25/1950–7/27/1953) and set the stage for the Cold War between the Americans and the Soviets.
The United Nations Command had withdrawn to Busan in the south following a North Korean attack supported by the Soviet Union, but this operation revitalized it. Troops landed at the port of Inchon, captured Seoul, and cut off North Korean supplies.

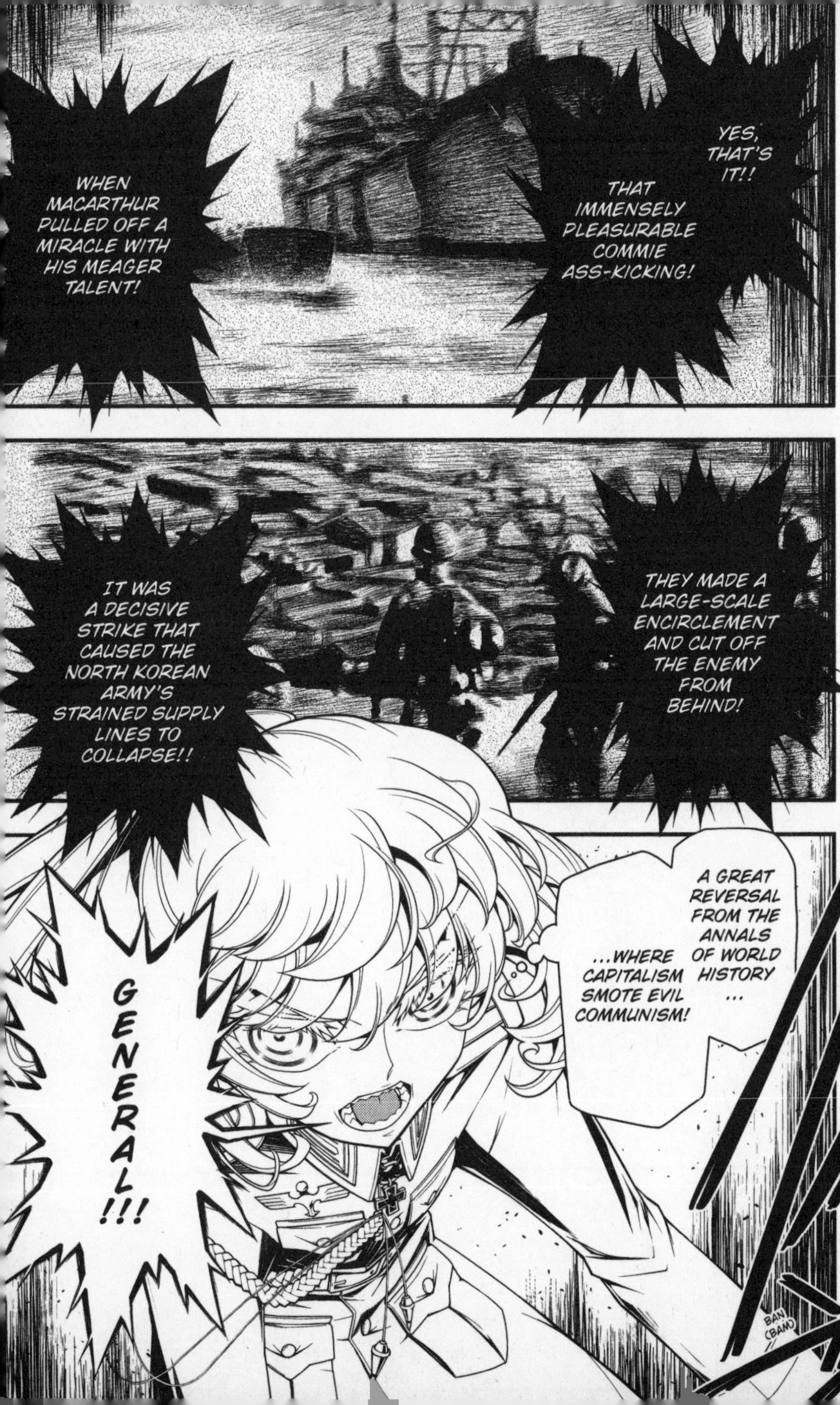
YES, THAT'S IT!!
THAT IMMENSELY PLEASURABLE COMMIE ASS-KICKING!
WHEN MACARTHUR PULLED OFF A MIRACLE WITH HIS MEAGER TALENT!
THEY MADE A LARGE-SCALE ENCIRCLEMENT AND CUT OFF THE ENEMY FROM BEHIND!
IT WAS A DECISIVE STRIKE THAT CAUSED THE NORTH KOREAN ARMY'S STRAINED SUPPLY LINES TO COLLAPSE!!
A GREAT REVERSAL FROM THE ANNALS OF WORLD HISTORY...
...WHERE CAPITALISM SMOTE EVIL COMMUNISM!
BAN (BAM)
GENERAL!!!

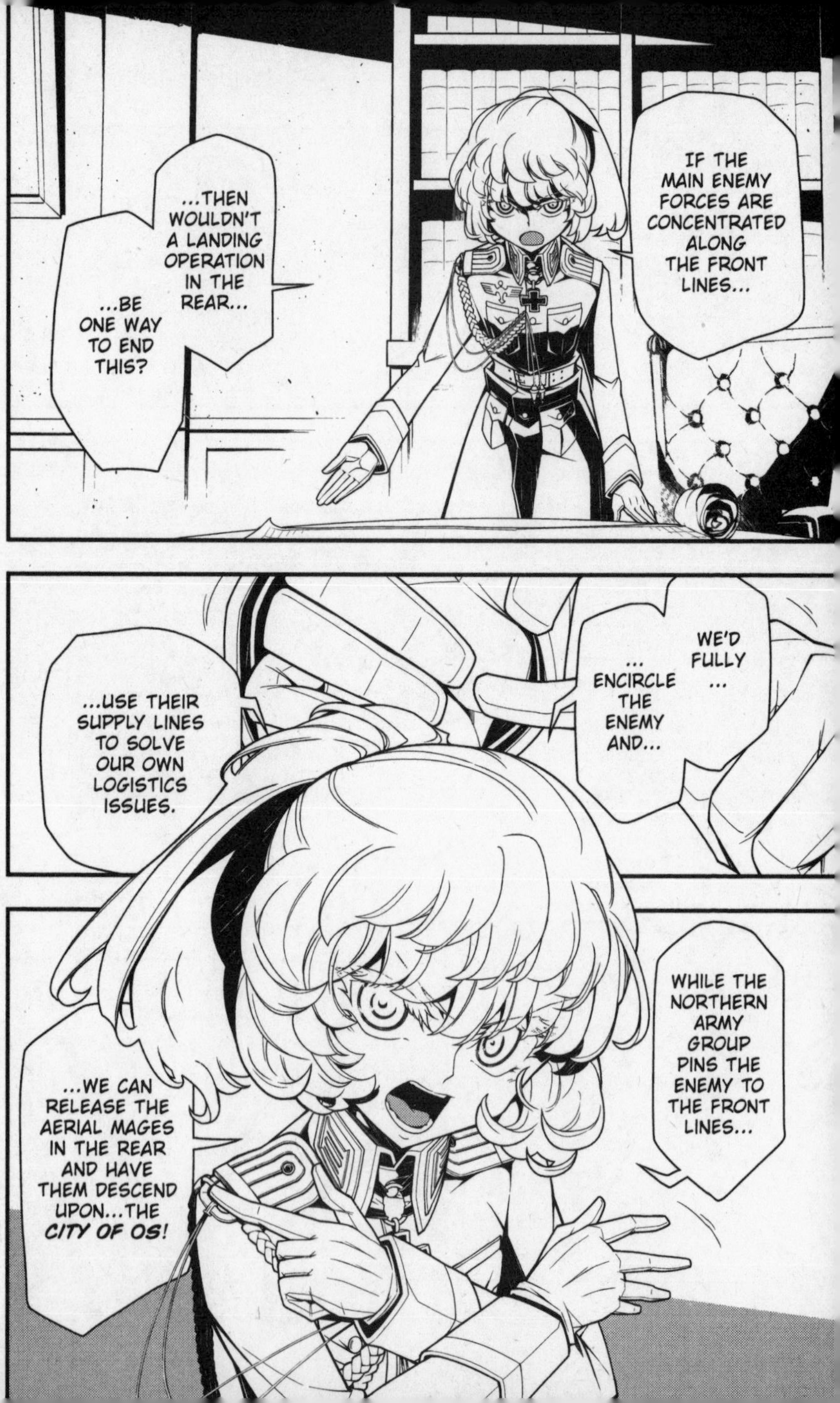
IF THE MAIN ENEMY FORCES ARE CONCENTRATED ALONG THE FRONT LINES...
...THEN WOULDN'T A LANDING OPERATION IN THE REAR...
...BE ONE WAY TO END THIS?
WE'D FULLY ...
... ENCIRCLE THE ENEMY AND...
...USE THEIR SUPPLY LINES TO SOLVE OUR OWN LOGISTICS ISSUES.
WHILE THE NORTHERN ARMY GROUP PINS THE ENEMY TO THE FRONT LINES...
...WE CAN RELEASE THE AERIAL MAGES IN THE REAR AND HAVE THEM DESCEND UPON...THE *CITY OF OS*!

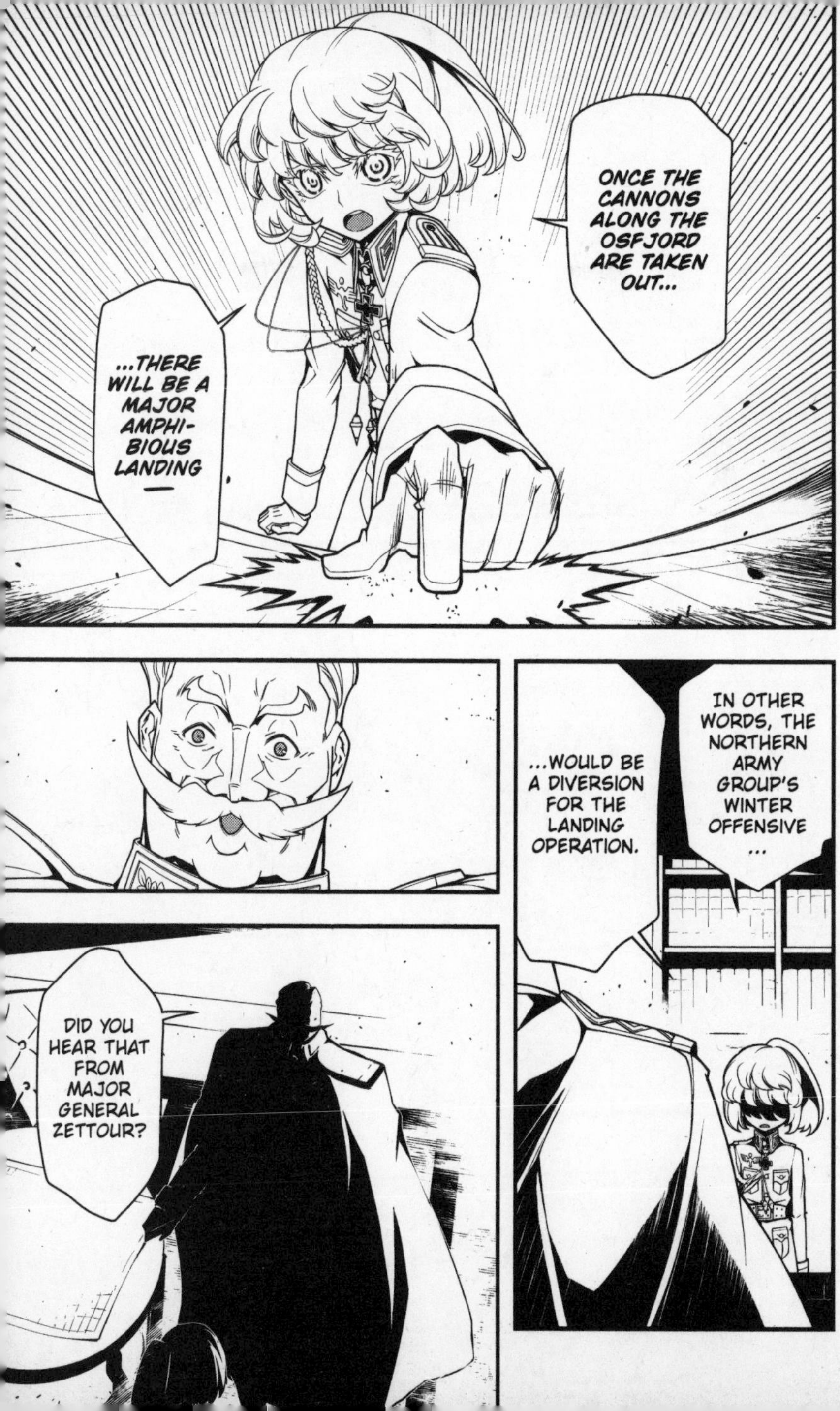
ONCE THE CANNONS ALONG THE OSFJORD ARE TAKEN OUT...
...THERE WILL BE A MAJOR AMPHIBIOUS LANDING—
IN OTHER WORDS, THE NORTHERN ARMY GROUP'S WINTER OFFENSIVE...
...WOULD BE A DIVERSION FOR THE LANDING OPERATION.
DID YOU HEAR THAT FROM MAJOR GENERAL ZETTOUR?

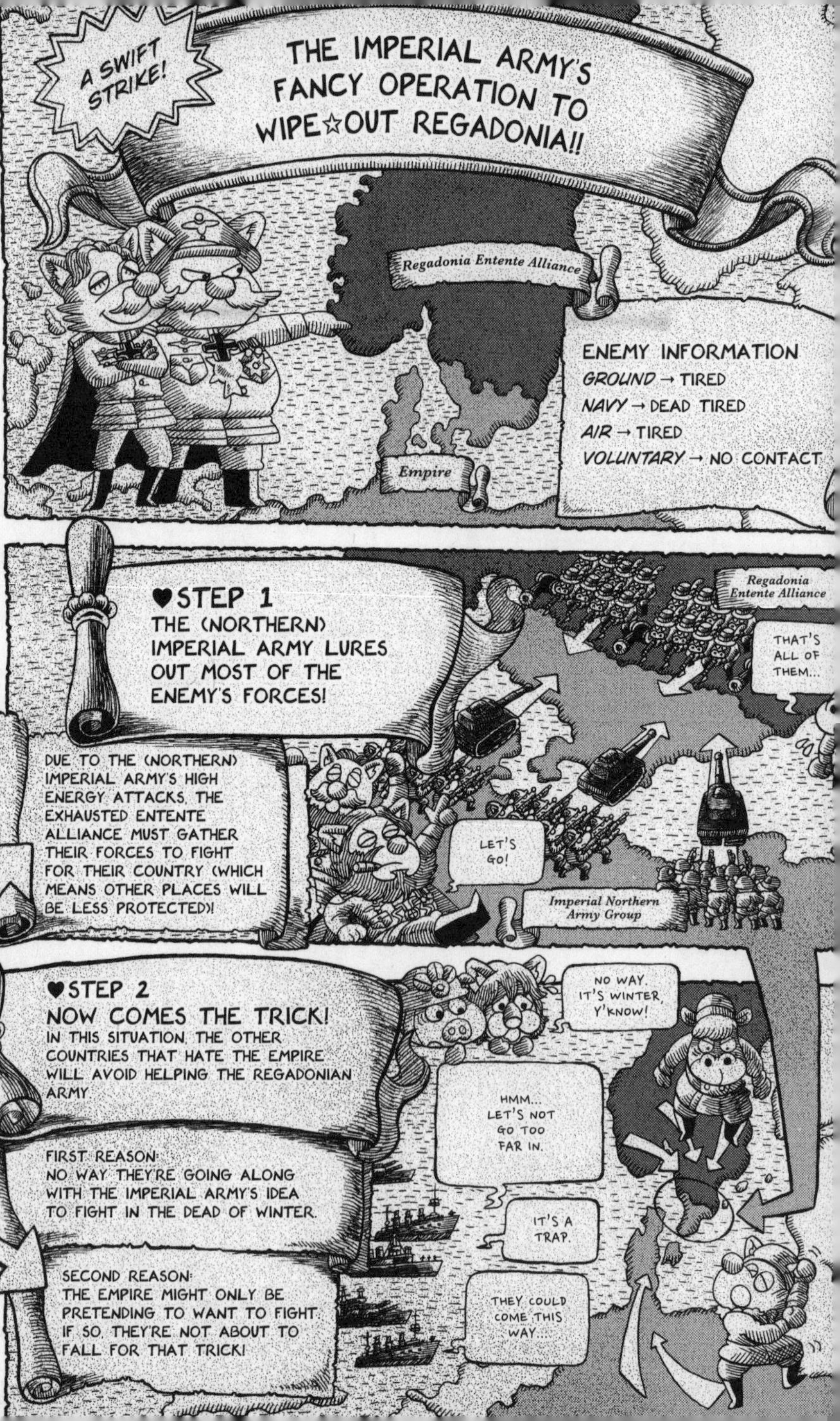
THE IMPERIAL ARMY'S FANCY OPERATION TO WIPE☆OUT REGADONIA!!
A SWIFT STRIKE!
Regadonia Entente Alliance
ENEMY INFORMATION
GROUND → TIRED
NAVY → DEAD TIRED
AIR → TIRED
VOLUNTARY → NO CONTACT
Empire
Regadonia Entente Alliance
THAT'S ALL OF THEM...
♥STEP 1
THE (NORTHERN) IMPERIAL ARMY LURES OUT MOST OF THE ENEMY'S FORCES!
LET'S GO!
Imperial Northern Army Group
DUE TO THE (NORTHERN) IMPERIAL ARMY'S HIGH ENERGY ATTACKS, THE EXHAUSTED ENTENTE ALLIANCE MUST GATHER THEIR FORCES TO FIGHT FOR THEIR COUNTRY (WHICH MEANS OTHER PLACES WILL BE LESS PROTECTED)!
NO WAY. IT'S WINTER, Y'KNOW!
HMM... LET'S NOT GO TOO FAR IN.
IT'S A TRAP.
THEY COULD COME THIS WAY...
♥STEP 2
NOW COMES THE TRICK!
IN THIS SITUATION, THE OTHER COUNTRIES THAT HATE THE EMPIRE WILL AVOID HELPING THE REGADONIAN ARMY.
FIRST REASON:
NO WAY THEY'RE GOING ALONG WITH THE IMPERIAL ARMY'S IDEA TO FIGHT IN THE DEAD OF WINTER.
SECOND REASON:
THE EMPIRE MIGHT ONLY BE PRETENDING TO WANT TO FIGHT. IF SO, THEY'RE NOT ABOUT TO FALL FOR THAT TRICK!

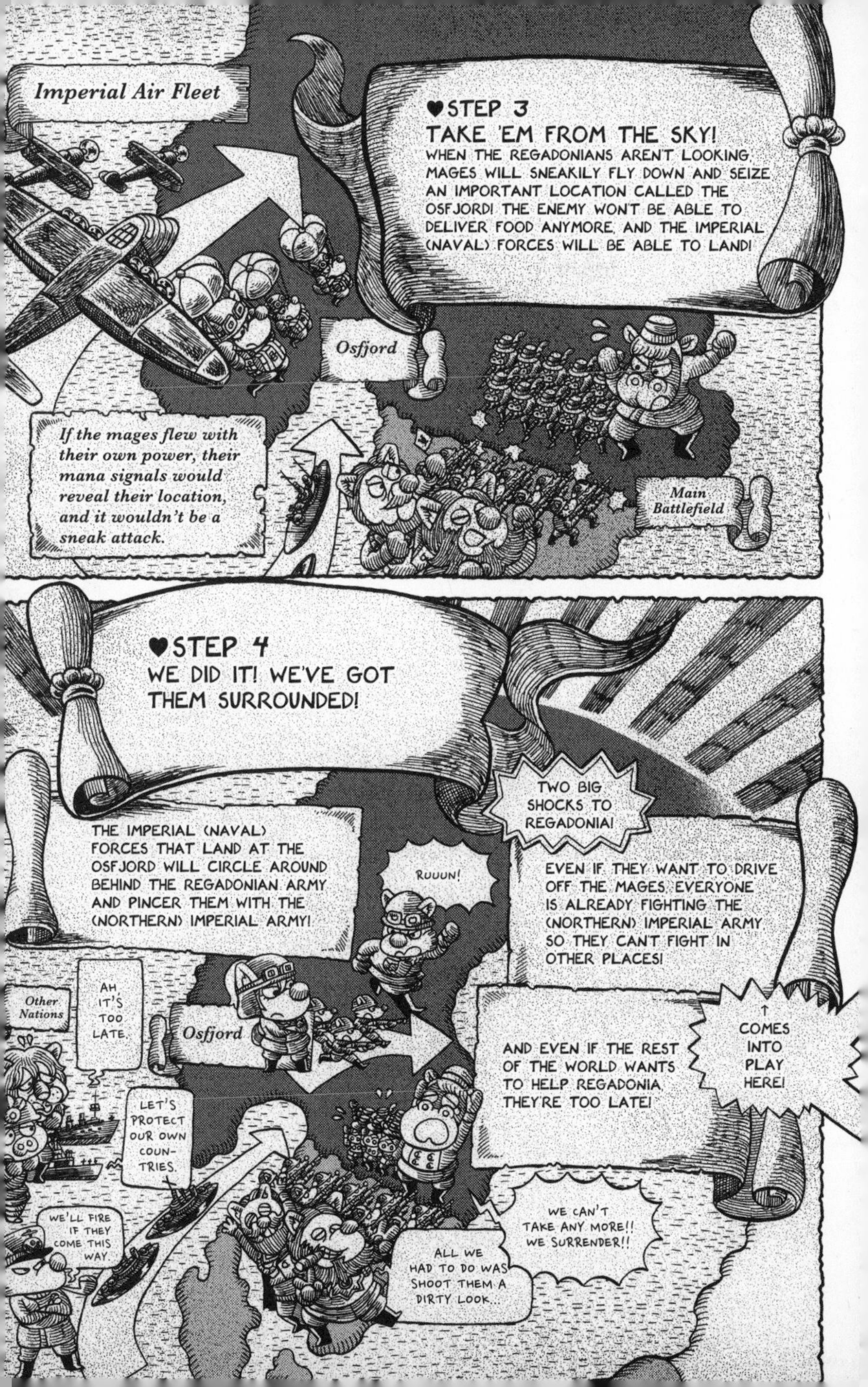
♥STEP 3
TAKE 'EM FROM THE SKY!
WHEN THE REGADONIANS AREN'T LOOKING, MAGES WILL SNEAKILY FLY DOWN AND SEIZE AN IMPORTANT LOCATION CALLED THE OSFJORD! THE ENEMY WON'T BE ABLE TO DELIVER FOOD ANYMORE, AND THE IMPERIAL (NAVAL) FORCES WILL BE ABLE TO LAND!
Imperial Air Fleet
Osfjord
Main Battlefield
If the mages flew with their own power, their mana signals would reveal their location, and it wouldn't be a sneak attack.
♥STEP 4
WE DID IT! WE'VE GOT THEM SURROUNDED!
TWO BIG SHOCKS TO REGADONIA!
EVEN IF THEY WANT TO DRIVE OFF THE MAGES, EVERYONE IS ALREADY FIGHTING THE (NORTHERN) IMPERIAL ARMY, SO THEY CAN'T FIGHT IN OTHER PLACES!
↑ COMES INTO PLAY HERE!
AND EVEN IF THE REST OF THE WORLD WANTS TO HELP REGADONIA, THEY'RE TOO LATE!
THE IMPERIAL (NAVAL) FORCES THAT LAND AT THE OSFJORD WILL CIRCLE AROUND BEHIND THE REGADONIAN ARMY AND PINCER THEM WITH THE (NORTHERN) IMPERIAL ARMY!
RUUUN!
Osfjord
Other Nations
AH, IT'S TOO LATE.
LET'S PROTECT OUR OWN COUN-TRIES.
WE CAN'T TAKE ANY MORE!! WE SURRENDER!!
ALL WE HAD TO DO WAS SHOOT THEM A DIRTY LOOK...
WE'LL FIRE IF THEY COME THIS WAY.

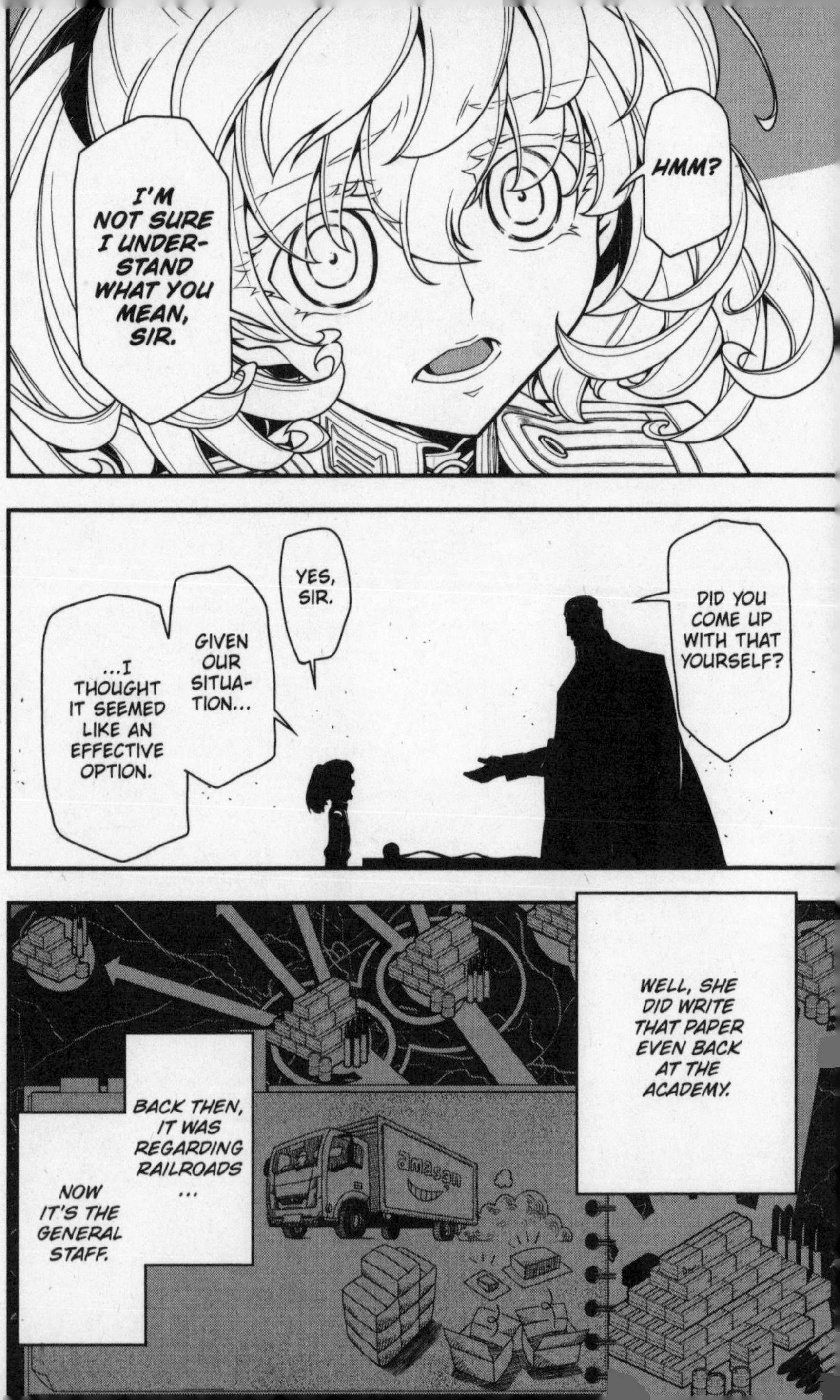
HMM?
I'M NOT SURE I UNDERSTAND WHAT YOU MEAN, SIR.
DID YOU COME UP WITH THAT YOURSELF?
YES, SIR.
GIVEN OUR SITUATION...
...I THOUGHT IT SEEMED LIKE AN EFFECTIVE OPTION.
WELL, SHE DID WRITE THAT PAPER EVEN BACK AT THE ACADEMY.
BACK THEN, IT WAS REGARDING RAILROADS...
NOW IT'S THE GENERAL STAFF.
amasan

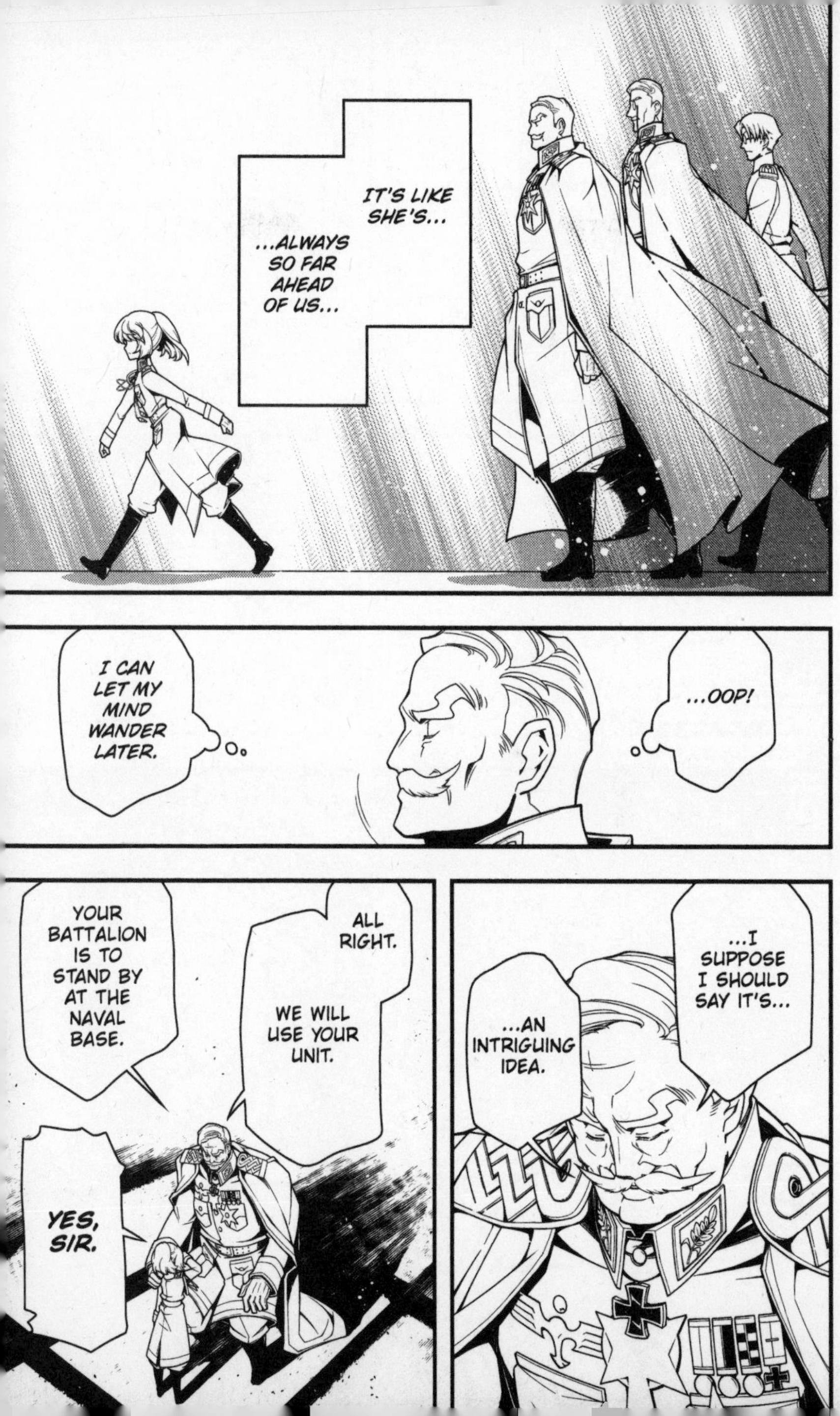
IT'S LIKE SHE'S...
...ALWAYS SO FAR AHEAD OF US...
...OOP!
I CAN LET MY MIND WANDER LATER.
...I SUPPOSE I SHOULD SAY IT'S...
...AN INTRIGUING IDEA.
ALL RIGHT.
WE WILL USE YOUR UNIT.
YOUR BATTALION IS TO STAND BY AT THE NAVAL BASE.
YES, SIR.

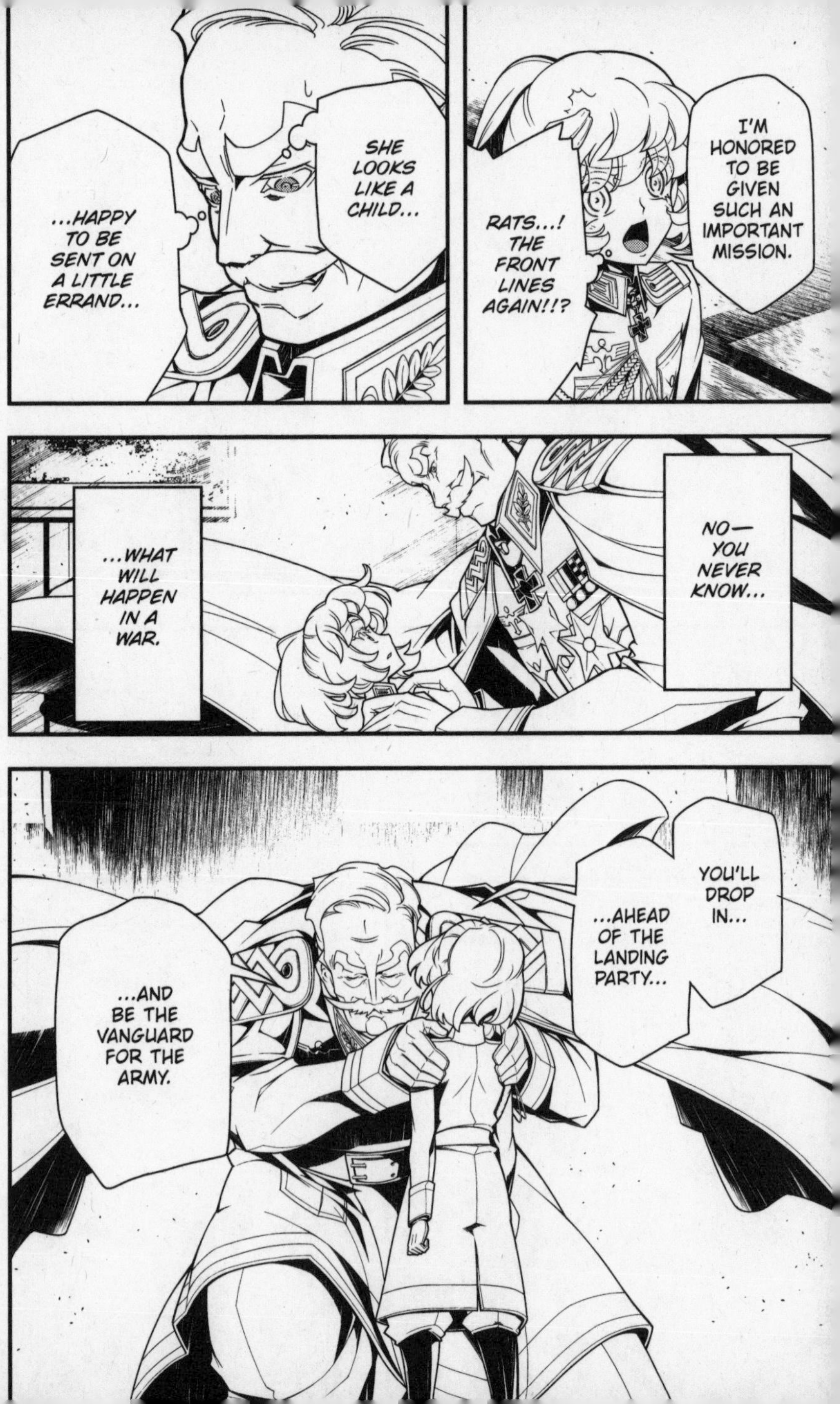
I'M HONORED TO BE GIVEN SUCH AN IMPORTANT MISSION.
RATS...! THE FRONT LINES AGAIN!!?
SHE LOOKS LIKE A CHILD...
...HAPPY TO BE SENT ON A LITTLE ERRAND...
NO— YOU NEVER KNOW...
...WHAT WILL HAPPEN IN A WAR.
YOU'LL DROP IN...
...AHEAD OF THE LANDING PARTY...
...AND BE THE VANGUARD FOR THE ARMY.

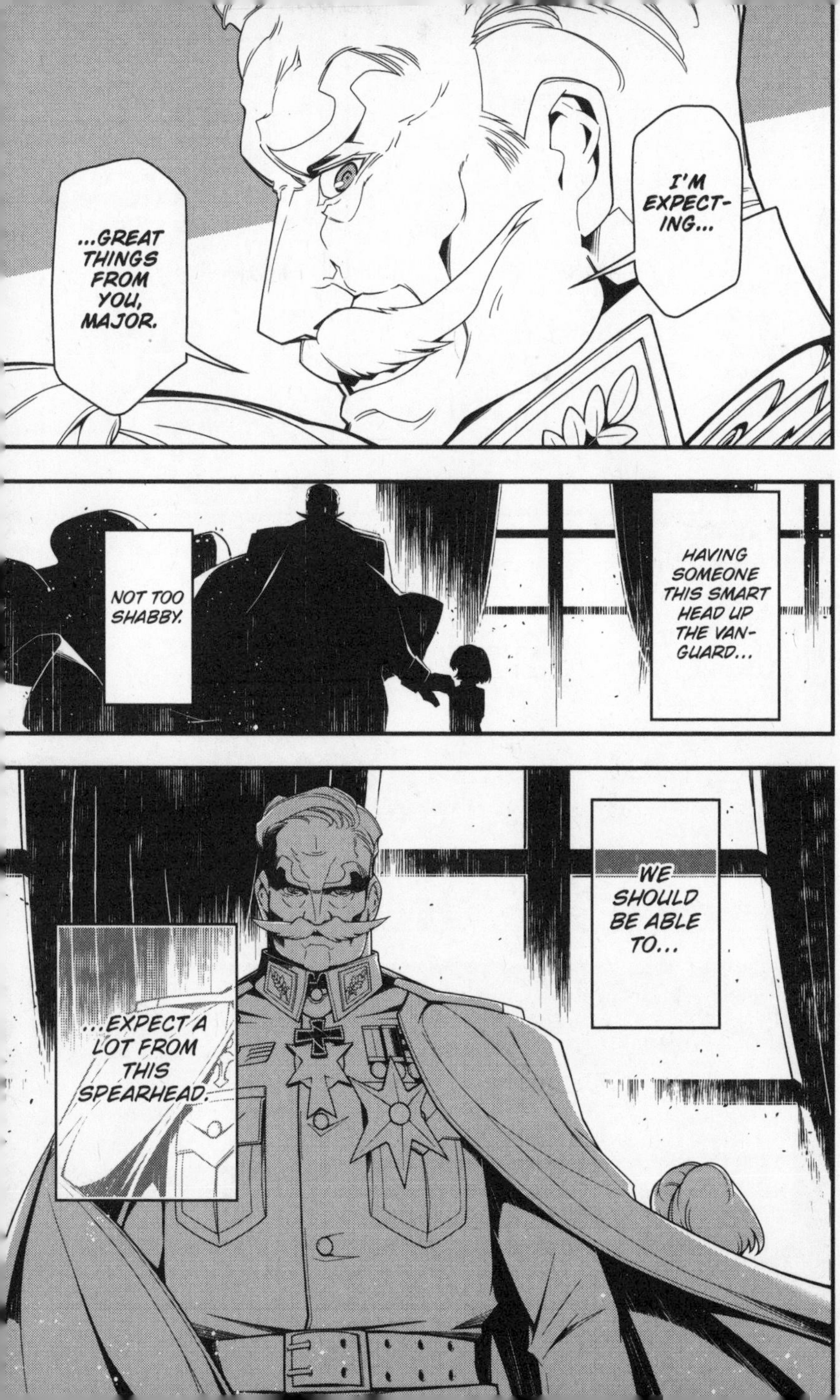
I'M EXPECT-ING...
...GREAT THINGS FROM YOU, MAJOR.
HAVING SOMEONE THIS SMART HEAD UP THE VAN-GUARD...
NOT TOO SHABBY.
WE SHOULD BE ABLE TO...
...EXPECT A LOT FROM THIS SPEARHEAD.

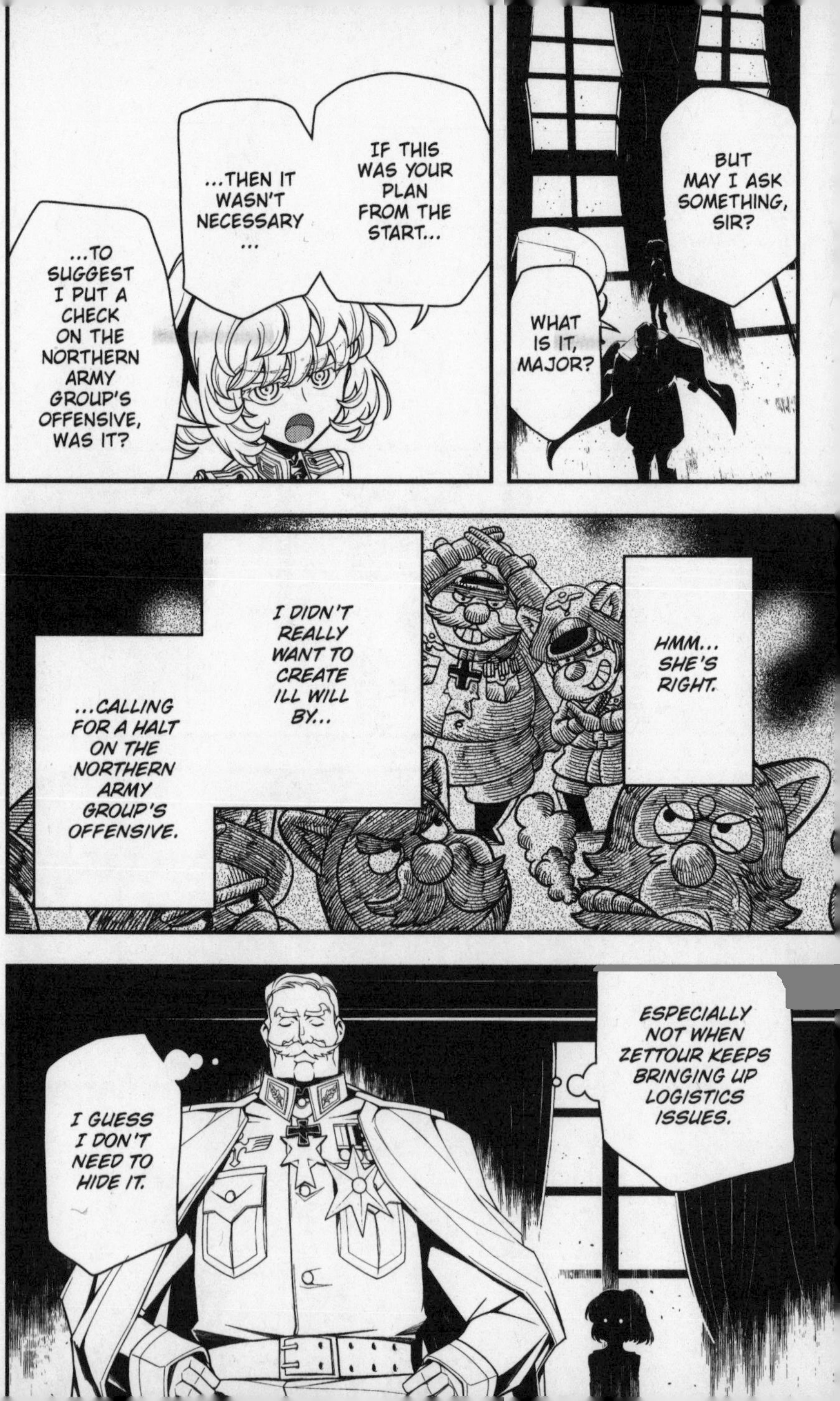
BUT MAY I ASK SOMETHING, SIR?
WHAT IS IT, MAJOR?
IF THIS WAS YOUR PLAN FROM THE START...
...THEN IT WASN'T NECESSARY...
...TO SUGGEST I PUT A CHECK ON THE NORTHERN ARMY GROUP'S OFFENSIVE, WAS IT?
HMM... SHE'S RIGHT.
I DIDN'T REALLY WANT TO CREATE ILL WILL BY...
...CALLING FOR A HALT ON THE NORTHERN ARMY GROUP'S OFFENSIVE.
ESPECIALLY NOT WHEN ZETTOUR KEEPS BRINGING UP LOGISTICS ISSUES.
I GUESS I DON'T NEED TO HIDE IT.

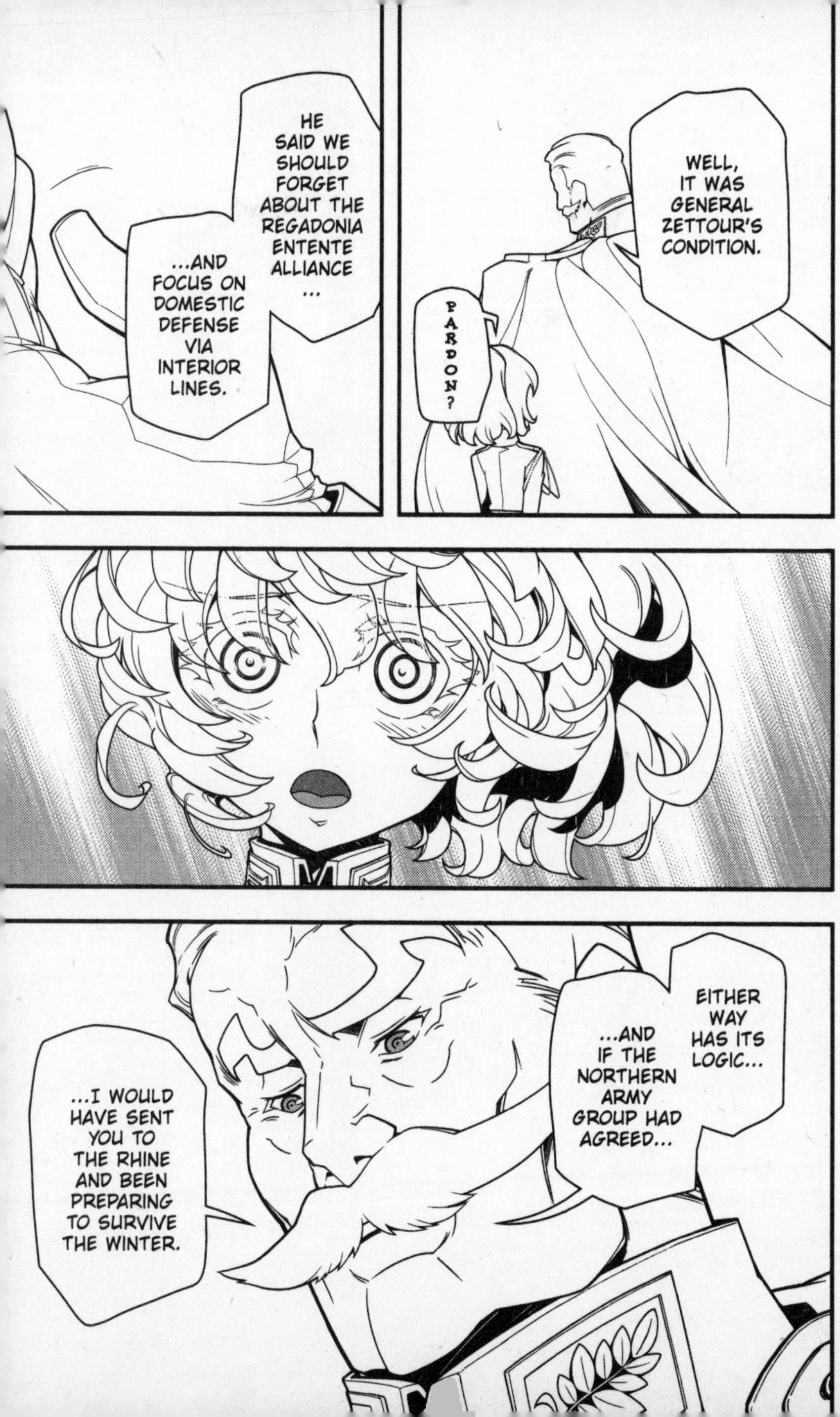
WELL, IT WAS GENERAL ZETTOUR'S CONDITION.
PARDON?
HE SAID WE SHOULD FORGET ABOUT THE REGADONIA ENTENTE ALLIANCE...
...AND FOCUS ON DOMESTIC DEFENSE VIA INTERIOR LINES.
EITHER WAY HAS ITS LOGIC...
...AND IF THE NORTHERN ARMY GROUP HAD AGREED...
...I WOULD HAVE SENT YOU TO THE RHINE AND BEEN PREPARING TO SURVIVE THE WINTER.

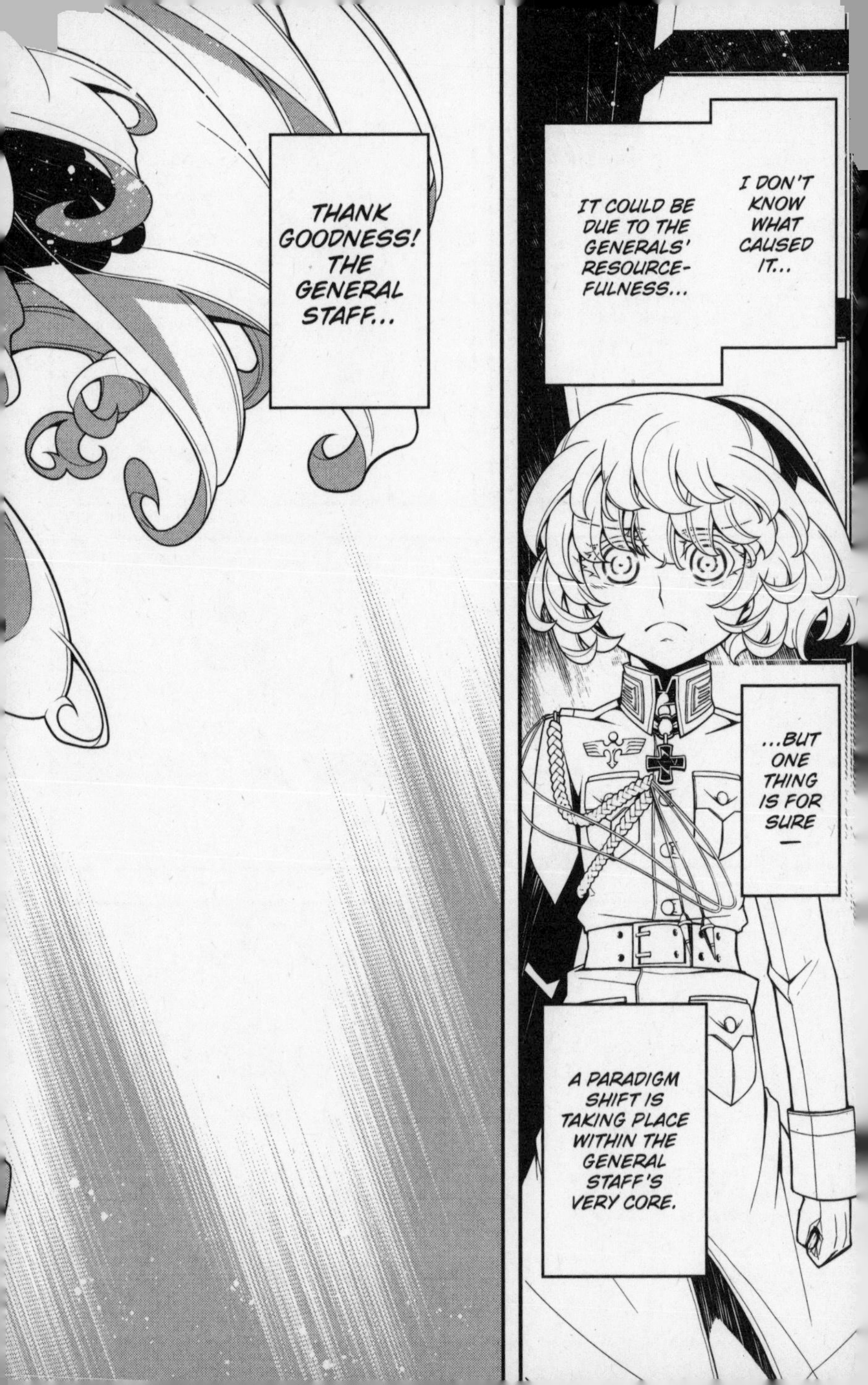
I DON'T KNOW WHAT CAUSED IT...
IT COULD BE DUE TO THE GENERALS' RESOURCE-FULNESS...
...BUT ONE THING IS FOR SURE —
A PARADIGM SHIFT IS TAKING PLACE WITHIN THE GENERAL STAFF'S VERY CORE.
THANK GOODNESS! THE GENERAL STAFF...

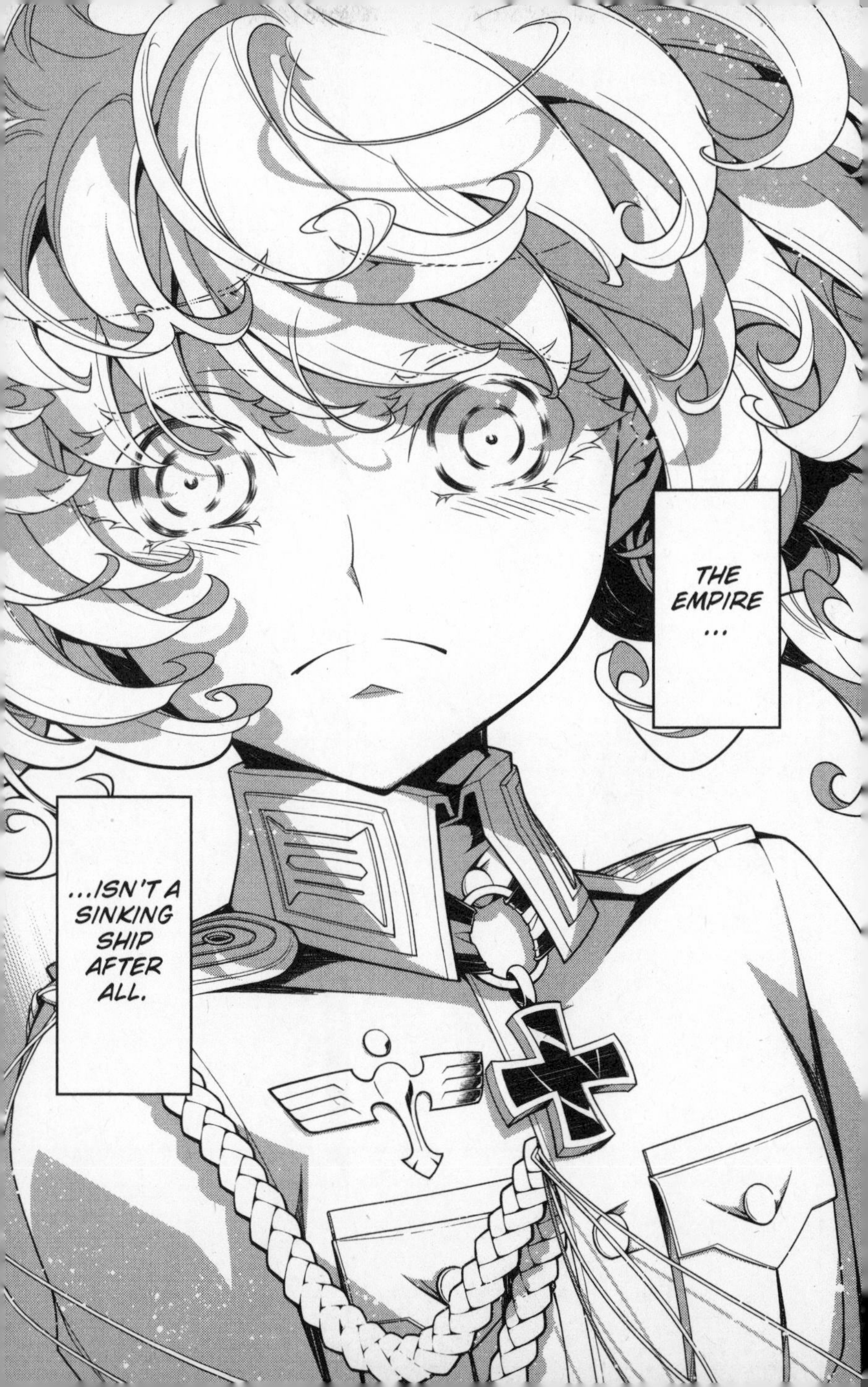
THE EMPIRE ...
...ISN'T A SINKING SHIP AFTER ALL.

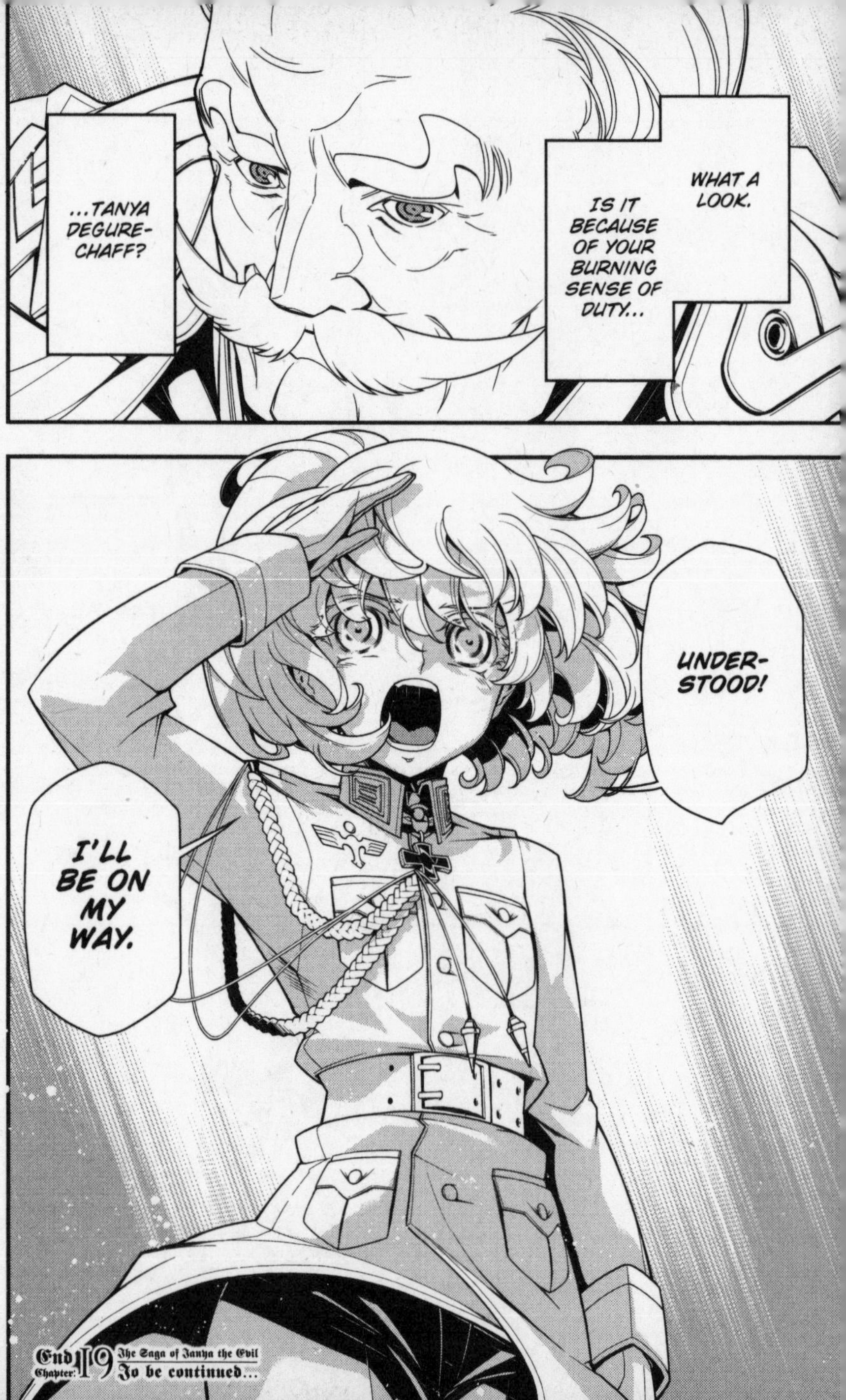
WHAT A LOOK.
IS IT BECAUSE OF YOUR BURNING SENSE OF DUTY...
...TANYA DEGURE-CHAFF?
UNDER-STOOD!
I'LL BE ON MY WAY.
End Chapter: 19 The Saga of Tanya the Evil To be continued...

Glossary Chapter 23

Plane-Hijacking Incident

The Yodogo Hijacking that occurred in March 1970.

Japan Airlines Flight 351 "Yodogo," bound for Itazuke (now Fukuoka) Airport from Haneda was hijacked by nine people from the communist group, the Red Army Faction. The hijackers held the staff and passengers hostage and demanded that the plane be flown to North Korea. Thanks to the captain and copilot's quick thinking, they managed to stop in Itazuke and South Korea's Gimpo International Airport, but they eventually headed to Pyeongyang as per the demands of the criminal gang. The nine hijackers took refuge in North Korea.

This was the first hijacking in Japan, and in response, the Punishment for the Unlawful Seizure of Aircraft Act (aka the Hijacking Prevention Law) was put into effect.

Corruption Scandal

The Lockheed bribery scandals that came to light in February 1976 and affected countries around the world.

The American aerospace company Lockheed paid huge bribes to high-ranking Japanese officials who worked for the government and in financial sectors surrounding the import of the TriStar passenger jet and the P-3C maritime surveillance aircraft. Besides the company executives who served as the go-between for Lockheed and the airlines, and the person who was seen as the fixer for government and financial matters, the former prime minister suspected of having money connections, Kakuei Tanaka, and Transport Minister Tomisaburō Hashimoto were arrested, charged, and found guilty.

Additionally, when one businessman was called to the Diet and said, "I have no memory of that," the phrase gained popularity, and ever since, the memories of Japanese politicians have gotten dramatically worse.

Two Oil Shocks

Two instances of worldwide economic chaos caused by soaring oil prices in 1973 and 1979.

When the Yom Kippur War broke out, the six member countries of OPEC agreed to raise the price on oil, and then OAPEC decided to prohibit oil exports to supporters of Israel, including the United States. As a result, oil prices in Japan jumped 213 percent, and the period of rapid economic growth drew to a close.

During this first oil shock, there was a fear that certain resources would run out. Due to the trade minister's call to conserve paper, a rumor started that there was going to be a paper shortage, and people began to stockpile toilet paper. The stockpiling extended to other daily necessities, and in the panic, soap, salt, soy sauce, sugar, and so on disappeared one after another from store shelves.

Glossary Chapter 24

The Soviet Union Invading Afghanistan

The Soviet Union's military interference in Afghanistan, which began in December 1979.

At the time in Afghanistan, a pro-Soviet communist administration was in power, but Islamic nationalists revolted. Fearing the rebellion would expand, the Soviet Union invaded. The move was criticized internationally, and the war dragged on for ten years and became one of the triggers for the collapse of the Soviet Union. Additionally, when the Soviet Union withdrew, the Taliban rose up out of the civil war that ensued, which led to further disruption across the world.

Adam Smith

An eighteenth-century Scottish philosopher and economist. Wrote "The Wealth of Nations," a crowning work of modern economics.

In "The Wealth of Nations," he explains that since people act in their greatest self-interest by nature, if statesmen could achieve liberal economics, citizens could choose the job that suits them best, and society would become more productive.

He also asserted that since market prices would be determined appropriately by the forces of supply and demand, if import taxes, bounties, and price war–limiting guilds were abolished, wealth would become evenly distributed.

Smith called these market principles "the invisible hand" and said that statesmen's jobs were to uphold the free market and maintain public safety and national security. This idea is called laissez-faire, and it is connected to neoliberal thinking, of which the Chicago school is an example.

The Chicago School

A school of economics based at the University of Chicago. The term refers to the second wave of thought that coalesced during the 1960s with key thinkers such as Milton Friedman and Gary Becker. Its neoclassical ideas can be traced back to Adam Smith. One of the group's characteristics was that they tried to analyze all sorts of societal phenomena using economic methods.

Milton Friedman, especially, argued for the broadening of laissez-faire ideas, saying that the postal service, education, and transportation should be left to the people and market forces. This "small government" thinking is said to be neoliberal, and it was incorporated by the Reagan administration in the United States and the Nakasone administration in Japan.

Gary Becker applied economic methodology to various societal issues such as crime, the drug trade, and politics. He thought that human actions could be analyzed as being the result of a logical choice for the individual. He also was the one who viewed human abilities as "human capital" and promoted that idea.

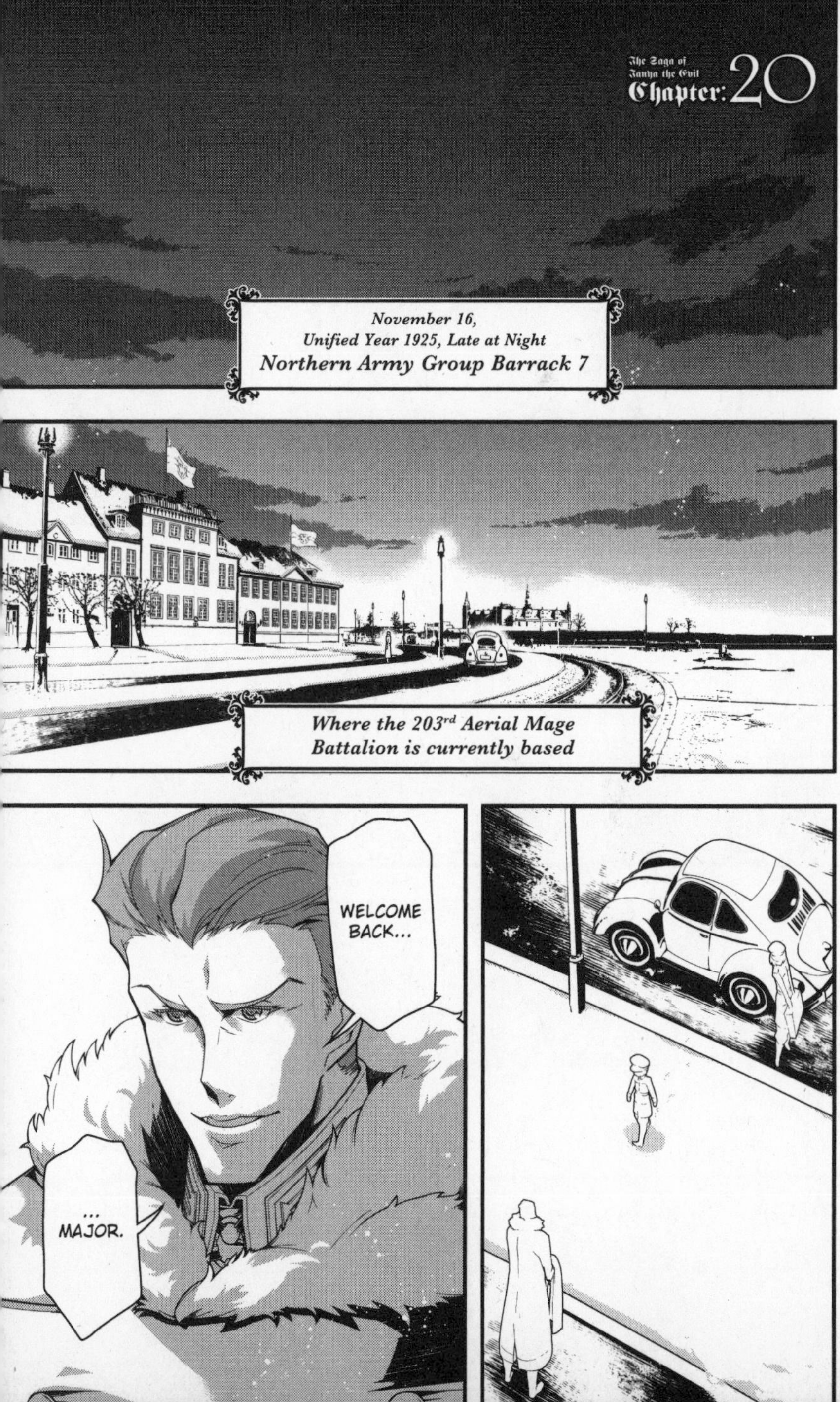
The Saga of Tanya the Evil
Chapter: 20
November 16,
Unified Year 1925, Late at Night
Northern Army Group Barrack 7
Where the 203rd Aerial Mage Battalion is currently based
WELCOME BACK...
... MAJOR.

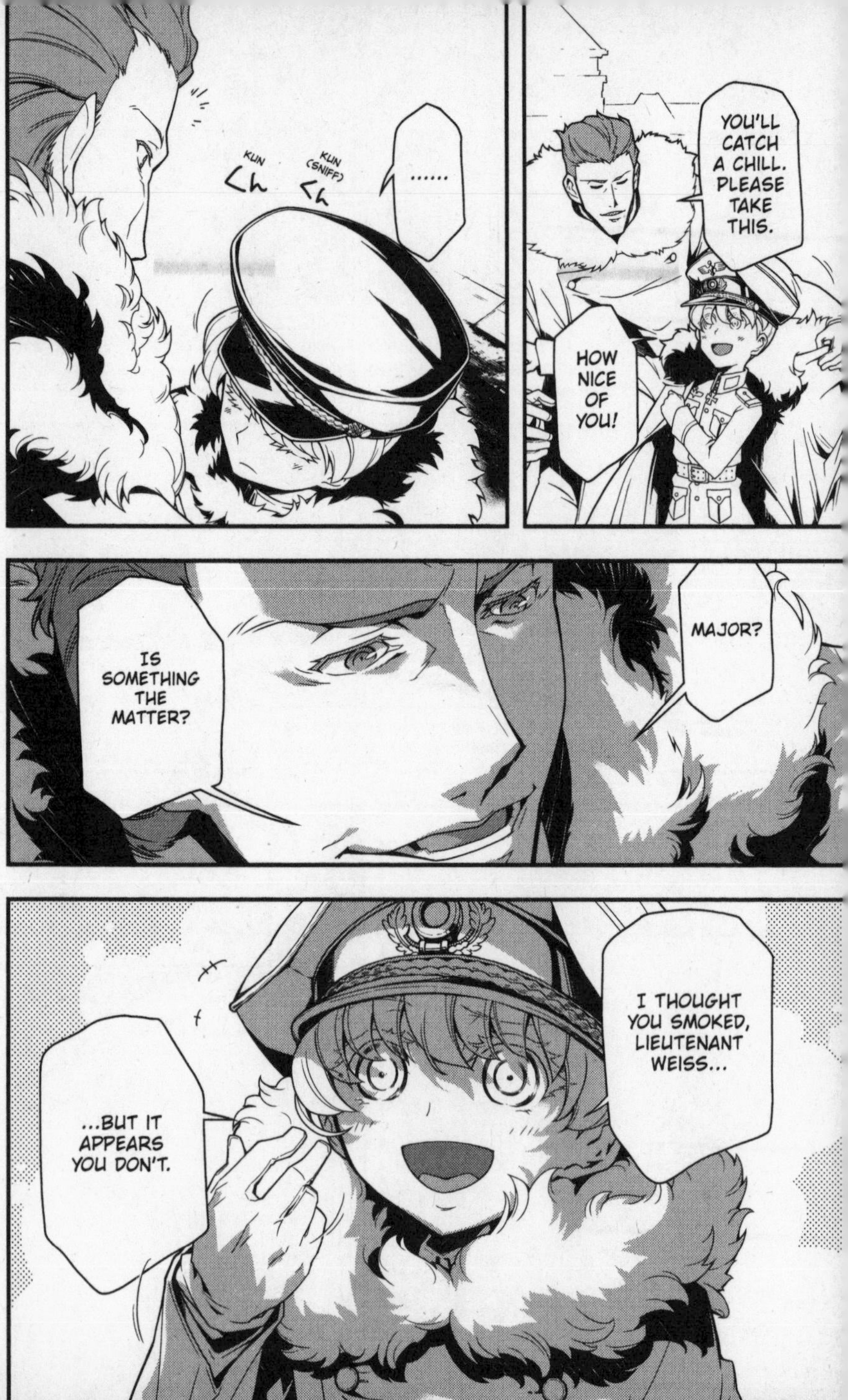
YOU'LL CATCH A CHILL. PLEASE TAKE THIS.
HOW NICE OF YOU!
......
KUN (SNIFF) くん
KUN くん
MAJOR?
IS SOMETHING THE MATTER?
I THOUGHT YOU SMOKED, LIEUTENANT WEISS...
...BUT IT APPEARS YOU DON'T.

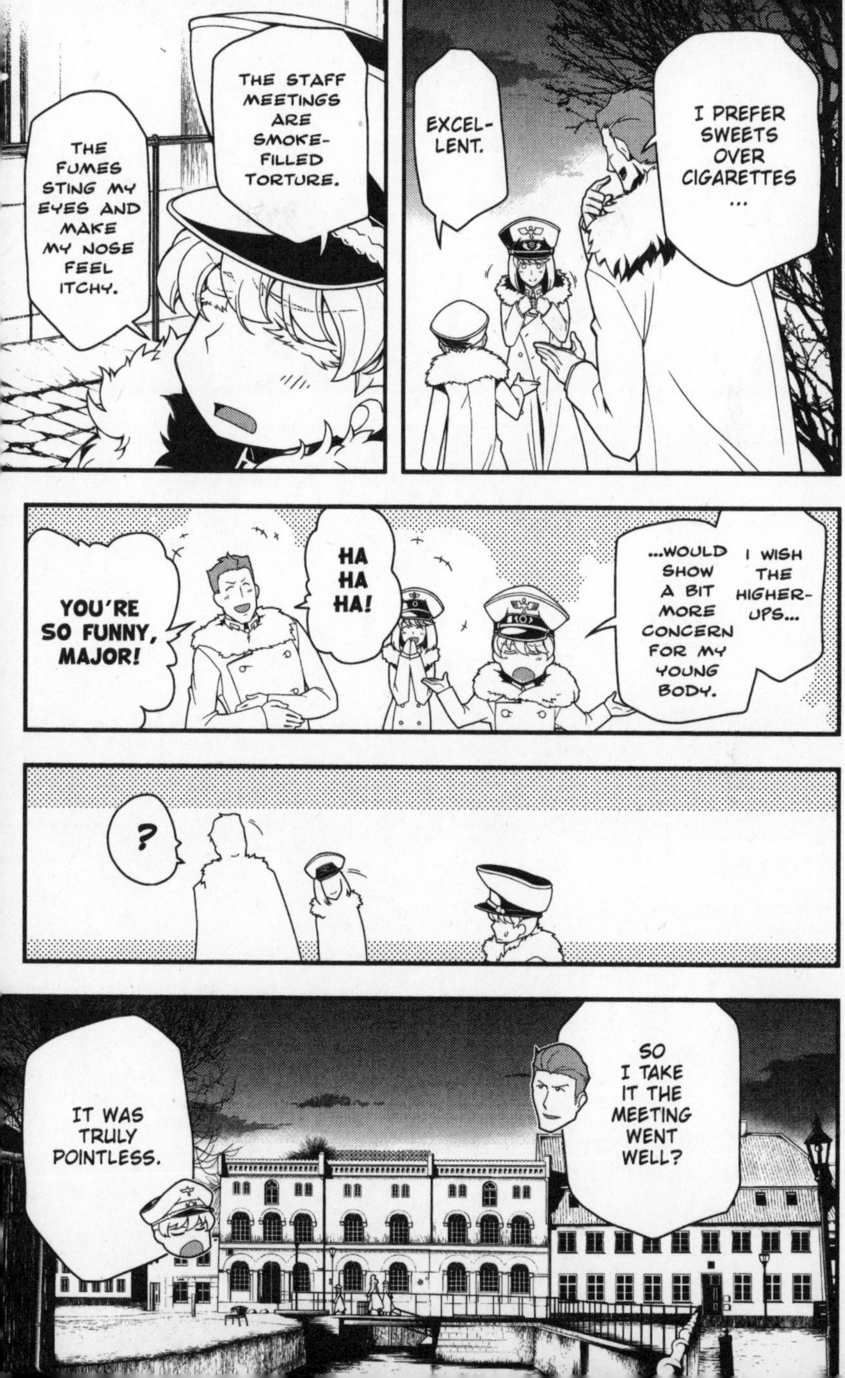
I PREFER SWEETS OVER CIGARETTES...
EXCEL-LENT.
THE STAFF MEETINGS ARE SMOKE-FILLED TORTURE.
THE FUMES STING MY EYES AND MAKE MY NOSE FEEL ITCHY.
I WISH THE HIGHER-UPS...
...WOULD SHOW A BIT MORE CONCERN FOR MY YOUNG BODY.
HA HA HA!
YOU'RE SO FUNNY, MAJOR!
?
SO I TAKE IT THE MEETING WENT WELL?
IT WAS TRULY POINTLESS.

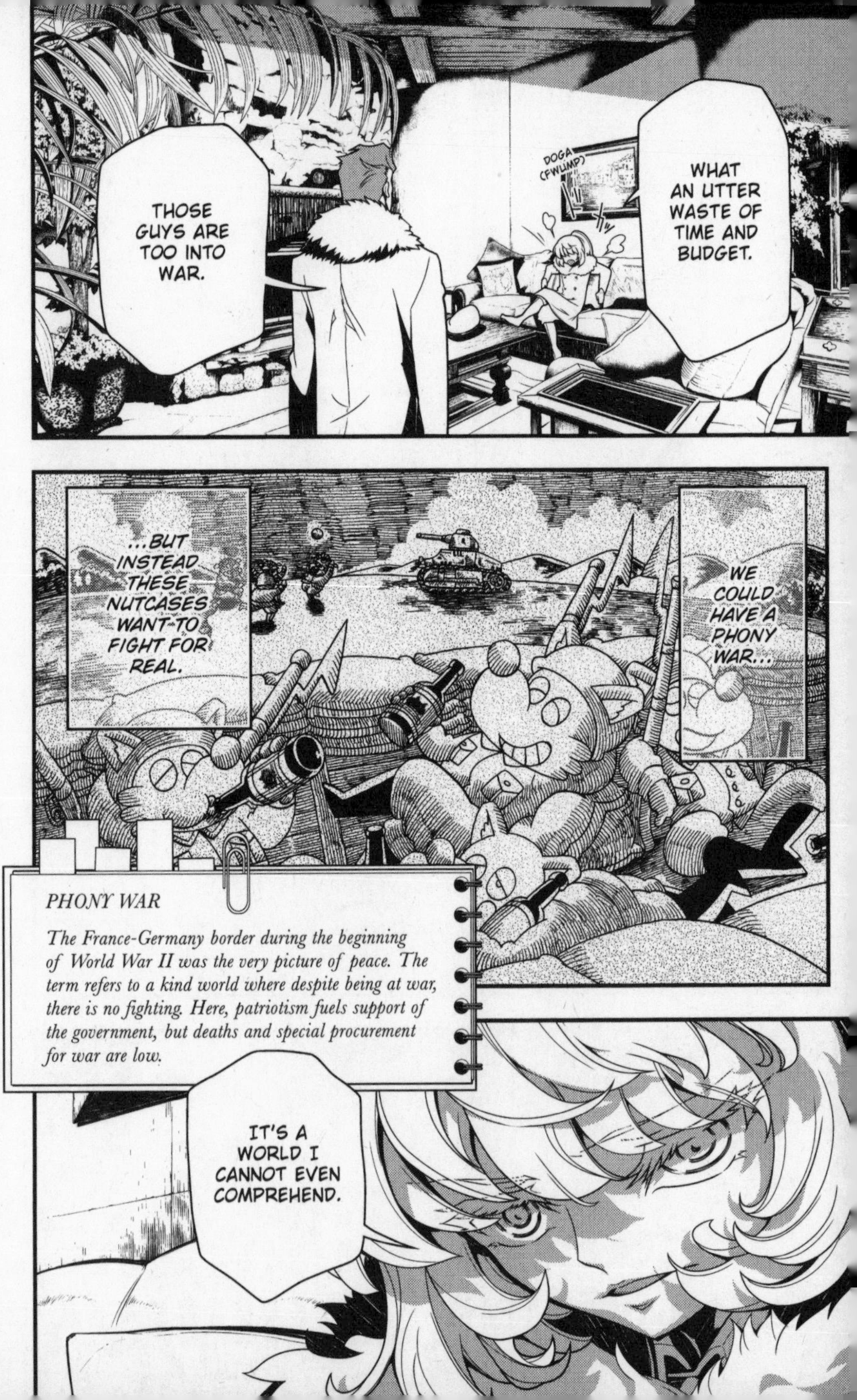
WHAT AN UTTER WASTE OF TIME AND BUDGET.
DOGA (FWUMP)
THOSE GUYS ARE TOO INTO WAR.
WE COULD HAVE A PHONY WAR...
...BUT INSTEAD THESE NUTCASES WANT TO FIGHT FOR REAL.
PHONY WAR
The France-Germany border during the beginning of World War II was the very picture of peace. The term refers to a kind world where despite being at war, there is no fighting. Here, patriotism fuels support of the government, but deaths and special procurement for war are low.
IT'S A WORLD I CANNOT EVEN COMPREHEND.

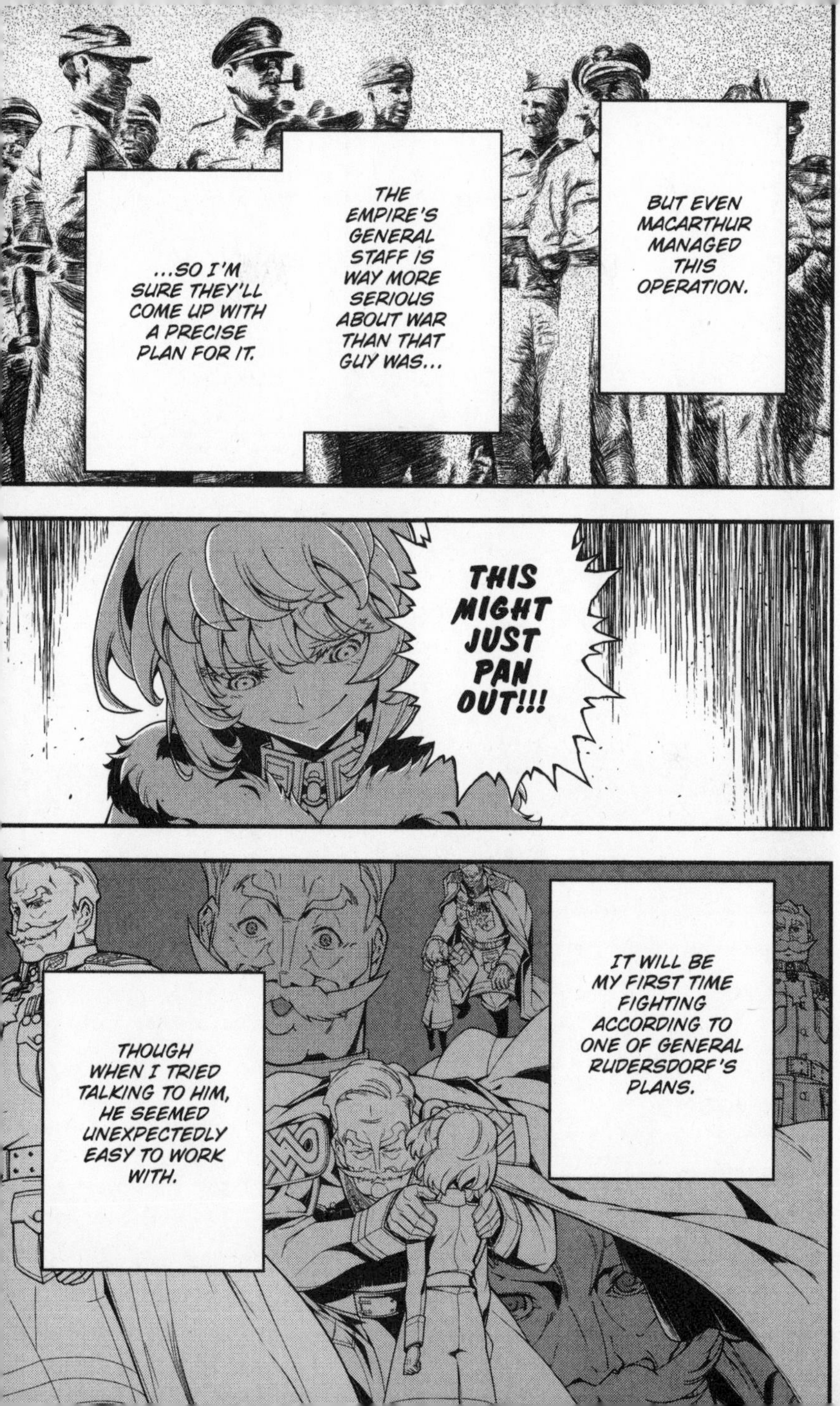
BUT EVEN MACARTHUR MANAGED THIS OPERATION.
THE EMPIRE'S GENERAL STAFF IS WAY MORE SERIOUS ABOUT WAR THAN THAT GUY WAS...
...SO I'M SURE THEY'LL COME UP WITH A PRECISE PLAN FOR IT.
THIS MIGHT JUST PAN OUT!!!
IT WILL BE MY FIRST TIME FIGHTING ACCORDING TO ONE OF GENERAL RUDERSDORF'S PLANS.
THOUGH WHEN I TRIED TALKING TO HIM, HE SEEMED UNEXPECTEDLY EASY TO WORK WITH.

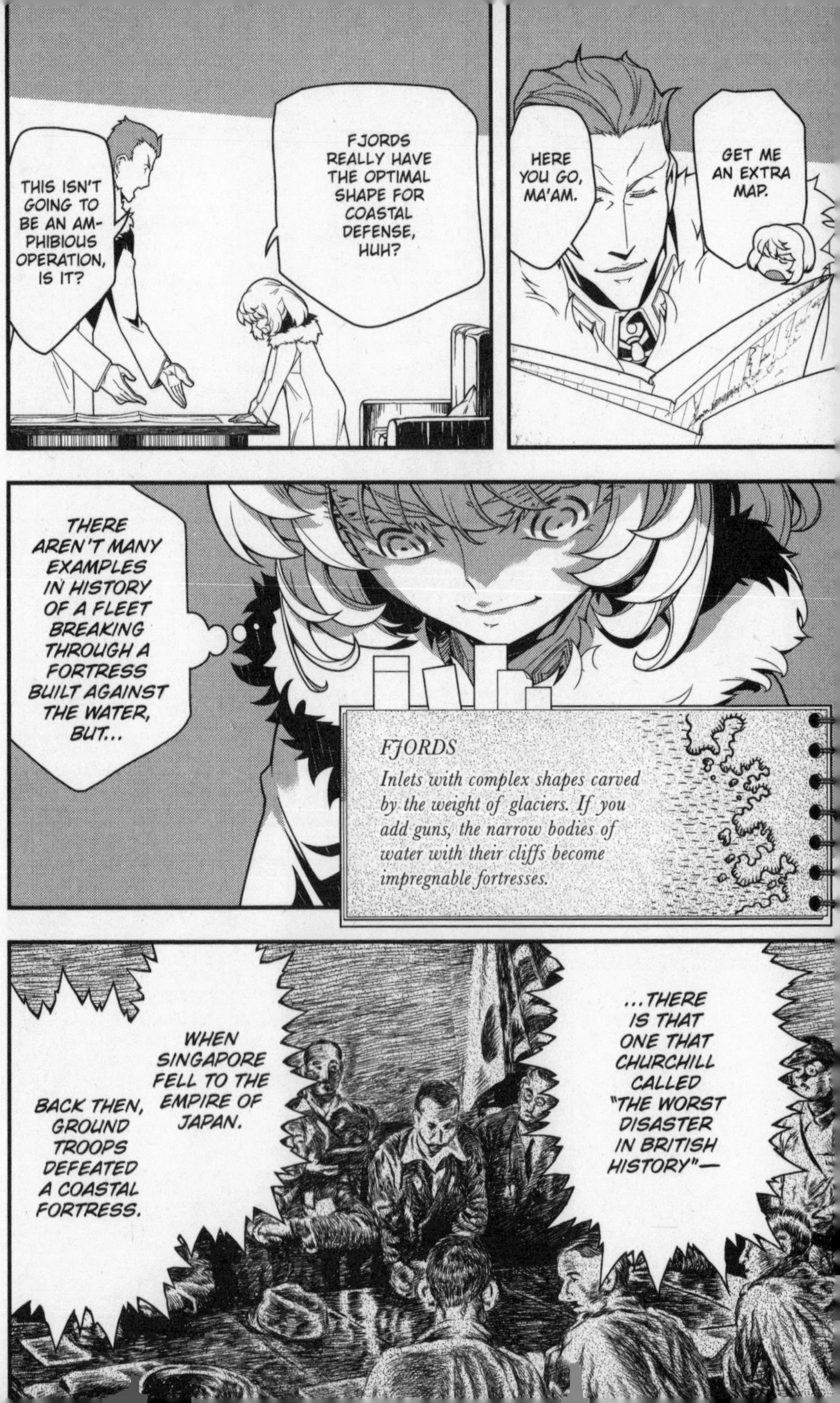
GET ME AN EXTRA MAP.
HERE YOU GO, MA'AM.
FJORDS REALLY HAVE THE OPTIMAL SHAPE FOR COASTAL DEFENSE, HUH?
THIS ISN'T GOING TO BE AN AM-PHIBIOUS OPERATION, IS IT?
THERE AREN'T MANY EXAMPLES IN HISTORY OF A FLEET BREAKING THROUGH A FORTRESS BUILT AGAINST THE WATER, BUT...
FJORDS
Inlets with complex shapes carved by the weight of glaciers. If you add guns, the narrow bodies of water with their cliffs become impregnable fortresses.
...THERE IS THAT ONE THAT CHURCHILL CALLED "THE WORST DISASTER IN BRITISH HISTORY"—
WHEN SINGAPORE FELL TO THE EMPIRE OF JAPAN.
BACK THEN, GROUND TROOPS DEFEATED A COASTAL FORTRESS.

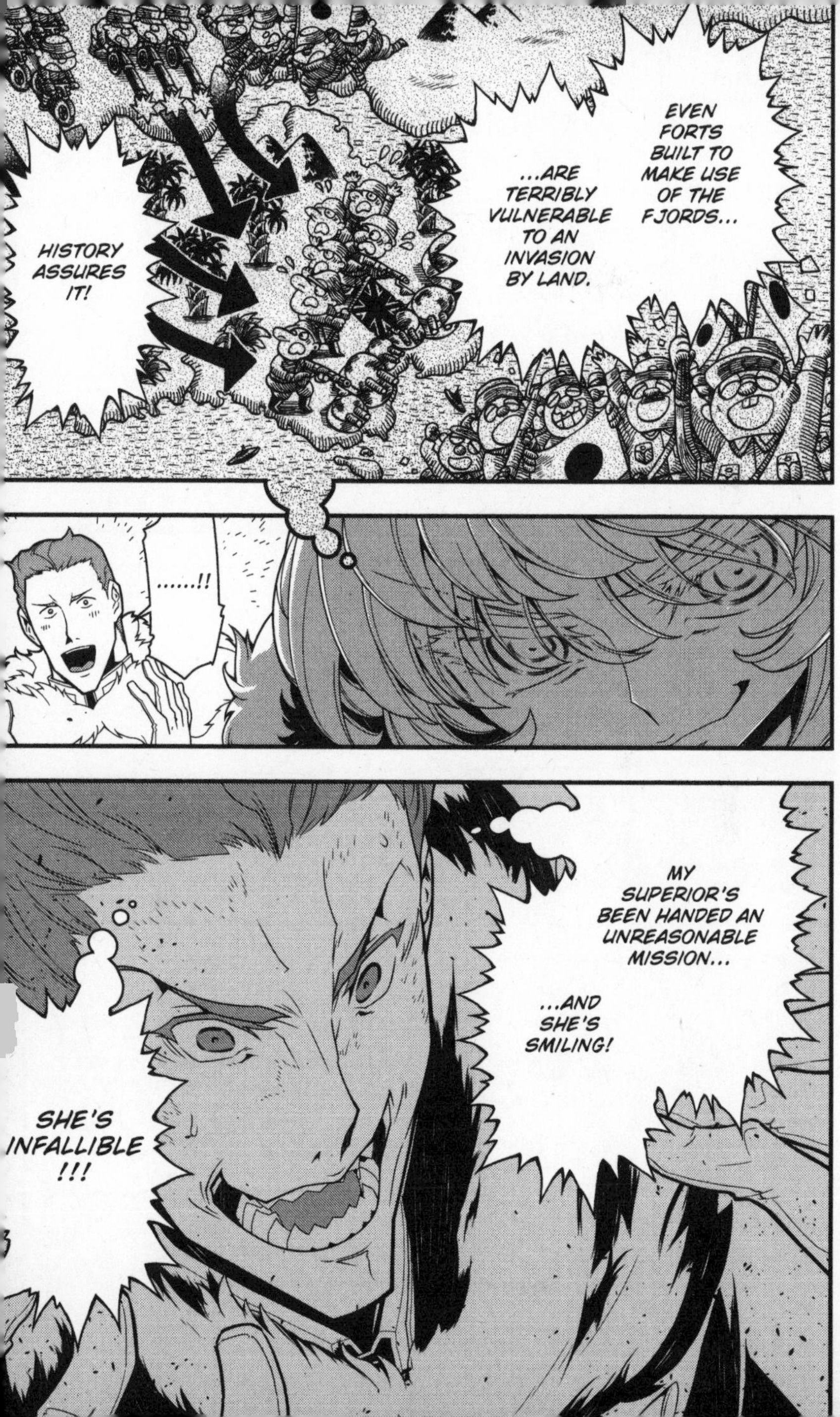

EVEN FORTS BUILT TO MAKE USE OF THE FJORDS...
...ARE TERRIBLY VULNERABLE TO AN INVASION BY LAND.
HISTORY ASSURES IT!
......!!
MY SUPERIOR'S BEEN HANDED AN UNREASONABLE MISSION...
...AND SHE'S SMILING!
SHE'S INFALLIBLE!!!

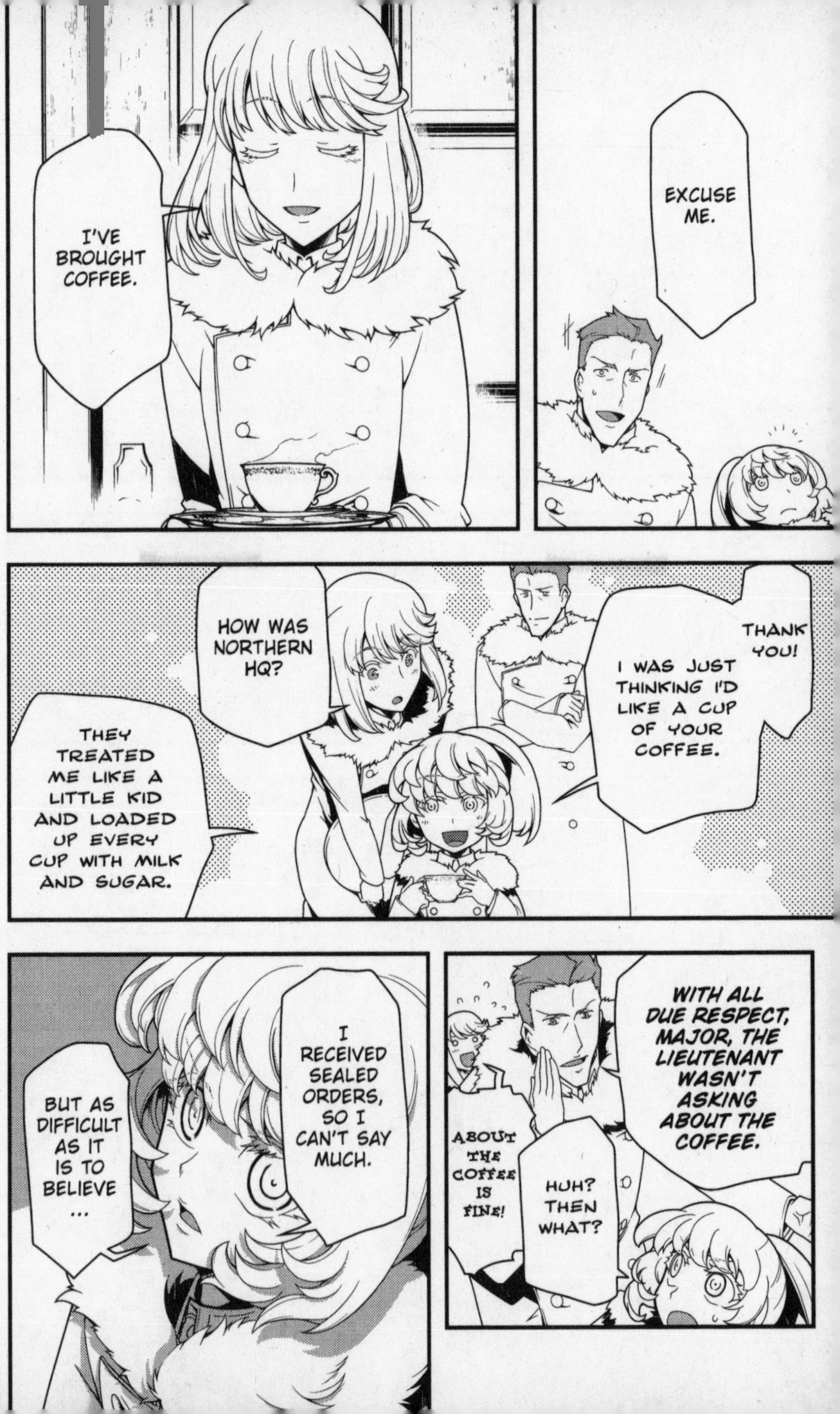
EXCUSE ME.
I'VE BROUGHT COFFEE.
THANK YOU!
I WAS JUST THINKING I'D LIKE A CUP OF YOUR COFFEE.
HOW WAS NORTHERN HQ?
THEY TREATED ME LIKE A LITTLE KID AND LOADED UP EVERY CUP WITH MILK AND SUGAR.
WITH ALL DUE RESPECT, MAJOR, THE LIEUTENANT WASN'T ASKING ABOUT THE COFFEE.
ABOUT THE COFFEE IS FINE!
HUH? THEN WHAT?
I RECEIVED SEALED ORDERS, SO I CAN'T SAY MUCH.
BUT AS DIFFICULT AS IT IS TO BELIEVE ...

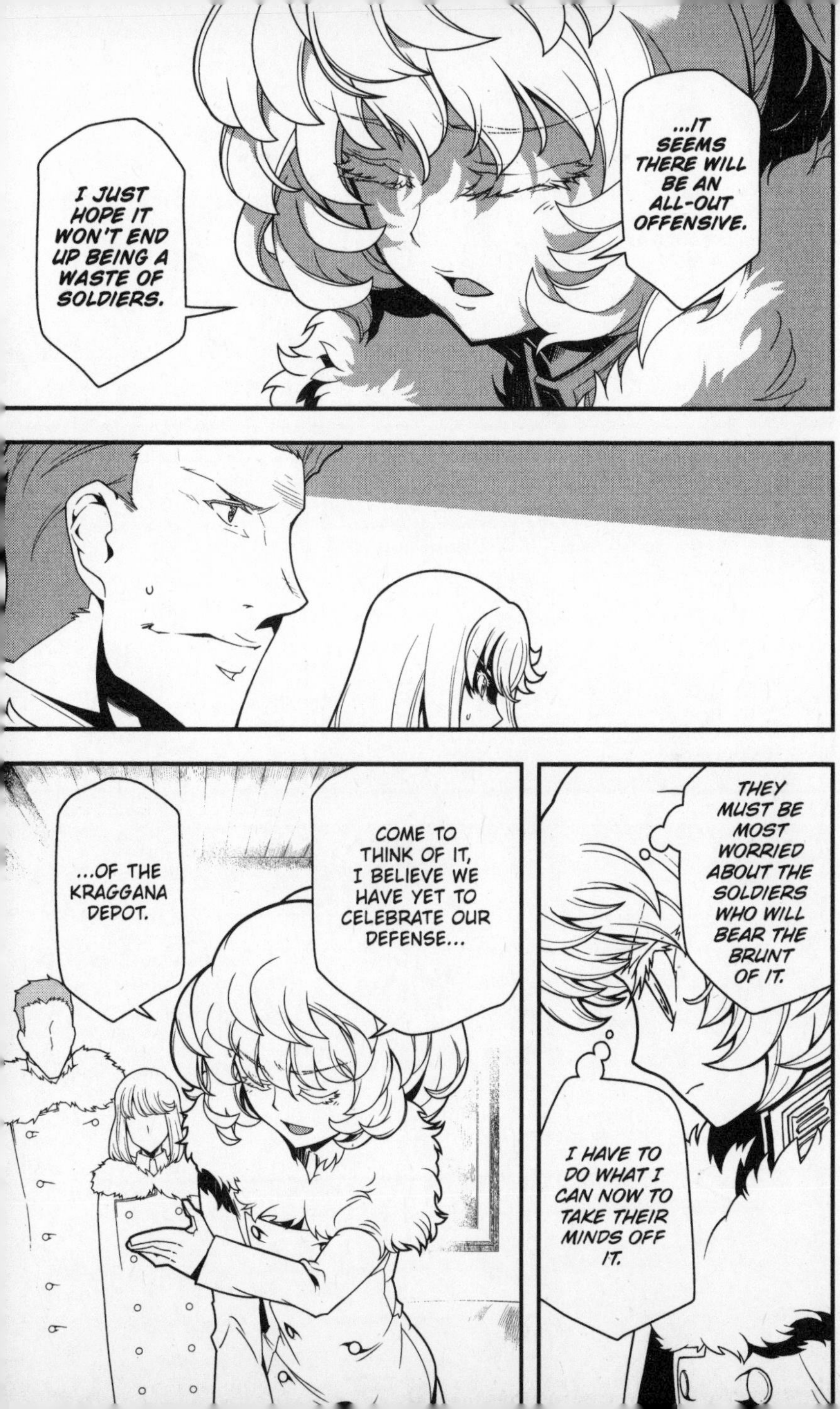
...IT SEEMS THERE WILL BE AN ALL-OUT OFFENSIVE.
I JUST HOPE IT WON'T END UP BEING A WASTE OF SOLDIERS.
THEY MUST BE MOST WORRIED ABOUT THE SOLDIERS WHO WILL BEAR THE BRUNT OF IT.
I HAVE TO DO WHAT I CAN NOW TO TAKE THEIR MINDS OFF IT.
COME TO THINK OF IT, I BELIEVE WE HAVE YET TO CELEBRATE OUR DEFENSE...
...OF THE KRAGGANA DEPOT.

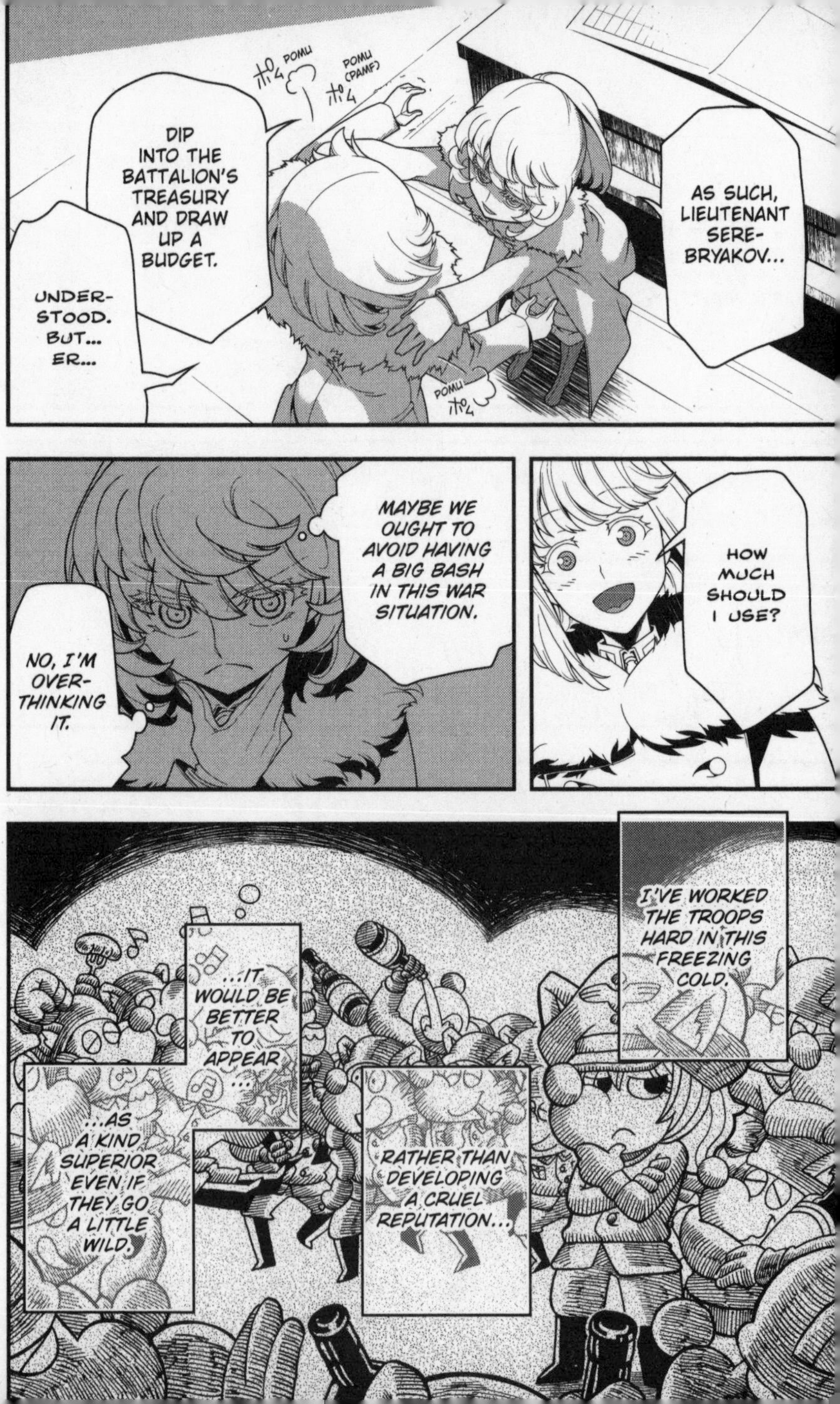
AS SUCH, LIEUTENANT SERE-BRYAKOV...
POMU (PAMF)
POMU
DIP INTO THE BATTALION'S TREASURY AND DRAW UP A BUDGET.
UNDER-STOOD. BUT... ER...
POMU
HOW MUCH SHOULD I USE?
MAYBE WE OUGHT TO AVOID HAVING A BIG BASH IN THIS WAR SITUATION.
NO, I'M OVER-THINKING IT.
I'VE WORKED THE TROOPS HARD IN THIS FREEZING COLD.
...IT WOULD BE BETTER TO APPEAR...
RATHER THAN DEVELOPING A CRUEL REPUTATION...
...AS A KIND SUPERIOR EVEN IF THEY GO A LITTLE WILD.

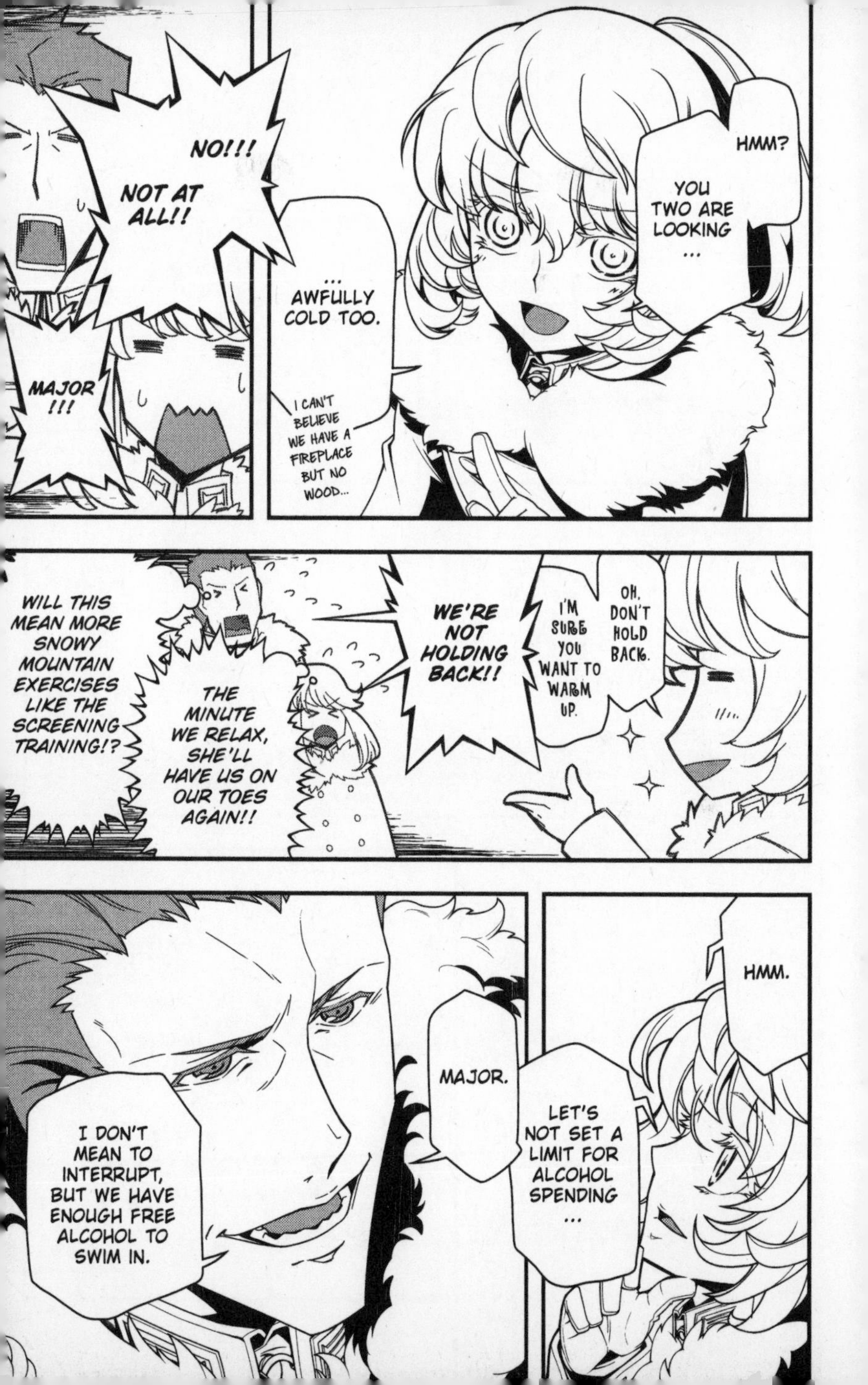
HMM?
YOU TWO ARE LOOKING ...
... AWFULLY COLD TOO.
I CAN'T BELIEVE WE HAVE A FIREPLACE BUT NO WOOD...
NO!!! NOT AT ALL!!
MAJOR!!!
OH, DON'T HOLD BACK.
I'M SURE YOU WANT TO WARM UP.
WE'RE NOT HOLDING BACK!!
THE MINUTE WE RELAX, SHE'LL HAVE US ON OUR TOES AGAIN!!
WILL THIS MEAN MORE SNOWY MOUNTAIN EXERCISES LIKE THE SCREENING TRAINING!?
HMM.
LET'S NOT SET A LIMIT FOR ALCOHOL SPENDING ...
MAJOR.
I DON'T MEAN TO INTERRUPT, BUT WE HAVE ENOUGH FREE ALCOHOL TO SWIM IN.

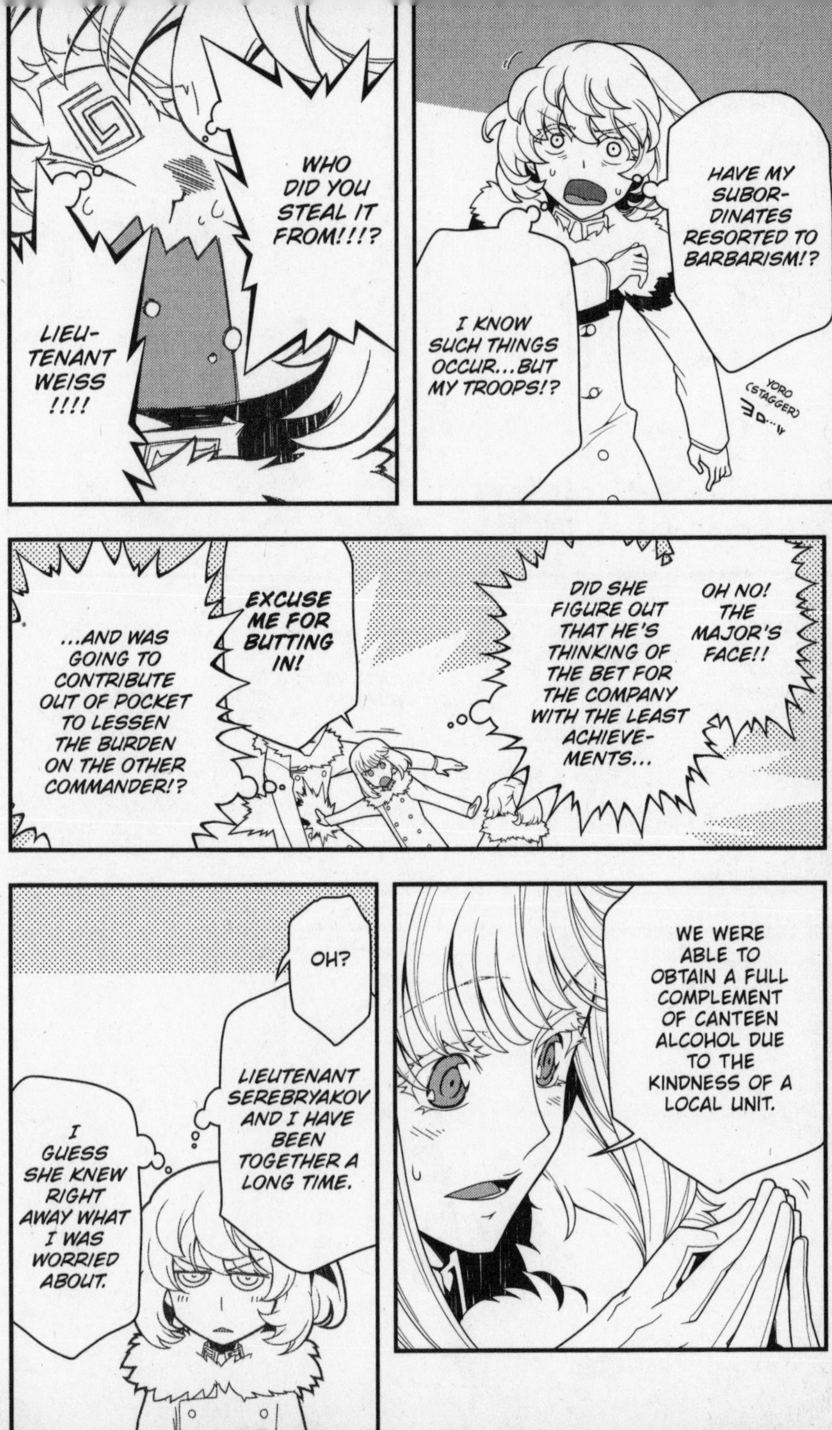
HAVE MY SUBORDINATES RESORTED TO BARBARISM!?
I KNOW SUCH THINGS OCCUR...BUT MY TROOPS!?
YORO (STAGGER)
WHO DID YOU STEAL IT FROM!!!?
LIEUTENANT WEISS!!!!
OH NO! THE MAJOR'S FACE!!
DID SHE FIGURE OUT THAT HE'S THINKING OF THE BET FOR THE COMPANY WITH THE LEAST ACHIEVEMENTS...
EXCUSE ME FOR BUTTING IN!
...AND WAS GOING TO CONTRIBUTE OUT OF POCKET TO LESSEN THE BURDEN ON THE OTHER COMMANDER!?
WE WERE ABLE TO OBTAIN A FULL COMPLEMENT OF CANTEEN ALCOHOL DUE TO THE KINDNESS OF A LOCAL UNIT.
OH?
LIEUTENANT SEREBRYAKOV AND I HAVE BEEN TOGETHER A LONG TIME.
I GUESS SHE KNEW RIGHT AWAY WHAT I WAS WORRIED ABOUT.

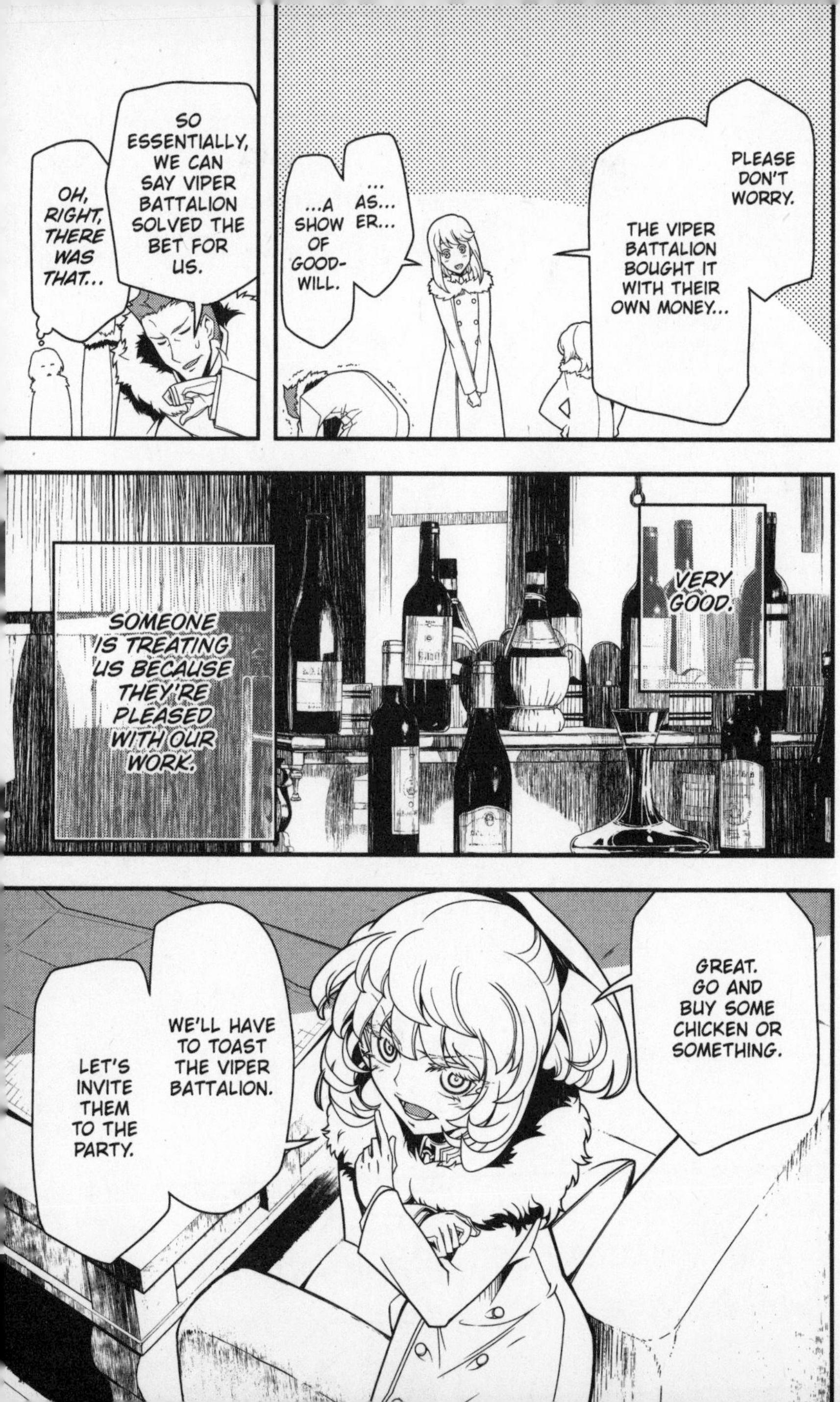
PLEASE DON'T WORRY.
THE VIPER BATTALION BOUGHT IT WITH THEIR OWN MONEY...
... AS... ER...
...A SHOW OF GOOD-WILL.
SO ESSENTIALLY, WE CAN SAY VIPER BATTALION SOLVED THE BET FOR US.
OH, RIGHT, THERE WAS THAT...
VERY GOOD.
SOMEONE IS TREATING US BECAUSE THEY'RE PLEASED WITH OUR WORK.
GREAT. GO AND BUY SOME CHICKEN OR SOMETHING.
WE'LL HAVE TO TOAST THE VIPER BATTALION.
LET'S INVITE THEM TO THE PARTY.

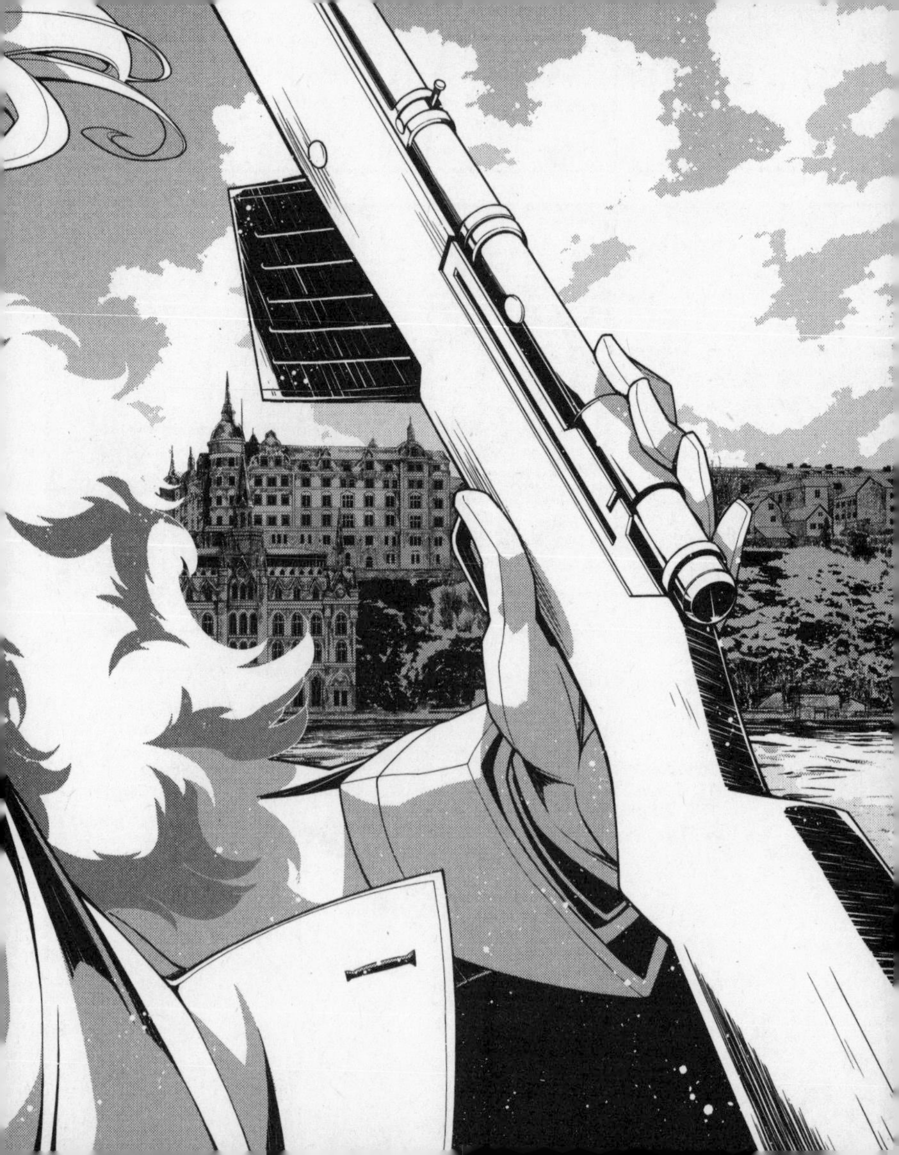

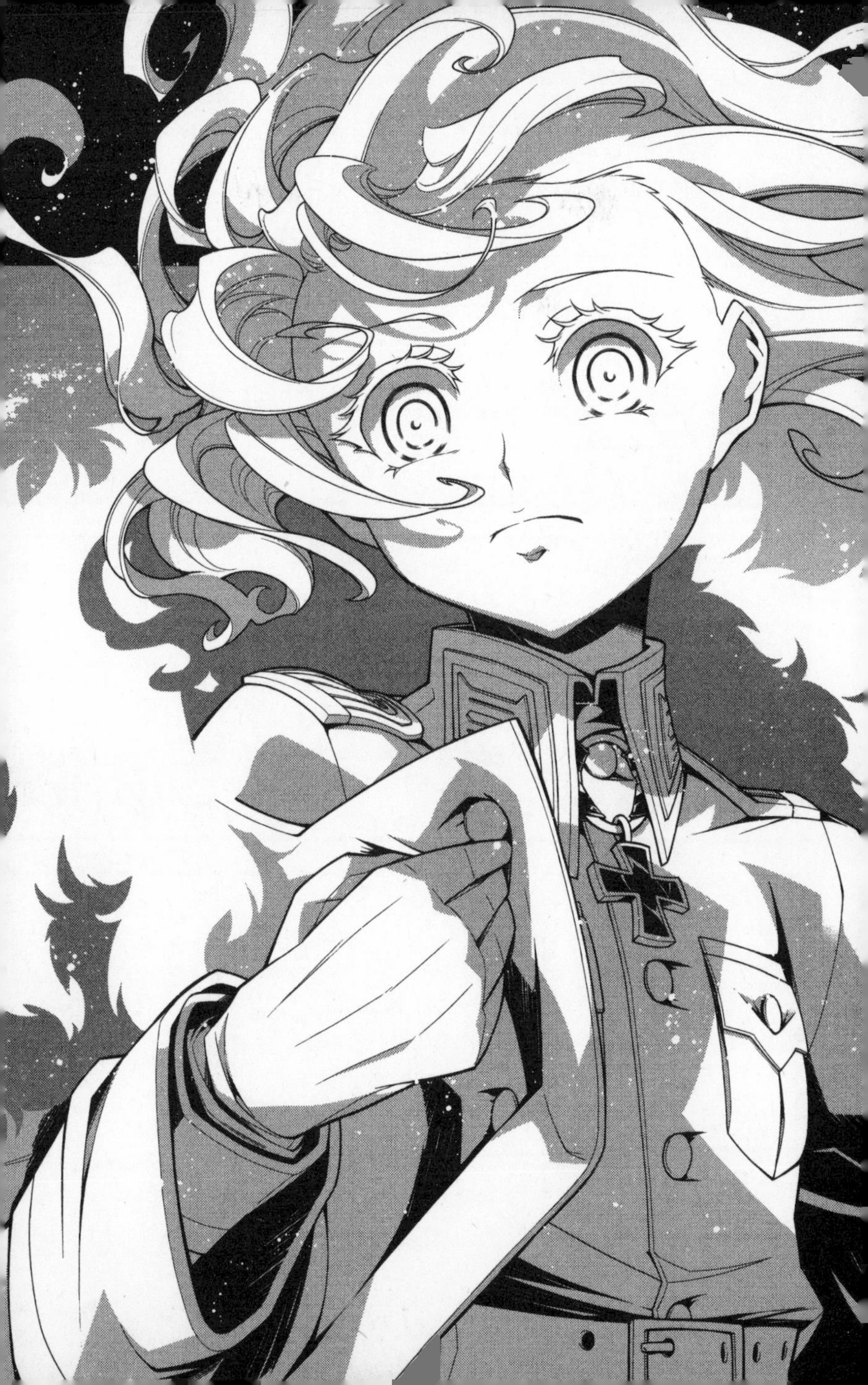

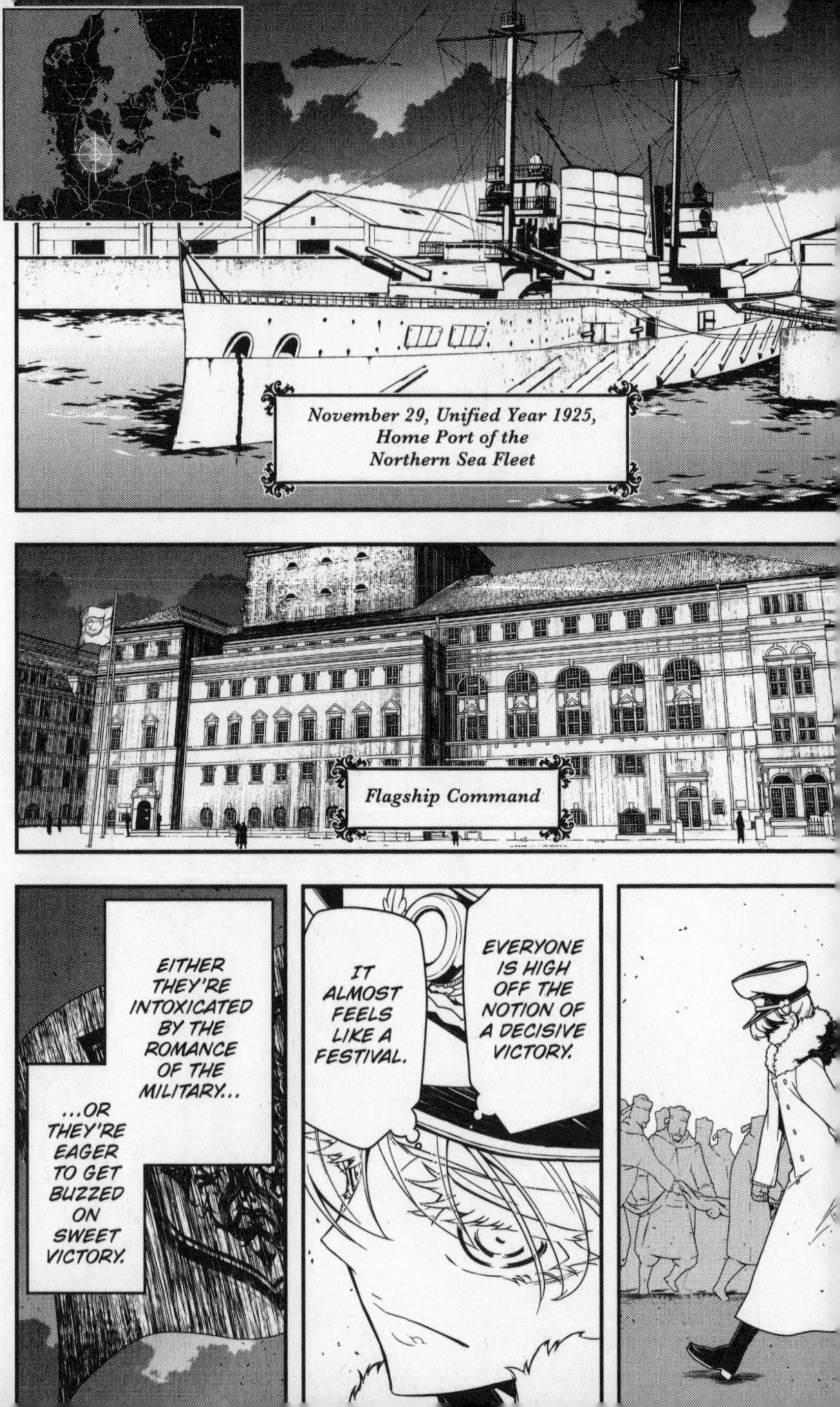
November 29, Unified Year 1925, Home Port of the Northern Sea Fleet
Flagship Command
EVERYONE IS HIGH OFF THE NOTION OF A DECISIVE VICTORY.
IT ALMOST FEELS LIKE A FESTIVAL.
EITHER THEY'RE INTOXICATED BY THE ROMANCE OF THE MILITARY...
...OR THEY'RE EAGER TO GET BUZZED ON SWEET VICTORY.

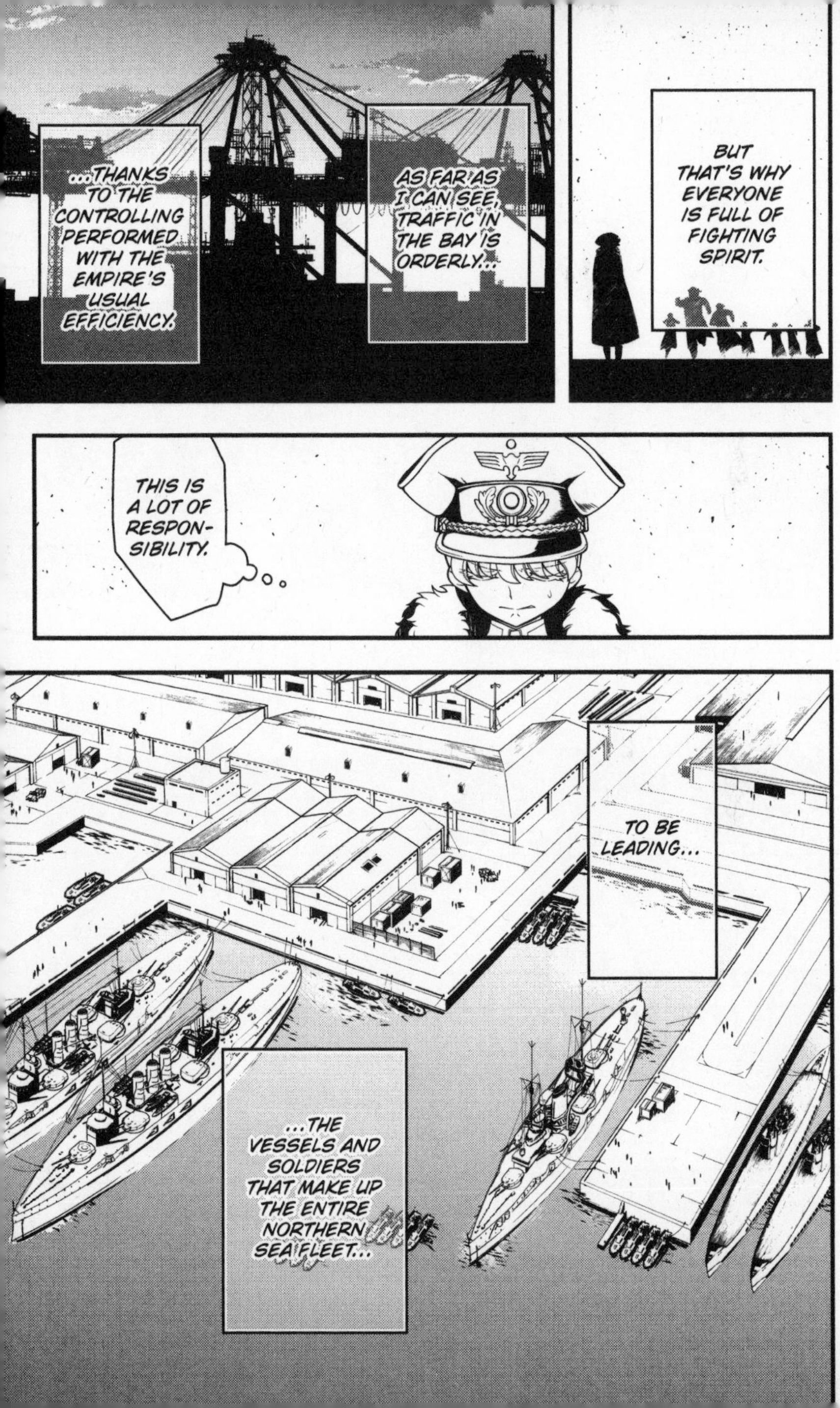
BUT THAT'S WHY EVERYONE IS FULL OF FIGHTING SPIRIT.
AS FAR AS I CAN SEE, TRAFFIC IN THE BAY IS ORDERLY...
...THANKS TO THE CONTROLLING PERFORMED WITH THE EMPIRE'S USUAL EFFICIENCY.
THIS IS A LOT OF RESPON-SIBILITY.
TO BE LEADING...
...THE VESSELS AND SOLDIERS THAT MAKE UP THE ENTIRE NORTHERN SEA FLEET...

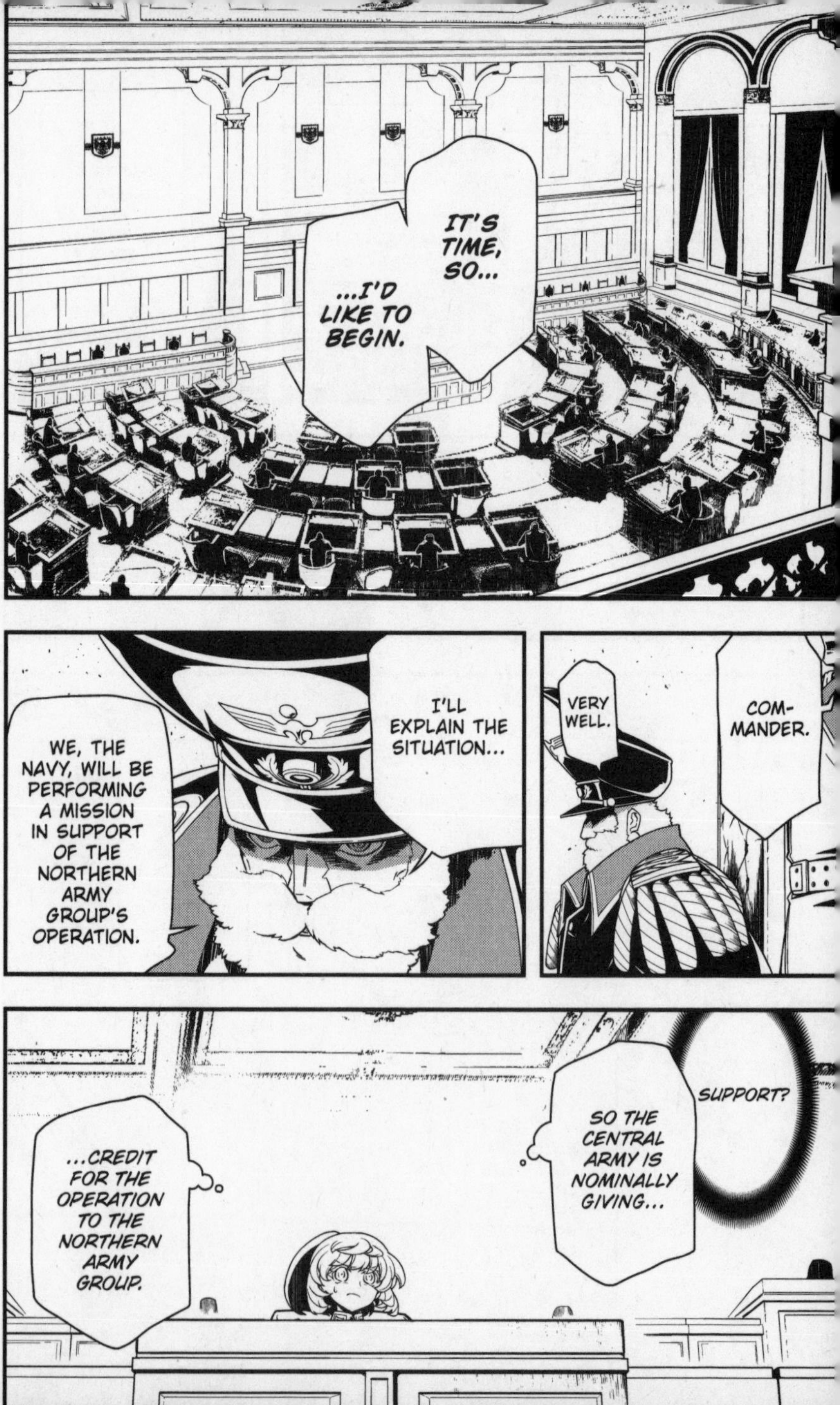
IT'S TIME, SO...
...I'D LIKE TO BEGIN.
COM-MANDER.
VERY WELL.
I'LL EXPLAIN THE SITUATION...
WE, THE NAVY, WILL BE PERFORMING A MISSION IN SUPPORT OF THE NORTHERN ARMY GROUP'S OPERATION.
SUPPORT?
SO THE CENTRAL ARMY IS NOMINALLY GIVING...
...CREDIT FOR THE OPERATION TO THE NORTHERN ARMY GROUP.

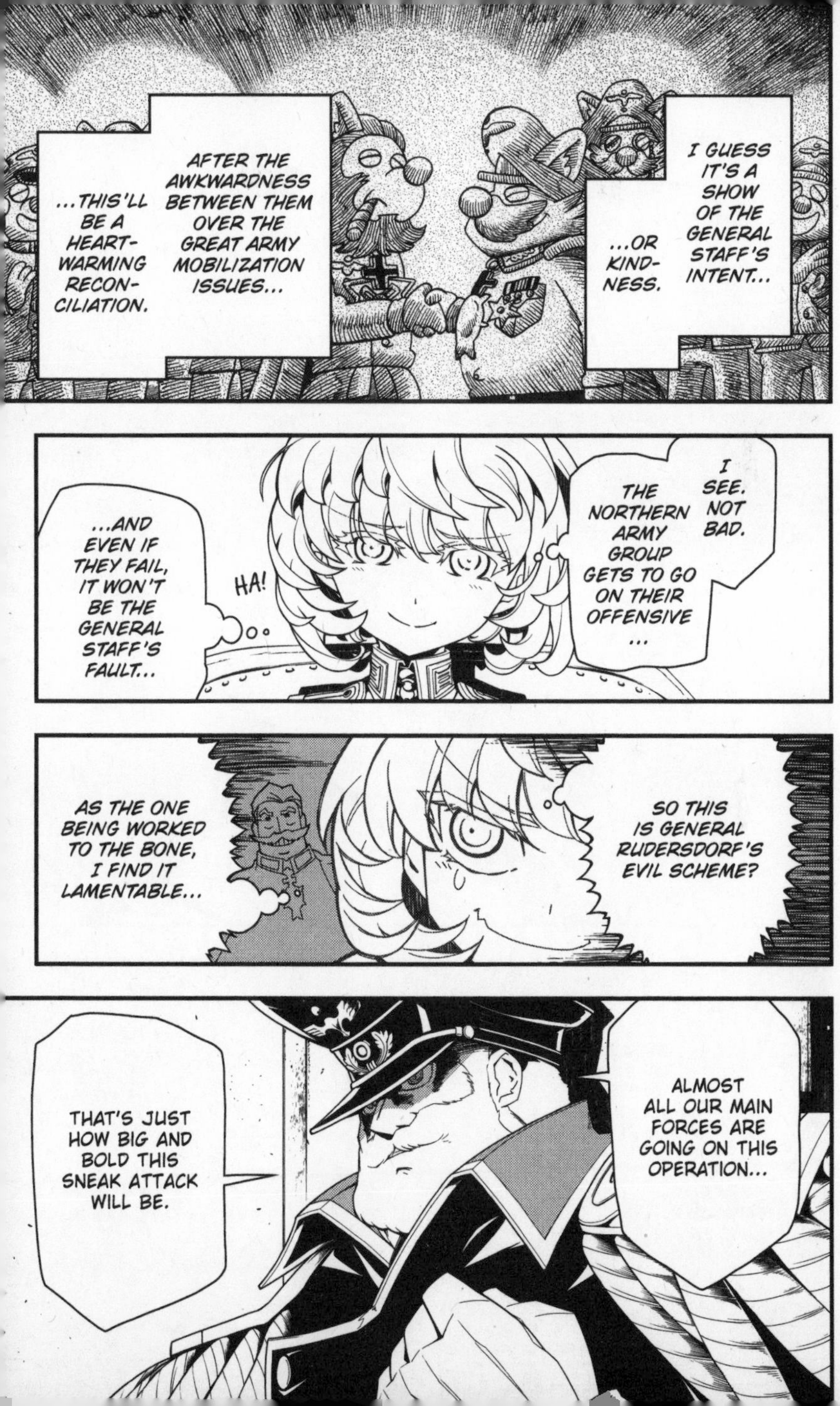
I GUESS IT'S A SHOW OF THE GENERAL STAFF'S INTENT...
...OR KINDNESS.
AFTER THE AWKWARDNESS BETWEEN THEM OVER THE GREAT ARMY MOBILIZATION ISSUES...
...THIS'LL BE A HEART-WARMING RECON-CILIATION.
I SEE. NOT BAD.
THE NORTHERN ARMY GROUP GETS TO GO ON THEIR OFFENSIVE...
HA!
...AND EVEN IF THEY FAIL, IT WON'T BE THE GENERAL STAFF'S FAULT...
SO THIS IS GENERAL RUDERSDORF'S EVIL SCHEME?
AS THE ONE BEING WORKED TO THE BONE, I FIND IT LAMENTABLE...
ALMOST ALL OUR MAIN FORCES ARE GOING ON THIS OPERATION...
THAT'S JUST HOW BIG AND BOLD THIS SNEAK ATTACK WILL BE.

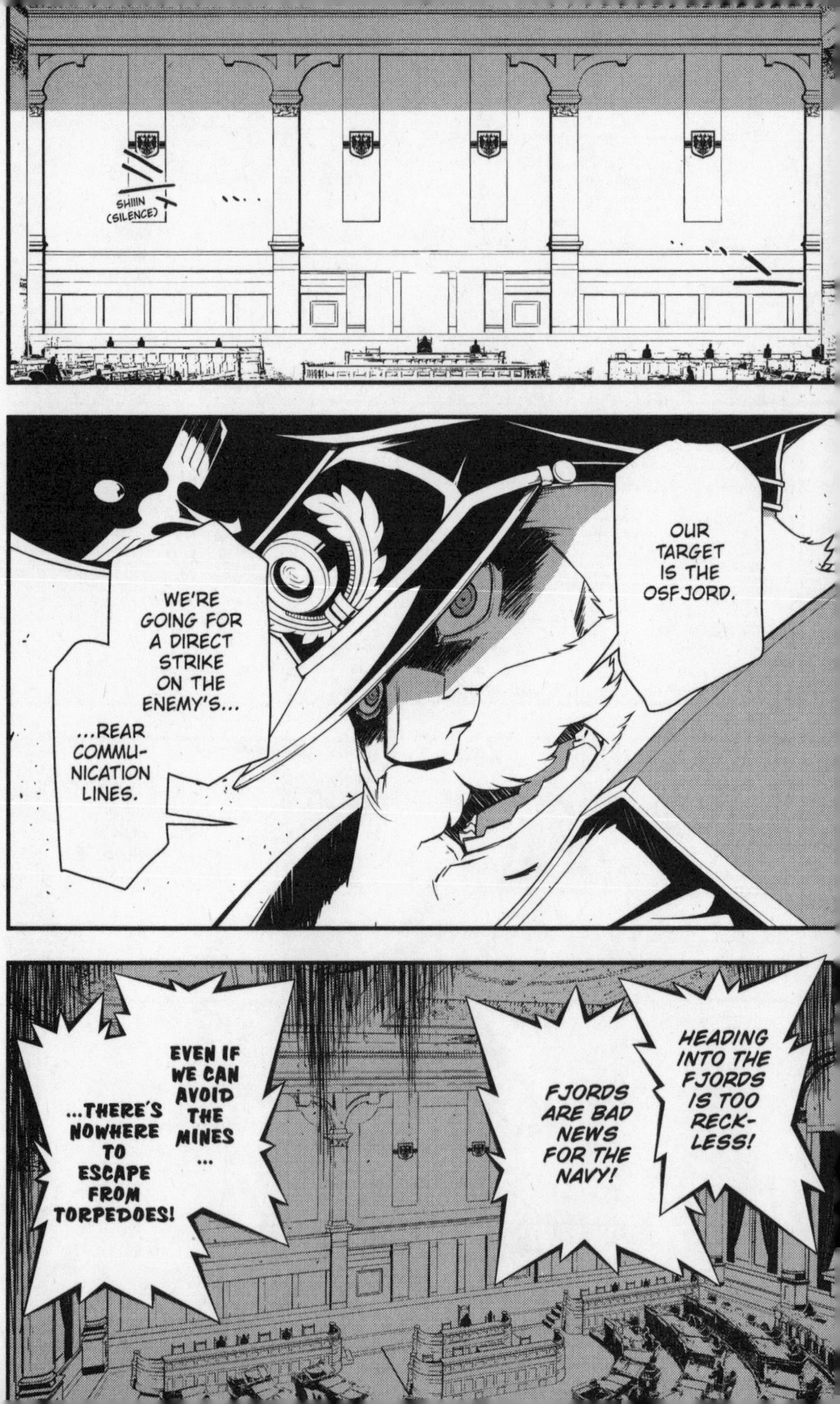
SHIIIN (SILENCE)
...
OUR TARGET IS THE OSFJORD.
WE'RE GOING FOR A DIRECT STRIKE ON THE ENEMY'S...
...REAR COMMUNICATION LINES.
HEADING INTO THE FJORDS IS TOO RECKLESS!
FJORDS ARE BAD NEWS FOR THE NAVY!
EVEN IF WE CAN AVOID THE MINES...
...THERE'S NOWHERE TO ESCAPE FROM TORPEDOES!

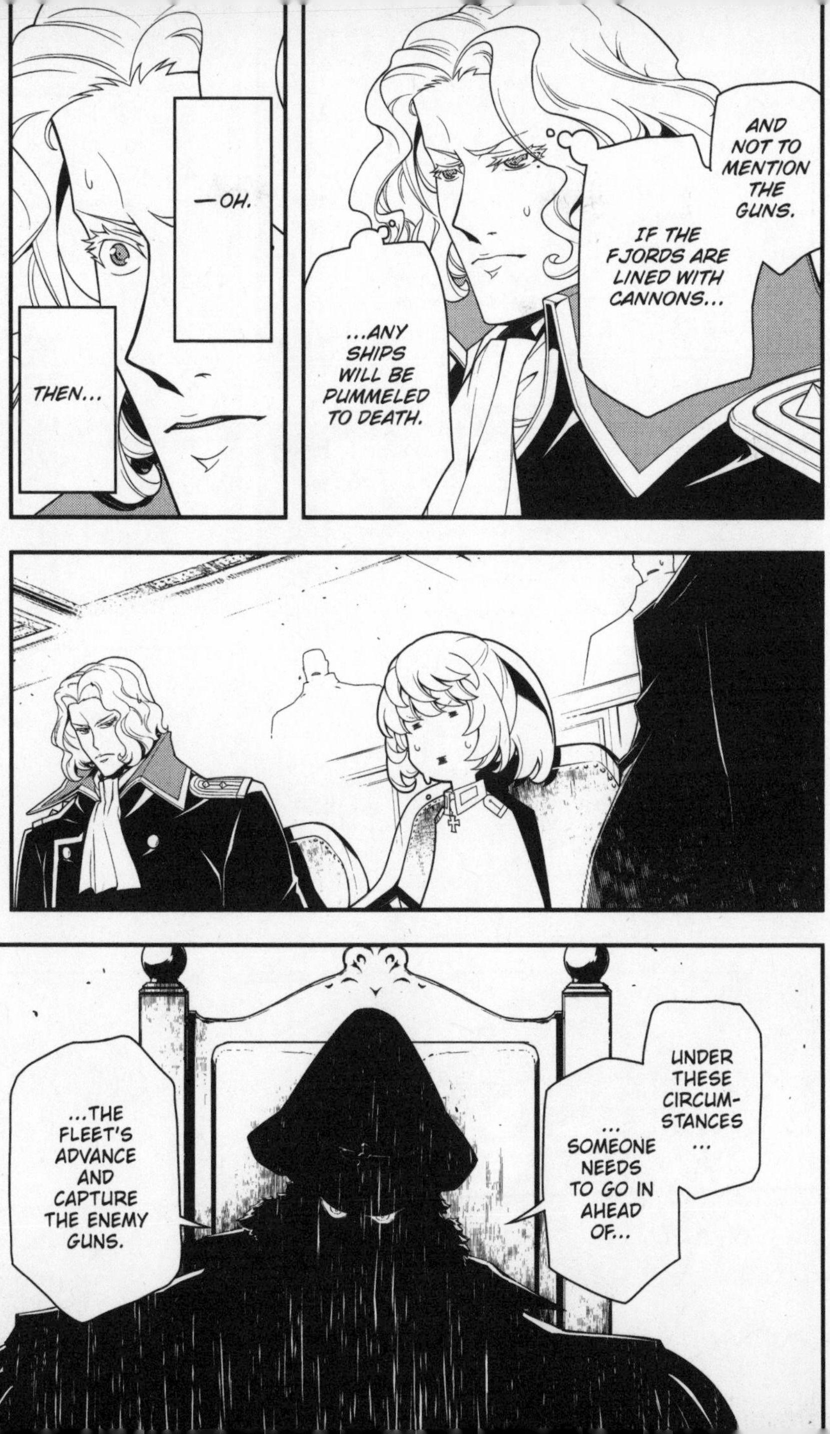
AND NOT TO MENTION THE GUNS.
IF THE FJORDS ARE LINED WITH CANNONS...
...ANY SHIPS WILL BE PUMMELED TO DEATH.
—OH.
THEN...
UNDER THESE CIRCUM-STANCES ...
... SOMEONE NEEDS TO GO IN AHEAD OF...
...THE FLEET'S ADVANCE AND CAPTURE THE ENEMY GUNS.

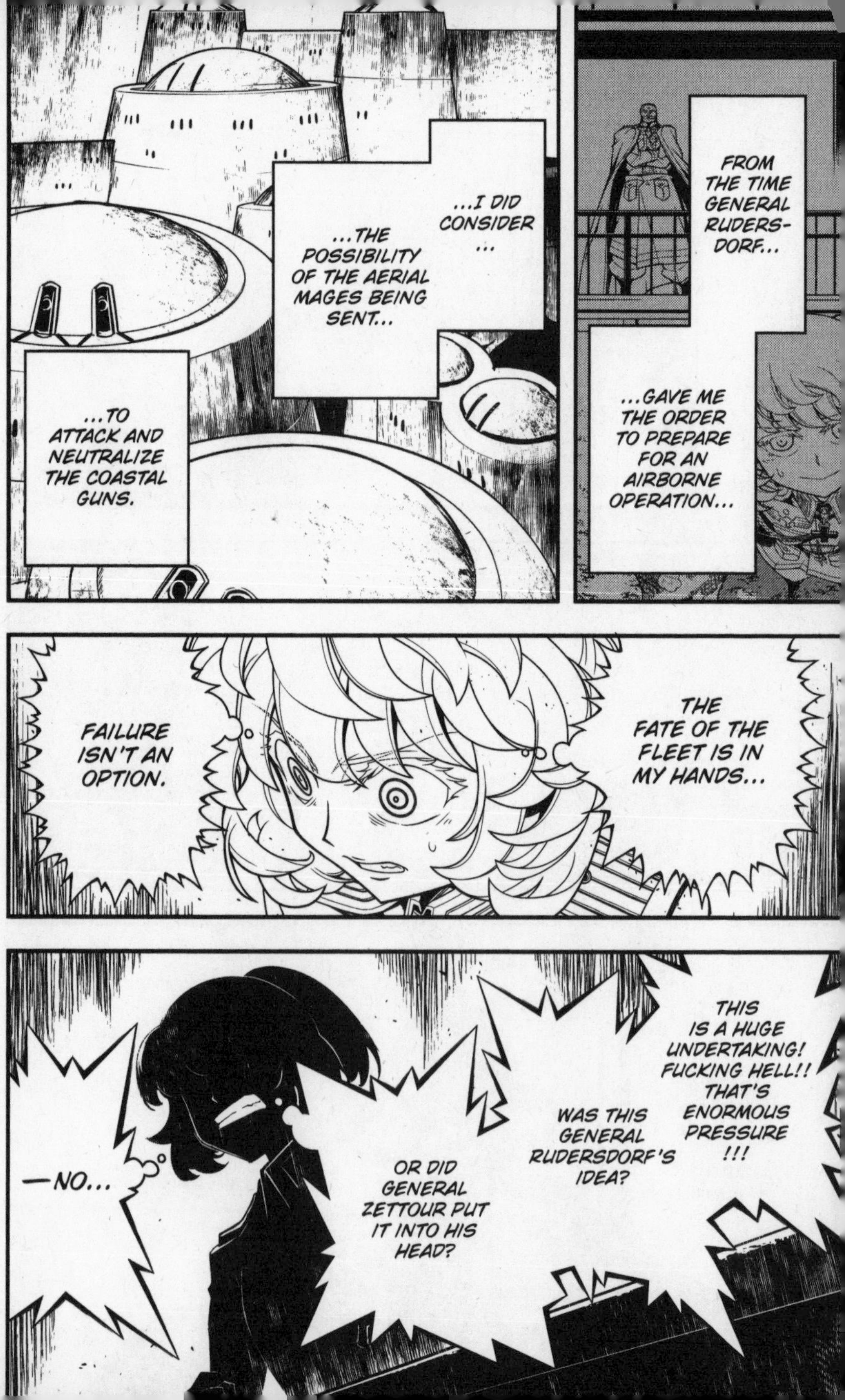
FROM THE TIME GENERAL RUDERS-DORF...
...GAVE ME THE ORDER TO PREPARE FOR AN AIRBORNE OPERATION...
...I DID CONSIDER ...
...THE POSSIBILITY OF THE AERIAL MAGES BEING SENT...
...TO ATTACK AND NEUTRALIZE THE COASTAL GUNS.
THE FATE OF THE FLEET IS IN MY HANDS...
FAILURE ISN'T AN OPTION.
THIS IS A HUGE UNDERTAKING! FUCKING HELL!! THAT'S ENORMOUS PRESSURE !!!
WAS THIS GENERAL RUDERSDORF'S IDEA?
OR DID GENERAL ZETTOUR PUT IT INTO HIS HEAD?
—NO...

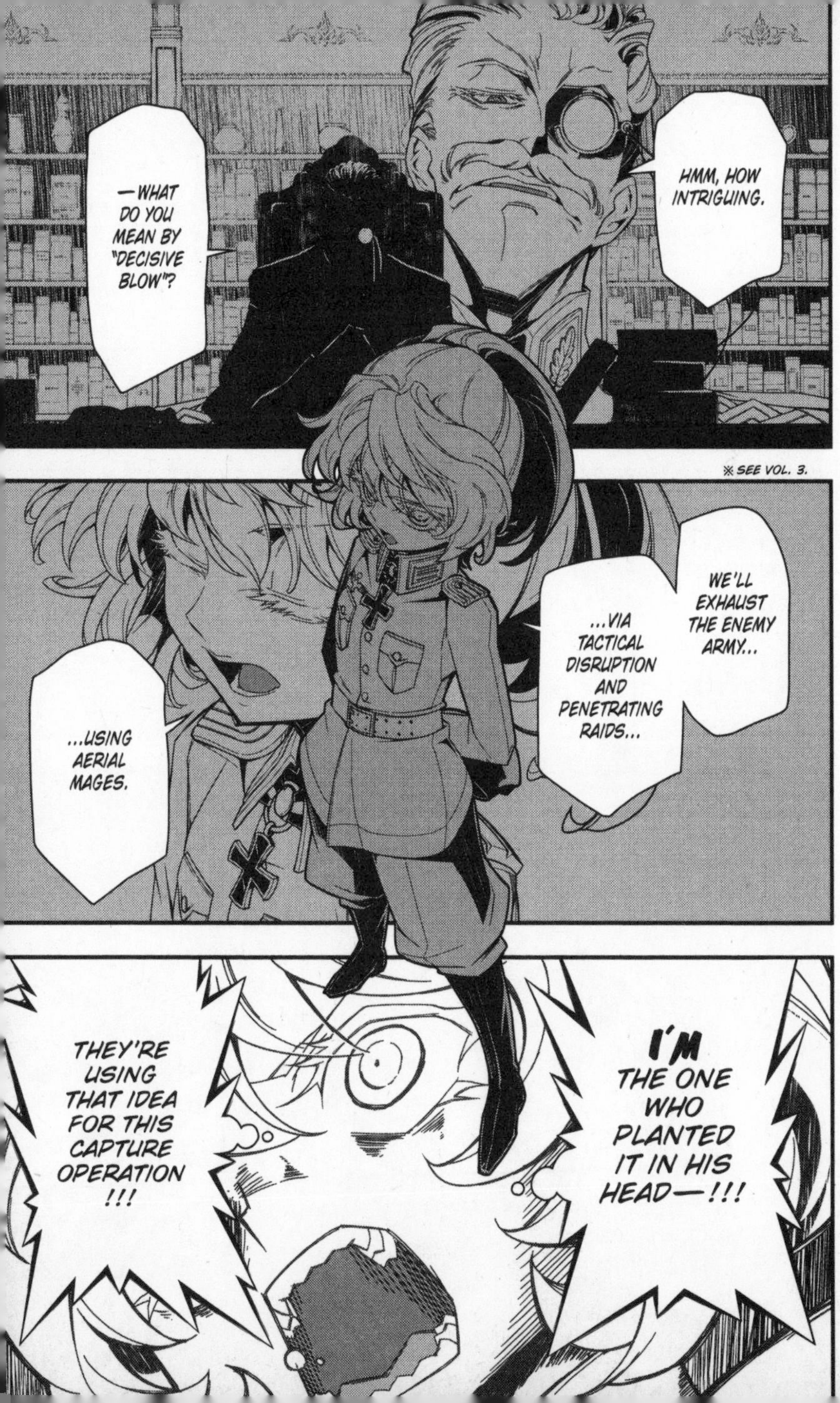
HMM, HOW INTRIGUING.
—WHAT DO YOU MEAN BY "DECISIVE BLOW"?
※ SEE VOL. 3.
WE'LL EXHAUST THE ENEMY ARMY...
...VIA TACTICAL DISRUPTION AND PENETRATING RAIDS...
...USING AERIAL MAGES.
I'M THE ONE WHO PLANTED IT IN HIS HEAD—!!!
THEY'RE USING THAT IDEA FOR THIS CAPTURE OPERATION!!!

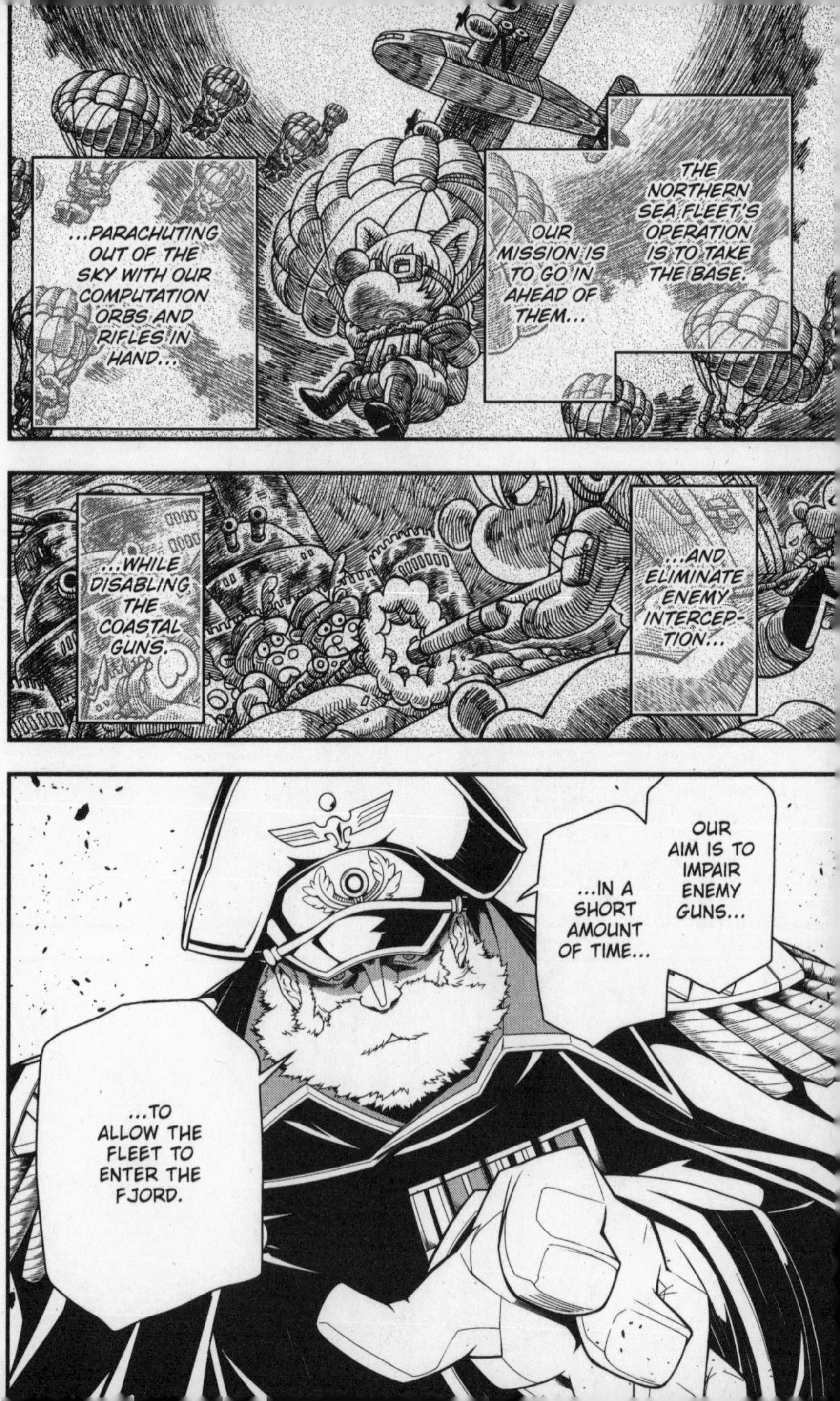
THE NORTHERN SEA FLEET'S OPERATION IS TO TAKE THE BASE.
OUR MISSION IS TO GO IN AHEAD OF THEM...
...PARACHUTING OUT OF THE SKY WITH OUR COMPUTATION ORBS AND RIFLES IN HAND...
...AND ELIMINATE ENEMY INTERCEPTION...
...WHILE DISABLING THE COASTAL GUNS.
OUR AIM IS TO IMPAIR ENEMY GUNS...
...IN A SHORT AMOUNT OF TIME...
...TO ALLOW THE FLEET TO ENTER THE FJORD.

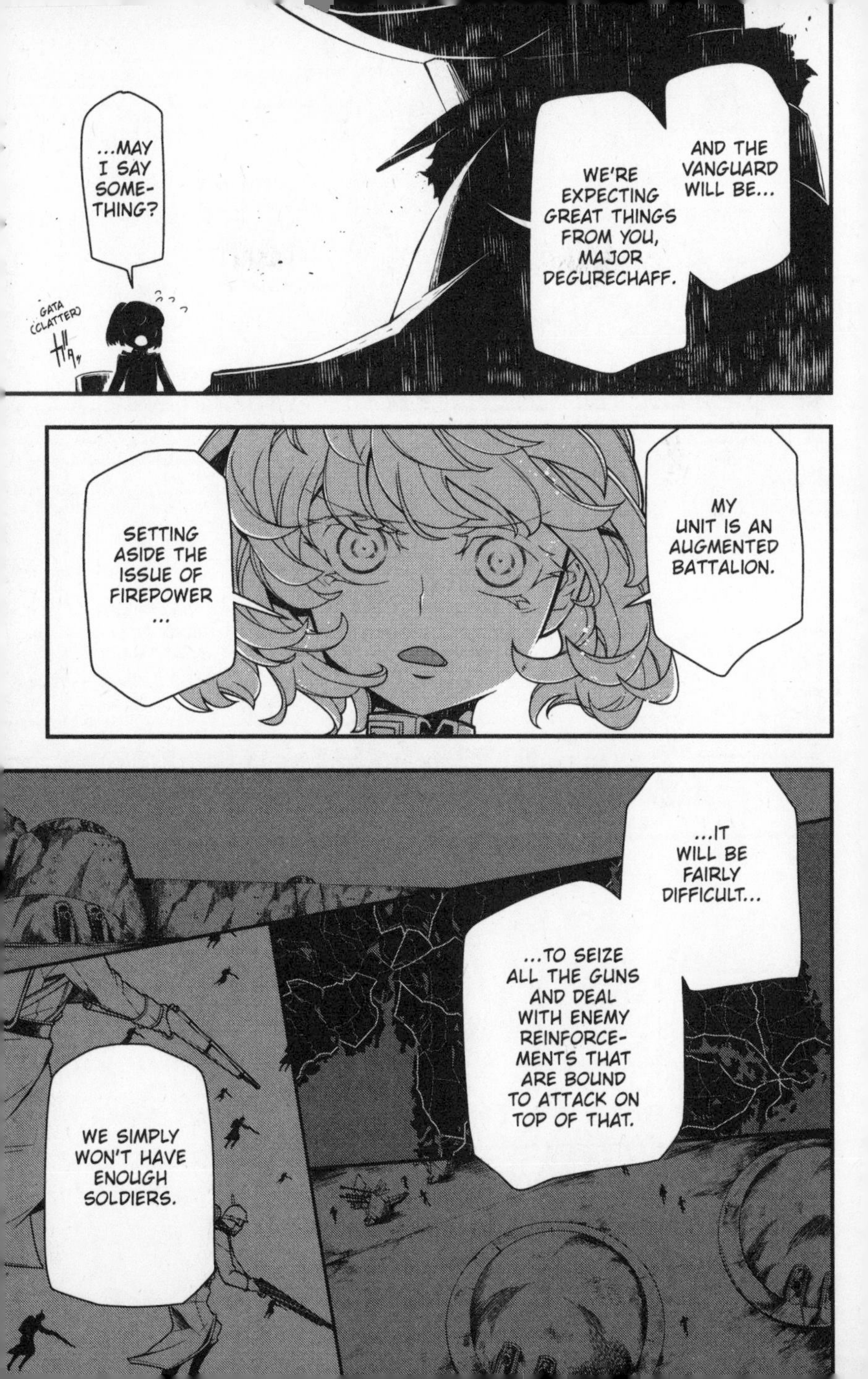
AND THE VANGUARD WILL BE...
WE'RE EXPECTING GREAT THINGS FROM YOU, MAJOR DEGURECHAFF.
...MAY I SAY SOMETHING?
GATA (CLATTER)
MY UNIT IS AN AUGMENTED BATTALION.
SETTING ASIDE THE ISSUE OF FIREPOWER...
...IT WILL BE FAIRLY DIFFICULT...
...TO SEIZE ALL THE GUNS AND DEAL WITH ENEMY REINFORCEMENTS THAT ARE BOUND TO ATTACK ON TOP OF THAT.
WE SIMPLY WON'T HAVE ENOUGH SOLDIERS.

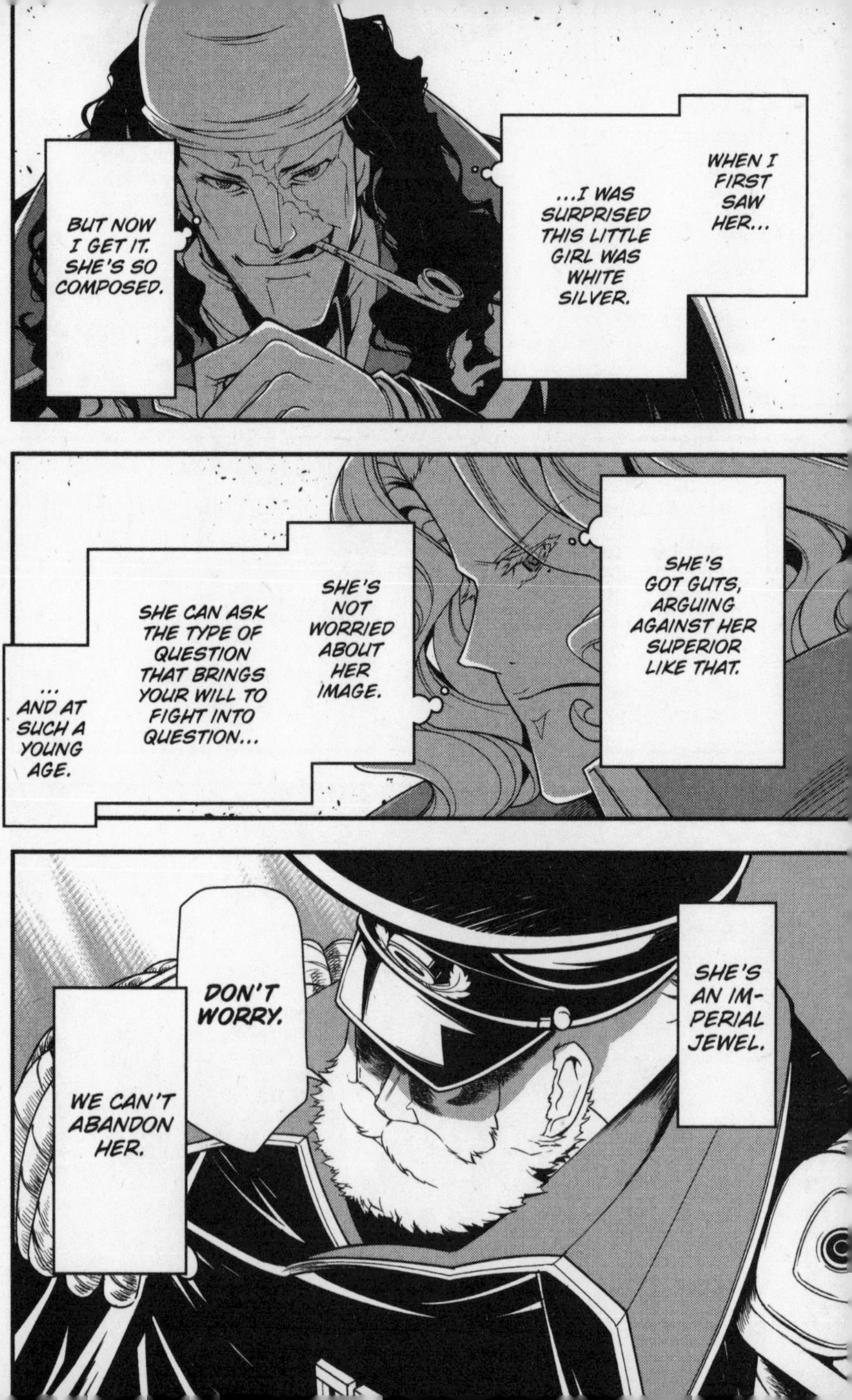
WHEN I FIRST SAW HER...
...I WAS SURPRISED THIS LITTLE GIRL WAS WHITE SILVER.
BUT NOW I GET IT. SHE'S SO COMPOSED.
SHE'S GOT GUTS, ARGUING AGAINST HER SUPERIOR LIKE THAT.
SHE'S NOT WORRIED ABOUT HER IMAGE.
SHE CAN ASK THE TYPE OF QUESTION THAT BRINGS YOUR WILL TO FIGHT INTO QUESTION...
...AND AT SUCH A YOUNG AGE.
SHE'S AN IMPERIAL JEWEL.
DON'T WORRY.
WE CAN'T ABANDON HER.

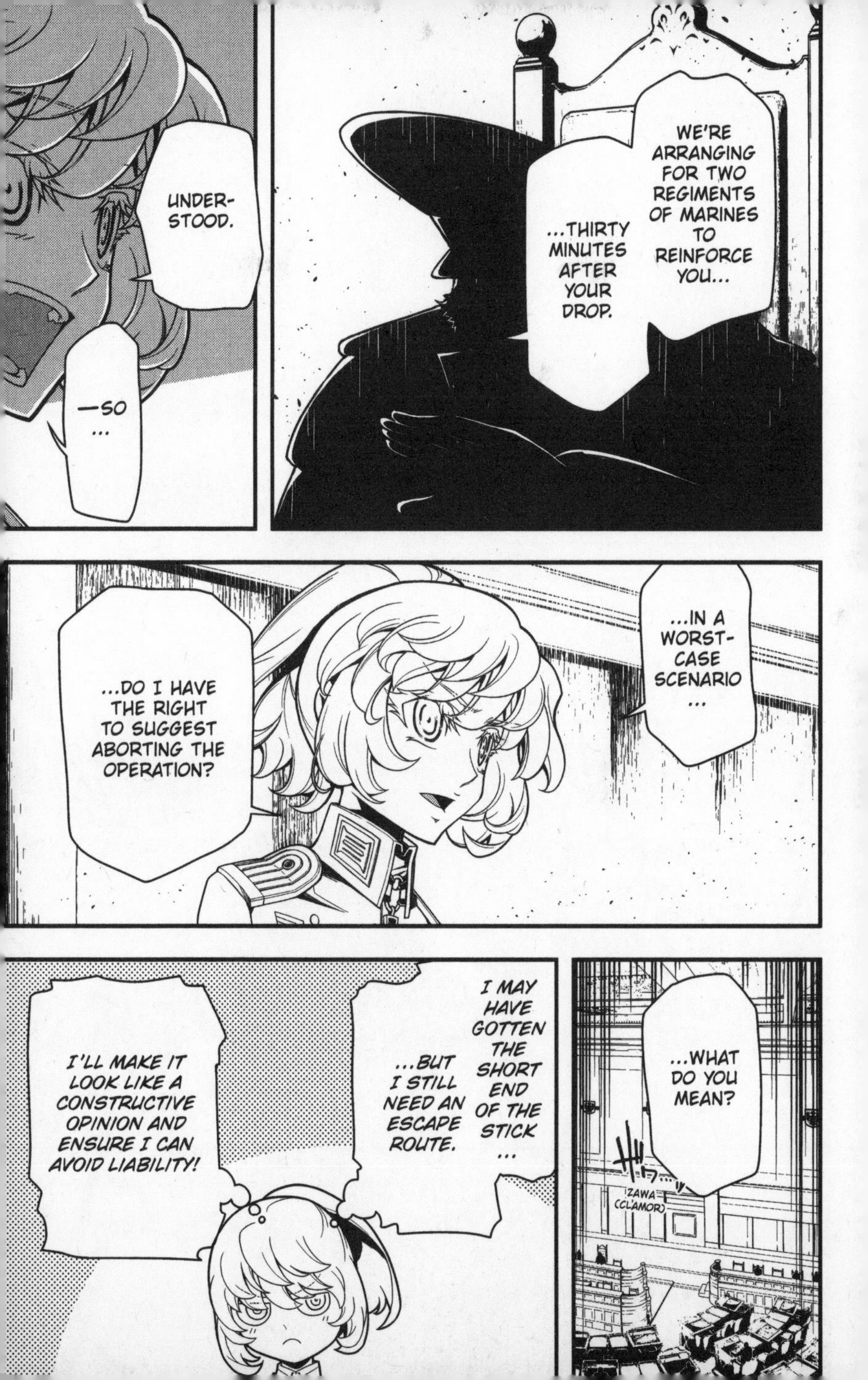
WE'RE ARRANGING FOR TWO REGIMENTS OF MARINES TO REINFORCE YOU...
...THIRTY MINUTES AFTER YOUR DROP.
UNDER-STOOD.
—SO ...
...IN A WORST-CASE SCENARIO ...
...DO I HAVE THE RIGHT TO SUGGEST ABORTING THE OPERATION?
...WHAT DO YOU MEAN?
ZAWA (CLAMOR)
I MAY HAVE GOTTEN THE SHORT END OF THE STICK ...
...BUT I STILL NEED AN ESCAPE ROUTE.
I'LL MAKE IT LOOK LIKE A CONSTRUCTIVE OPINION AND ENSURE I CAN AVOID LIABILITY!

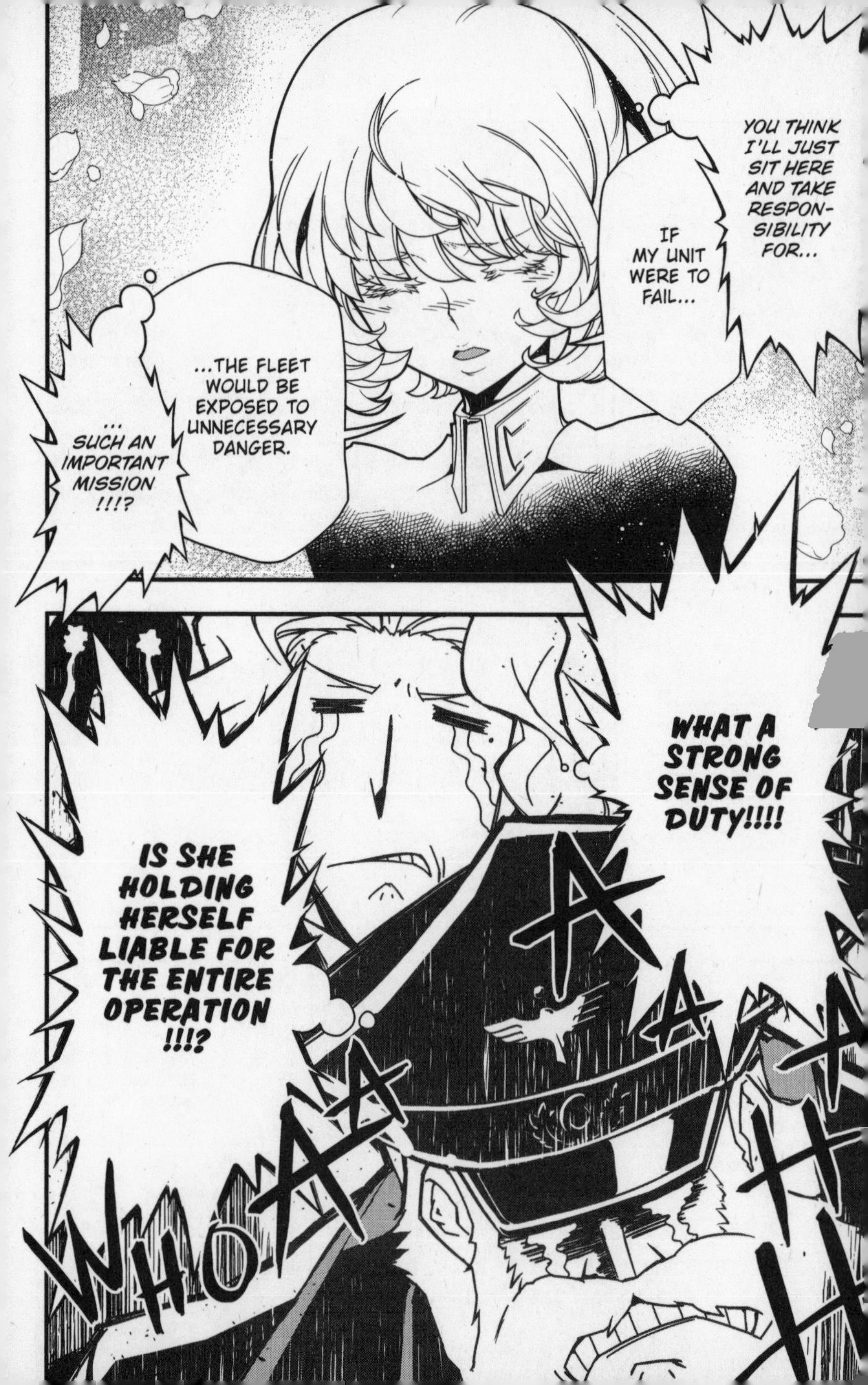
YOU THINK I'LL JUST SIT HERE AND TAKE RESPON-SIBILITY FOR...
IF MY UNIT WERE TO FAIL...
...THE FLEET WOULD BE EXPOSED TO UNNECESSARY DANGER.
...SUCH AN IMPORTANT MISSION!!!?
WHAT A STRONG SENSE OF DUTY!!!!
IS SHE HOLDING HERSELF LIABLE FOR THE ENTIRE OPERATION!!!?
WHOAAAAAHH

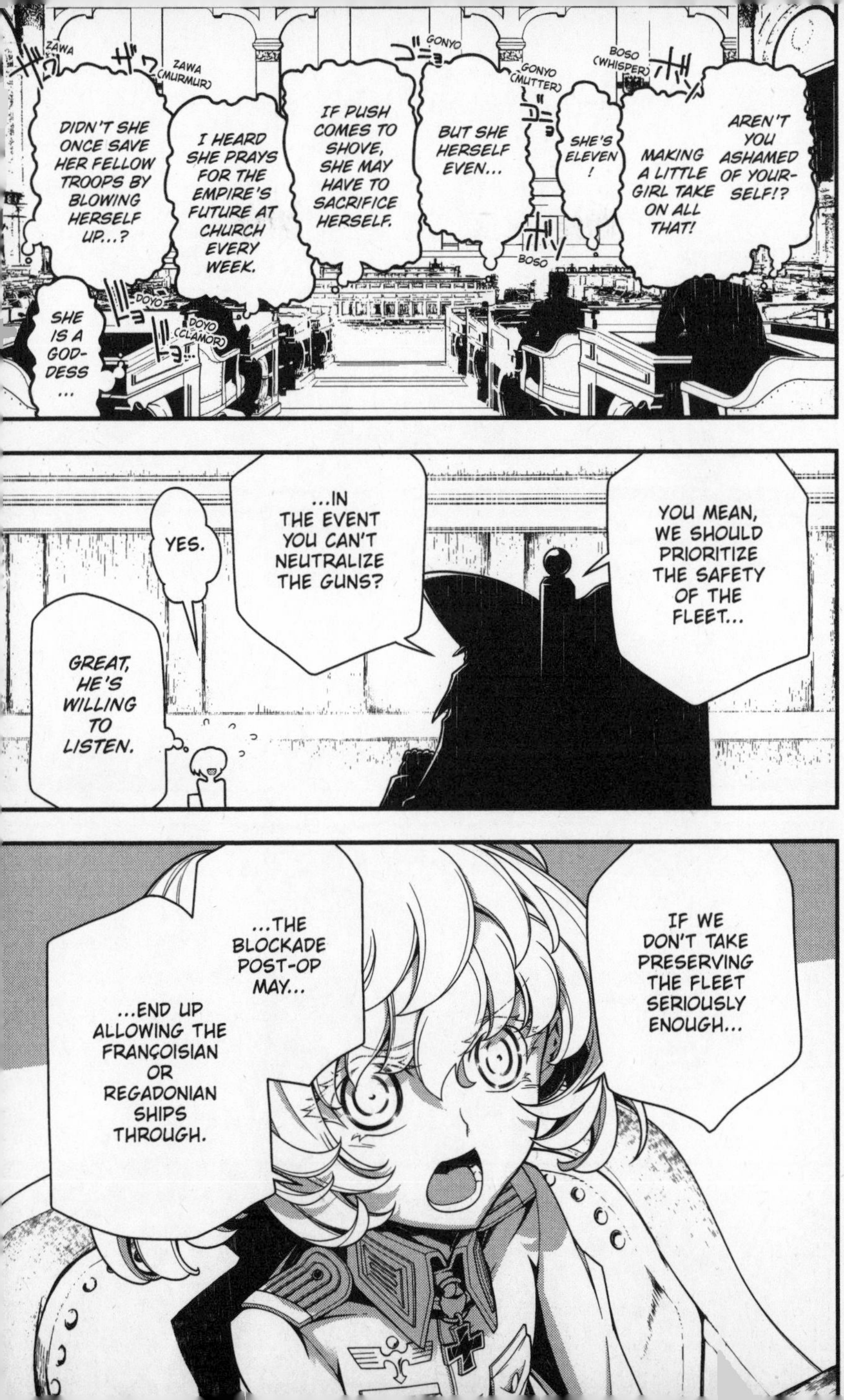
BOSO (WHISPER)
AREN'T YOU ASHAMED OF YOURSELF!?
MAKING A LITTLE GIRL TAKE ON ALL THAT!
SHE'S ELEVEN!
BOSO
GONYO (MUTTER)
BUT SHE HERSELF EVEN...
GONYO
IF PUSH COMES TO SHOVE, SHE MAY HAVE TO SACRIFICE HERSELF.
ZAWA (MURMUR)
I HEARD SHE PRAYS FOR THE EMPIRE'S FUTURE AT CHURCH EVERY WEEK.
ZAWA
DIDN'T SHE ONCE SAVE HER FELLOW TROOPS BY BLOWING HERSELF UP...?
DOYO (CLAMOR)
DOYO
SHE IS A GOD-DESS...
YOU MEAN, WE SHOULD PRIORITIZE THE SAFETY OF THE FLEET...
...IN THE EVENT YOU CAN'T NEUTRALIZE THE GUNS?
YES.
GREAT, HE'S WILLING TO LISTEN.
IF WE DON'T TAKE PRESERVING THE FLEET SERIOUSLY ENOUGH...
...THE BLOCKADE POST-OP MAY...
...END UP ALLOWING THE FRANÇOISIAN OR REGADONIAN SHIPS THROUGH.

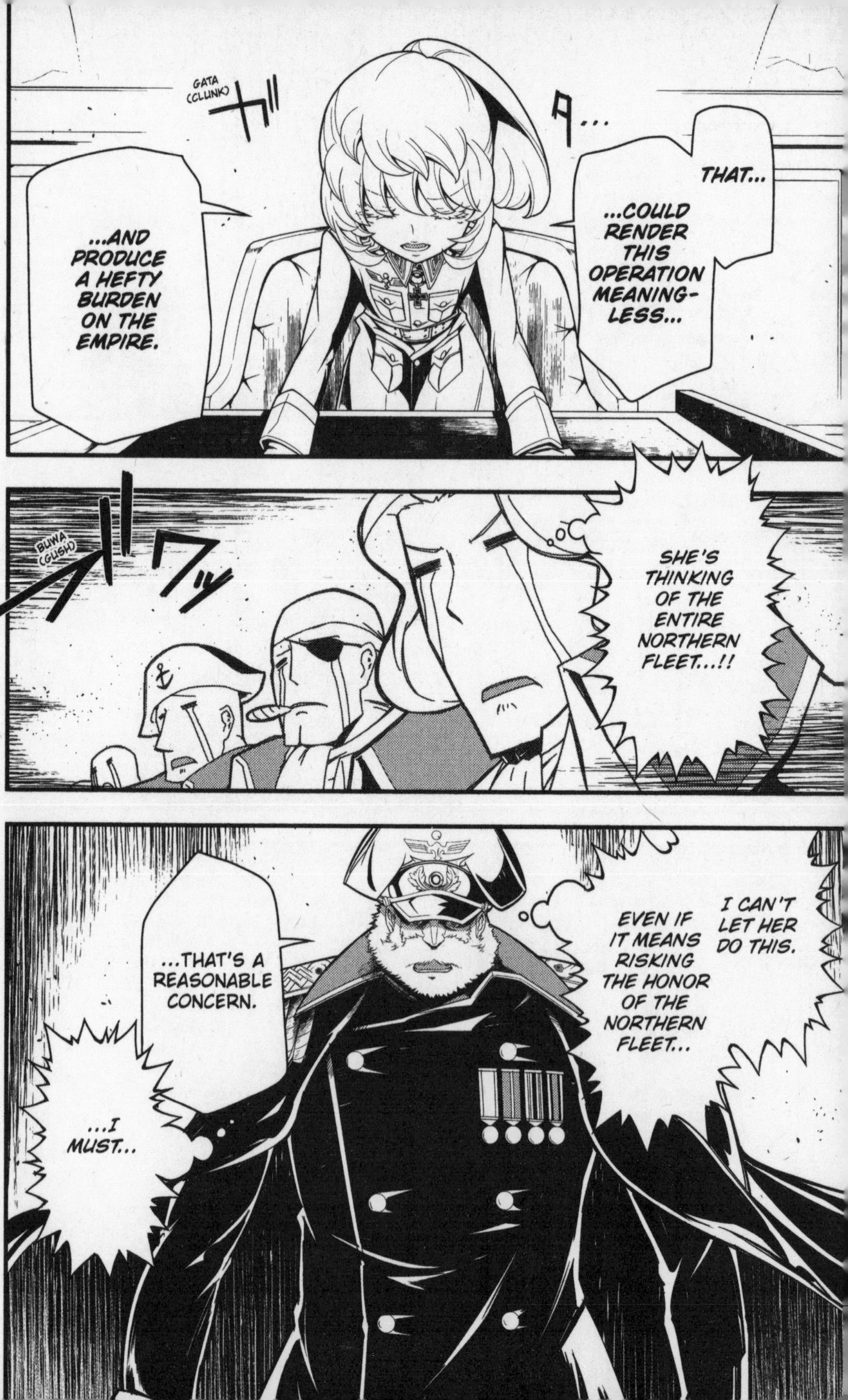
THAT...
...COULD RENDER THIS OPERATION MEANING-LESS...
...AND PRODUCE A HEFTY BURDEN ON THE EMPIRE.
GATA (CLUNK)
SHE'S THINKING OF THE ENTIRE NORTHERN FLEET...!!
BUWA (GUSH)
I CAN'T LET HER DO THIS.
EVEN IF IT MEANS RISKING THE HONOR OF THE NORTHERN FLEET...
...THAT'S A REASONABLE CONCERN.
...I MUST...

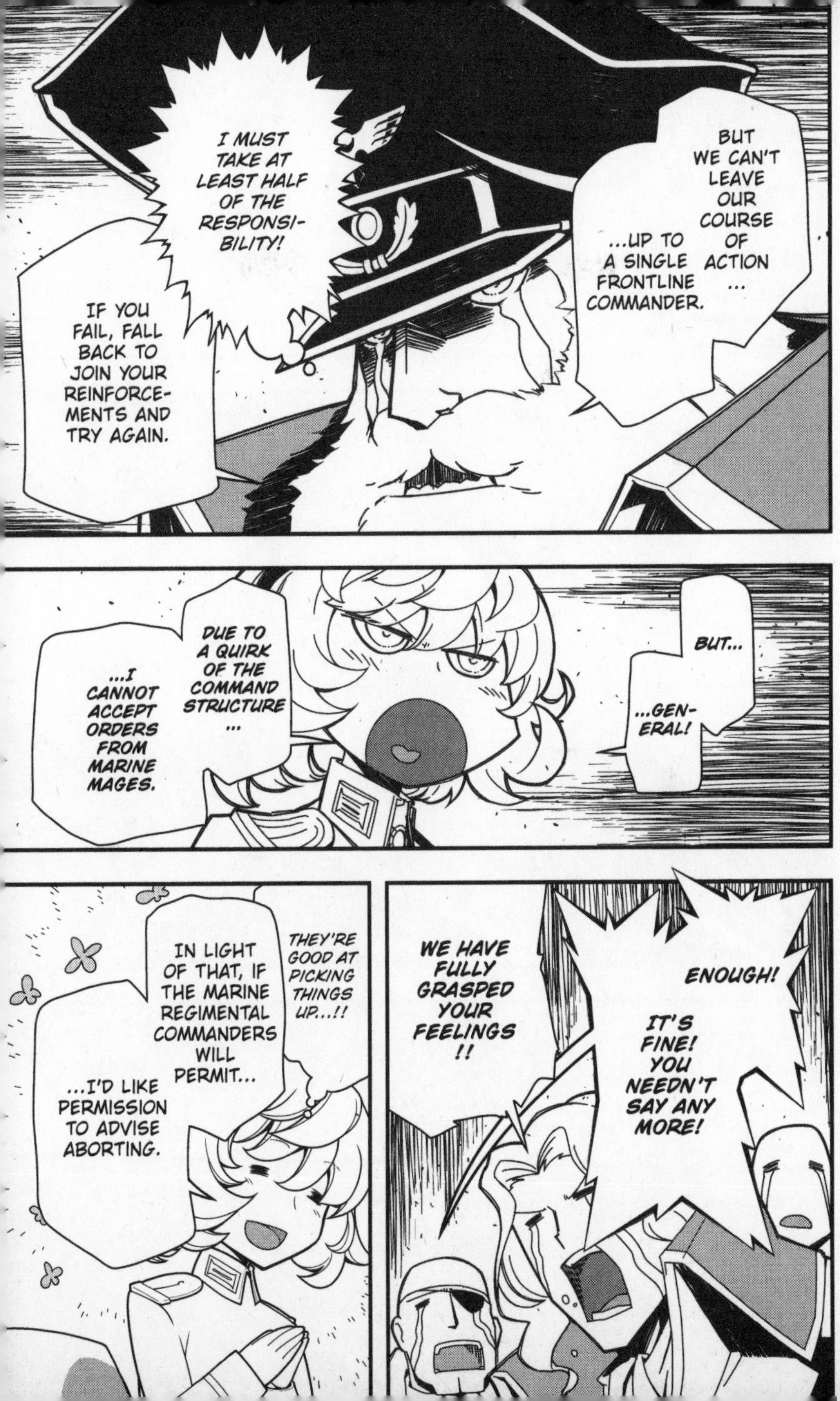

BUT WE CAN'T LEAVE OUR COURSE OF ACTION ...
...UP TO A SINGLE FRONTLINE COMMANDER.
I MUST TAKE AT LEAST HALF OF THE RESPONSI-BILITY!
IF YOU FAIL, FALL BACK TO JOIN YOUR REINFORCE-MENTS AND TRY AGAIN.
BUT...
...GEN-ERAL!
DUE TO A QUIRK OF THE COMMAND STRUCTURE ...
...I CANNOT ACCEPT ORDERS FROM MARINE MAGES.
ENOUGH!
IT'S FINE! YOU NEEDN'T SAY ANY MORE!
WE HAVE FULLY GRASPED YOUR FEELINGS !!
THEY'RE GOOD AT PICKING THINGS UP...!!
IN LIGHT OF THAT, IF THE MARINE REGIMENTAL COMMANDERS WILL PERMIT...
...I'D LIKE PERMISSION TO ADVISE ABORTING.

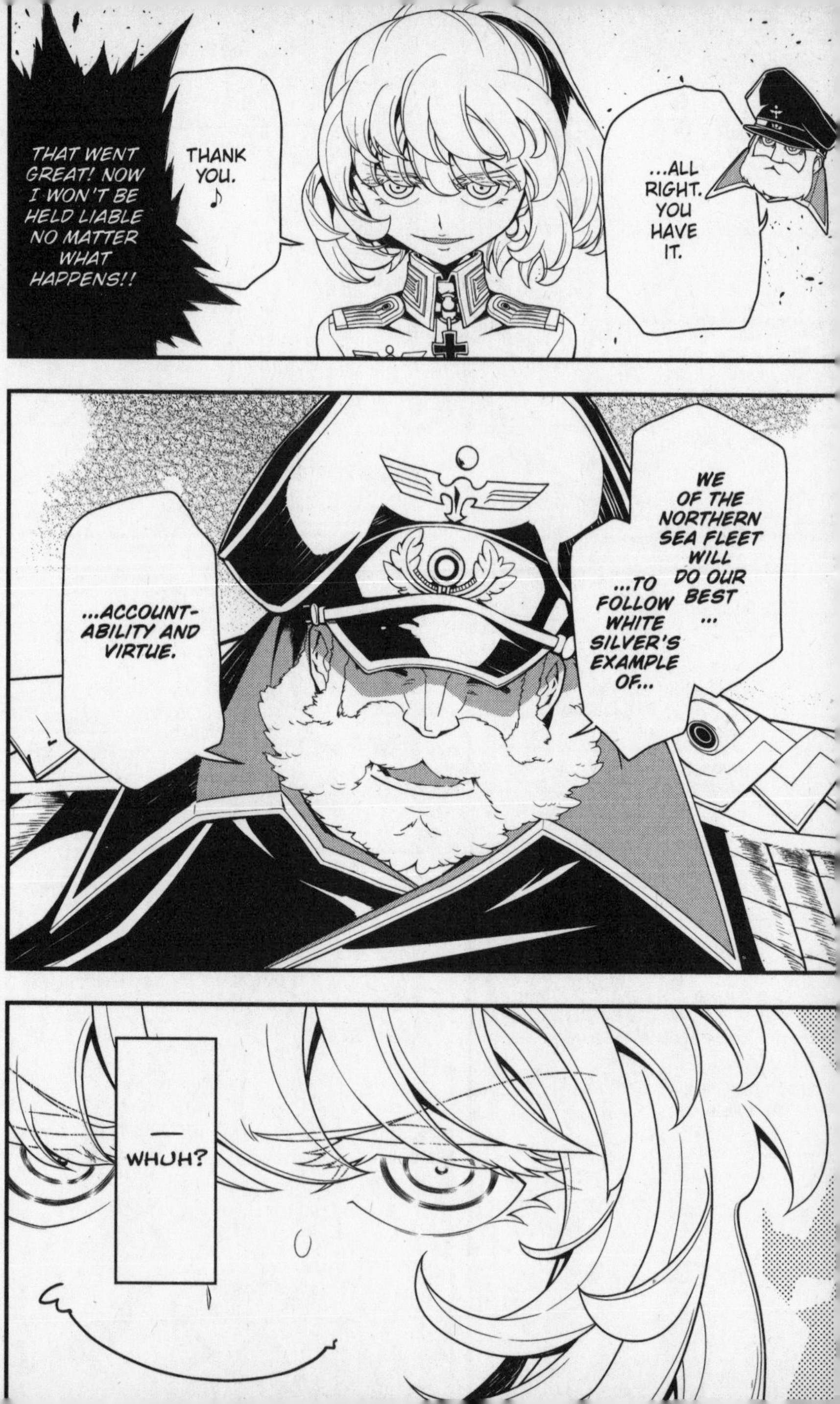
...ALL RIGHT. YOU HAVE IT.
THANK YOU. ♪
THAT WENT GREAT! NOW I WON'T BE HELD LIABLE NO MATTER WHAT HAPPENS!!
WE OF THE NORTHERN SEA FLEET WILL DO OUR BEST ...
...TO FOLLOW WHITE SILVER'S EXAMPLE OF...
...ACCOUNT-ABILITY AND VIRTUE.
— WHUH?

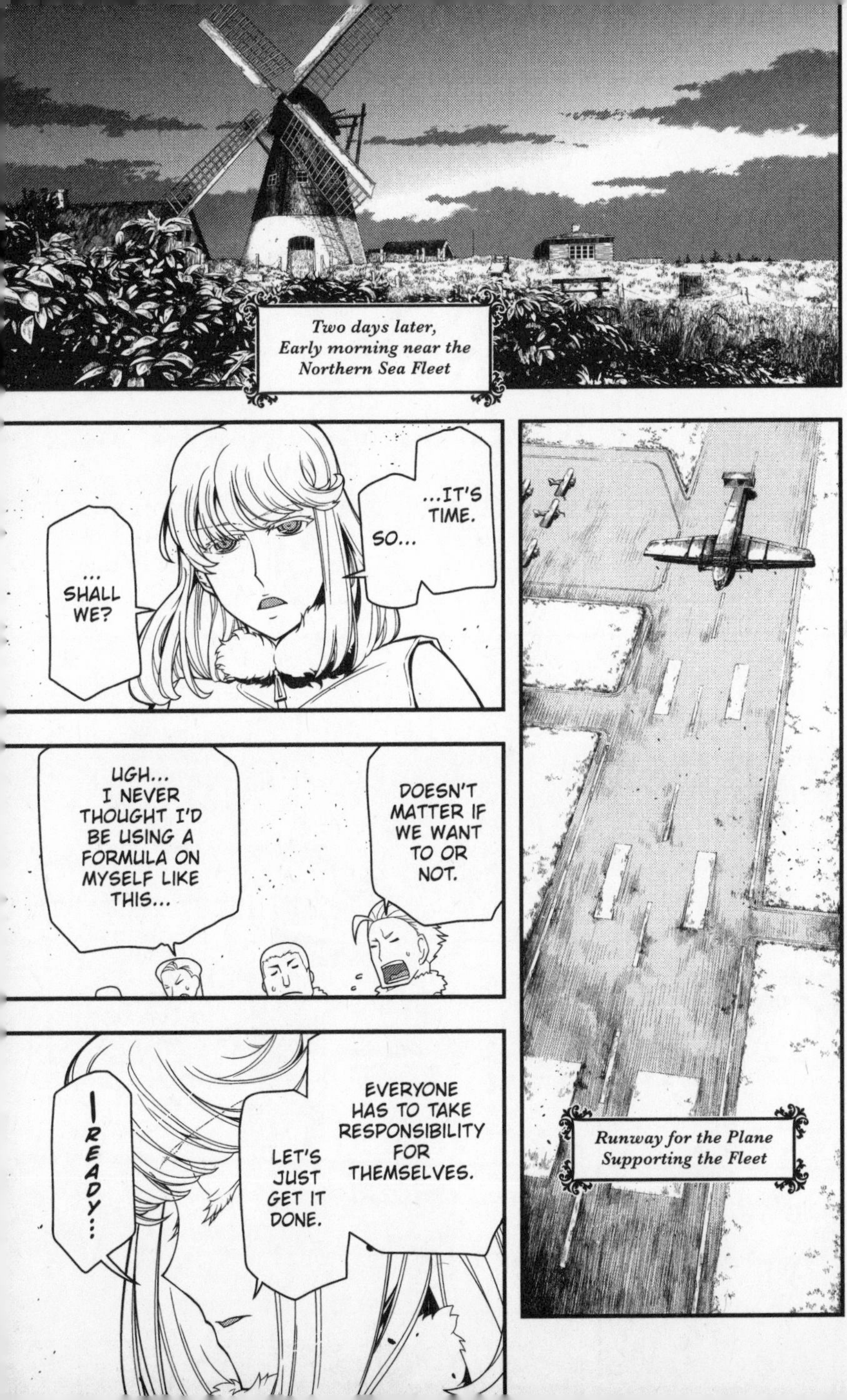
Two days later, Early morning near the Northern Sea Fleet
Runway for the Plane Supporting the Fleet
...IT'S TIME. SO...
... SHALL WE?
DOESN'T MATTER IF WE WANT TO OR NOT.
UGH... I NEVER THOUGHT I'D BE USING A FORMULA ON MYSELF LIKE THIS...
EVERYONE HAS TO TAKE RESPONSIBILITY FOR THEMSELVES. LET'S JUST GET IT DONE.
READY...

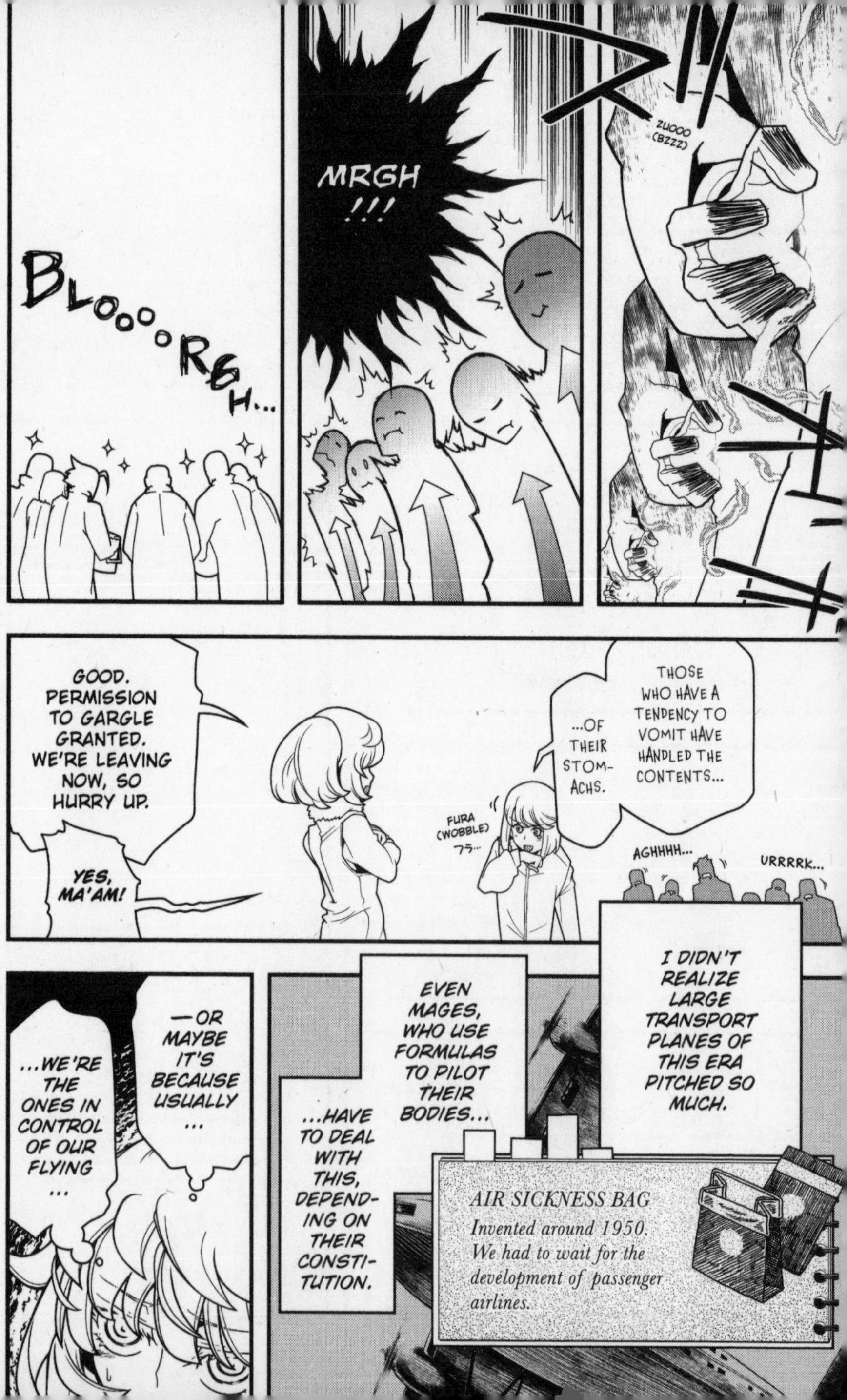
ZUOOO (BZZZ)
MRGH!!!
BLOOOORGH...
THOSE WHO HAVE A TENDENCY TO VOMIT HAVE HANDLED THE CONTENTS...
...OF THEIR STOMACHS.
FURA (WOBBLE)
URRRRK...
AGHHHH...
GOOD. PERMISSION TO GARGLE GRANTED. WE'RE LEAVING NOW, SO HURRY UP.
YES, MA'AM!
I DIDN'T REALIZE LARGE TRANSPORT PLANES OF THIS ERA PITCHED SO MUCH.
EVEN MAGES, WHO USE FORMULAS TO PILOT THEIR BODIES...
...HAVE TO DEAL WITH THIS, DEPENDING ON THEIR CONSTITUTION.
AIR SICKNESS BAG
Invented around 1950. We had to wait for the development of passenger airlines.
—OR MAYBE IT'S BECAUSE USUALLY...
...WE'RE THE ONES IN CONTROL OF OUR FLYING...

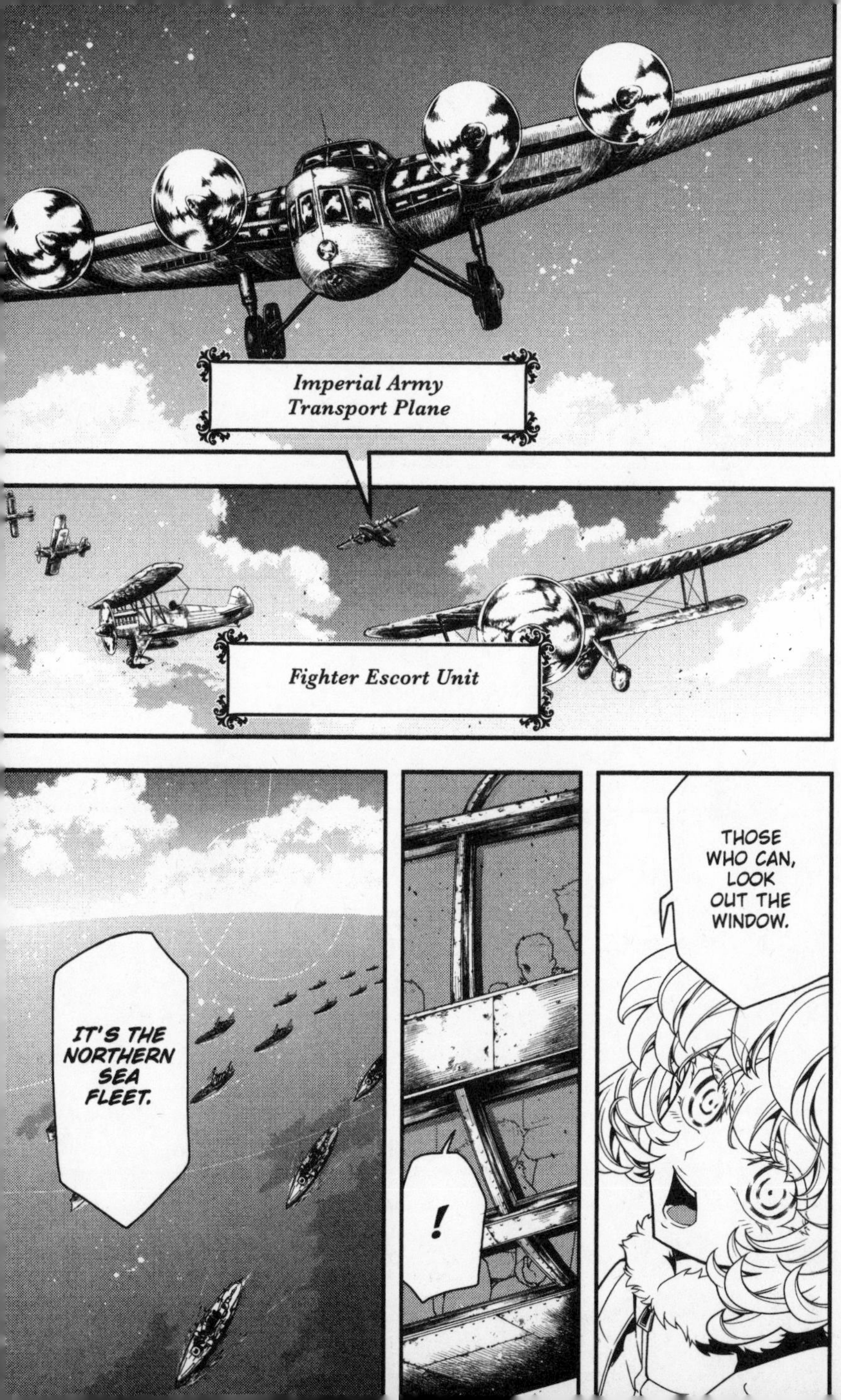
Imperial Army Transport Plane
Fighter Escort Unit
THOSE WHO CAN, LOOK OUT THE WINDOW.
!
IT'S THE NORTHERN SEA FLEET.

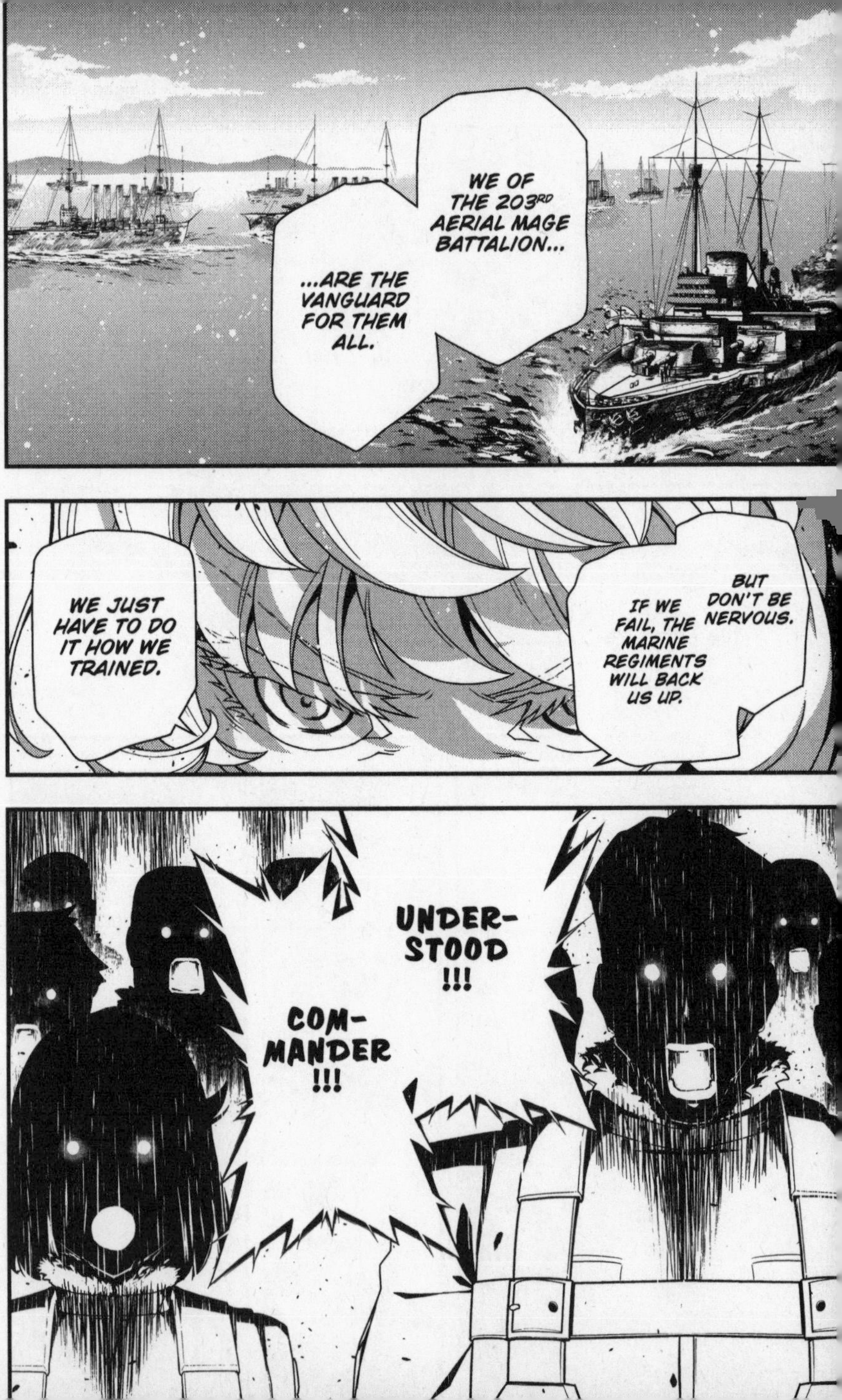
WE OF THE 203RD AERIAL MAGE BATTALION...
...ARE THE VANGUARD FOR THEM ALL.
BUT DON'T BE NERVOUS.
IF WE FAIL, THE MARINE REGIMENTS WILL BACK US UP.
WE JUST HAVE TO DO IT HOW WE TRAINED.
UNDER-STOOD!!!
COM-MANDER!!!

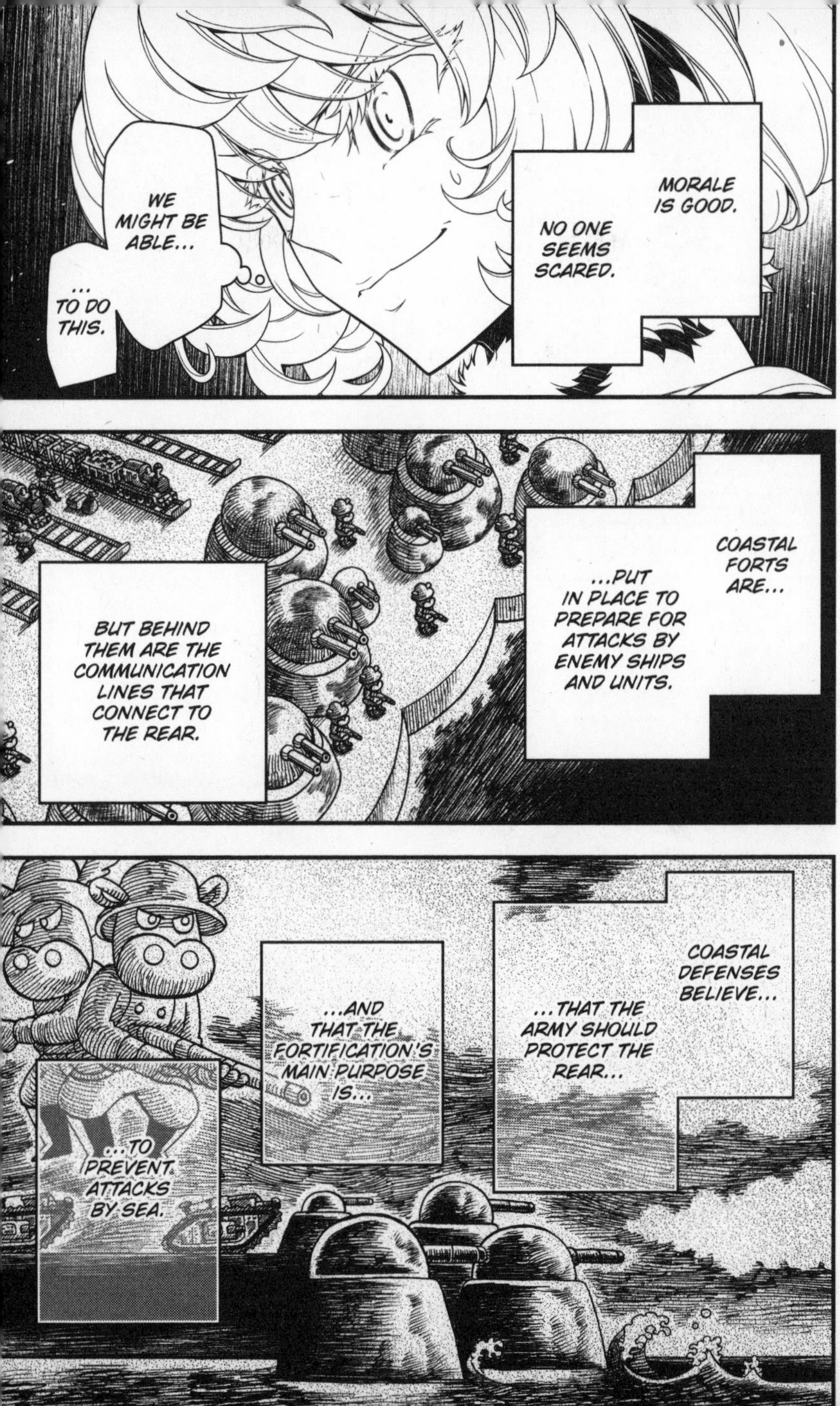
MORALE IS GOOD.
NO ONE SEEMS SCARED.
WE MIGHT BE ABLE...
...TO DO THIS.
COASTAL FORTS ARE...
...PUT IN PLACE TO PREPARE FOR ATTACKS BY ENEMY SHIPS AND UNITS.
BUT BEHIND THEM ARE THE COMMUNICATION LINES THAT CONNECT TO THE REAR.
COASTAL DEFENSES BELIEVE...
...THAT THE ARMY SHOULD PROTECT THE REAR...
...AND THAT THE FORTIFICATION'S MAIN PURPOSE IS...
...TO PREVENT ATTACKS BY SEA.

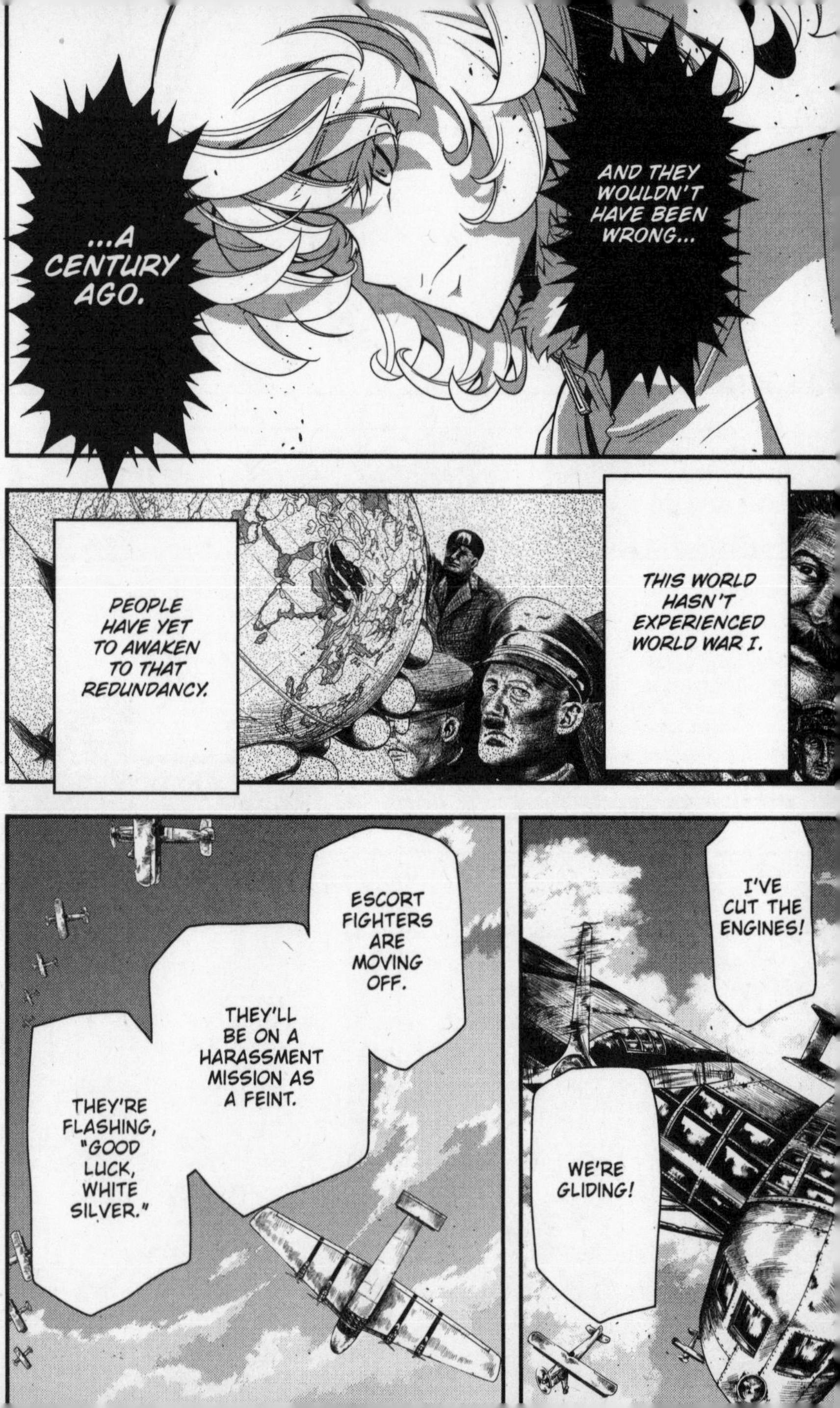
AND THEY WOULDN'T HAVE BEEN WRONG...
...A CENTURY AGO.
THIS WORLD HASN'T EXPERIENCED WORLD WAR I.
PEOPLE HAVE YET TO AWAKEN TO THAT REDUNDANCY.
I'VE CUT THE ENGINES!
WE'RE GLIDING!
ESCORT FIGHTERS ARE MOVING OFF.
THEY'LL BE ON A HARASSMENT MISSION AS A FEINT.
THEY'RE FLASHING, "GOOD LUCK, WHITE SILVER."

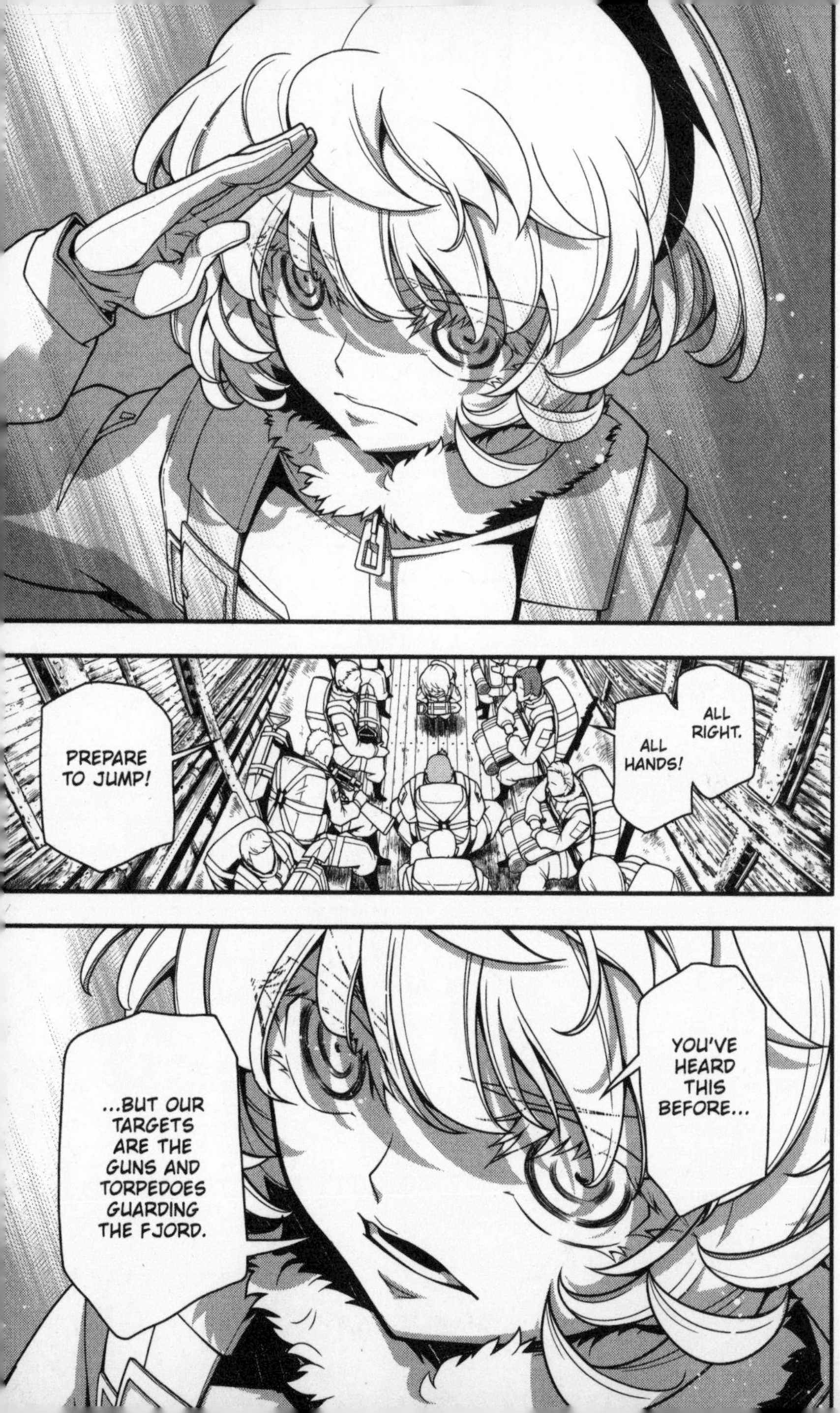
ALL RIGHT. ALL HANDS!
PREPARE TO JUMP!
YOU'VE HEARD THIS BEFORE...
...BUT OUR TARGETS ARE THE GUNS AND TORPEDOES GUARDING THE FJORD.

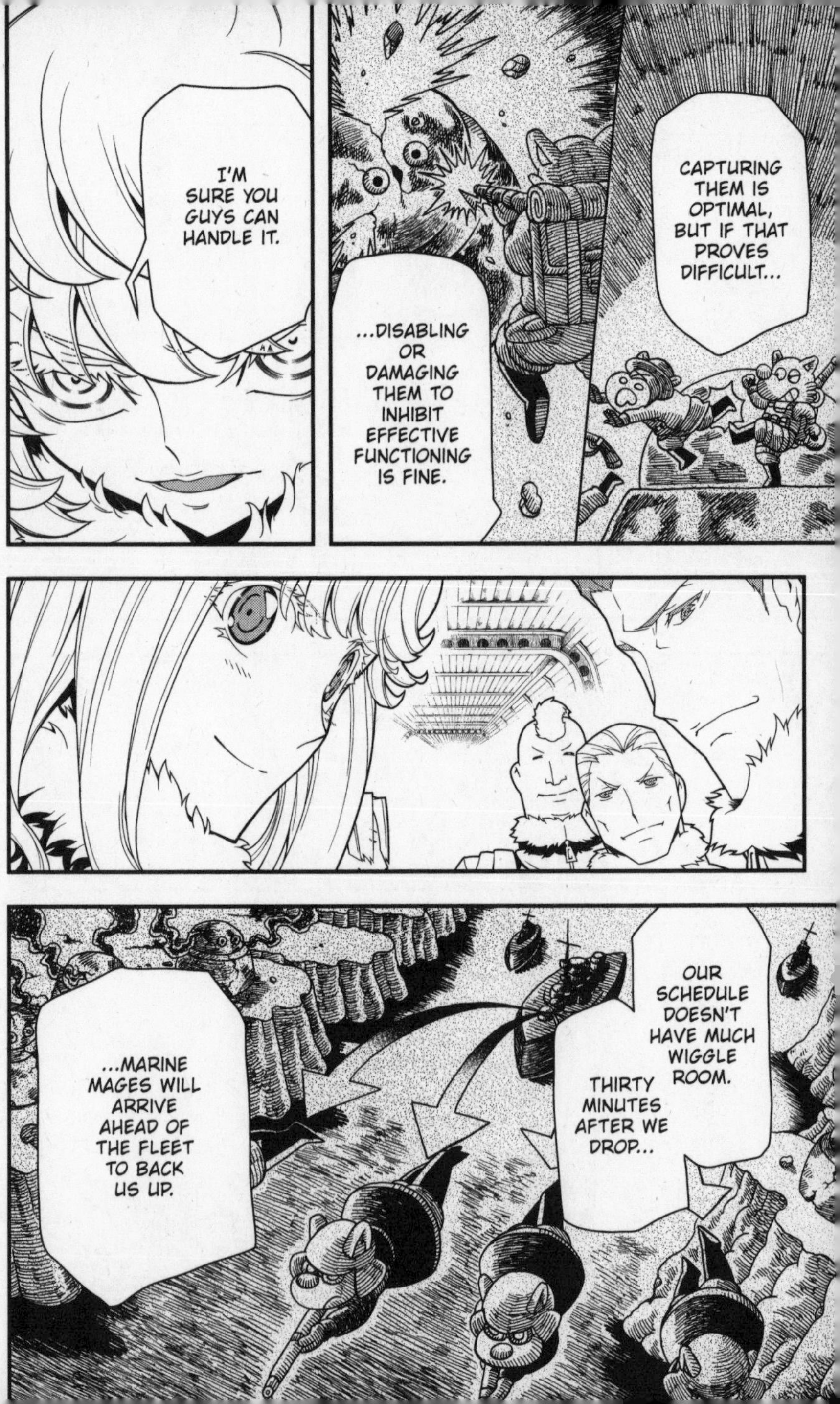
CAPTURING THEM IS OPTIMAL, BUT IF THAT PROVES DIFFICULT...
...DISABLING OR DAMAGING THEM TO INHIBIT EFFECTIVE FUNCTIONING IS FINE.
I'M SURE YOU GUYS CAN HANDLE IT.
OUR SCHEDULE DOESN'T HAVE MUCH WIGGLE ROOM.
THIRTY MINUTES AFTER WE DROP...
...MARINE MAGES WILL ARRIVE AHEAD OF THE FLEET TO BACK US UP.

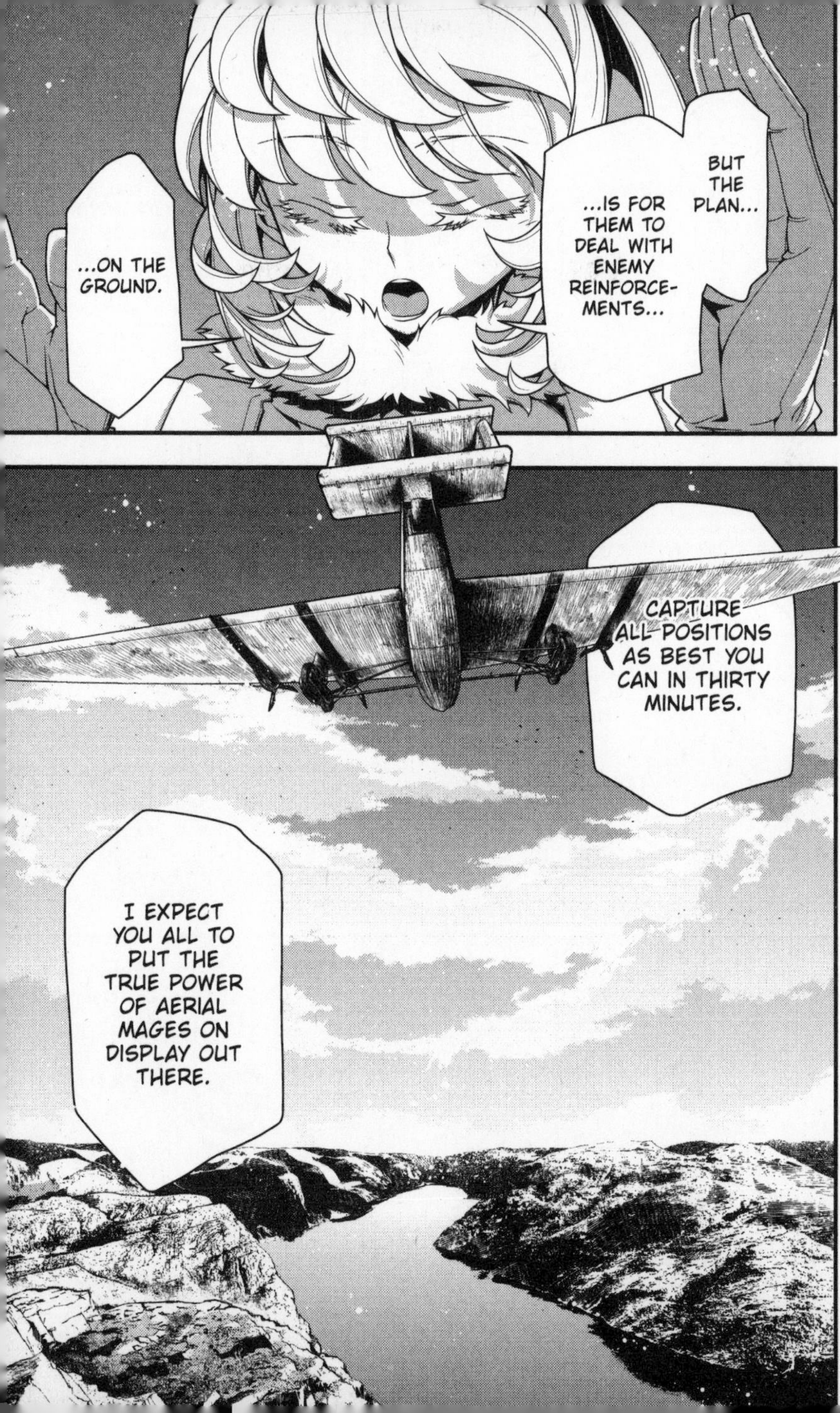
BUT THE PLAN...
...IS FOR THEM TO DEAL WITH ENEMY REINFORCE-MENTS...
...ON THE GROUND.
CAPTURE ALL POSITIONS AS BEST YOU CAN IN THIRTY MINUTES.
I EXPECT YOU ALL TO PUT THE TRUE POWER OF AERIAL MAGES ON DISPLAY OUT THERE.

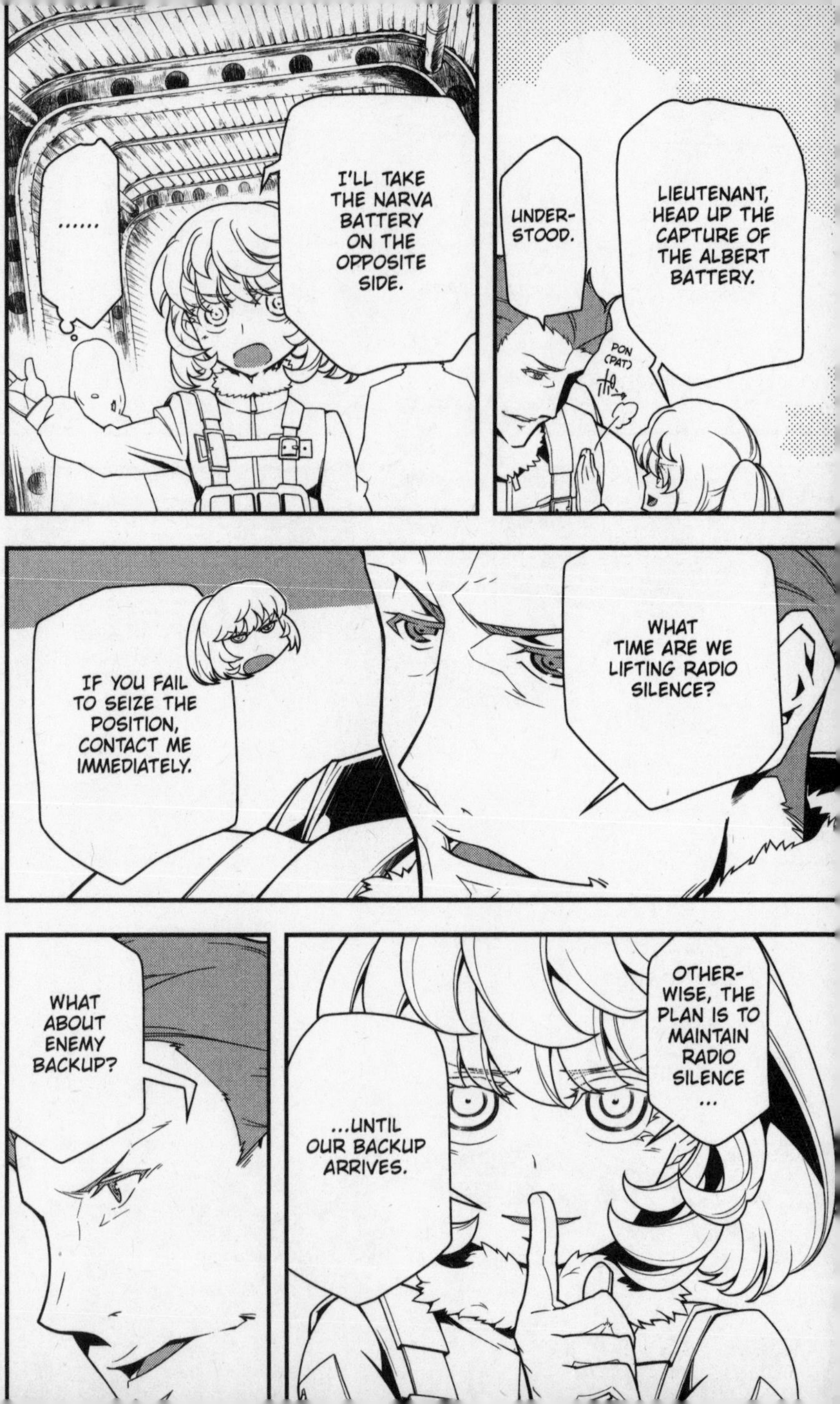
LIEUTENANT, HEAD UP THE CAPTURE OF THE ALBERT BATTERY.
PON (PAT)
UNDER-STOOD.
I'LL TAKE THE NARVA BATTERY ON THE OPPOSITE SIDE.
......
WHAT TIME ARE WE LIFTING RADIO SILENCE?
IF YOU FAIL TO SEIZE THE POSITION, CONTACT ME IMMEDIATELY.
OTHER-WISE, THE PLAN IS TO MAINTAIN RADIO SILENCE ...
...UNTIL OUR BACKUP ARRIVES.
WHAT ABOUT ENEMY BACKUP?

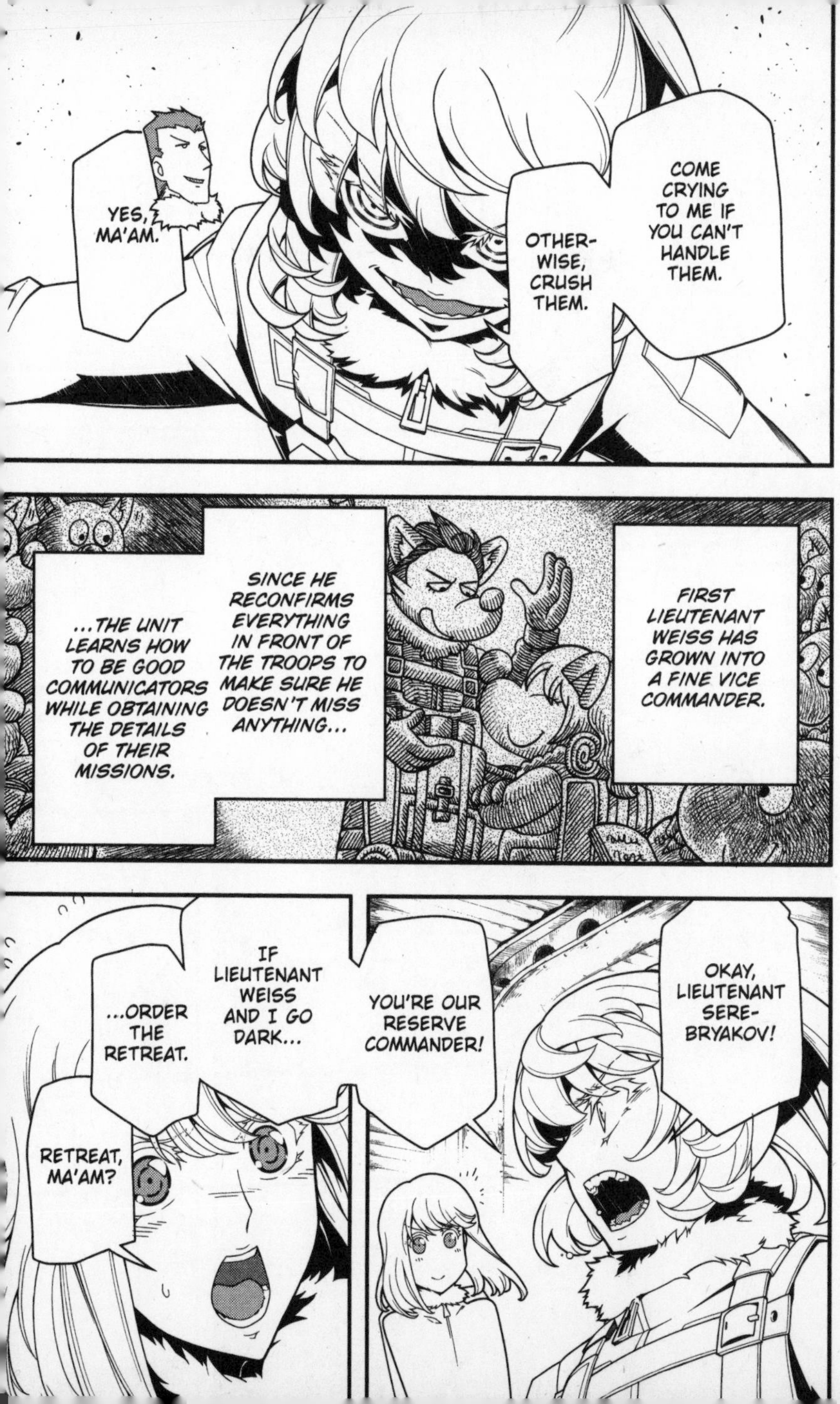
COME CRYING TO ME IF YOU CAN'T HANDLE THEM.
OTHER-WISE, CRUSH THEM.
YES, MA'AM.
FIRST LIEUTENANT WEISS HAS GROWN INTO A FINE VICE COMMANDER.
SINCE HE RECONFIRMS EVERYTHING IN FRONT OF THE TROOPS TO MAKE SURE HE DOESN'T MISS ANYTHING...
...THE UNIT LEARNS HOW TO BE GOOD COMMUNICATORS WHILE OBTAINING THE DETAILS OF THEIR MISSIONS.
OKAY, LIEUTENANT SERE-BRYAKOV!
YOU'RE OUR RESERVE COMMANDER!
IF LIEUTENANT WEISS AND I GO DARK...
...ORDER THE RETREAT.
RETREAT, MA'AM?

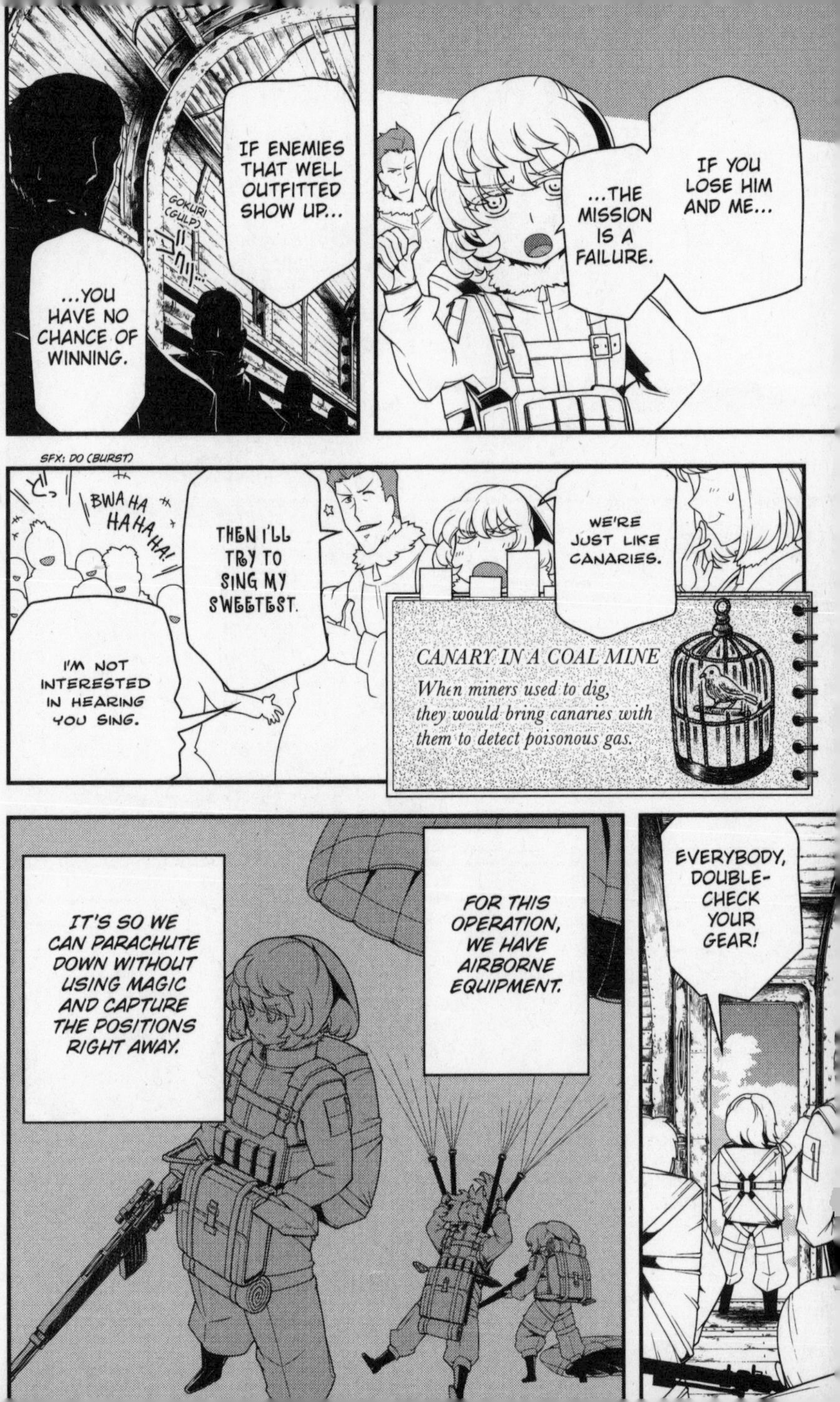
IF YOU LOSE HIM AND ME...
...THE MISSION IS A FAILURE.
IF ENEMIES THAT WELL OUTFITTED SHOW UP...
GOKURI (GULP)
...YOU HAVE NO CHANCE OF WINNING.
SFX: DO (BURST)
WE'RE JUST LIKE CANARIES.
CANARY IN A COAL MINE
When miners used to dig, they would bring canaries with them to detect poisonous gas.
THEN I'LL TRY TO SING MY SWEETEST.
BWA HA HA HA HA!
I'M NOT INTERESTED IN HEARING YOU SING.
EVERYBODY, DOUBLE-CHECK YOUR GEAR!
FOR THIS OPERATION, WE HAVE AIRBORNE EQUIPMENT.
IT'S SO WE CAN PARACHUTE DOWN WITHOUT USING MAGIC AND CAPTURE THE POSITIONS RIGHT AWAY.

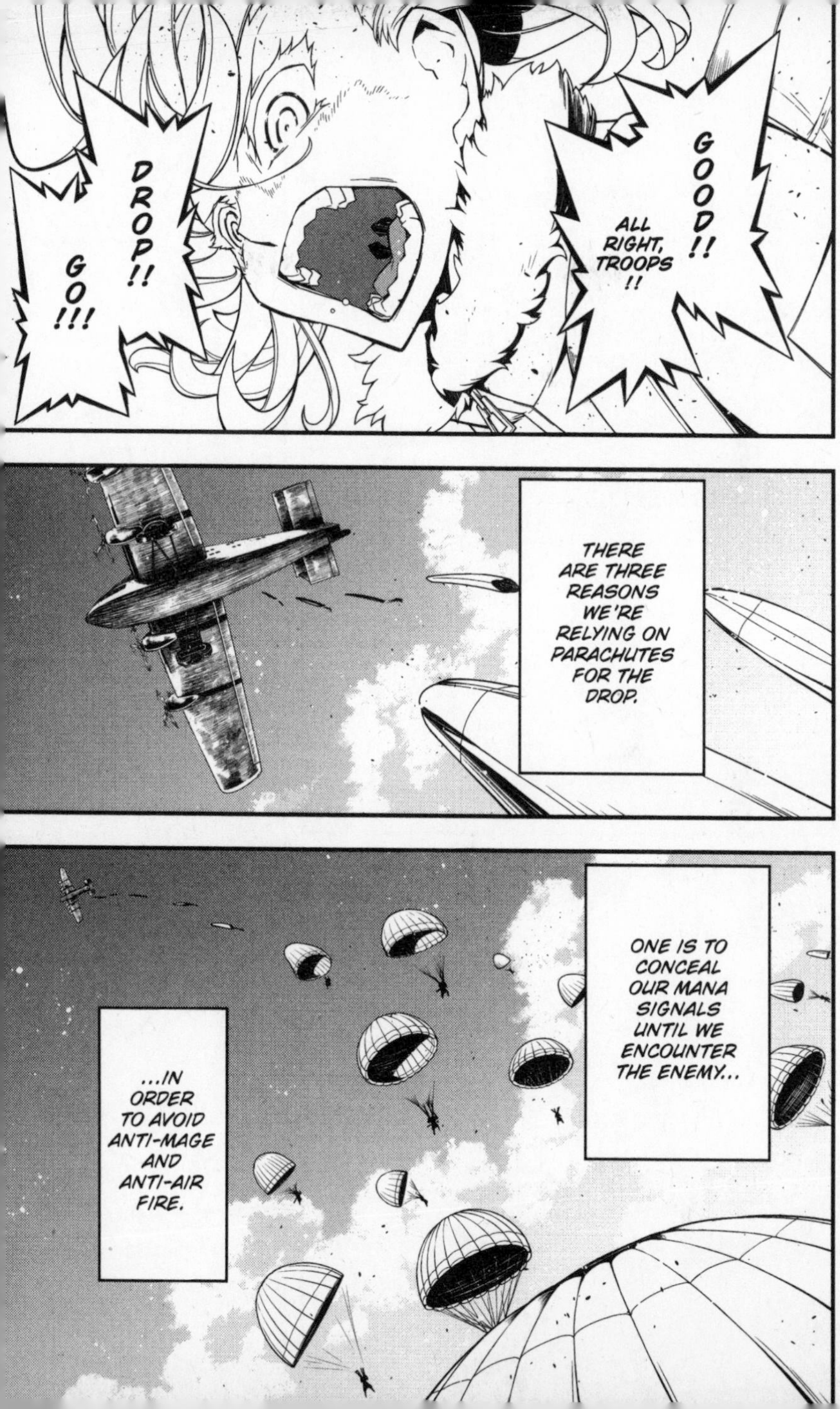
GOOD!!
ALL RIGHT, TROOPS!!
DROP!!
GO!!!
THERE ARE THREE REASONS WE'RE RELYING ON PARACHUTES FOR THE DROP.
ONE IS TO CONCEAL OUR MANA SIGNALS UNTIL WE ENCOUNTER THE ENEMY...
...IN ORDER TO AVOID ANTI-MAGE AND ANTI-AIR FIRE.

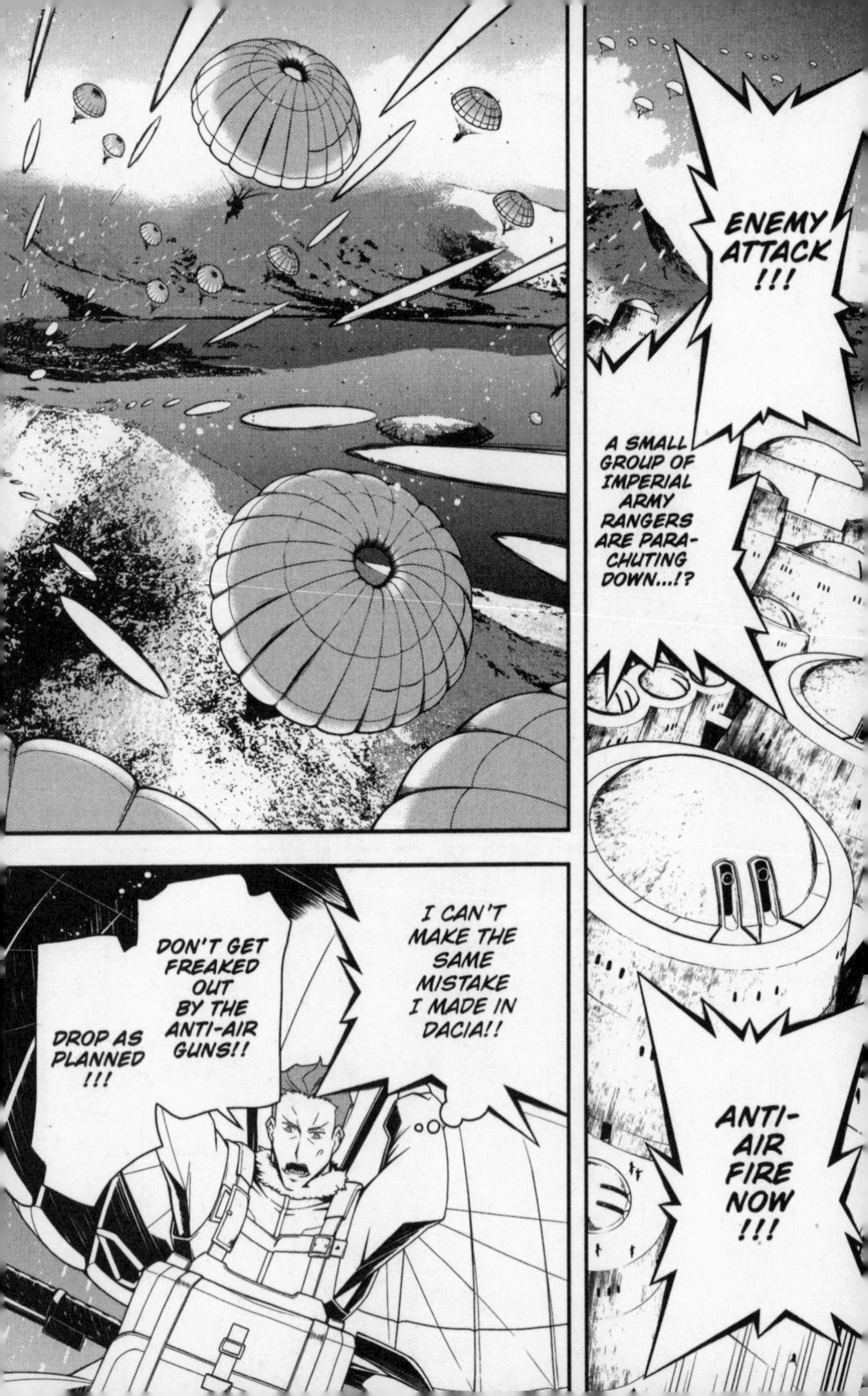
ENEMY ATTACK!!!
A SMALL GROUP OF IMPERIAL ARMY RANGERS ARE PARA-CHUTING DOWN...!?
ANTI-AIR FIRE NOW!!!
I CAN'T MAKE THE SAME MISTAKE I MADE IN DACIA!!
DON'T GET FREAKED OUT BY THE ANTI-AIR GUNS!!
DROP AS PLANNED!!!

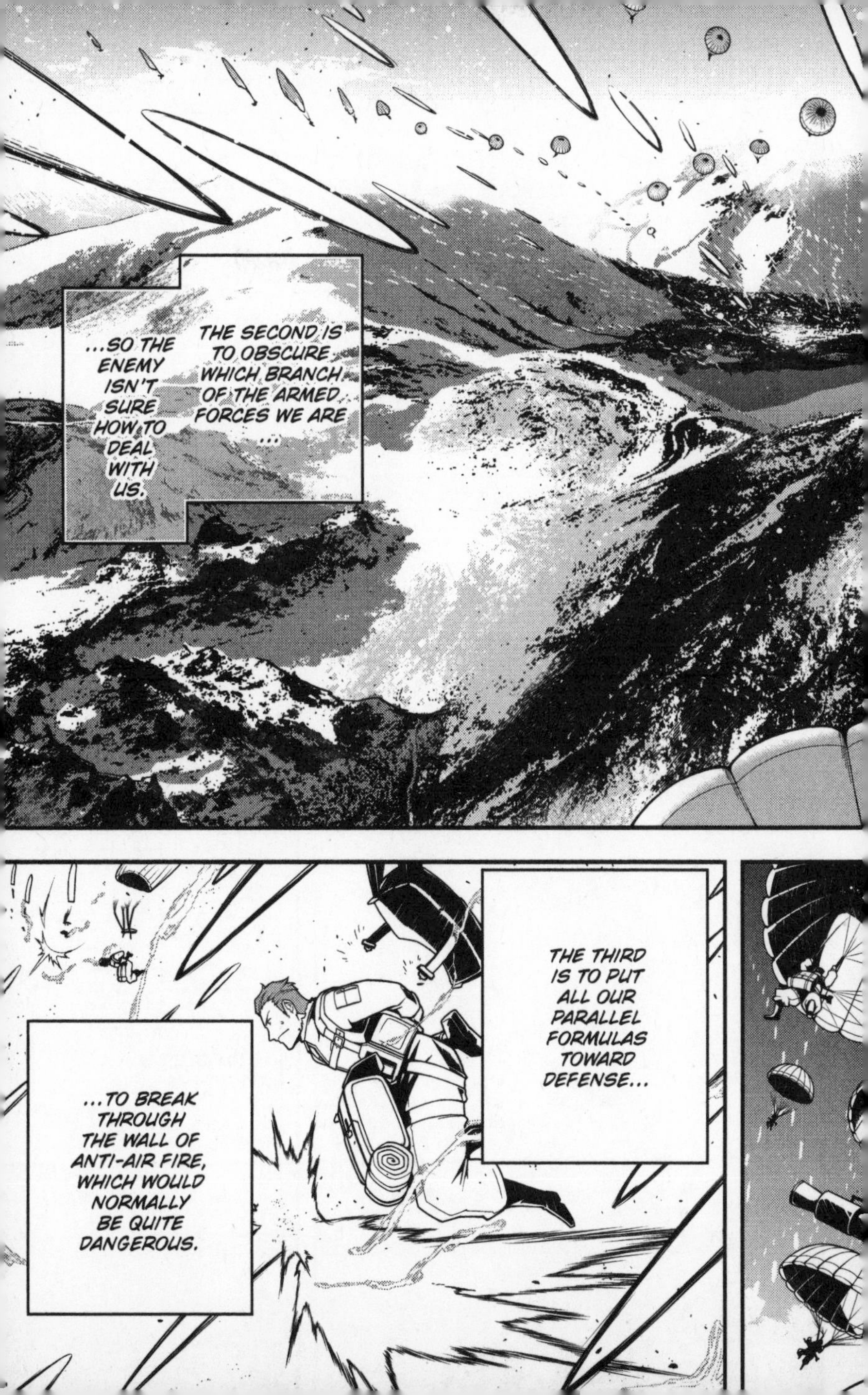
THE SECOND IS TO OBSCURE WHICH BRANCH OF THE ARMED FORCES WE ARE ...
...SO THE ENEMY ISN'T SURE HOW TO DEAL WITH US.
THE THIRD IS TO PUT ALL OUR PARALLEL FORMULAS TOWARD DEFENSE...
...TO BREAK THROUGH THE WALL OF ANTI-AIR FIRE, WHICH WOULD NORMALLY BE QUITE DANGEROUS.

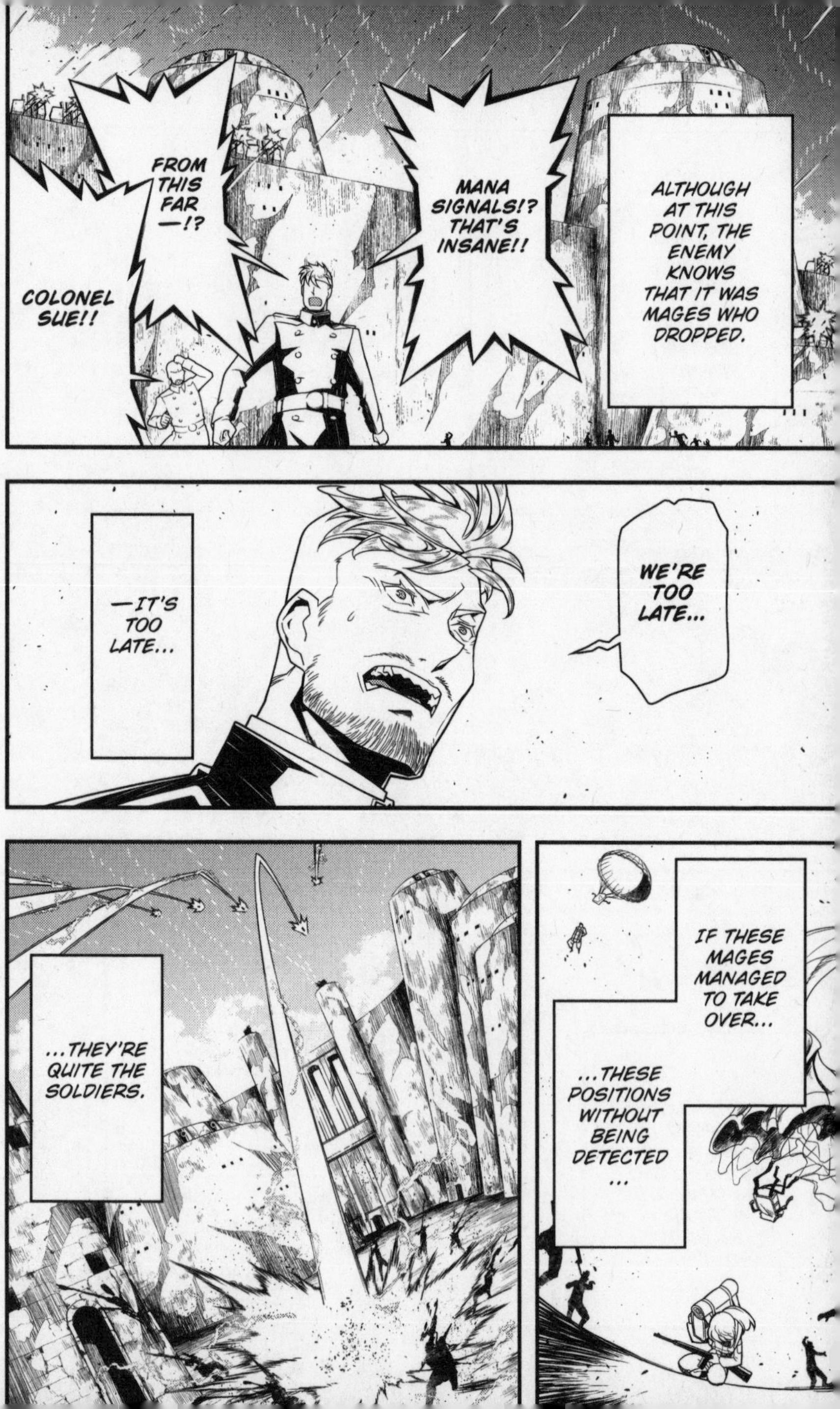
ALTHOUGH AT THIS POINT, THE ENEMY KNOWS THAT IT WAS MAGES WHO DROPPED.
MANA SIGNALS!? THAT'S INSANE!!
FROM THIS FAR—!?
COLONEL SUE!!
WE'RE TOO LATE...
—IT'S TOO LATE...
IF THESE MAGES MANAGED TO TAKE OVER...
...THESE POSITIONS WITHOUT BEING DETECTED...
...THEY'RE QUITE THE SOLDIERS.

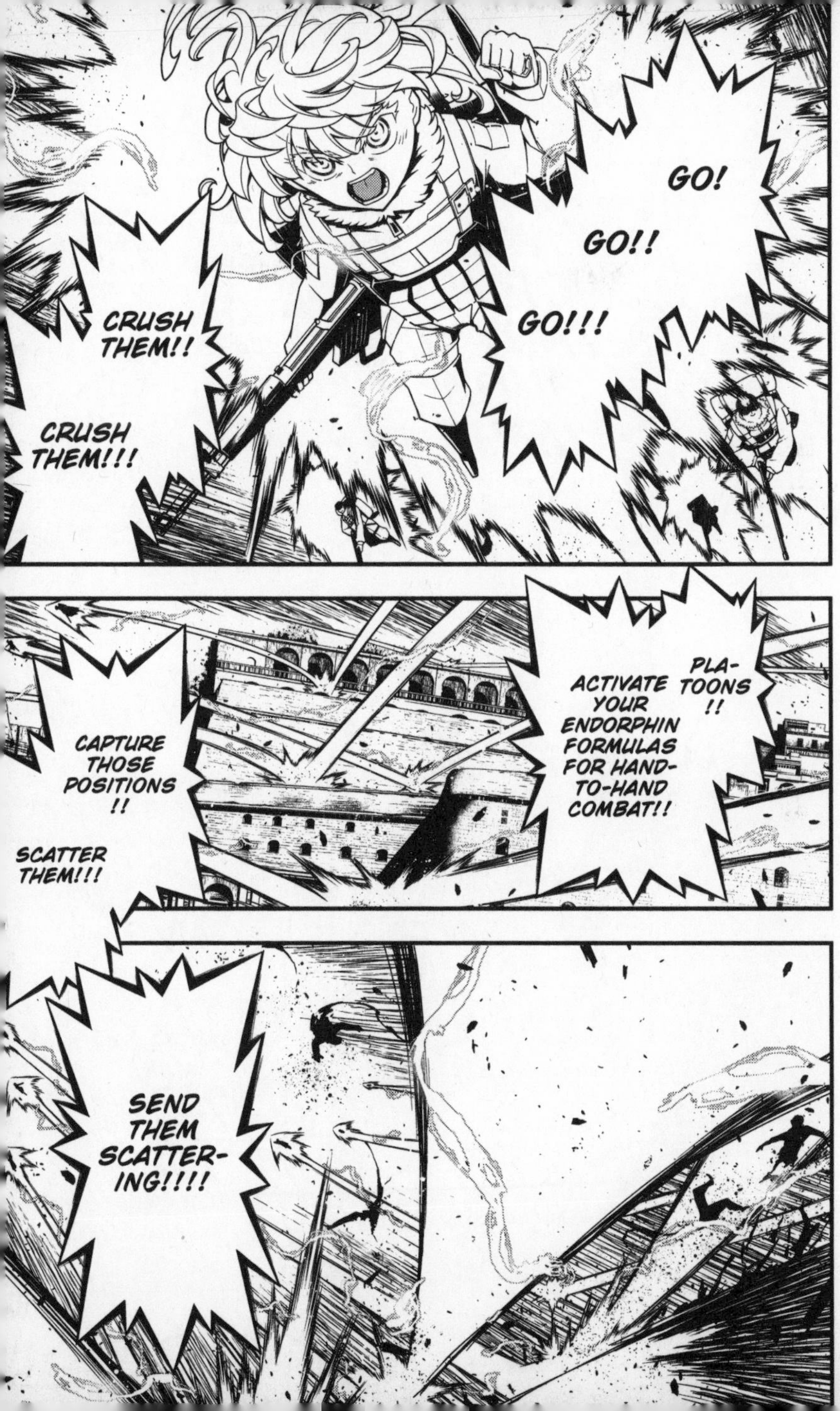
GO! GO!! GO!!!
CRUSH THEM!! CRUSH THEM!!!
PLA-TOONS!! ACTIVATE YOUR ENDORPHIN FORMULAS FOR HAND-TO-HAND COMBAT!!
CAPTURE THOSE POSITIONS!! SCATTER THEM!!!
SEND THEM SCATTER-ING!!!!

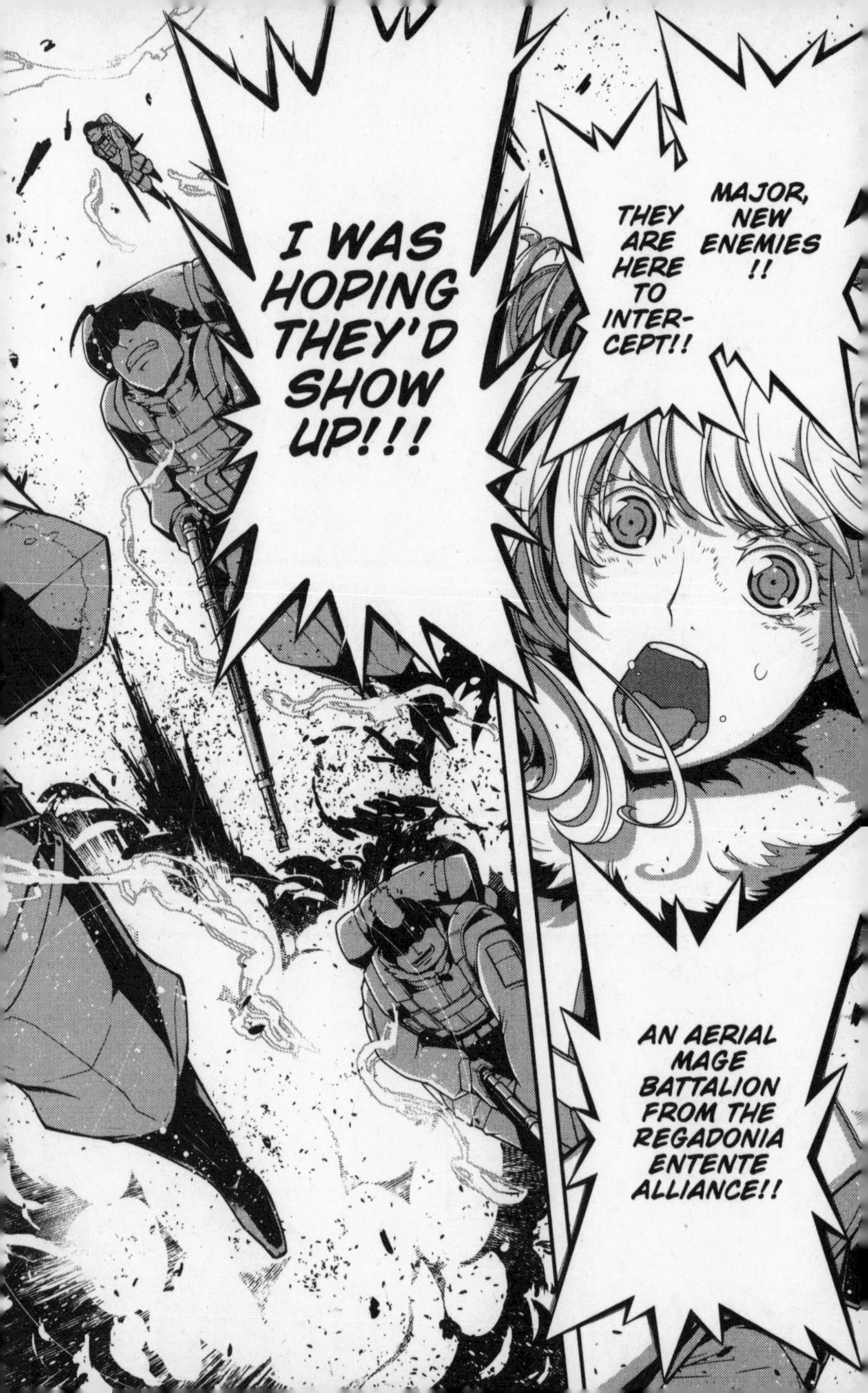
MAJOR, NEW ENEMIES!!
THEY ARE HERE TO INTER-CEPT!!
I WAS HOPING THEY'D SHOW UP!!!
AN AERIAL MAGE BATTALION FROM THE REGADONIA ENTENTE ALLIANCE!!

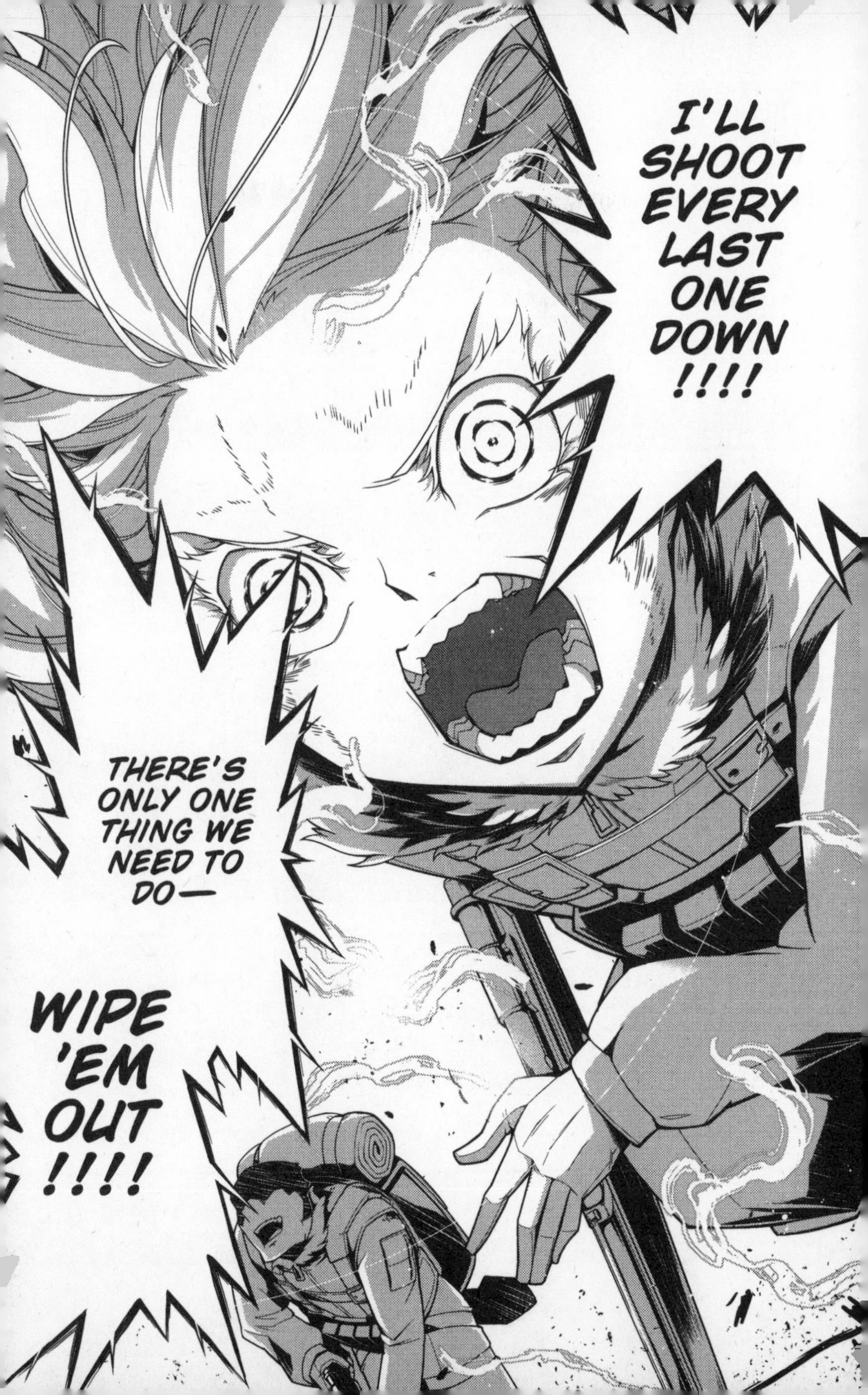
I'LL SHOOT EVERY LAST ONE DOWN !!!!
THERE'S ONLY ONE THING WE NEED TO DO—
WIPE 'EM OUT !!!!

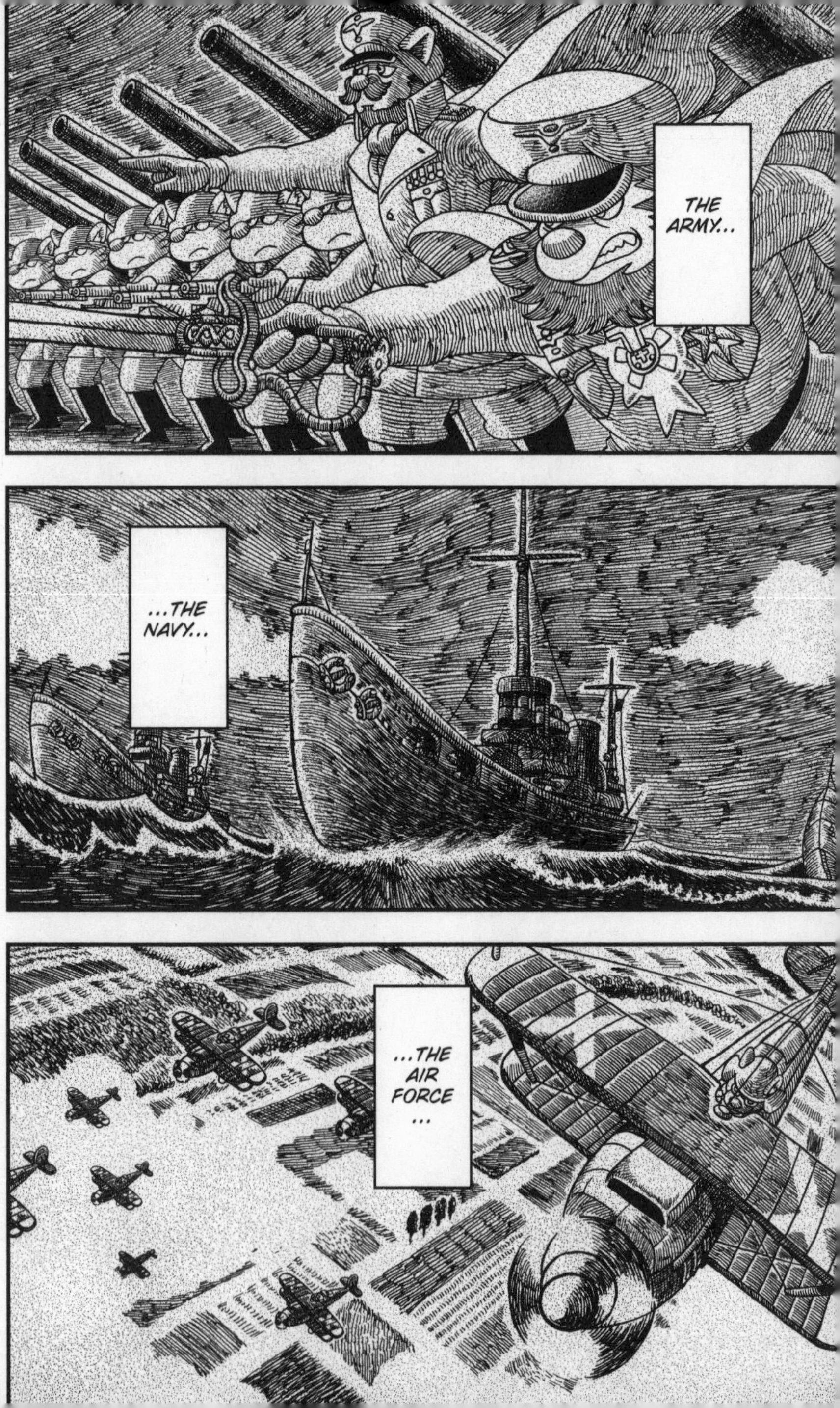
THE ARMY...
...THE NAVY...
...THE AIR FORCE ...

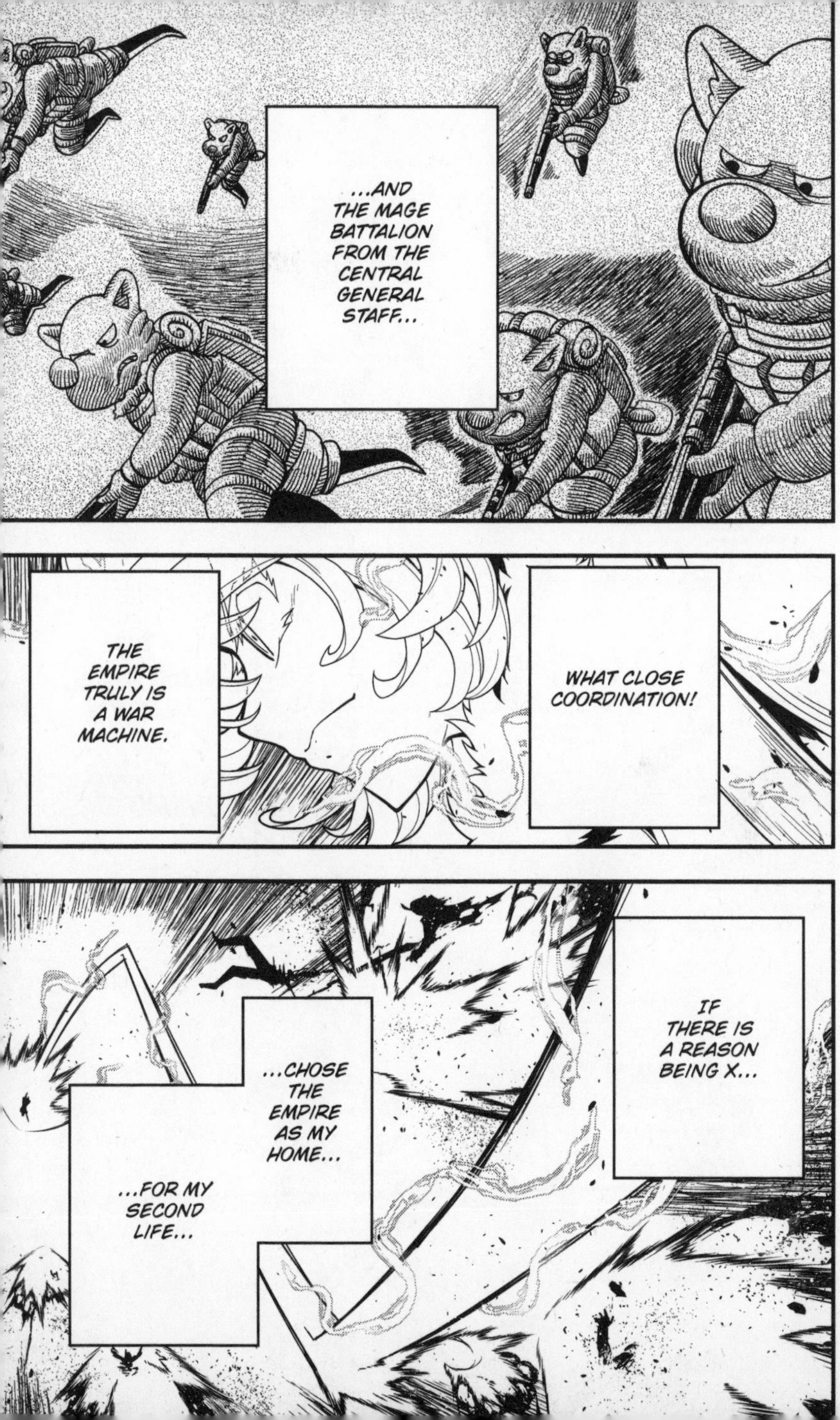
...AND THE MAGE BATTALION FROM THE CENTRAL GENERAL STAFF...
WHAT CLOSE COORDINATION!
THE EMPIRE TRULY IS A WAR MACHINE.
IF THERE IS A REASON BEING X...
...CHOSE THE EMPIRE AS MY HOME...
...FOR MY SECOND LIFE...

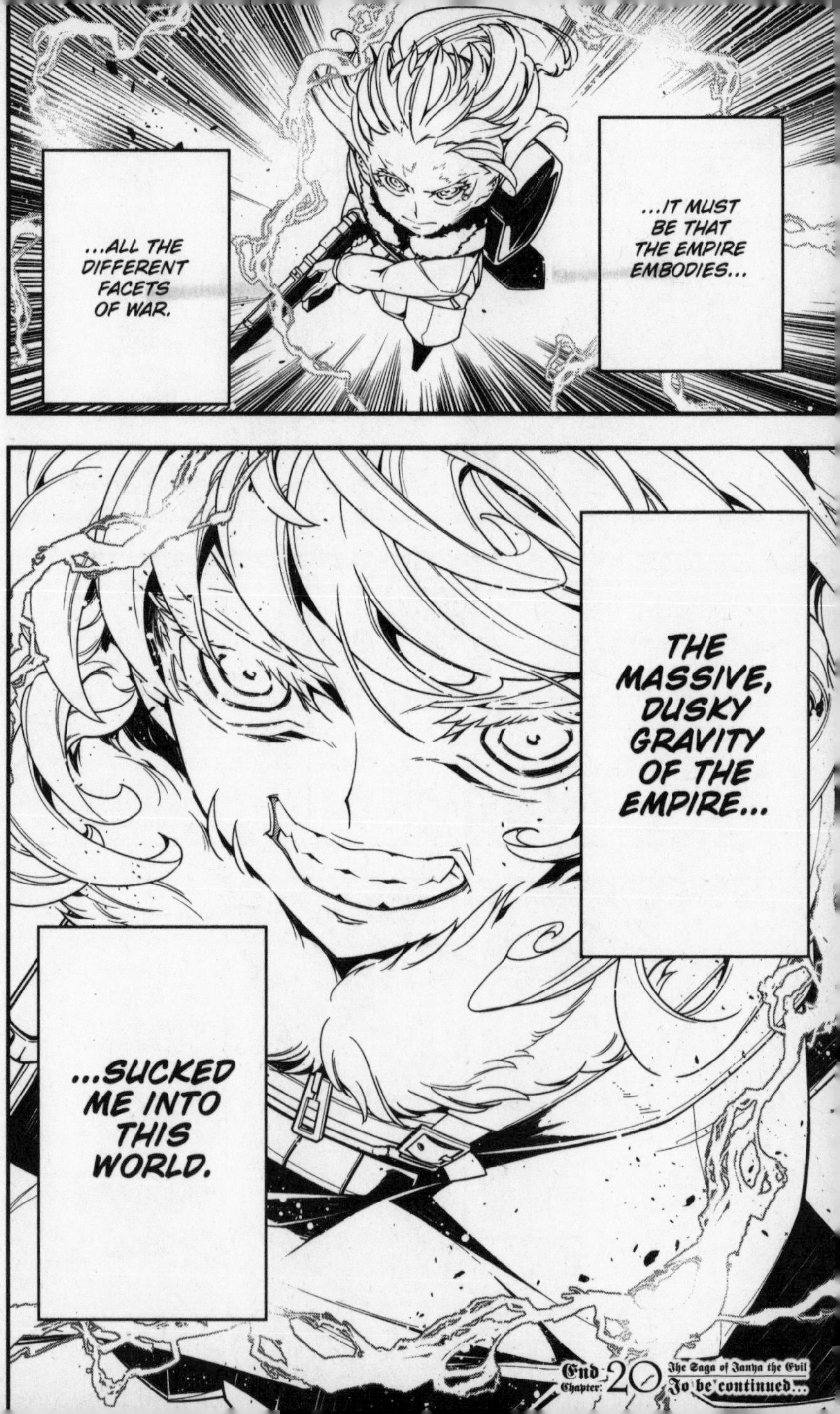
...IT MUST BE THAT THE EMPIRE EMBODIES...
...ALL THE DIFFERENT FACETS OF WAR.
THE MASSIVE, DUSKY GRAVITY OF THE EMPIRE...
...SUCKED ME INTO THIS WORLD.
End Chapter: 20
The Saga of Tanya the Evil
To be continued...

Glossary Chapter 25

Amphibious Warfare

Fighting to land on territory the enemy controls. A direct attack on coastal fortifications is called an "amphibious assault."

By its nature, it gives a huge advantage to the defending side, since the attacking side is crossing wide-open water. For that reason, it's necessary to have plenty of supporting bombardments from air or naval units until the ground forces land; an amphibious assault is only possible if the army, navy, and air force cooperate.

Normally, each branch has its own chain of command, and they often don't get along very well, so the operation depends on how well the units can be brought together.

Sealed Orders

Orders which, for confidentiality, may only be read or opened by a certain person. The time at or situation in which they're to be opened may also be decided beforehand.

The Fall of Singapore

The operation early on in the Pacific War during which the Imperial Japanese Army captured Singapore from the British.

Located on the southern tip of the Malaysian peninsula, Singapore is surrounded on three sides by water and separated from the peninsula on the north by the Johore Strait. The natural stronghold was called the "Gibraltar of the East." However, its defenses mainly consisted of guns facing the ocean. The area facing north toward Malaysia was relatively weak, so the Japanese cut through the peninsula and crossed the Johore Strait in an amphibious operation.

When the Japanese reached Johore, they deceived the British as to where they were planning to land and suppressed the coast with bombs and shells. Thanks to the feint, the troops were able to cross the mangrove area in the northwest and invade Singapore. The British had a position in the interior at Bukit Timah, which was higher ground, but the Japanese broke through after a fierce fight and arrived at the final defensive line outside the city. At that point, they were out of ammunition, but the British were cut off from their reservoir when they lost Bukit Timah, so their water shortage was growing too severe. As a result, they surrendered, and the battle ended.

The number of British troops that surrendered, including those who surrendered on the Malaysian peninsula, was 130,000, making it the largest defeat in British history.

Glossary Chapter 26

Canteen

Stores set up in barracks or ships to sell goods to military people and civilian employees of the military.

In the army, they're usually located at the regiment's barracks, and in the navy, on a large ship. They sell everything from food and drinks (alcohol, sweets, and so on) to hand towels and toothbrushes, writing utensils and clothing, cigarettes, and postcards. There's an adjoining salon for the troops to relax in, and it's not just for eating and drinking—they can read newspapers or magazines and enjoy card games and other leisure activities as well.

The operation of canteens differs between countries and armies, but in the Imperial Japanese Navy, the officers and the paymaster formed a canteen committee, and a canteen chief was selected from the noncommissioned officers to actually do the selling. The money for purchasing goods generally came out of the ship's noncommissioned officers' pockets, and when the ship pulled into port, the canteen committee would purchase things from civilian businesses or navy support organizations and then set hours and sell them on the ship. Buyers didn't pay in cash but filled out a form so the amount would be taken out of their salary. It's said that sometimes during battles the canteen would be open for free food and drinks.

Marines

Soldiers specialized in land combat who serve on ships.

Unlike sailors, who operate ships and fight naval battles, marines serve in amphibious operations, on response teams, or in special ops, and so on. They have a separate chain of command from the regular navy, but their place and role in the military is different depending on the country. In some places, they belong in the broad definition of the navy, and in others, they are either with the army or are in a category distinct from the army, navy, and air force. Some countries have separate airborne units.

Originally, before counter-ship combat was developed, they were the ground troops who would board a ship to fight hand to hand. Once naval cannons and other counter-ship weapons improved, the sailors and navy became the stars of maritime battles; marines served in missions for public safety or security in colonial territories. Then, when military technology advanced again, demand for amphibious assaults grew, and the marines arrived at their reputation as both land- and sea-going troops.

Radio Silence

Prohibiting communication via radio waves so one's position isn't revealed. It also prevents maneuvers leaking due to an increase or decrease in messages or a change in the ratio of encoded to plain messages.

Communication during radio silence can be achieved via signal shots, semaphores, or Morse code flashed with a light.

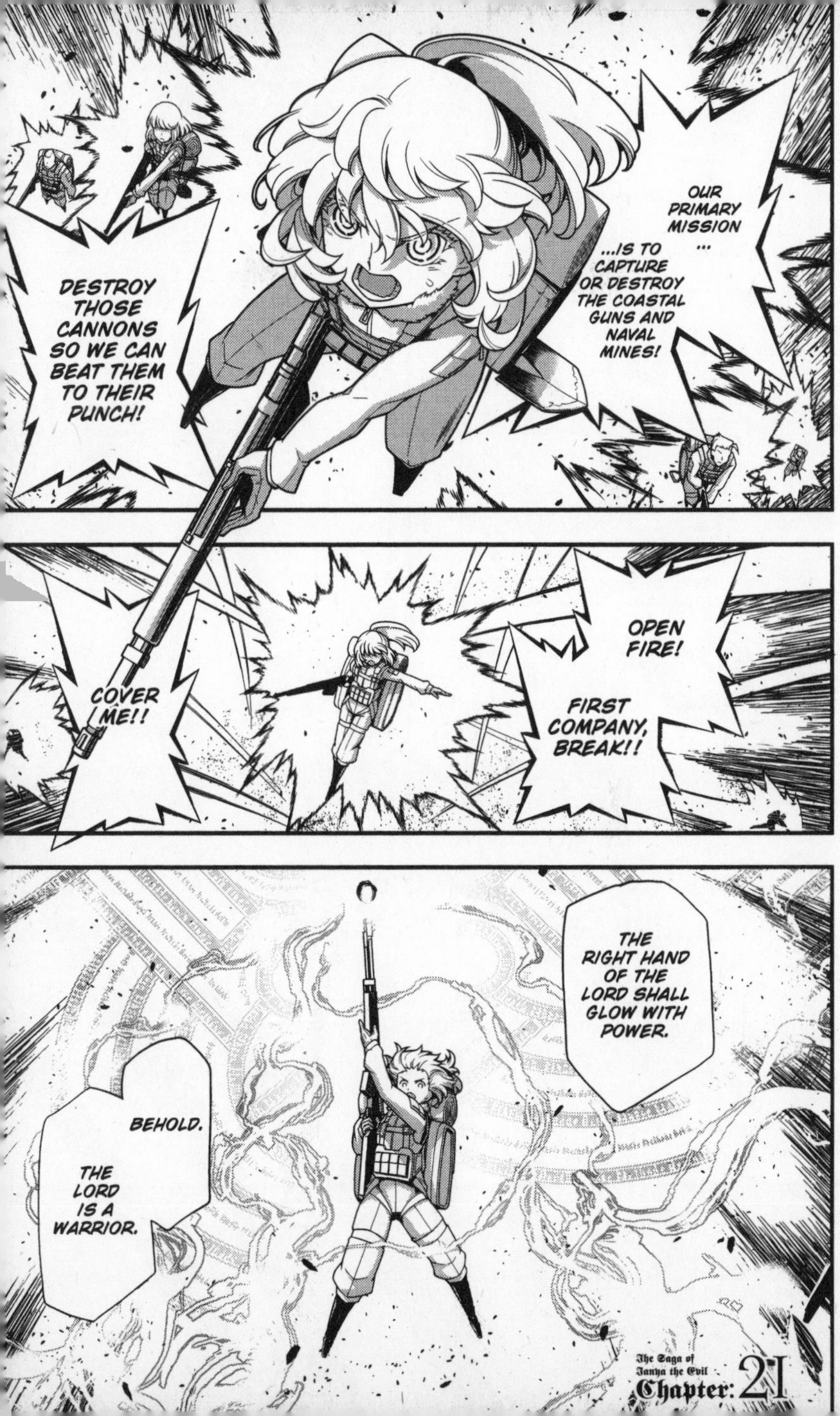
OUR PRIMARY MISSION ...
...IS TO CAPTURE OR DESTROY THE COASTAL GUNS AND NAVAL MINES!
DESTROY THOSE CANNONS SO WE CAN BEAT THEM TO THEIR PUNCH!
OPEN FIRE!
FIRST COMPANY, BREAK!!
COVER ME!!
THE RIGHT HAND OF THE LORD SHALL GLOW WITH POWER.
BEHOLD.
THE LORD IS A WARRIOR.
The Saga of Tanya the Evil
Chapter: 21

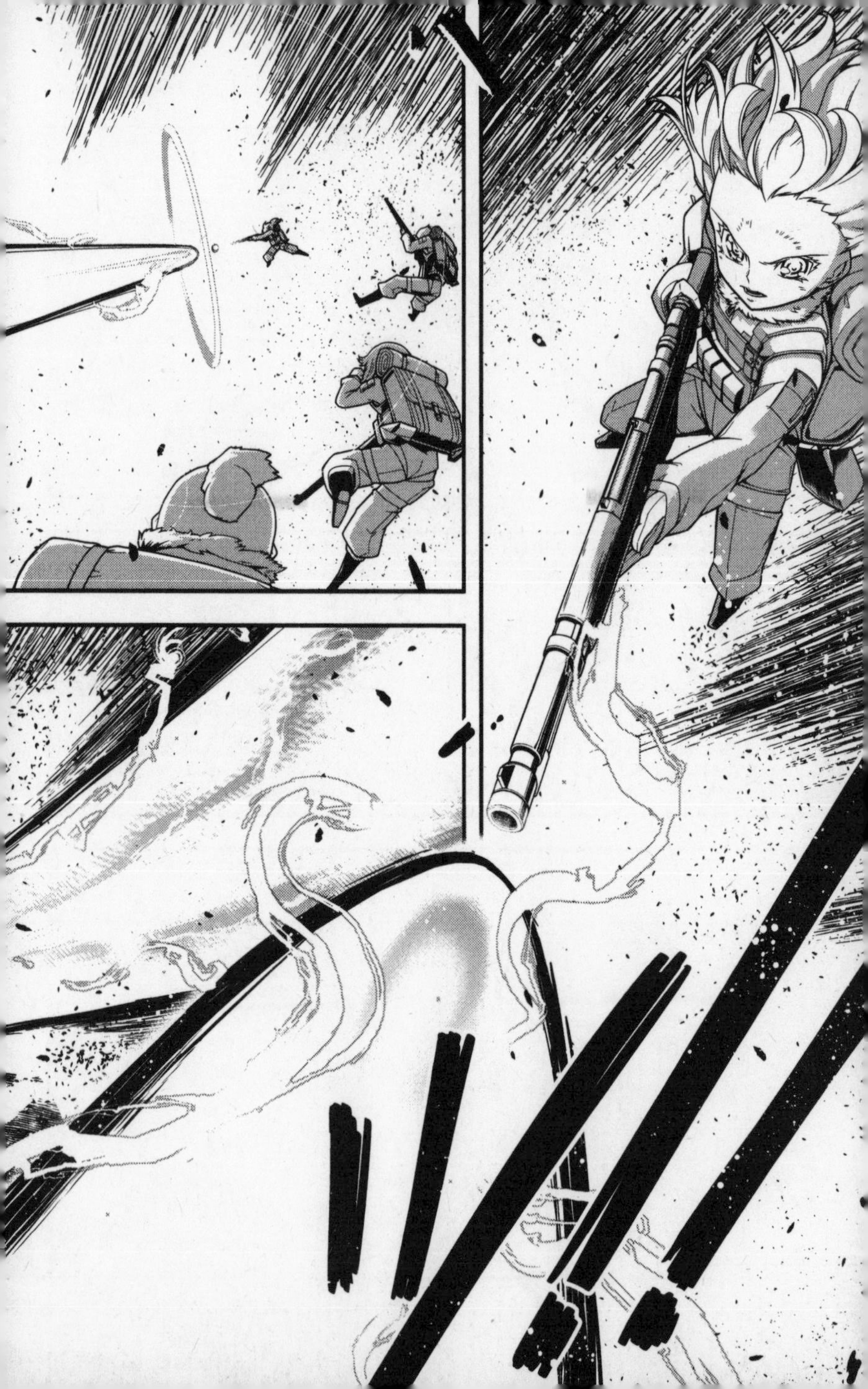

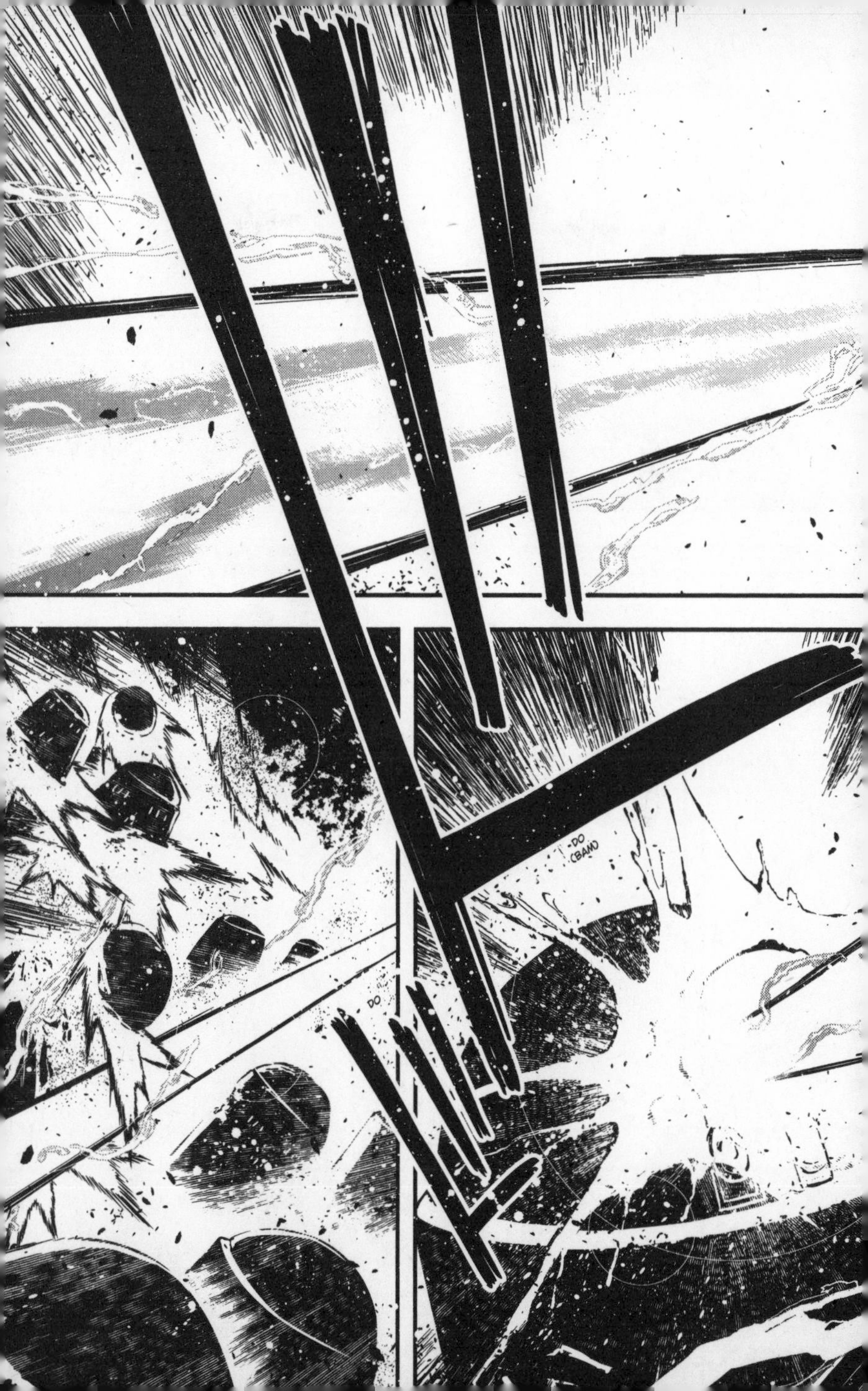
-DO
(BAM)
DO

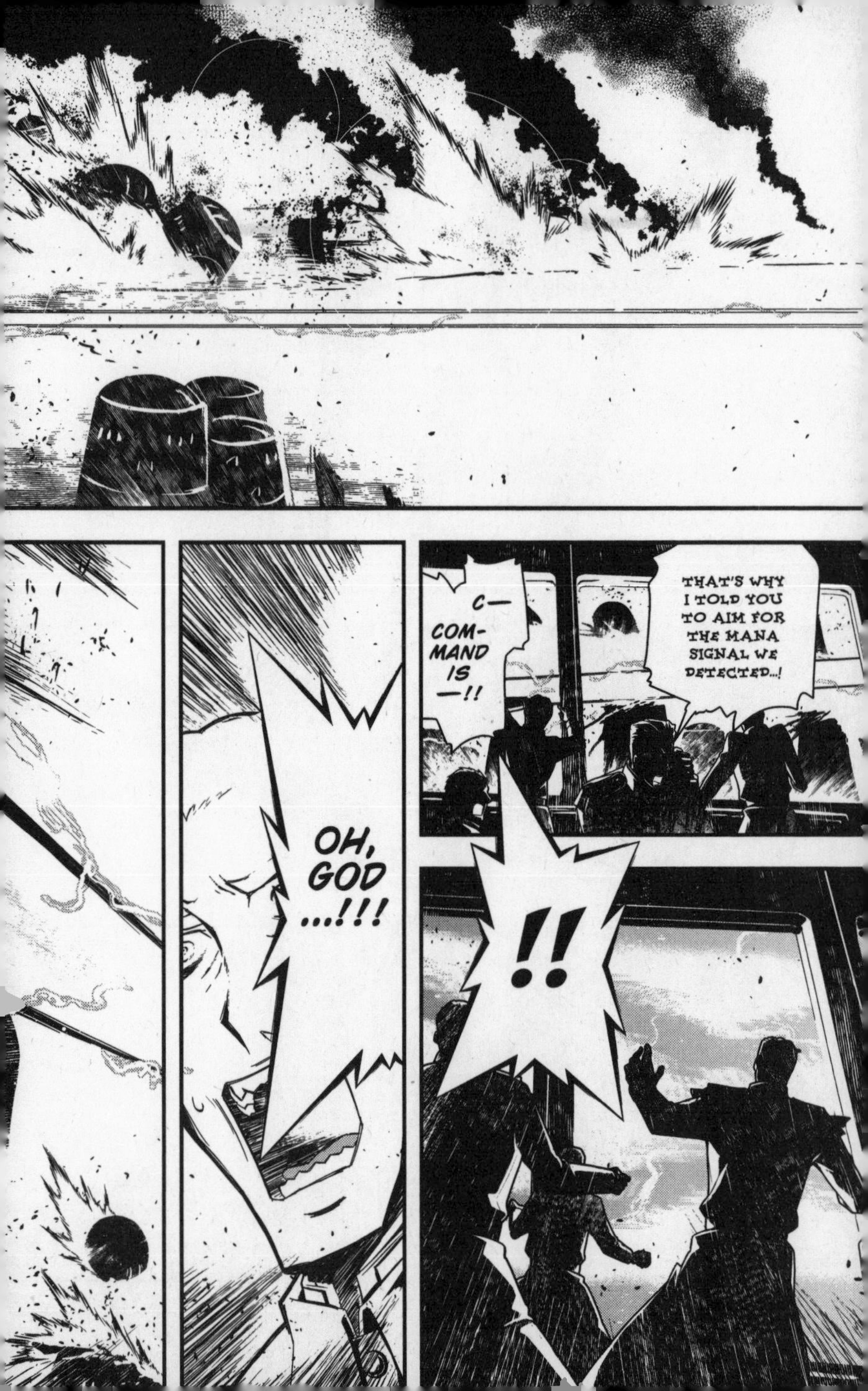
THAT'S WHY I TOLD YOU TO AIM FOR THE MANA SIGNAL WE DETECTED...!
C— COMMAND IS —!!
!!
OH, GOD ...!!!

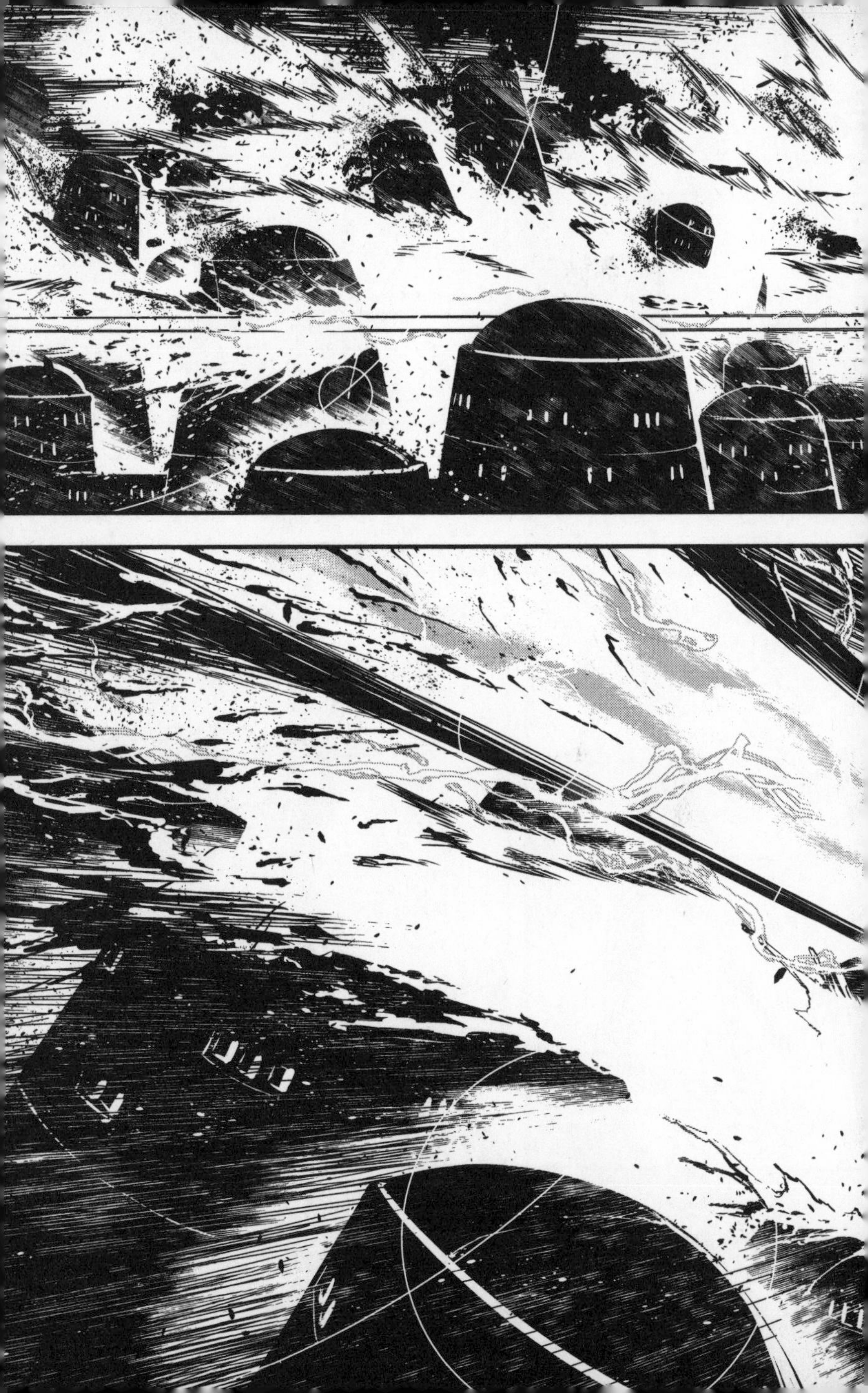

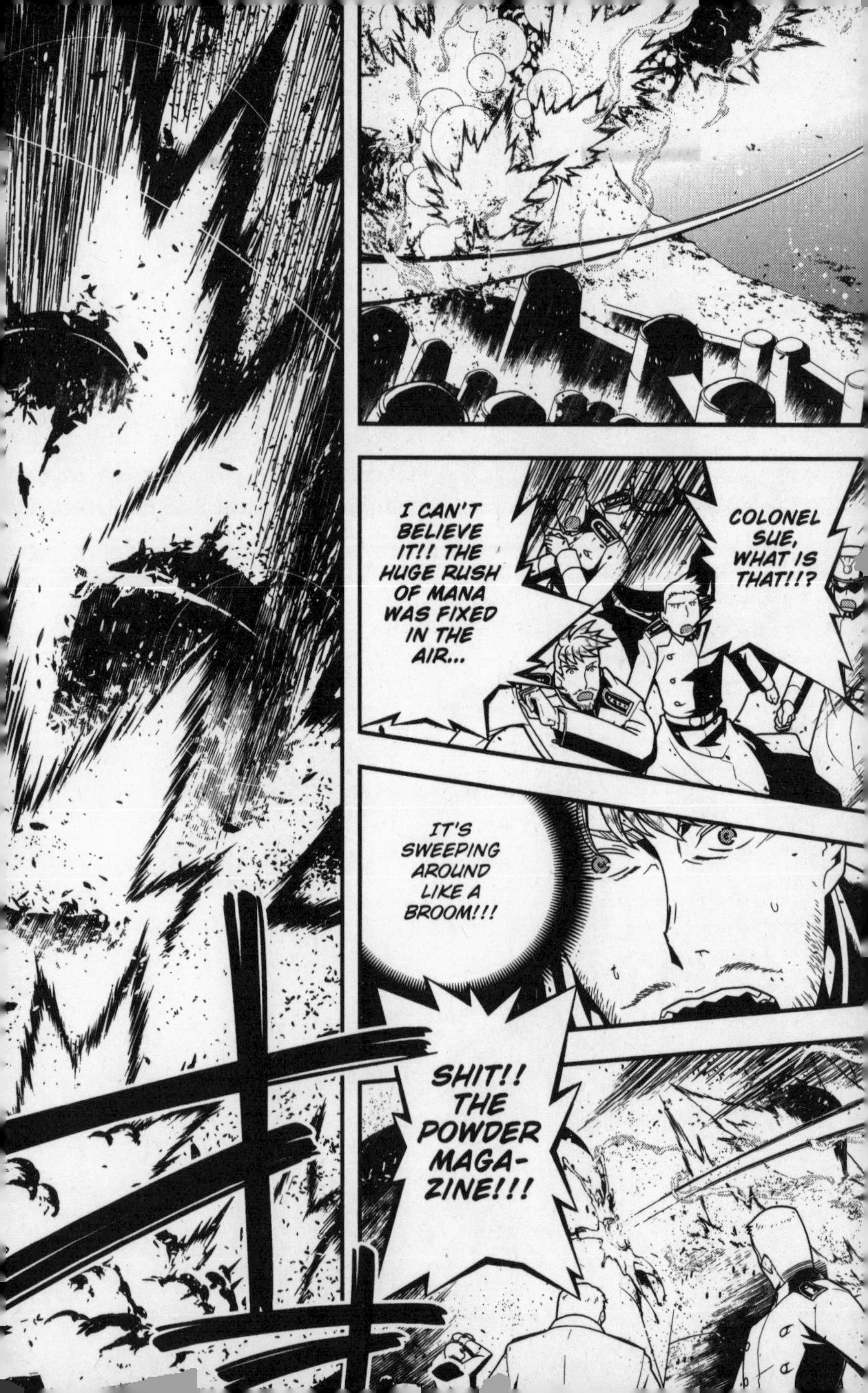
COLONEL SUE, WHAT IS THAT!!?
I CAN'T BELIEVE IT!! THE HUGE RUSH OF MANA WAS FIXED IN THE AIR...
IT'S SWEEPING AROUND LIKE A BROOM!!!
SHIT!! THE POWDER MAGA-ZINE!!!

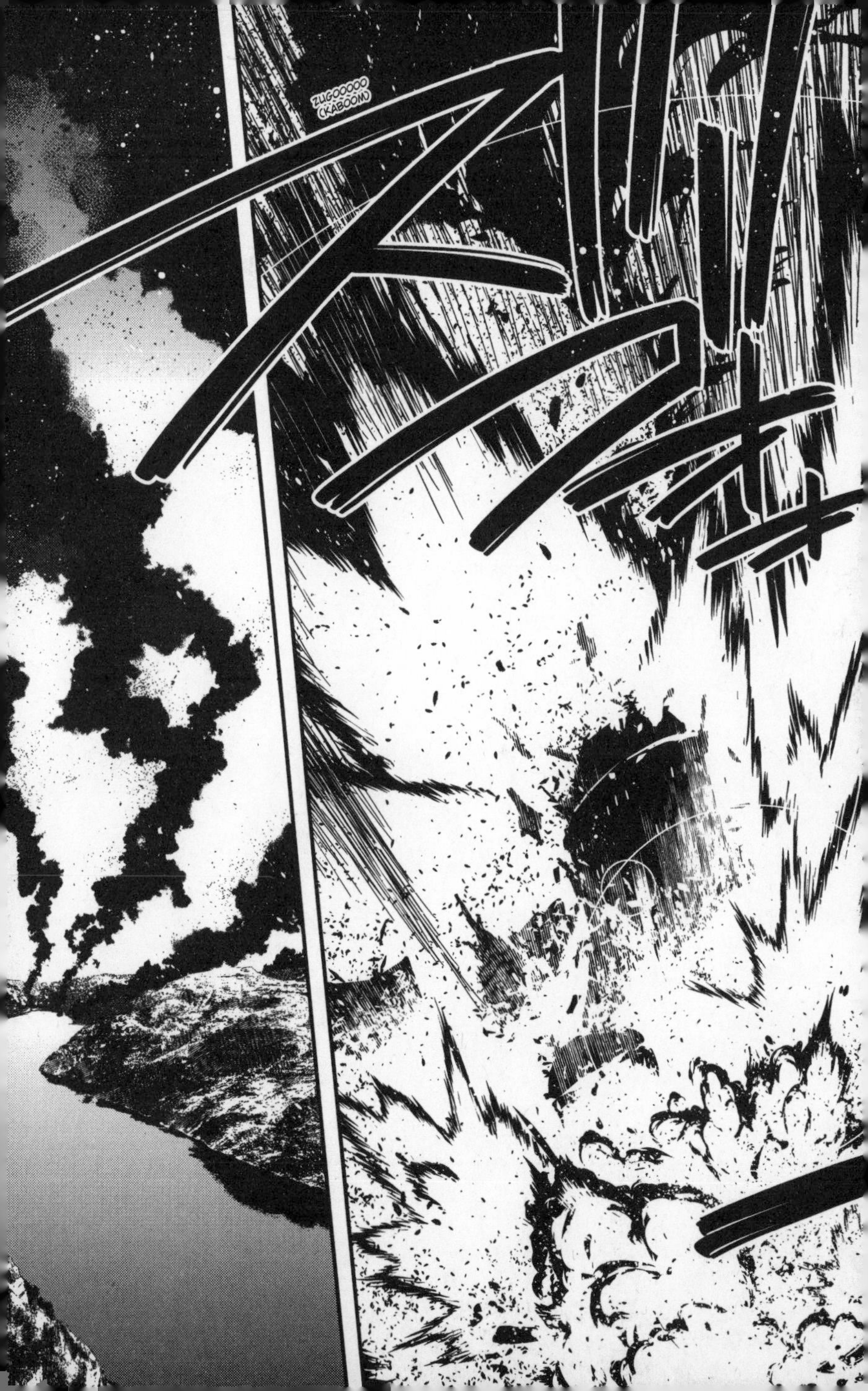
ZUGOOOOO
(KABOOM)

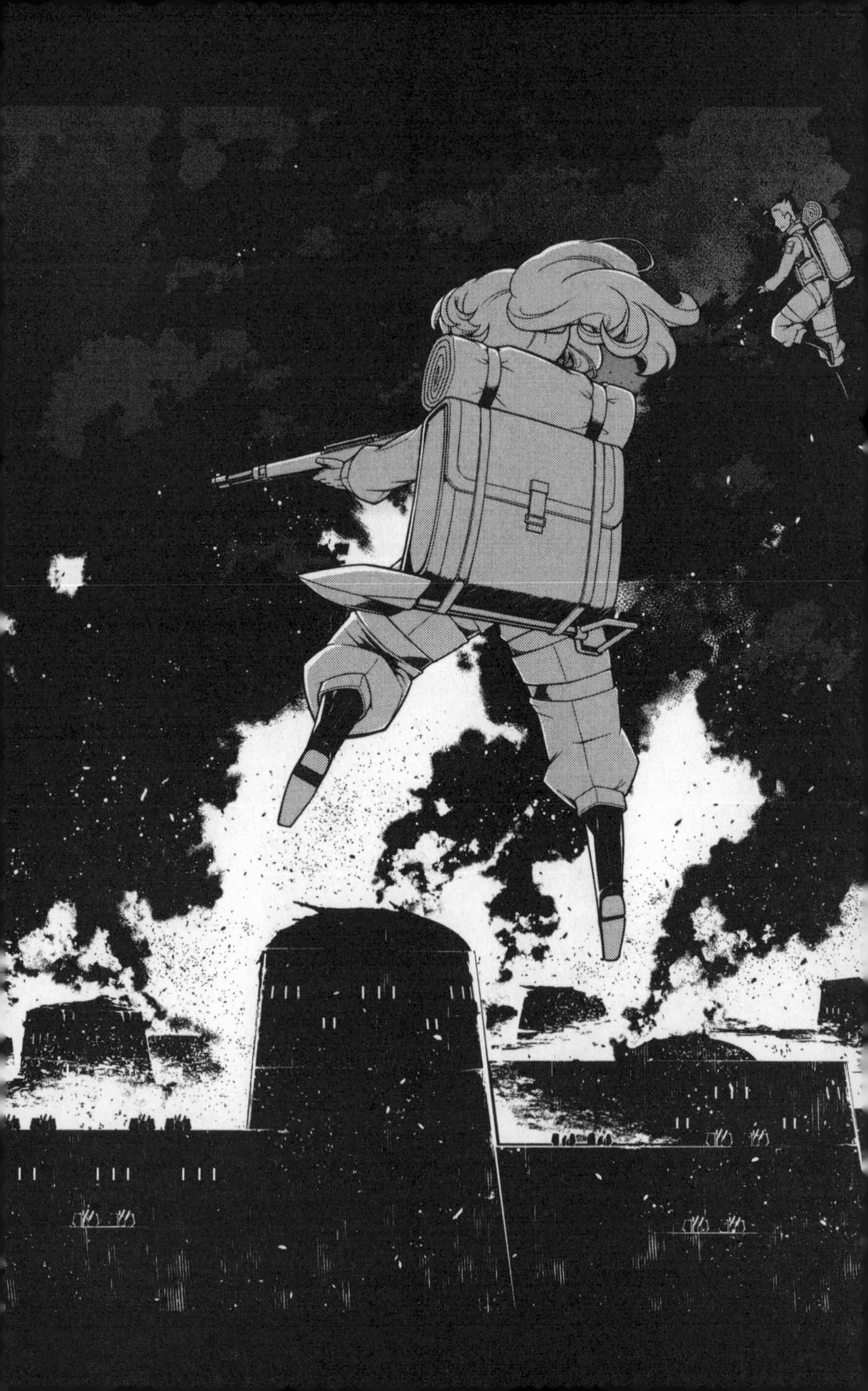

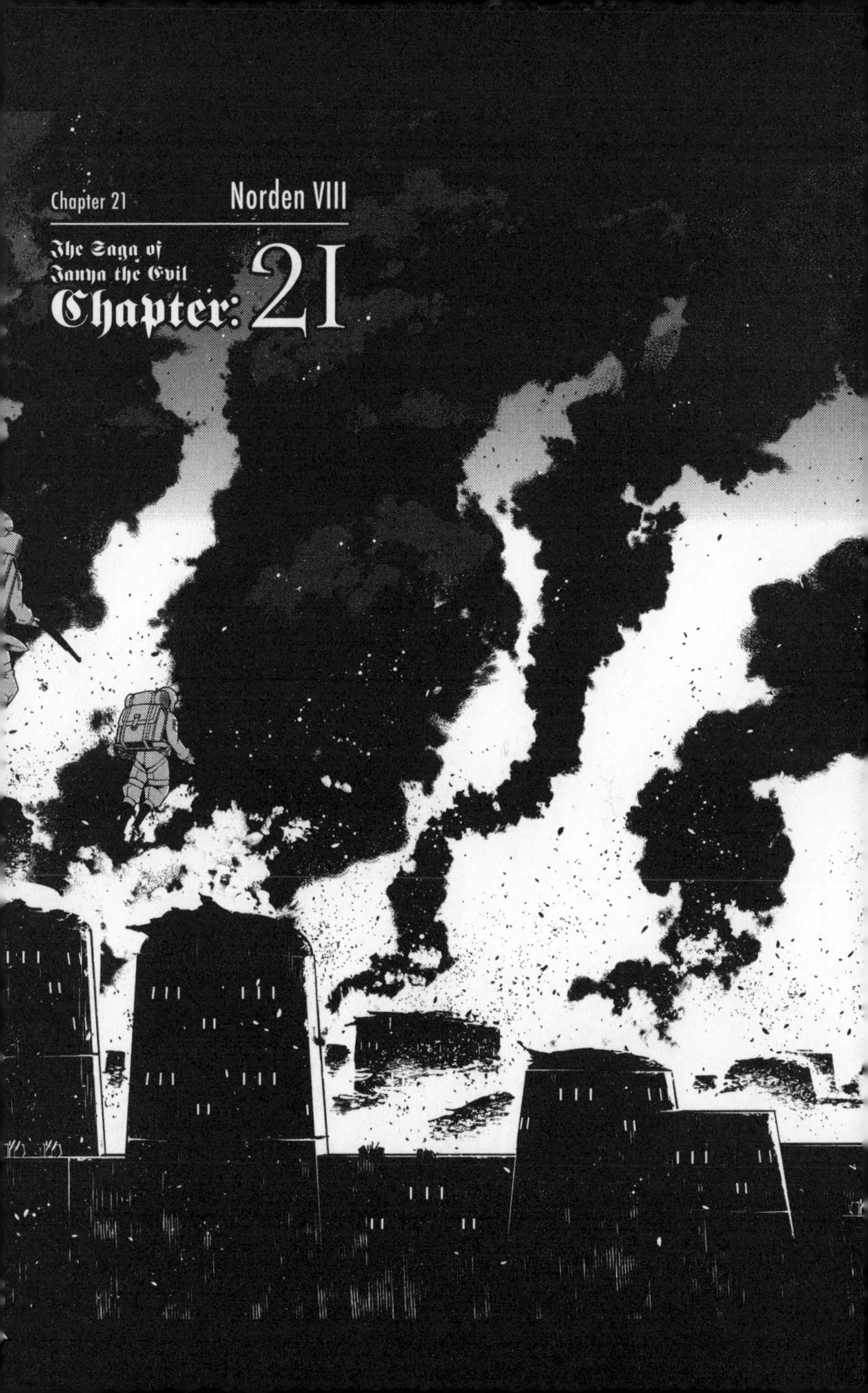
Chapter 21
Norden VIII
The Saga of Tanya the Evil
Chapter: 21

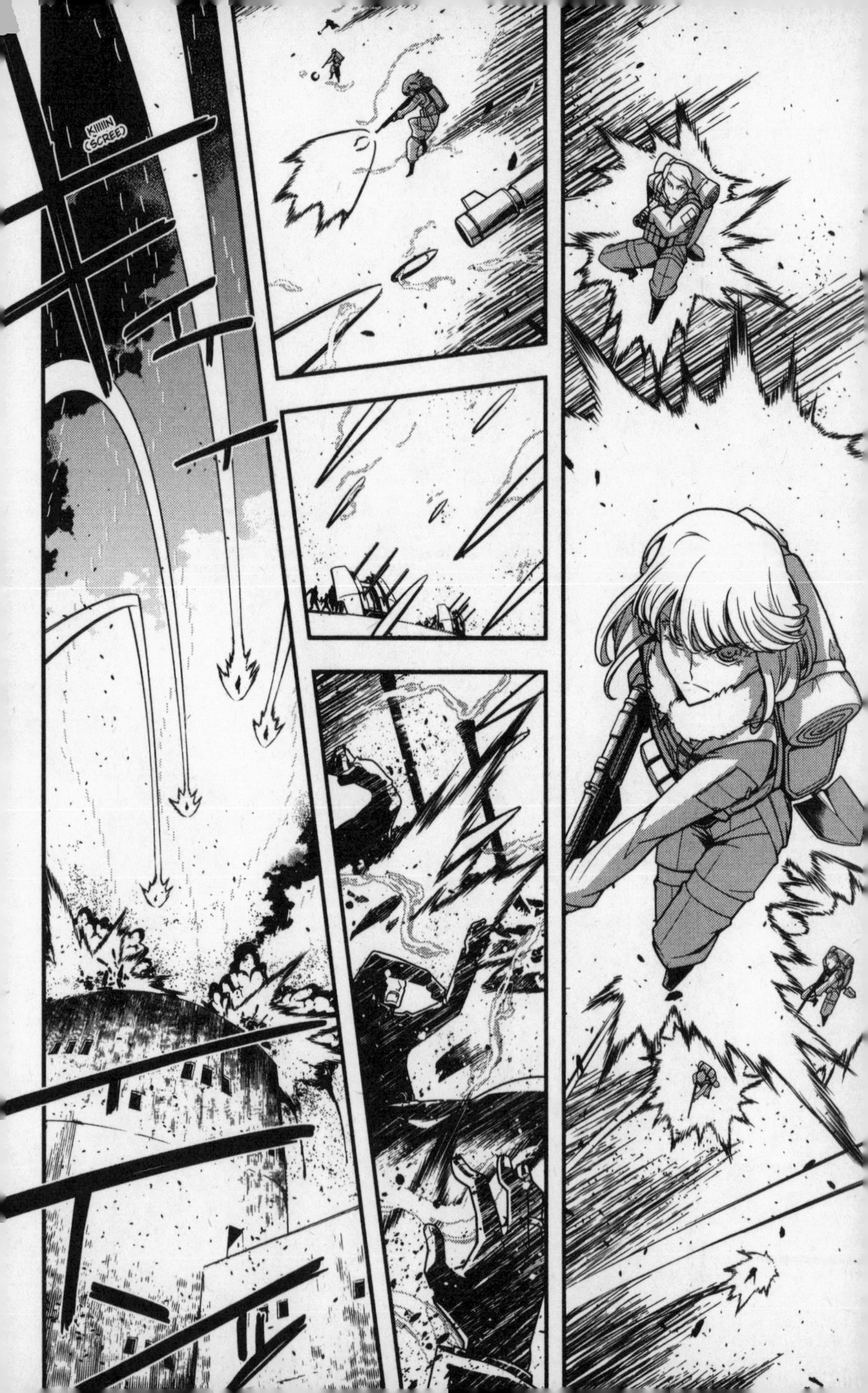
KIIIIN
(SCREE)

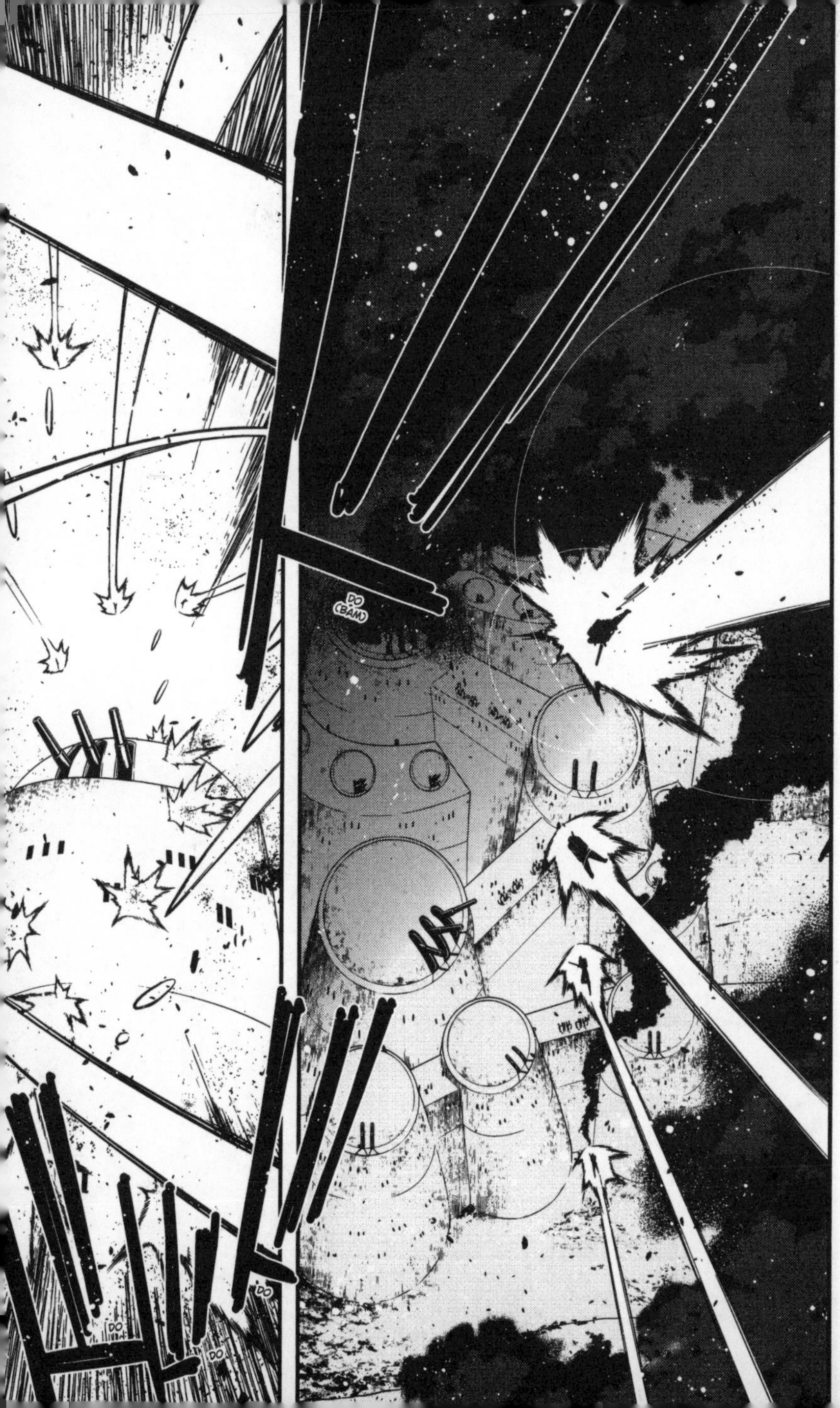
DO (BAM)
DO
DO
DO

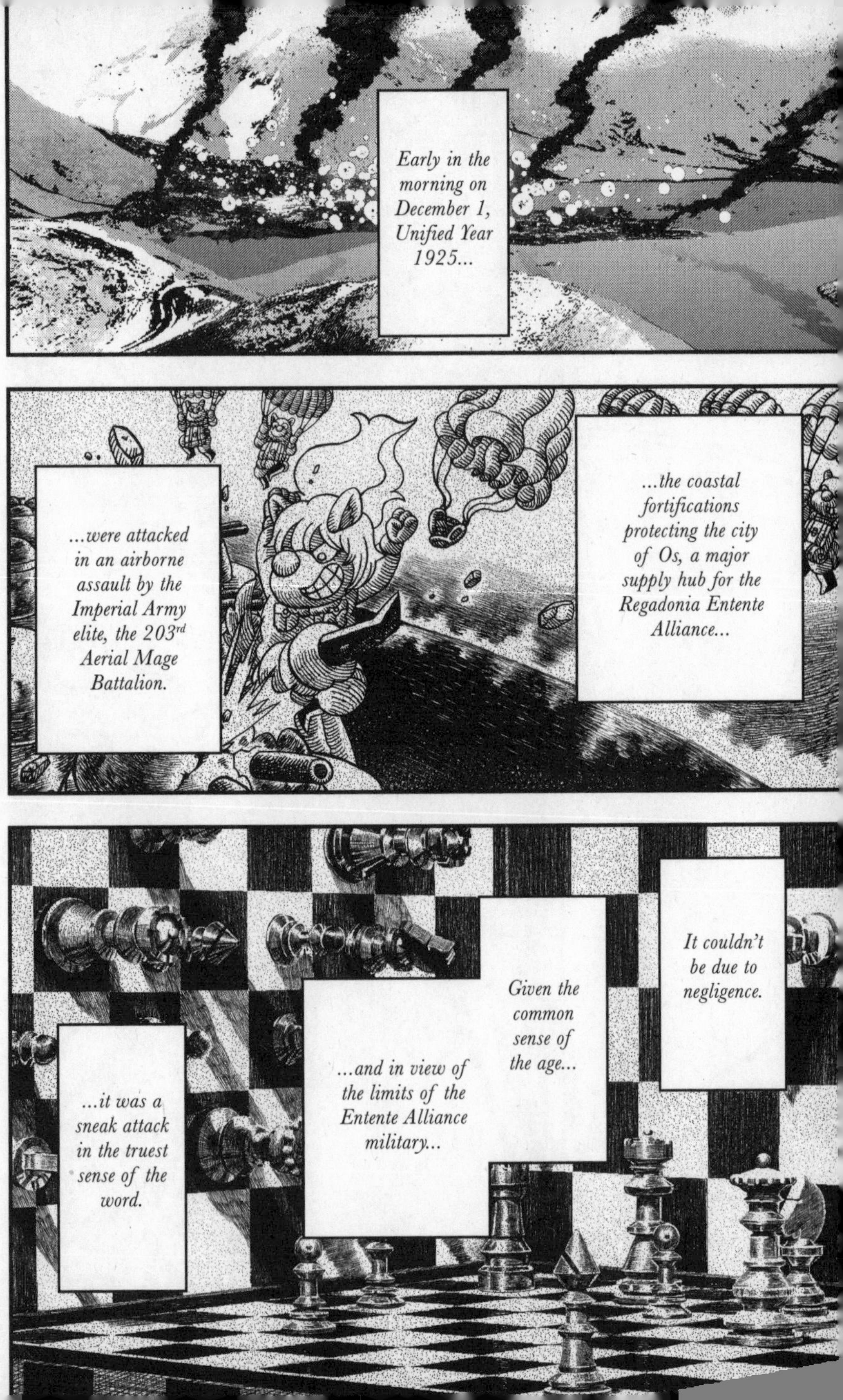
Early in the morning on December 1, Unified Year 1925...
...the coastal fortifications protecting the city of Os, a major supply hub for the Regadonia Entente Alliance...
...were attacked in an airborne assault by the Imperial Army elite, the 203rd Aerial Mage Battalion.
It couldn't be due to negligence.
Given the common sense of the age...
...and in view of the limits of the Entente Alliance military...
...it was a sneak attack in the truest sense of the word.

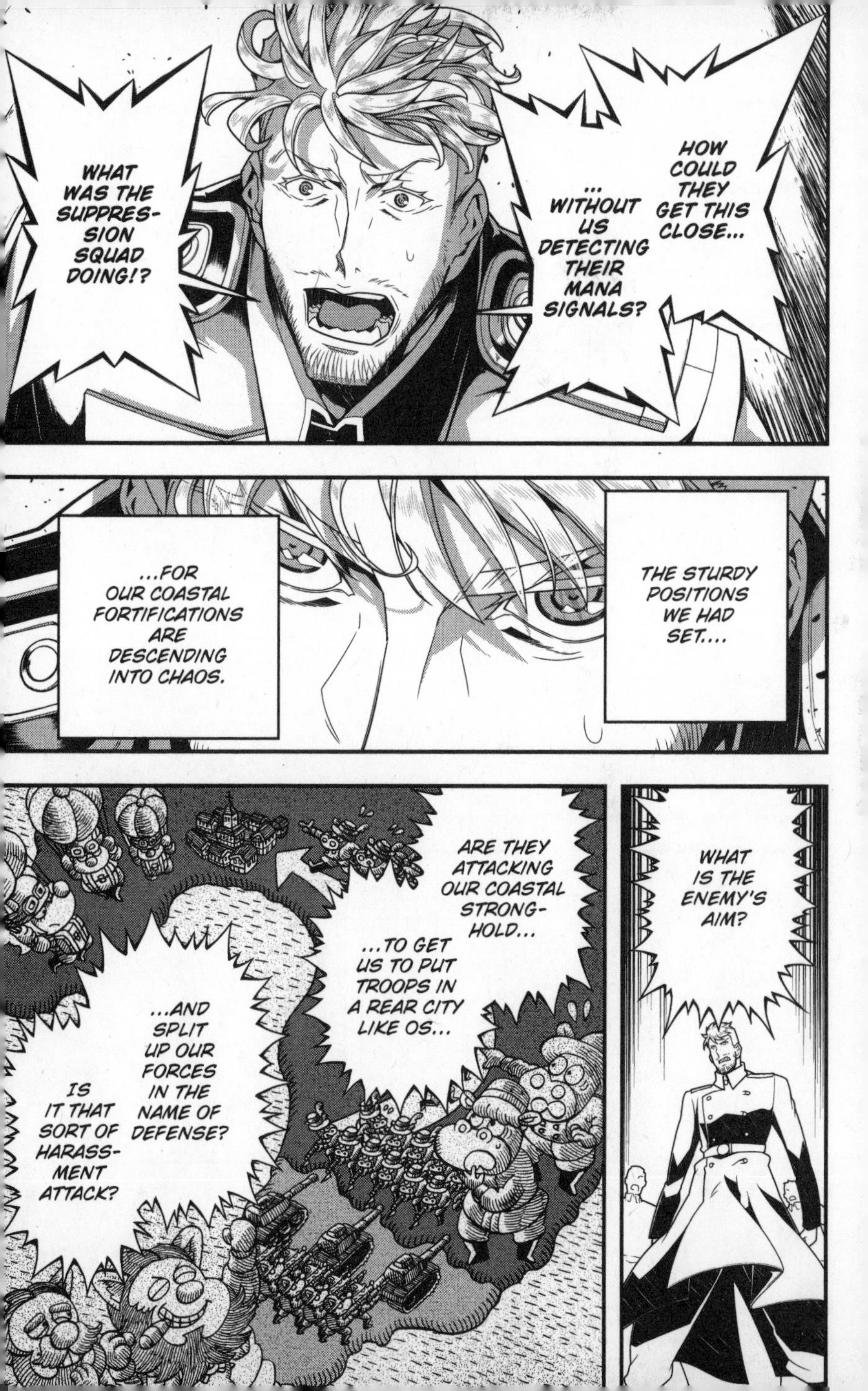
HOW COULD THEY GET THIS CLOSE...
...WITHOUT US DETECTING THEIR MANA SIGNALS?
WHAT WAS THE SUPPRESSION SQUAD DOING!?
THE STURDY POSITIONS WE HAD SET....
...FOR OUR COASTAL FORTIFICATIONS ARE DESCENDING INTO CHAOS.
WHAT IS THE ENEMY'S AIM?
ARE THEY ATTACKING OUR COASTAL STRONGHOLD...
...TO GET US TO PUT TROOPS IN A REAR CITY LIKE OS...
...AND SPLIT UP OUR FORCES IN THE NAME OF DEFENSE?
IS IT THAT SORT OF HARASSMENT ATTACK?

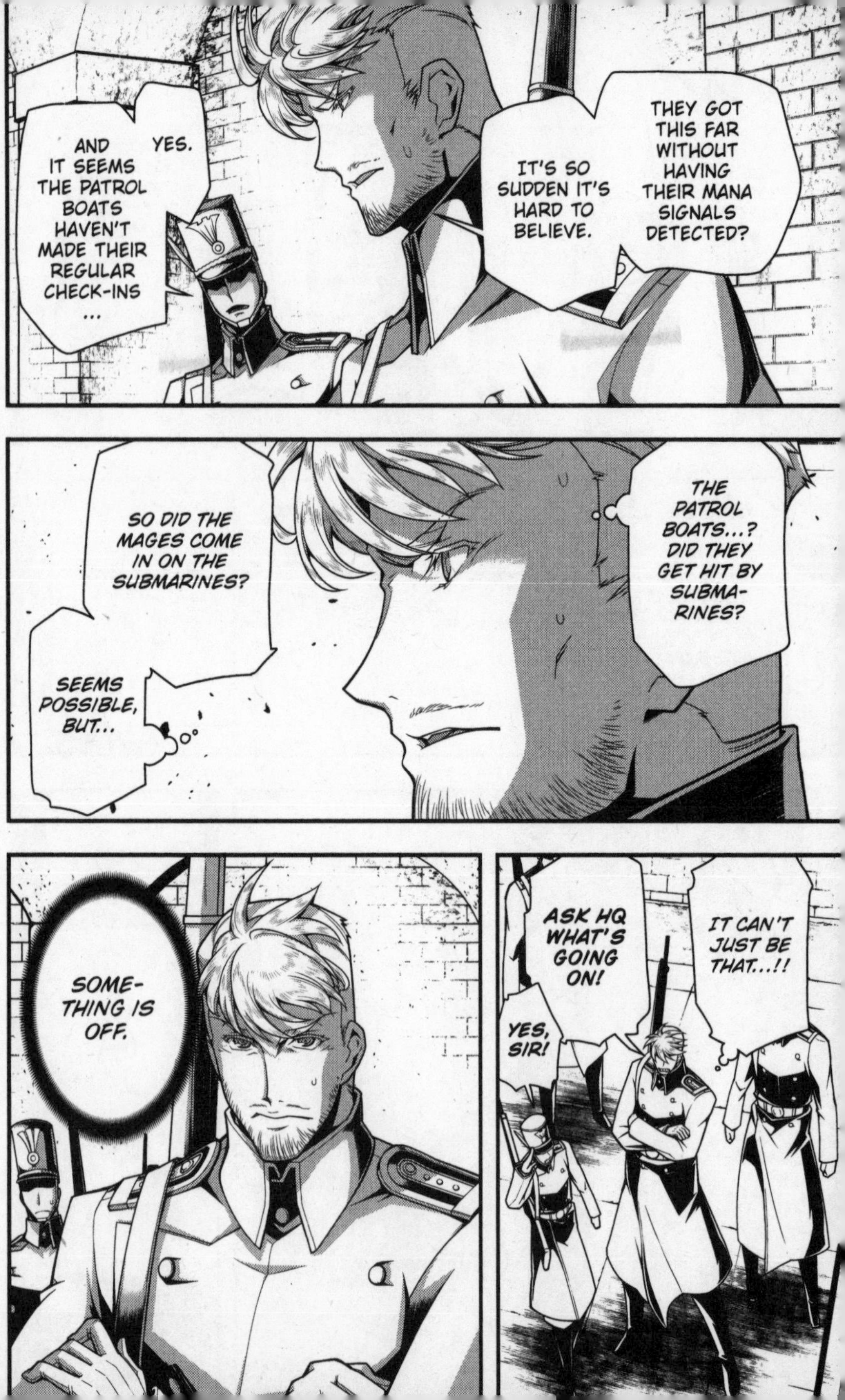
THEY GOT THIS FAR WITHOUT HAVING THEIR MANA SIGNALS DETECTED?
IT'S SO SUDDEN IT'S HARD TO BELIEVE.
YES.
AND IT SEEMS THE PATROL BOATS HAVEN'T MADE THEIR REGULAR CHECK-INS ...
THE PATROL BOATS...? DID THEY GET HIT BY SUBMA-RINES?
SO DID THE MAGES COME IN ON THE SUBMARINES?
SEEMS POSSIBLE, BUT...
IT CAN'T JUST BE THAT...!!
ASK HQ WHAT'S GOING ON!
YES, SIR!
SOME-THING IS OFF.

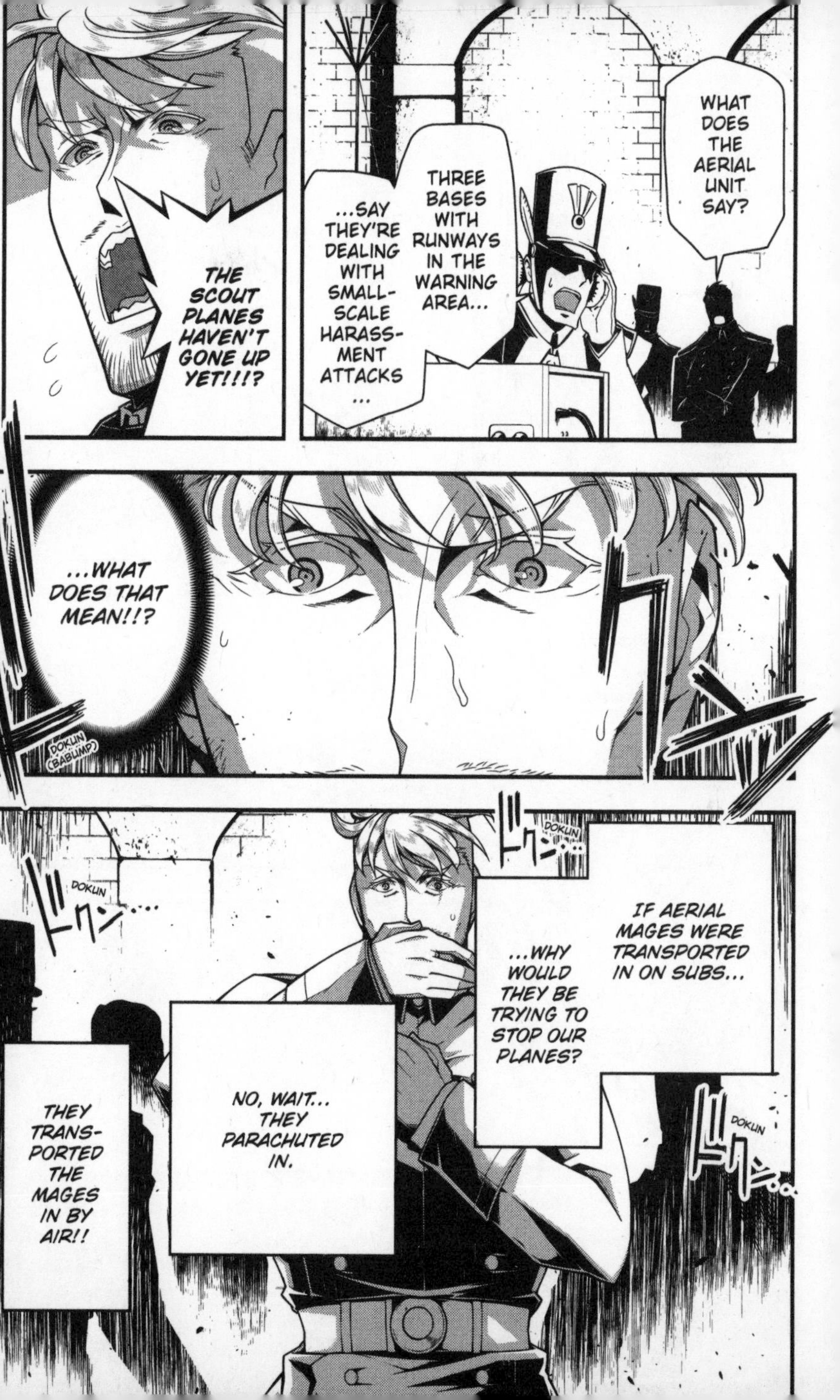
WHAT DOES THE AERIAL UNIT SAY?
THREE BASES WITH RUNWAYS IN THE WARNING AREA...
...SAY THEY'RE DEALING WITH SMALL-SCALE HARASSMENT ATTACKS...
THE SCOUT PLANES HAVEN'T GONE UP YET!!!?
...WHAT DOES THAT MEAN!!?
DOKUN (BABUMP)
DOKUN
IF AERIAL MAGES WERE TRANSPORTED IN ON SUBS...
...WHY WOULD THEY BE TRYING TO STOP OUR PLANES?
DOKUN
DOKUN
NO, WAIT... THEY PARACHUTED IN.
THEY TRANSPORTED THE MAGES IN BY AIR!!

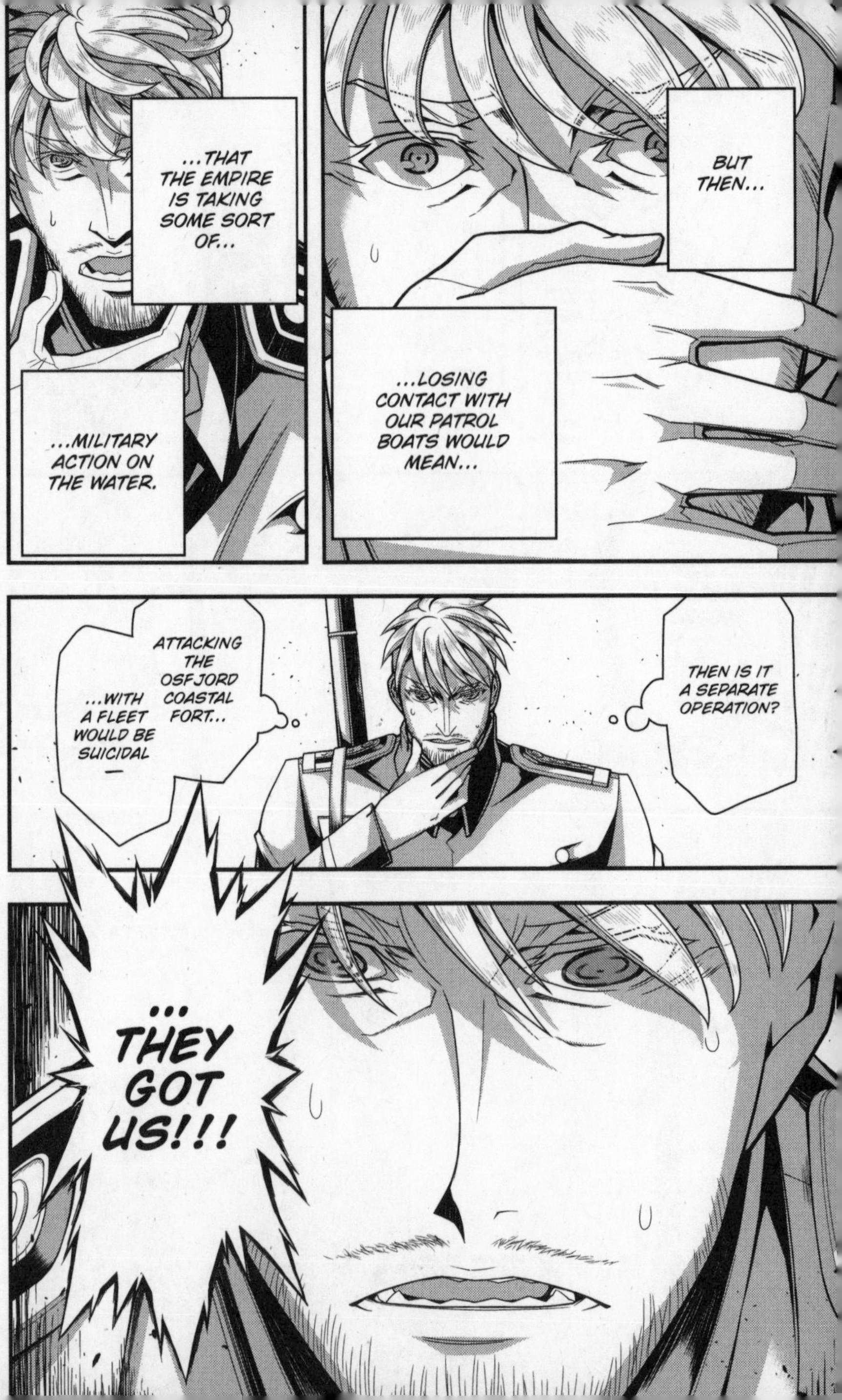
BUT THEN...
...LOSING CONTACT WITH OUR PATROL BOATS WOULD MEAN...
...THAT THE EMPIRE IS TAKING SOME SORT OF...
...MILITARY ACTION ON THE WATER.
THEN IS IT A SEPARATE OPERATION?
ATTACKING THE OSFJORD COASTAL FORT...
...WITH A FLEET WOULD BE SUICIDAL—
...THEY GOT US!!!

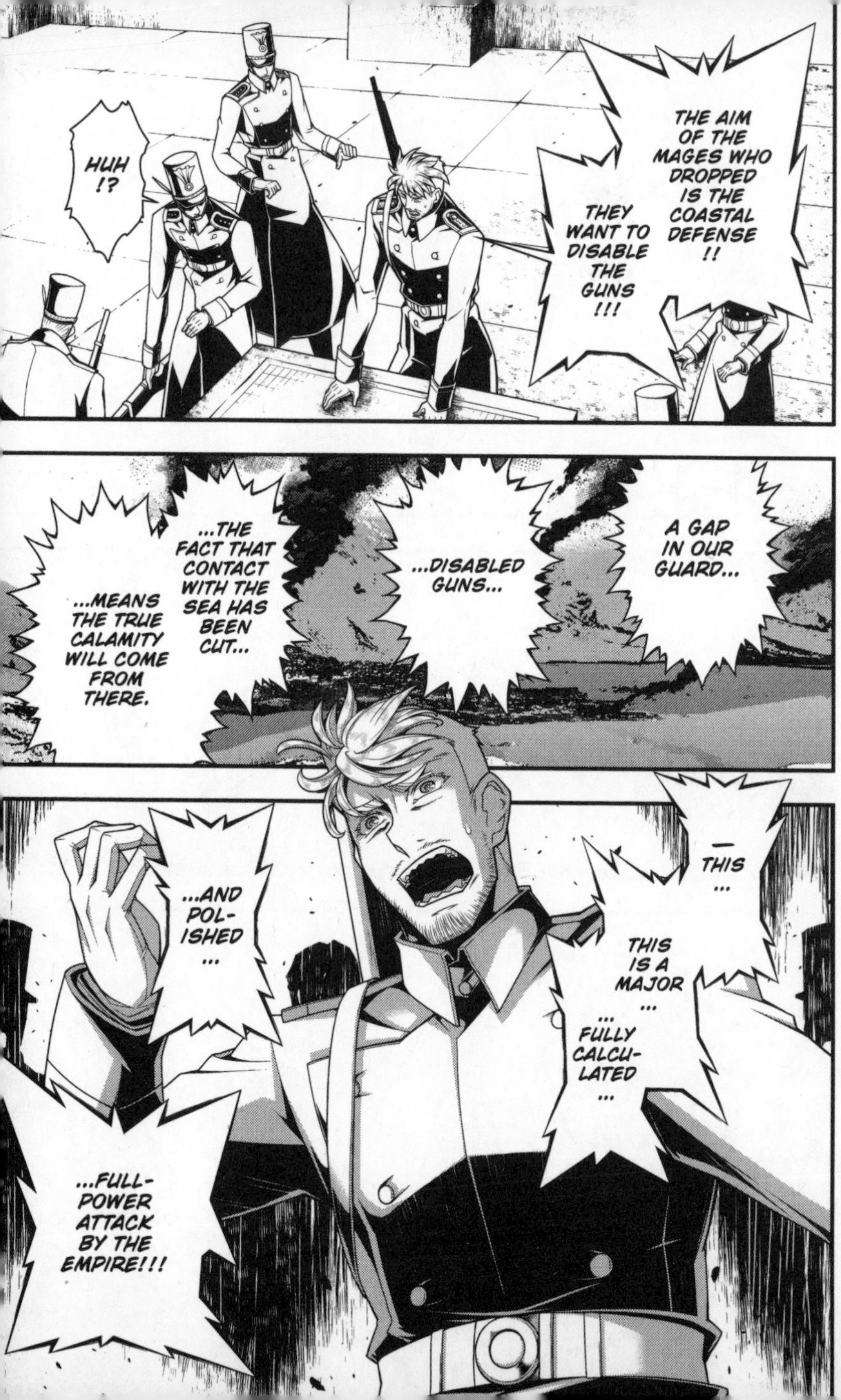
THE AIM OF THE MAGES WHO DROPPED IS THE COASTAL DEFENSE!!
THEY WANT TO DISABLE THE GUNS!!!
HUH!?
A GAP IN OUR GUARD...
...DISABLED GUNS...
...THE FACT THAT CONTACT WITH THE SEA HAS BEEN CUT...
...MEANS THE TRUE CALAMITY WILL COME FROM THERE.
—THIS...
THIS IS A MAJOR...
...FULLY CALCULATED...
...AND POL-ISHED...
...FULL-POWER ATTACK BY THE EMPIRE!!!

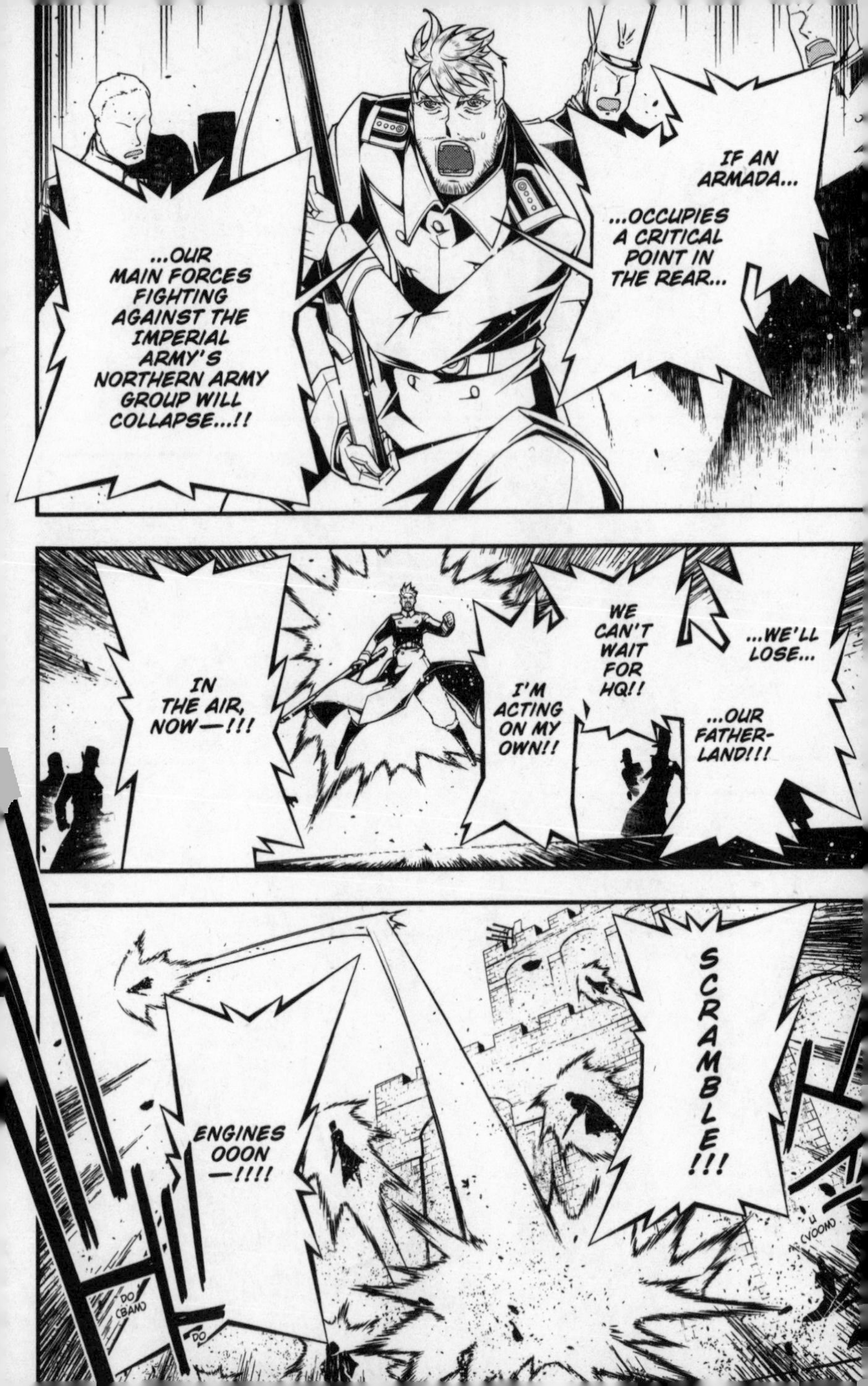
IF AN ARMADA...
...OCCUPIES A CRITICAL POINT IN THE REAR...
...OUR MAIN FORCES FIGHTING AGAINST THE IMPERIAL ARMY'S NORTHERN ARMY GROUP WILL COLLAPSE...!!
...WE'LL LOSE...
...OUR FATHERLAND!!!
WE CAN'T WAIT FOR HQ!!
I'M ACTING ON MY OWN!!
IN THE AIR, NOW—!!!
SCRAMBLE!!!
(VOOM)
ENGINES OOON—!!!!
DO (BAM)
DO

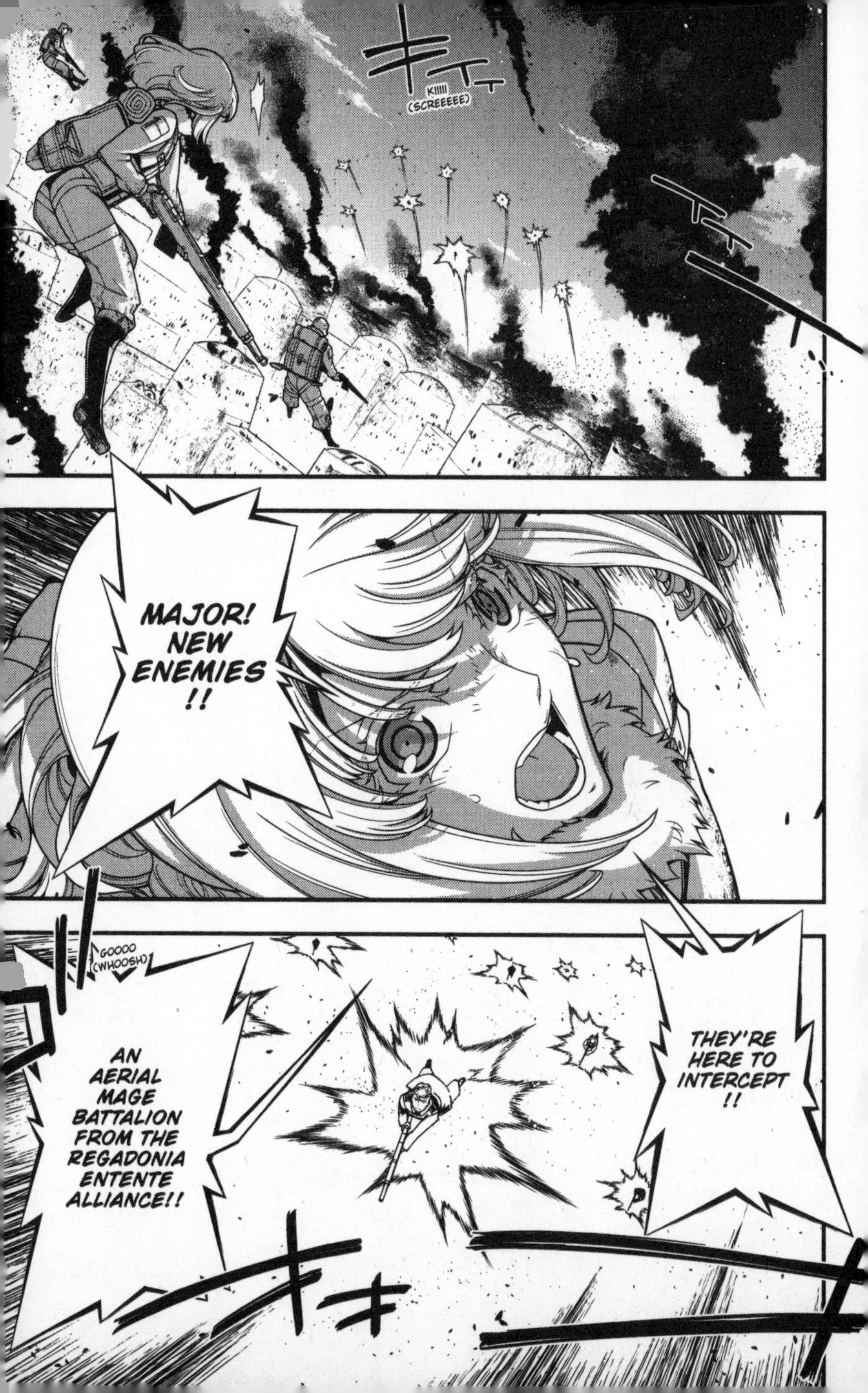
KIIIII
(SCREEEEE)
MAJOR! NEW ENEMIES!!
THEY'RE HERE TO INTERCEPT!!
GOOOO
(WHOOSH)
AN AERIAL MAGE BATTALION FROM THE REGADONIA ENTENTE ALLIANCE!!

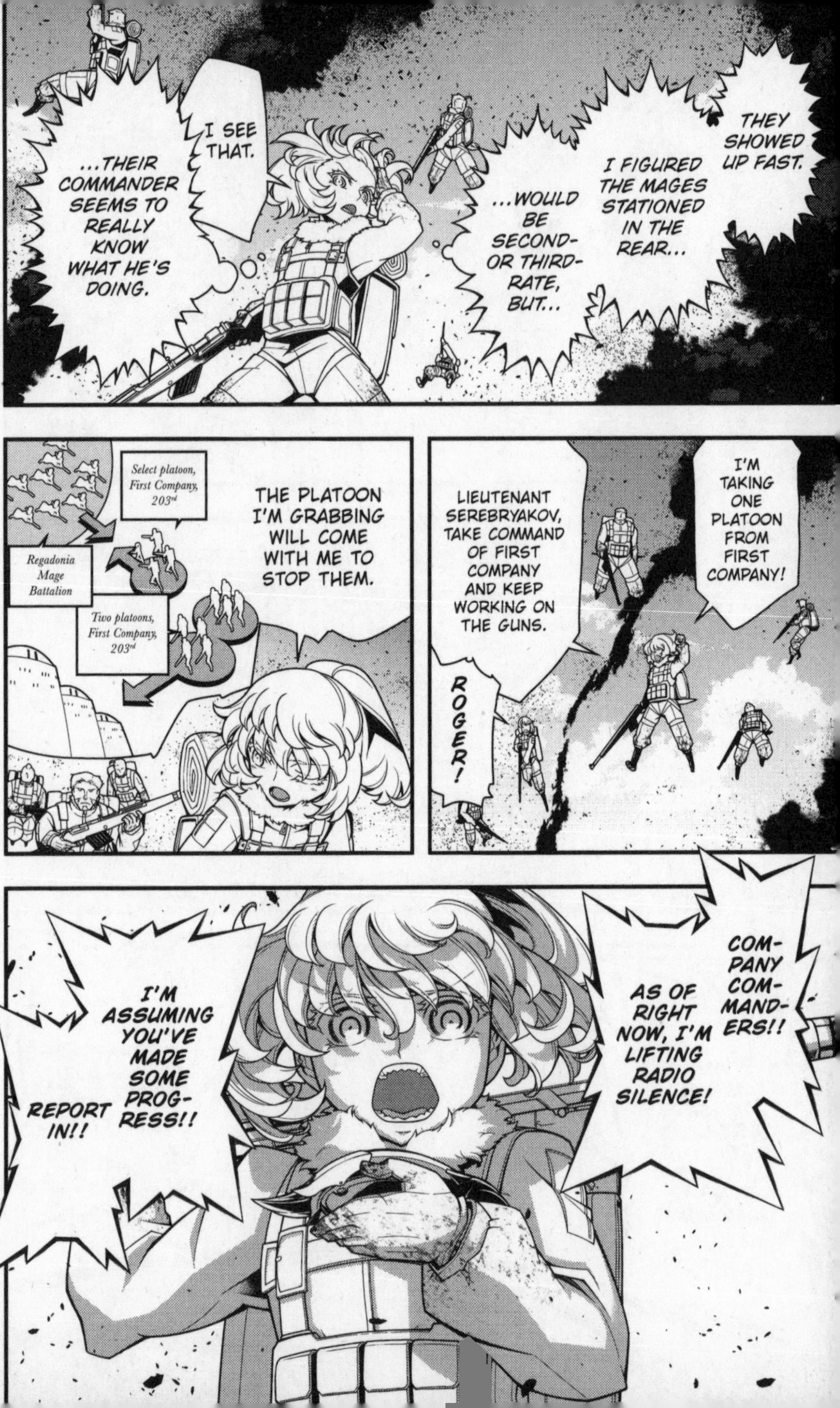
THEY SHOWED UP FAST.
I FIGURED THE MAGES STATIONED IN THE REAR...
...WOULD BE SECOND- OR THIRD-RATE, BUT...
I SEE THAT.
...THEIR COMMANDER SEEMS TO REALLY KNOW WHAT HE'S DOING.
I'M TAKING ONE PLATOON FROM FIRST COMPANY!
LIEUTENANT SEREBRYAKOV, TAKE COMMAND OF FIRST COMPANY AND KEEP WORKING ON THE GUNS.
ROGER!
THE PLATOON I'M GRABBING WILL COME WITH ME TO STOP THEM.
Select platoon, First Company, 203rd
Regadonia Mage Battalion
Two platoons, First Company, 203rd
COMPANY COMMANDERS!!
AS OF RIGHT NOW, I'M LIFTING RADIO SILENCE!
I'M ASSUMING YOU'VE MADE SOME PROGRESS!!
REPORT IN!!

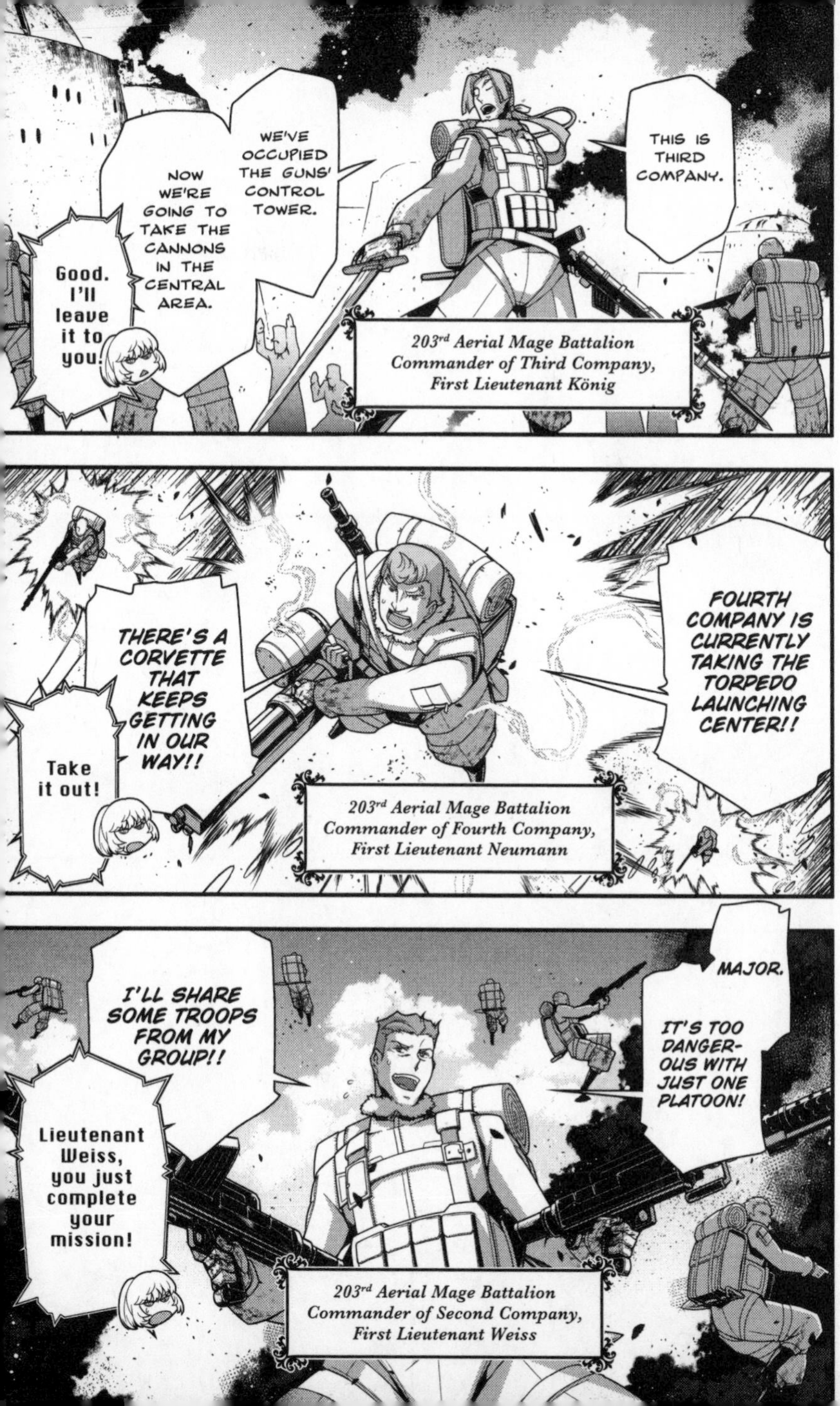
THIS IS THIRD COMPANY.
WE'VE OCCUPIED THE GUNS' CONTROL TOWER.
NOW WE'RE GOING TO TAKE THE CANNONS IN THE CENTRAL AREA.
203rd Aerial Mage Battalion Commander of Third Company, First Lieutenant König
Good. I'll leave it to you!
FOURTH COMPANY IS CURRENTLY TAKING THE TORPEDO LAUNCHING CENTER!!
THERE'S A CORVETTE THAT KEEPS GETTING IN OUR WAY!!
203rd Aerial Mage Battalion Commander of Fourth Company, First Lieutenant Neumann
Take it out!
MAJOR.
IT'S TOO DANGER-OUS WITH JUST ONE PLATOON!
I'LL SHARE SOME TROOPS FROM MY GROUP!!
Lieutenant Weiss, you just complete your mission!
203rd Aerial Mage Battalion Commander of Second Company, First Lieutenant Weiss

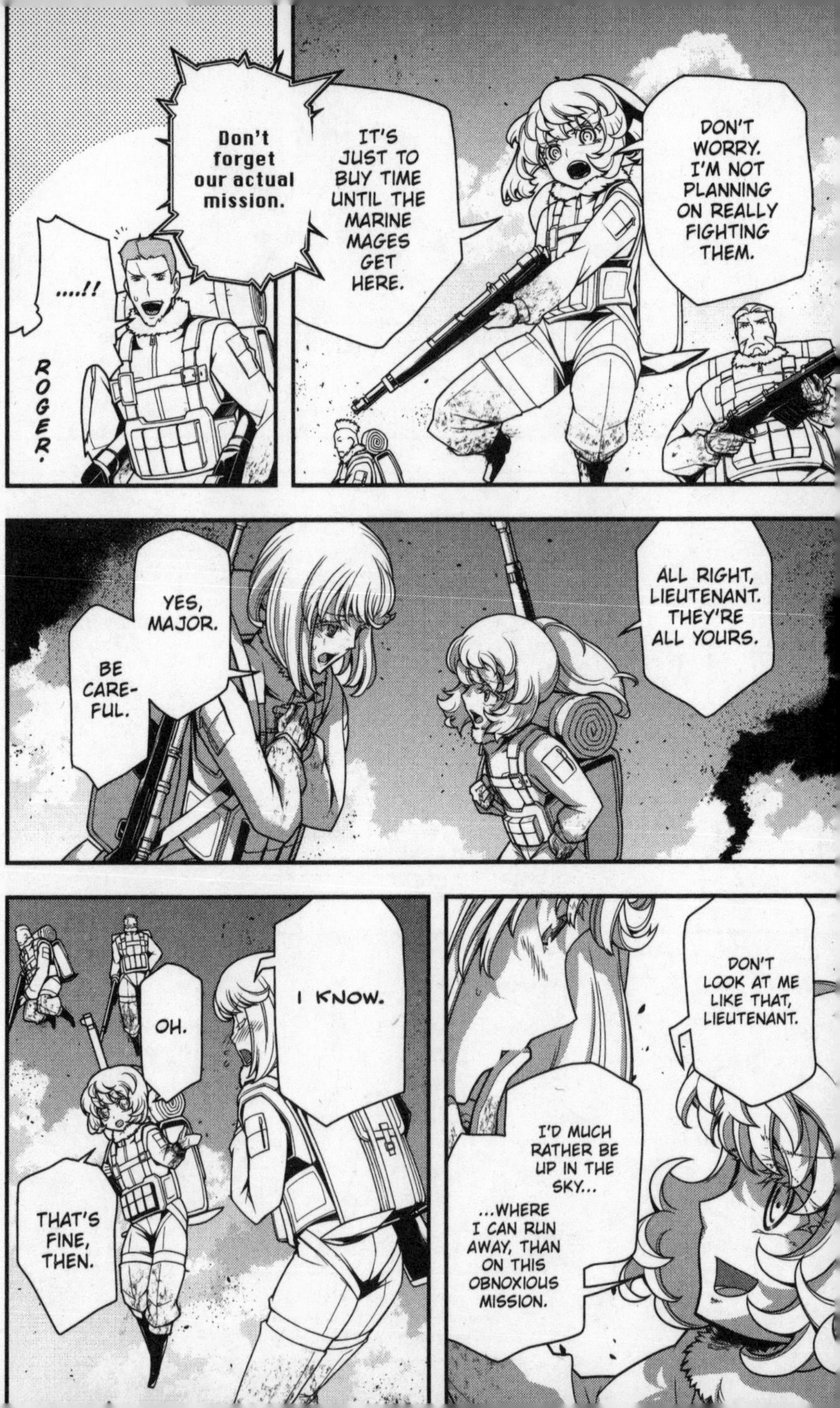
DON'T WORRY. I'M NOT PLANNING ON REALLY FIGHTING THEM.
IT'S JUST TO BUY TIME UNTIL THE MARINE MAGES GET HERE.
Don't forget our actual mission.
....!!
ROGER.
ALL RIGHT, LIEUTENANT. THEY'RE ALL YOURS.
YES, MAJOR.
BE CARE-FUL.
DON'T LOOK AT ME LIKE THAT, LIEUTENANT.
I'D MUCH RATHER BE UP IN THE SKY...
...WHERE I CAN RUN AWAY, THAN ON THIS OBNOXIOUS MISSION.
I KNOW.
OH.
THAT'S FINE, THEN.

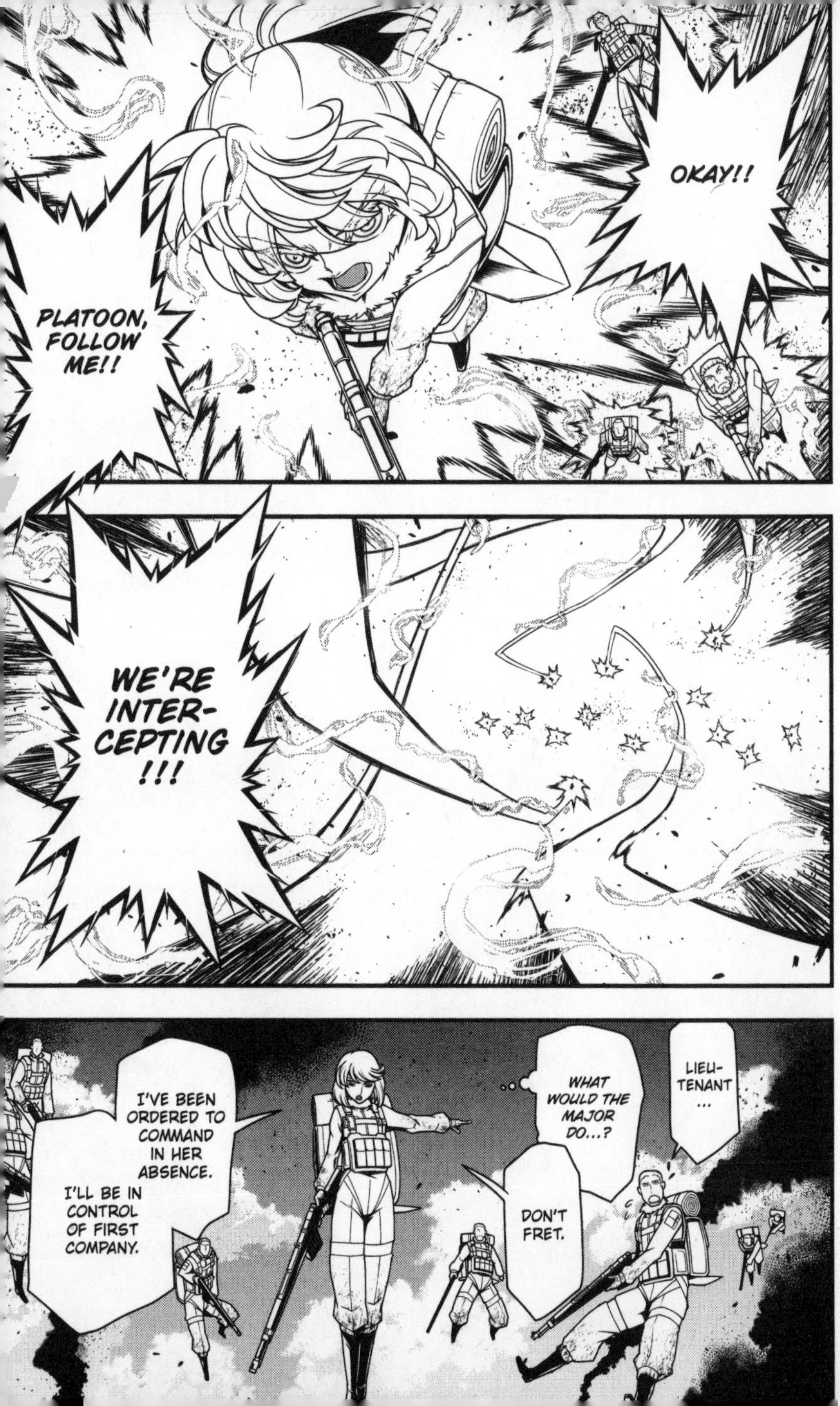
OKAY!!
PLATOON, FOLLOW ME!!
WE'RE INTERCEPTING!!!
LIEUTENANT...
WHAT WOULD THE MAJOR DO...?
DON'T FRET.
I'VE BEEN ORDERED TO COMMAND IN HER ABSENCE.
I'LL BE IN CONTROL OF FIRST COMPANY.

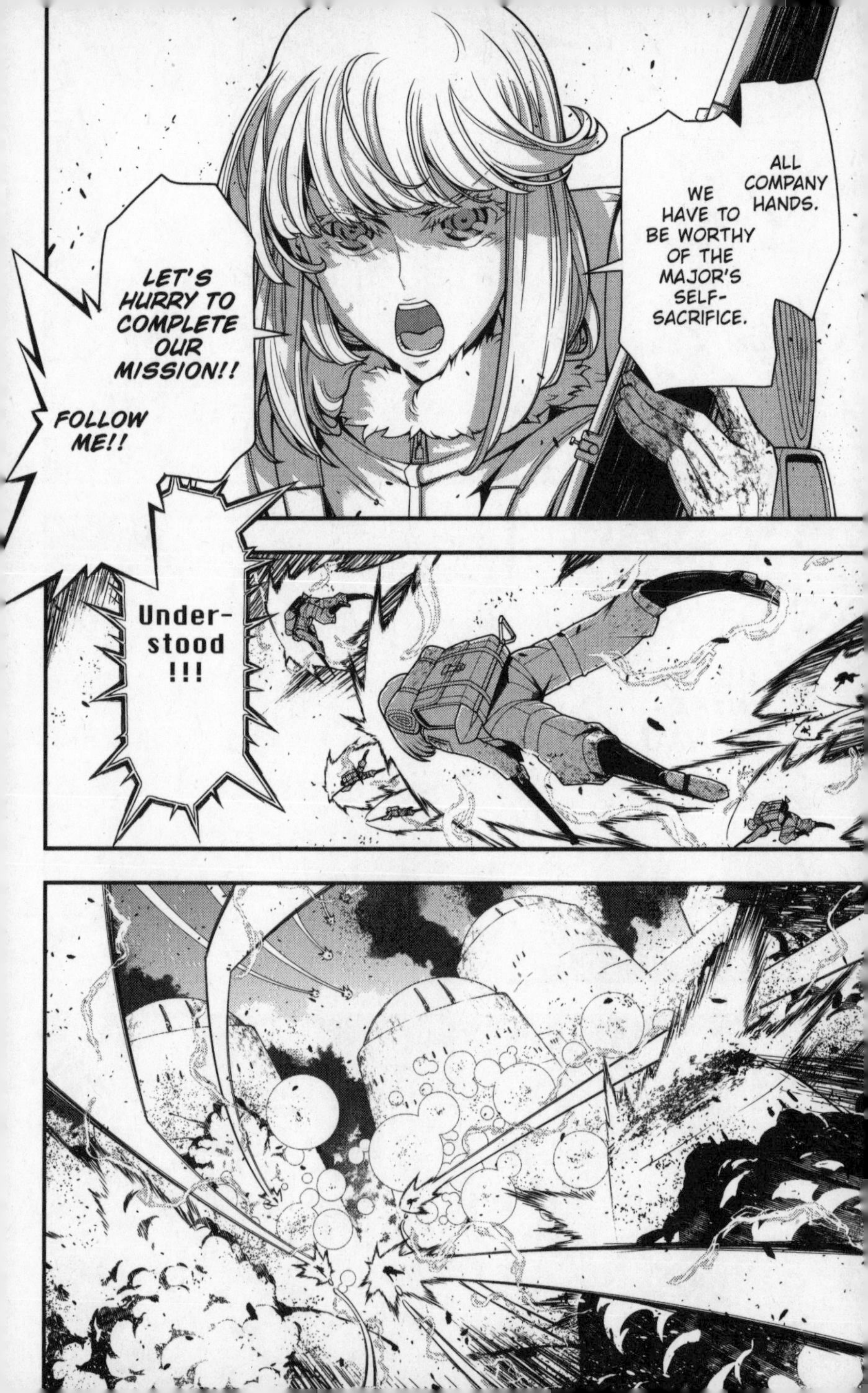
ALL COMPANY HANDS.
WE HAVE TO BE WORTHY OF THE MAJOR'S SELF-SACRIFICE.
LET'S HURRY TO COMPLETE OUR MISSION!!
FOLLOW ME!!
Under-stood!!!

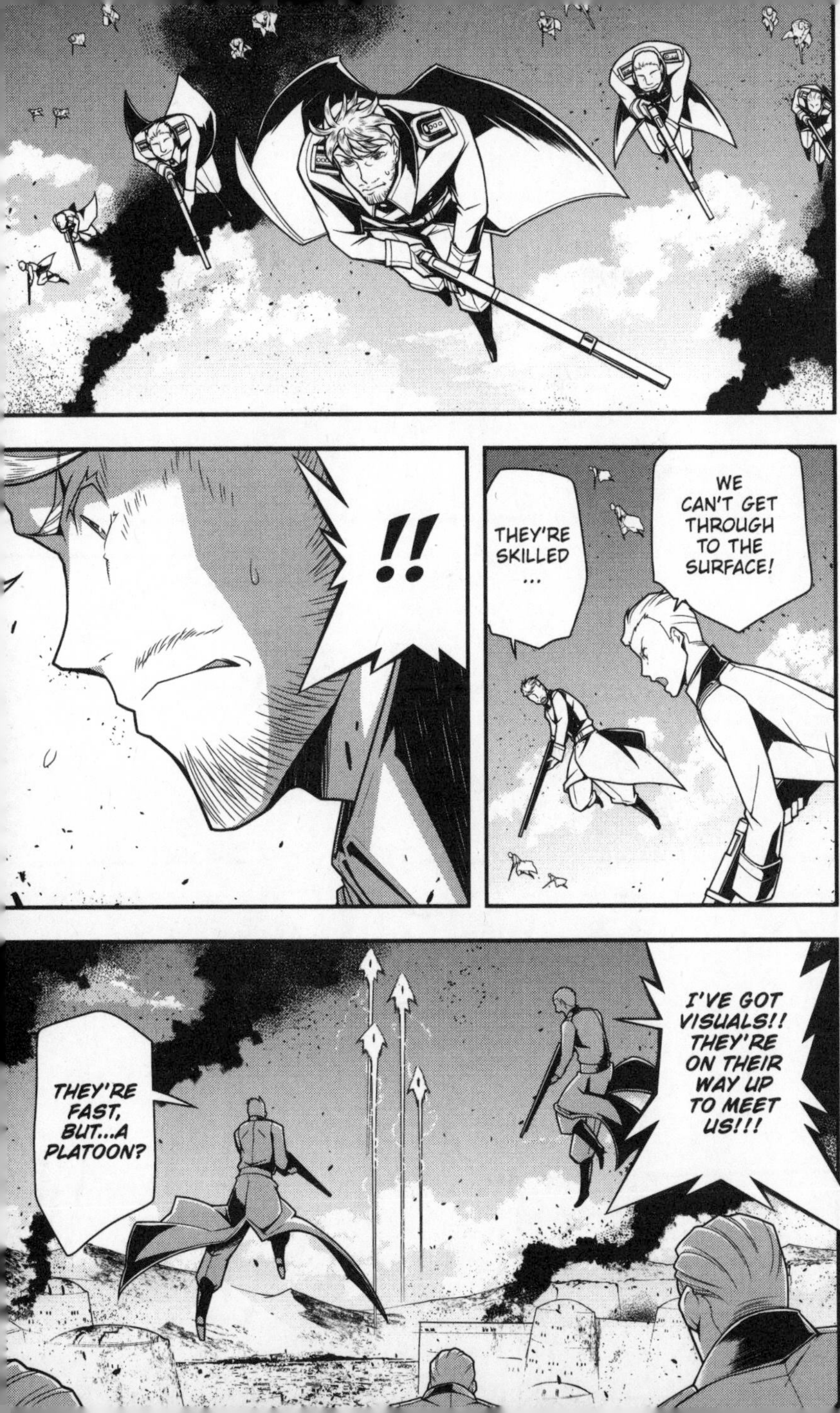
WE CAN'T GET THROUGH TO THE SURFACE!
THEY'RE SKILLED...
!!
I'VE GOT VISUALS!! THEY'RE ON THEIR WAY UP TO MEET US!!!
THEY'RE FAST, BUT...A PLATOON?

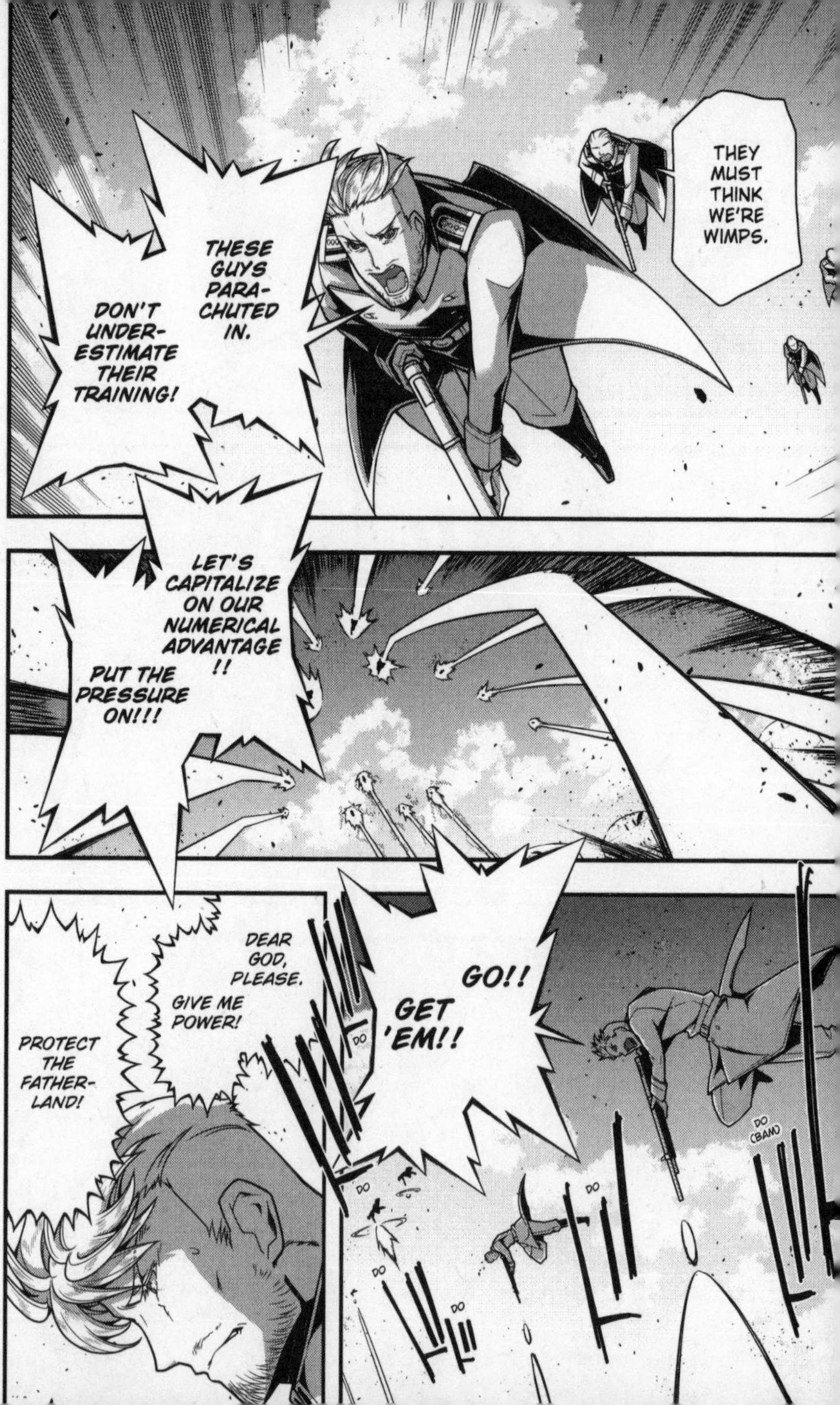
THEY MUST THINK WE'RE WIMPS.
THESE GUYS PARACHUTED IN.
DON'T UNDERESTIMATE THEIR TRAINING!
LET'S CAPITALIZE ON OUR NUMERICAL ADVANTAGE!!
PUT THE PRESSURE ON!!!
GO!!
GET 'EM!!
DO
DO (BAM)
DO
DO
DO
DO
DEAR GOD, PLEASE.
GIVE ME POWER!
PROTECT THE FATHERLAND!

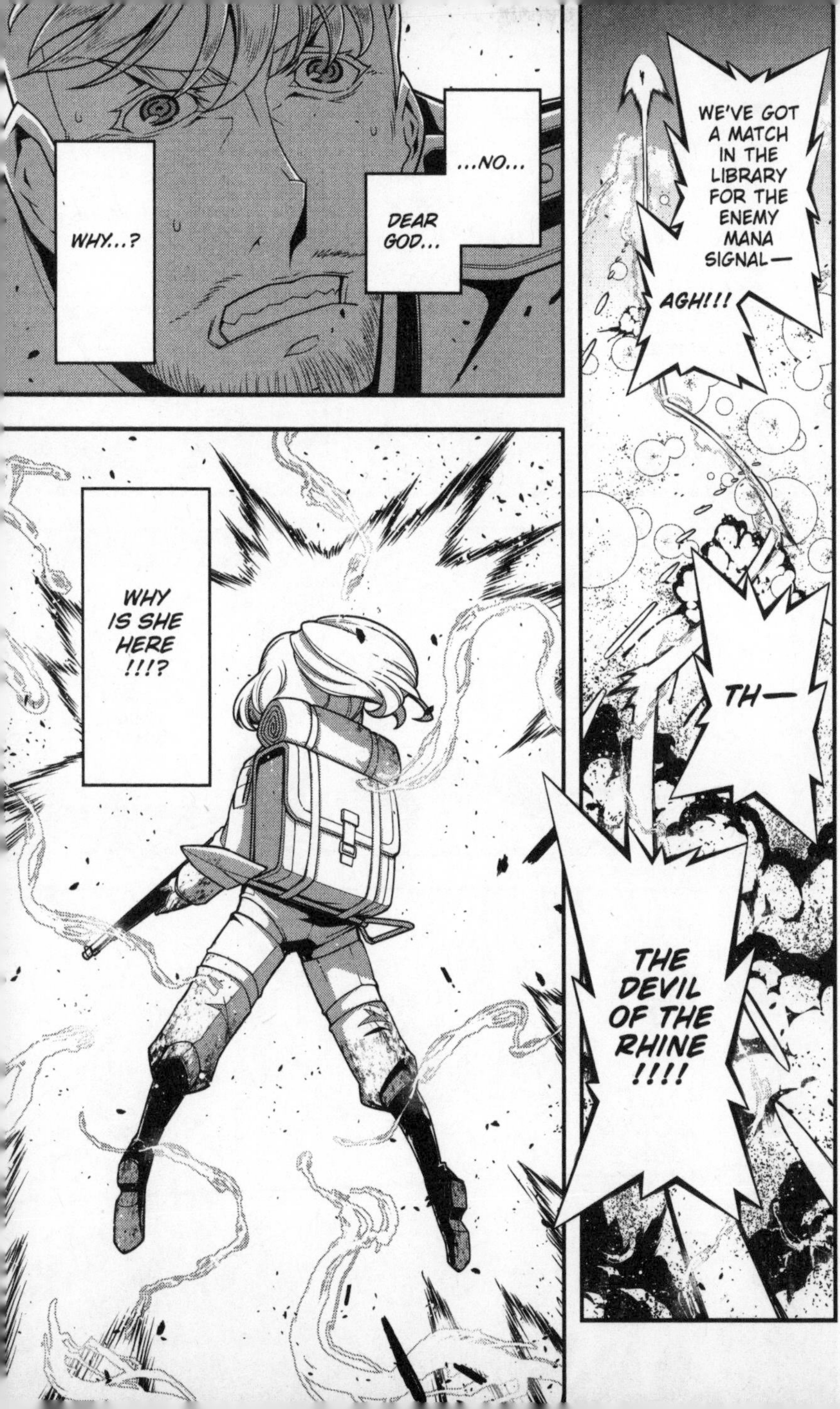
WE'VE GOT A MATCH IN THE LIBRARY FOR THE ENEMY MANA SIGNAL—
AGH!!!
TH—
THE DEVIL OF THE RHINE !!!!
...NO...
DEAR GOD...
WHY...?
WHY IS SHE HERE !!!?

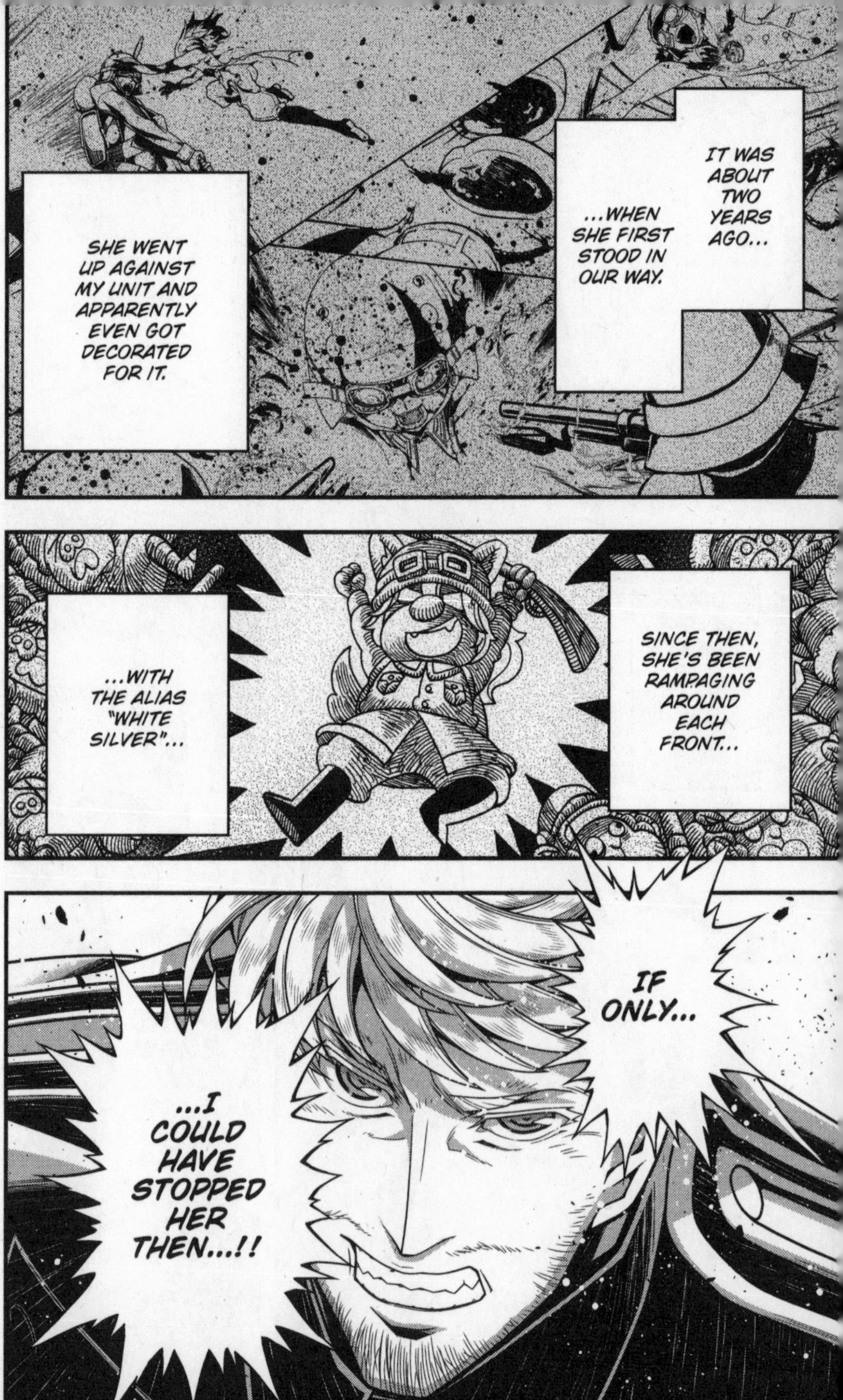
IT WAS ABOUT TWO YEARS AGO...
...WHEN SHE FIRST STOOD IN OUR WAY.
SHE WENT UP AGAINST MY UNIT AND APPARENTLY EVEN GOT DECORATED FOR IT.
SINCE THEN, SHE'S BEEN RAMPAGING AROUND EACH FRONT...
...WITH THE ALIAS "WHITE SILVER"...
IF ONLY...
...I COULD HAVE STOPPED HER THEN...!!

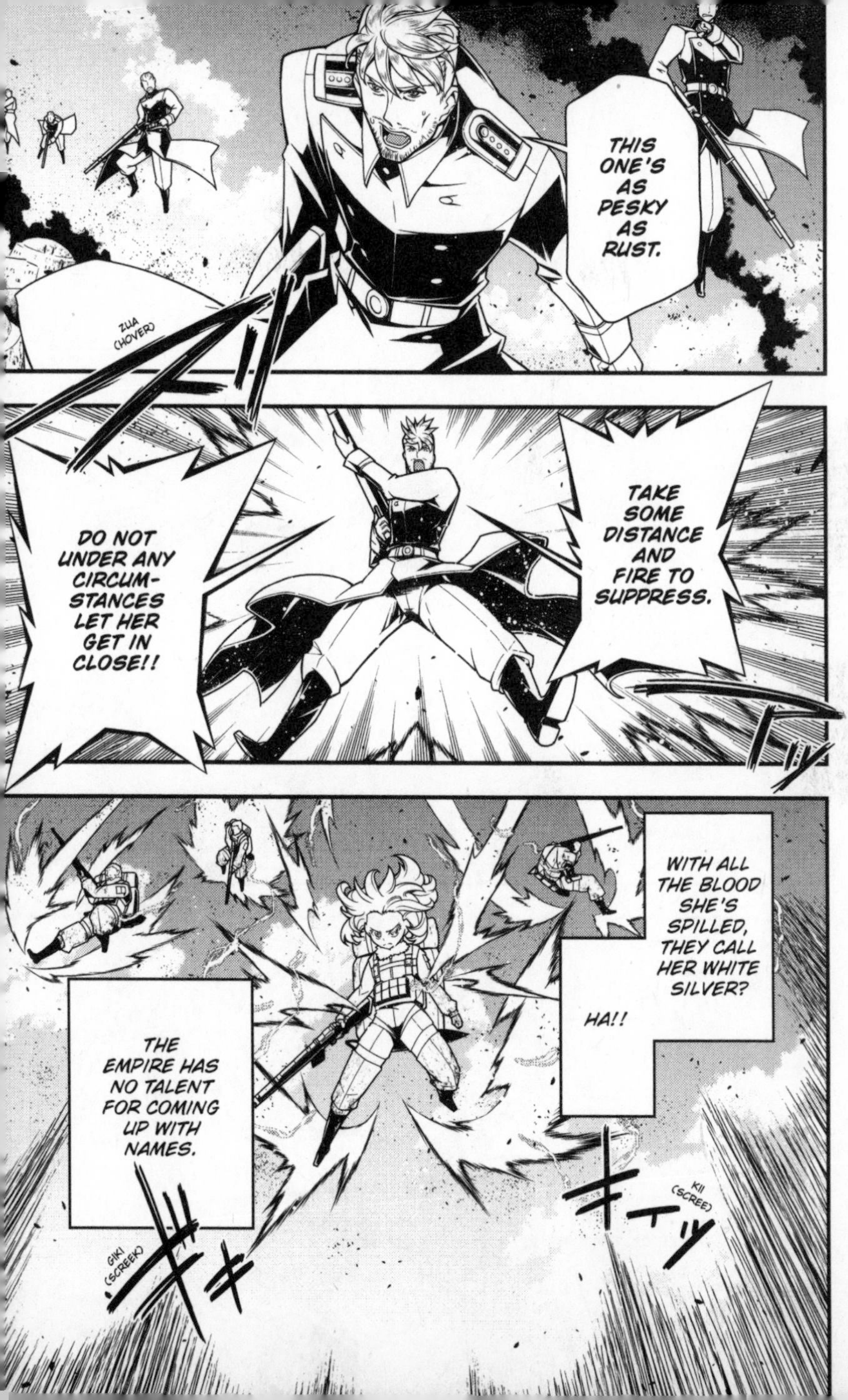
THIS ONE'S AS PESKY AS RUST.
ZUA (HOVER)
TAKE SOME DISTANCE AND FIRE TO SUPPRESS.
DO NOT UNDER ANY CIRCUM-STANCES LET HER GET IN CLOSE!!
WITH ALL THE BLOOD SHE'S SPILLED, THEY CALL HER WHITE SILVER?
HA!!
THE EMPIRE HAS NO TALENT FOR COMING UP WITH NAMES.
KII (SCREE)
GIKI (SCREEK)

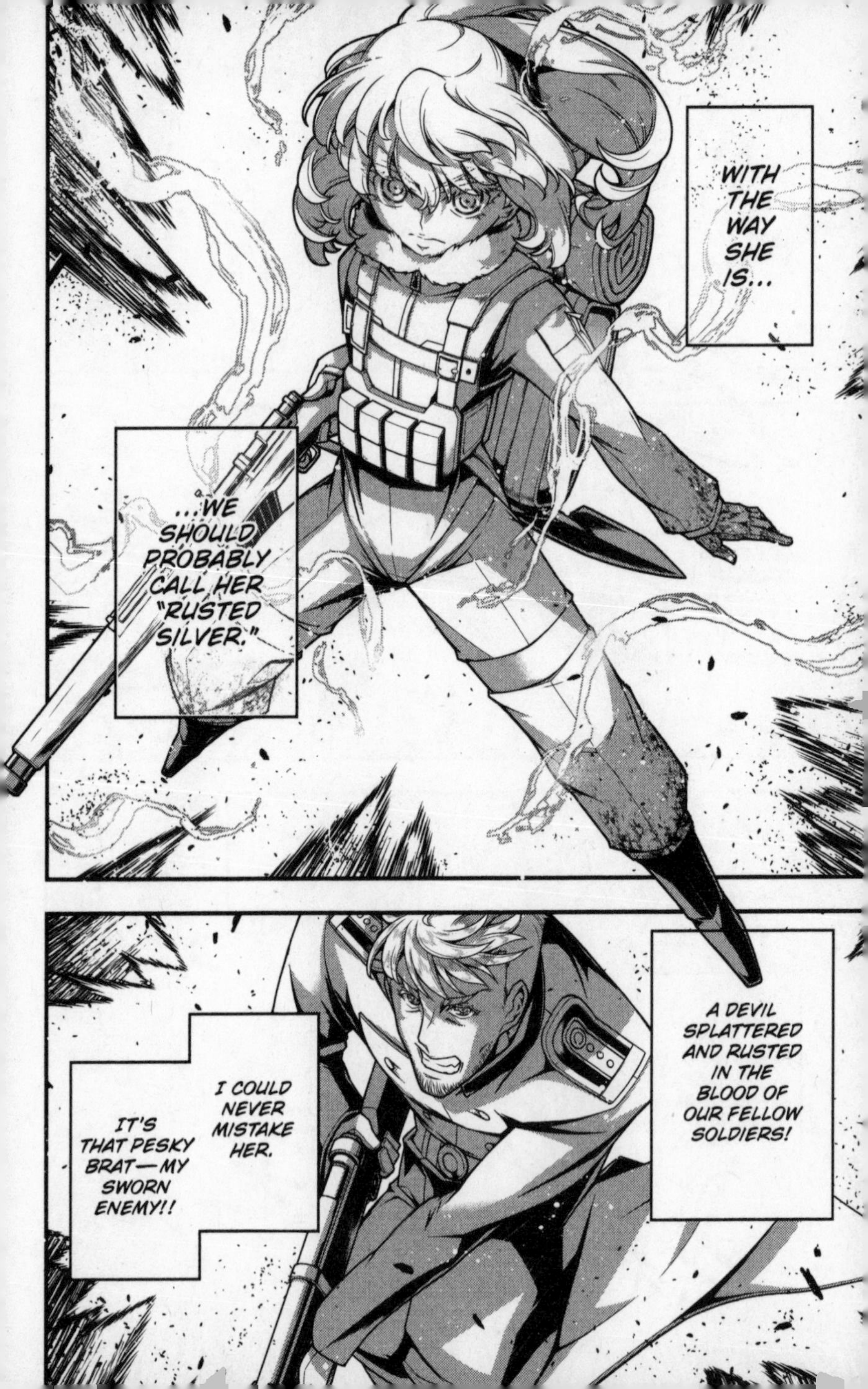
WITH THE WAY SHE IS...
...WE SHOULD PROBABLY CALL HER "RUSTED SILVER."
A DEVIL SPLATTERED AND RUSTED IN THE BLOOD OF OUR FELLOW SOLDIERS!
I COULD NEVER MISTAKE HER.
IT'S THAT PESKY BRAT—MY SWORN ENEMY!!

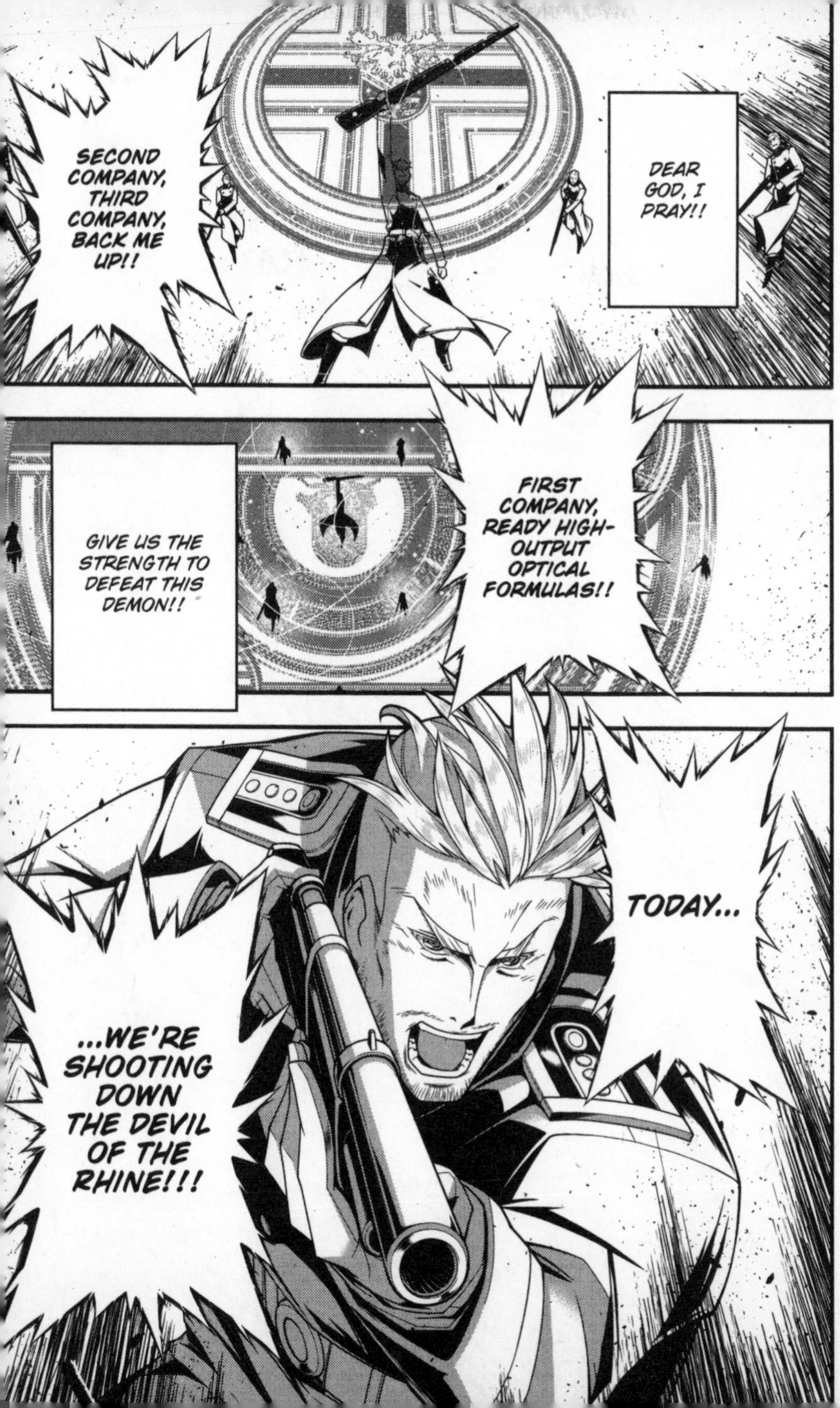
DEAR GOD, I PRAY!!
SECOND COMPANY, THIRD COMPANY, BACK ME UP!!
FIRST COMPANY, READY HIGH-OUTPUT OPTICAL FORMULAS!!
GIVE US THE STRENGTH TO DEFEAT THIS DEMON!!
TODAY...
...WE'RE SHOOTING DOWN THE DEVIL OF THE RHINE!!!

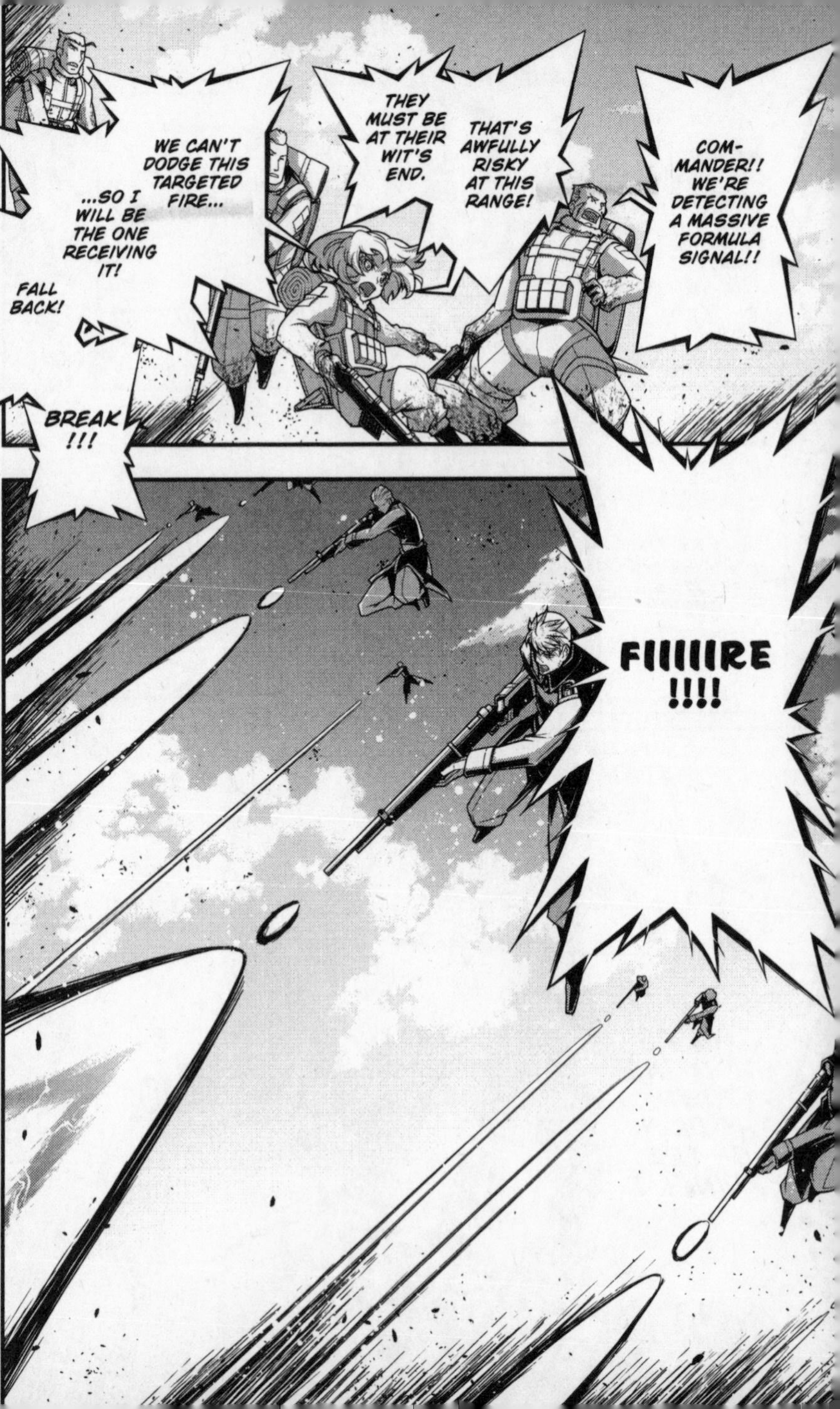
COM-MANDER!! WE'RE DETECTING A MASSIVE FORMULA SIGNAL!!
THAT'S AWFULLY RISKY AT THIS RANGE!
THEY MUST BE AT THEIR WIT'S END.
WE CAN'T DODGE THIS TARGETED FIRE...
...SO I WILL BE THE ONE RECEIVING IT!
FALL BACK!
BREAK!!!
FIIIIIRE!!!!

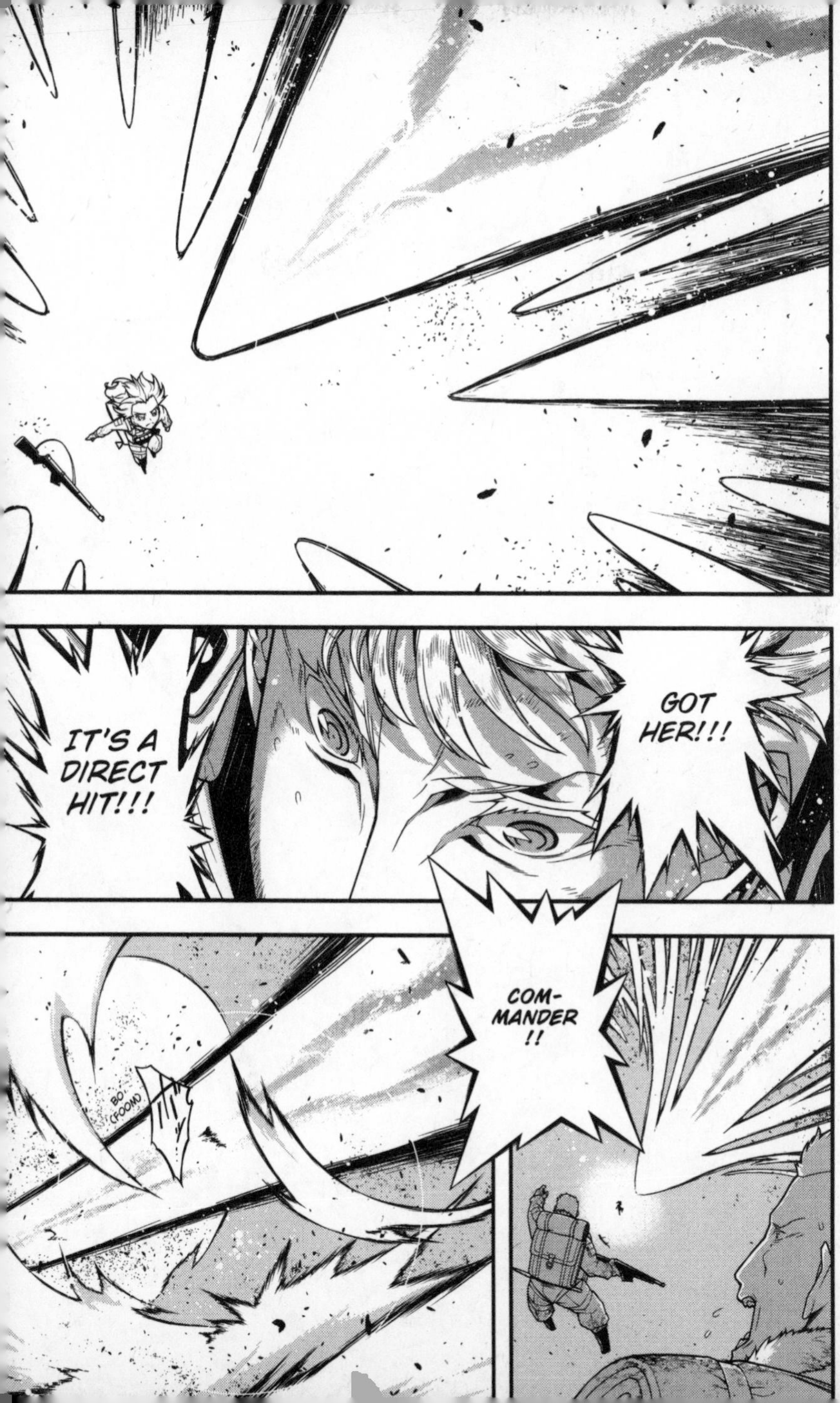
GOT HER!!!
IT'S A DIRECT HIT!!!
COM-MANDER !!
BO
(FOOM)

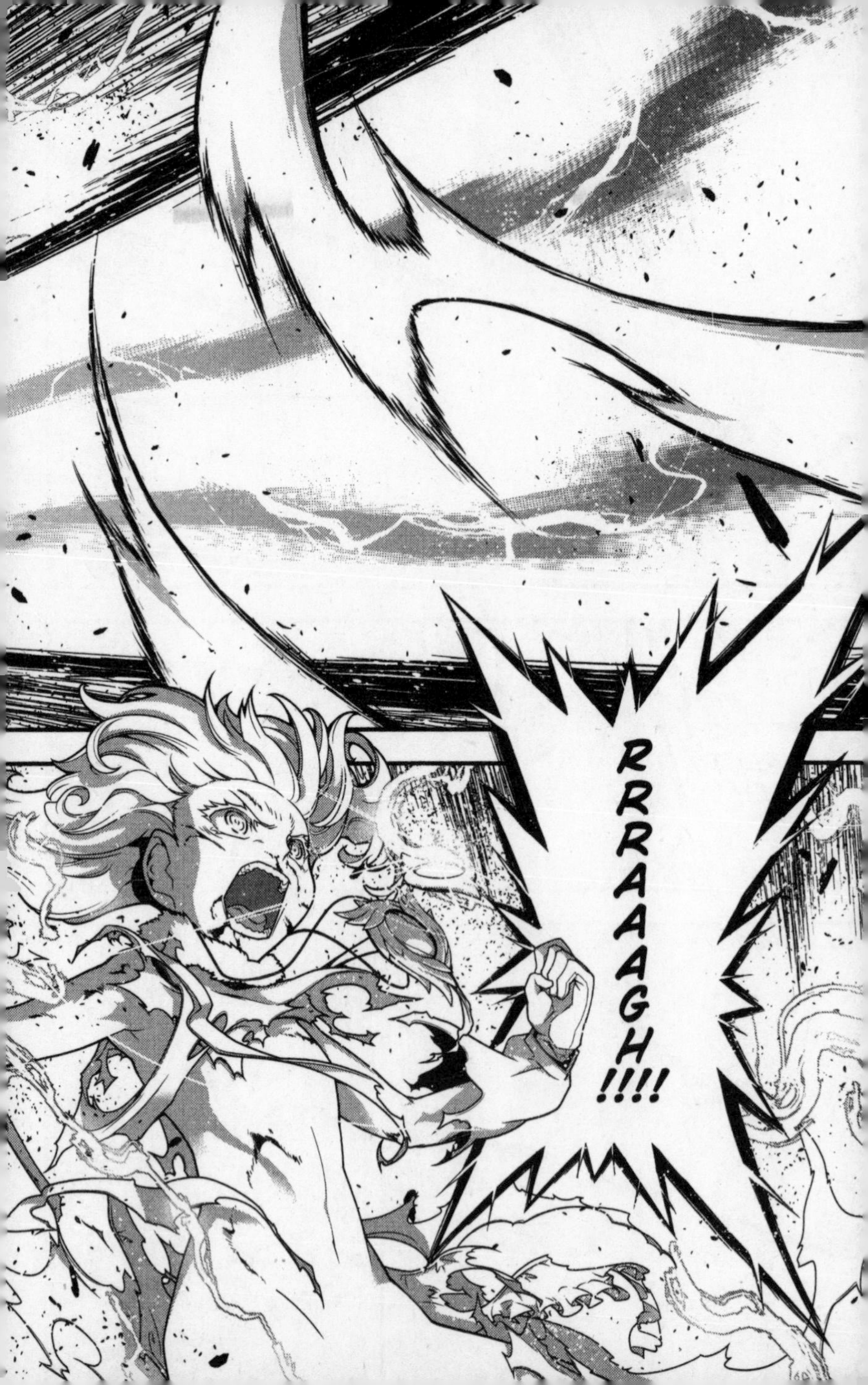
RRRAAAAGH!!!!

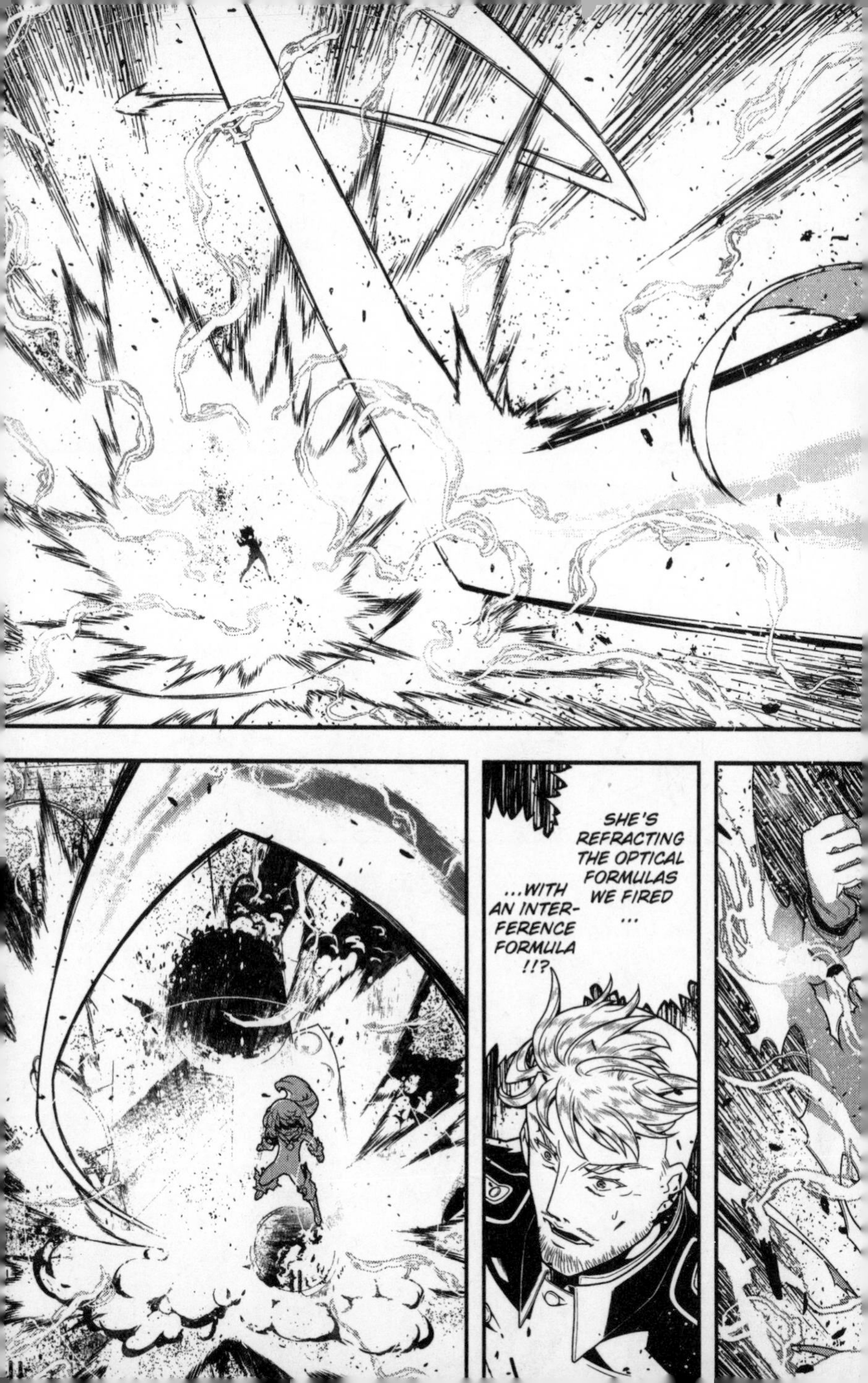
SHE'S REFRACTING THE OPTICAL FORMULAS WE FIRED ...
...WITH AN INTER-FERENCE FORMULA !!?

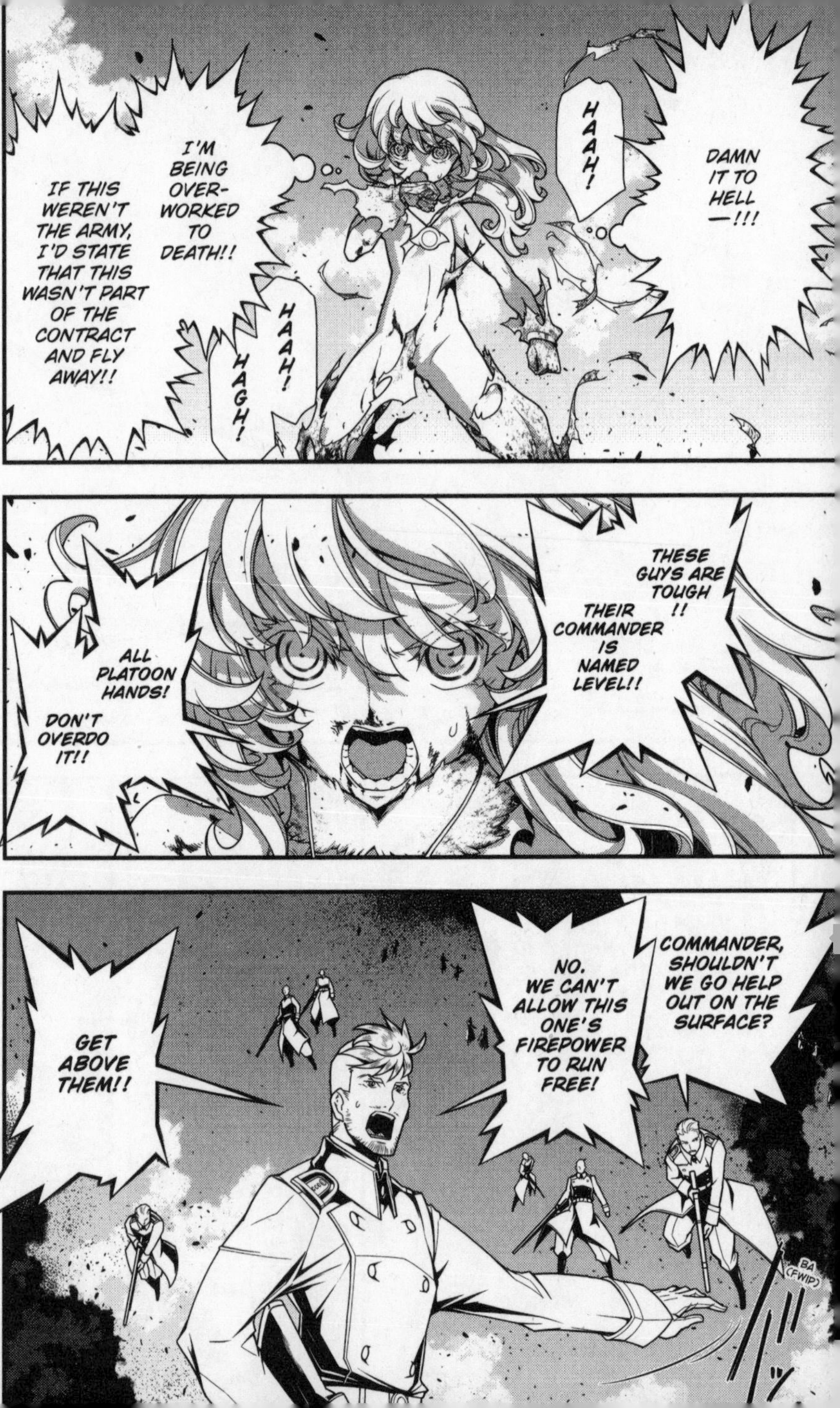
DAMN IT TO HELL—!!!
HAAAH!
I'M BEING OVER-WORKED TO DEATH!!
HAAAH! HAGH!
IF THIS WEREN'T THE ARMY, I'D STATE THAT THIS WASN'T PART OF THE CONTRACT AND FLY AWAY!!
THESE GUYS ARE TOUGH!!
THEIR COMMANDER IS NAMED LEVEL!!
ALL PLATOON HANDS!
DON'T OVERDO IT!!
COMMANDER, SHOULDN'T WE GO HELP OUT ON THE SURFACE?
NO. WE CAN'T ALLOW THIS ONE'S FIREPOWER TO RUN FREE!
GET ABOVE THEM!!
BA (FWIP)

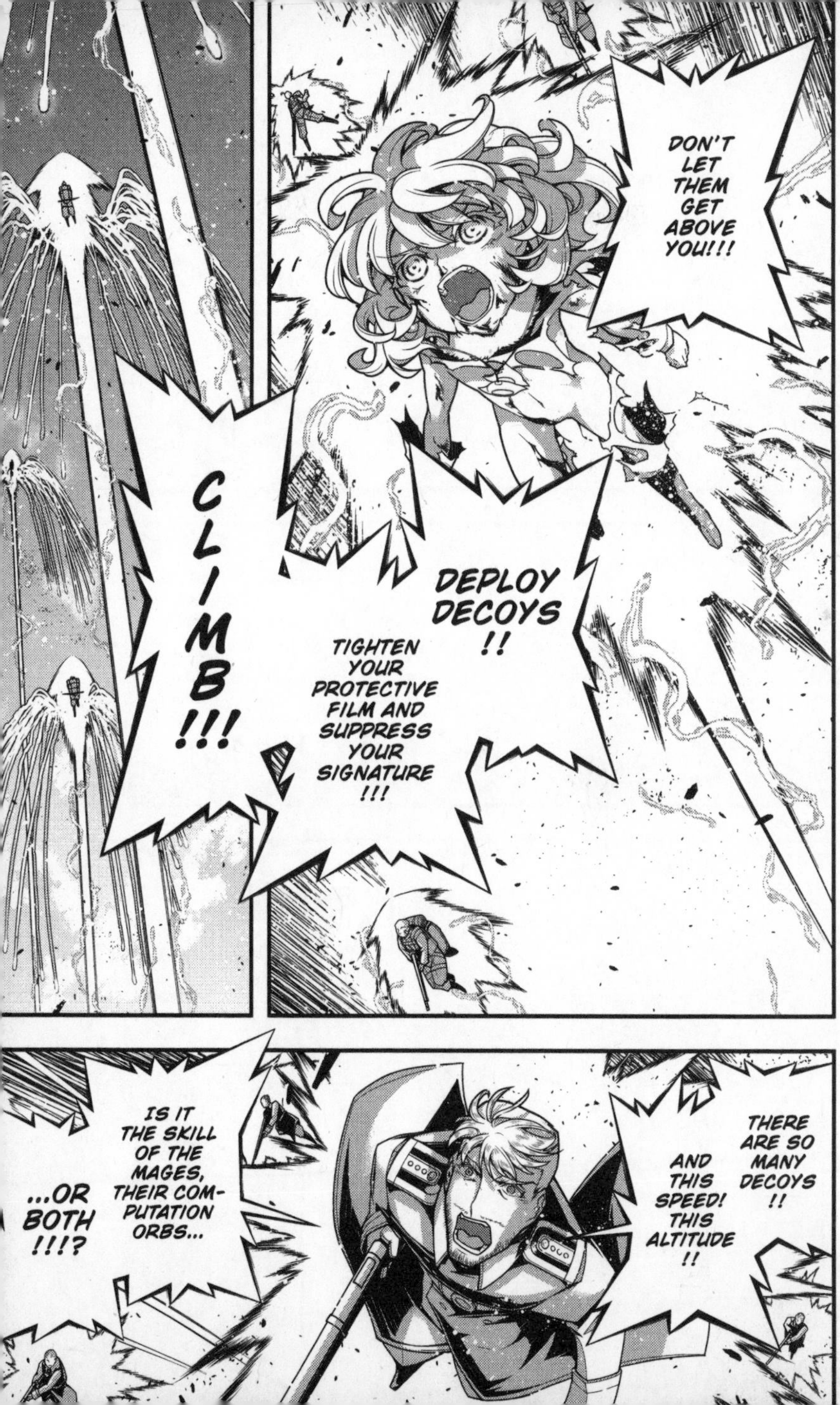
DON'T LET THEM GET ABOVE YOU!!!
DEPLOY DECOYS!!
TIGHTEN YOUR PROTECTIVE FILM AND SUPPRESS YOUR SIGNATURE!!!
CLIMB!!!
THERE ARE SO MANY DECOYS!!
AND THIS SPEED! THIS ALTITUDE!!
IS IT THE SKILL OF THE MAGES, THEIR COMPUTATION ORBS...
...OR BOTH!!!?

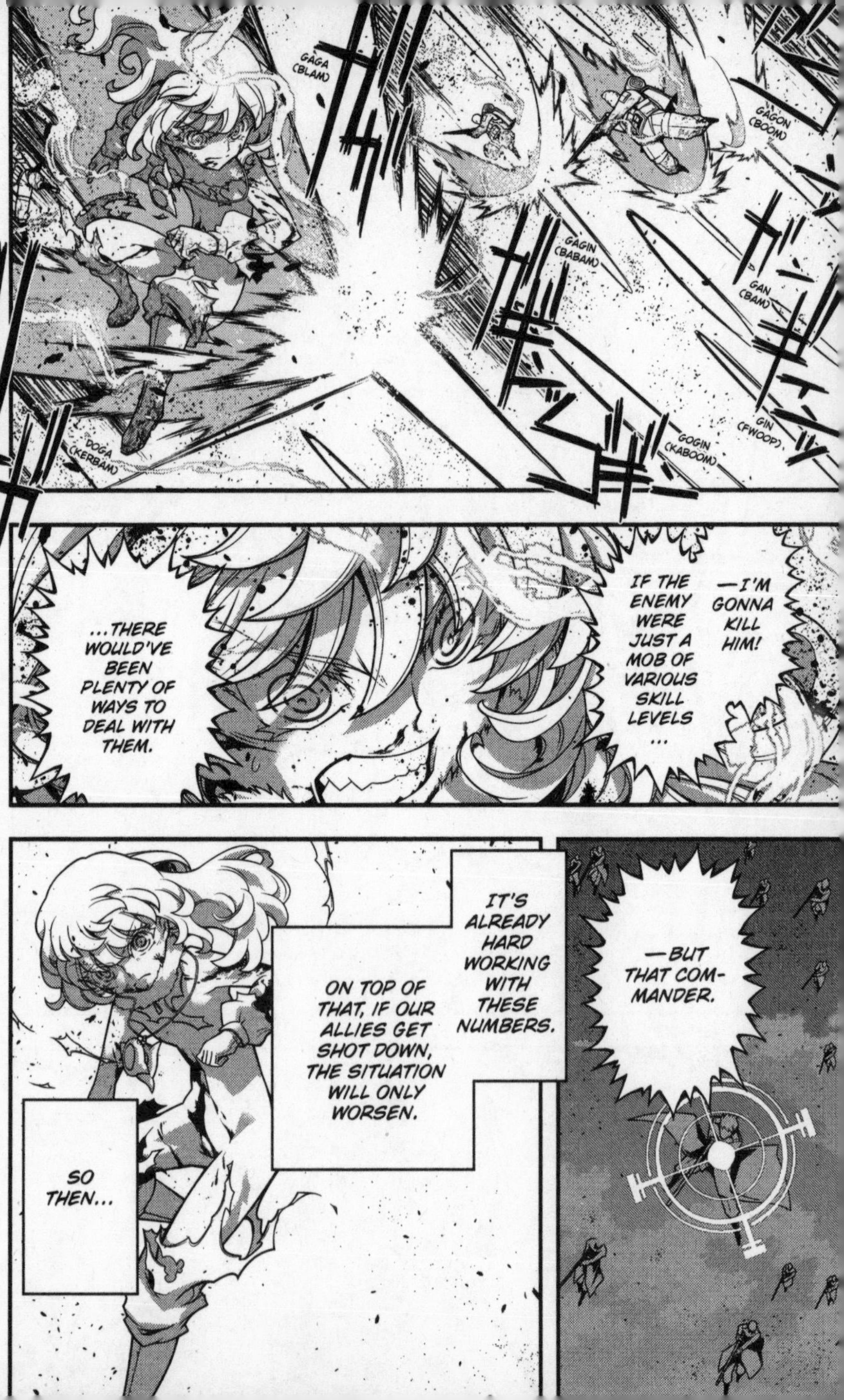
GAGON (BOOM)
GAGA (BLAM)
GAN (BAM)
GAGIN (BABAM)
GIN (FWOOP)
GOGIN (KABOOM)
DOGA (KERBAM)
—I'M GONNA KILL HIM!
IF THE ENEMY WERE JUST A MOB OF VARIOUS SKILL LEVELS...
...THERE WOULD'VE BEEN PLENTY OF WAYS TO DEAL WITH THEM.
—BUT THAT COMMANDER.
IT'S ALREADY HARD WORKING WITH THESE NUMBERS.
ON TOP OF THAT, IF OUR ALLIES GET SHOT DOWN, THE SITUATION WILL ONLY WORSEN.
SO THEN...

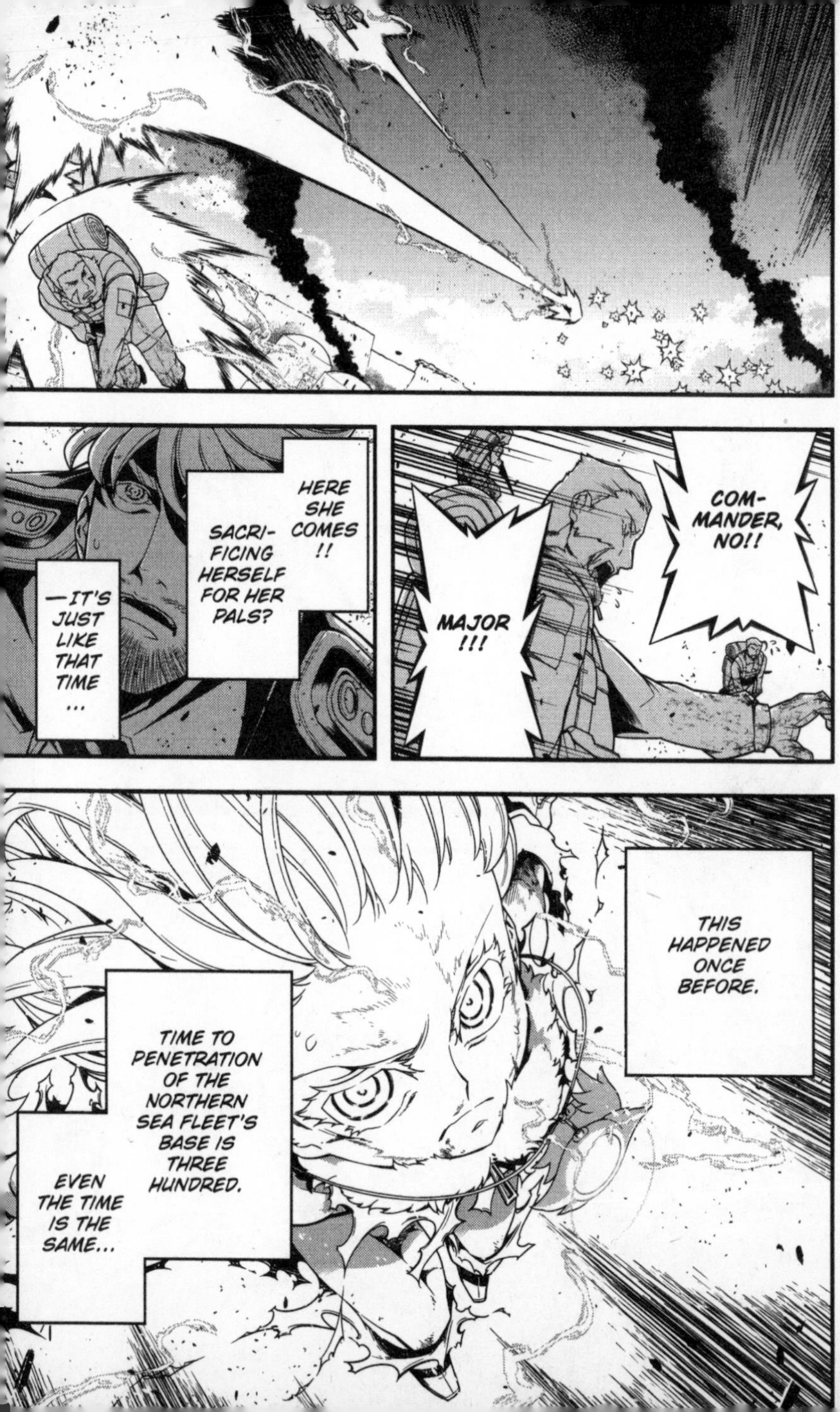
COM-MANDER, NO!!
MAJOR!!!
HERE SHE COMES!!
SACRI-FICING HERSELF FOR HER PALS?
—IT'S JUST LIKE THAT TIME...
THIS HAPPENED ONCE BEFORE.
TIME TO PENETRATION OF THE NORTHERN SEA FLEET'S BASE IS THREE HUNDRED.
EVEN THE TIME IS THE SAME...

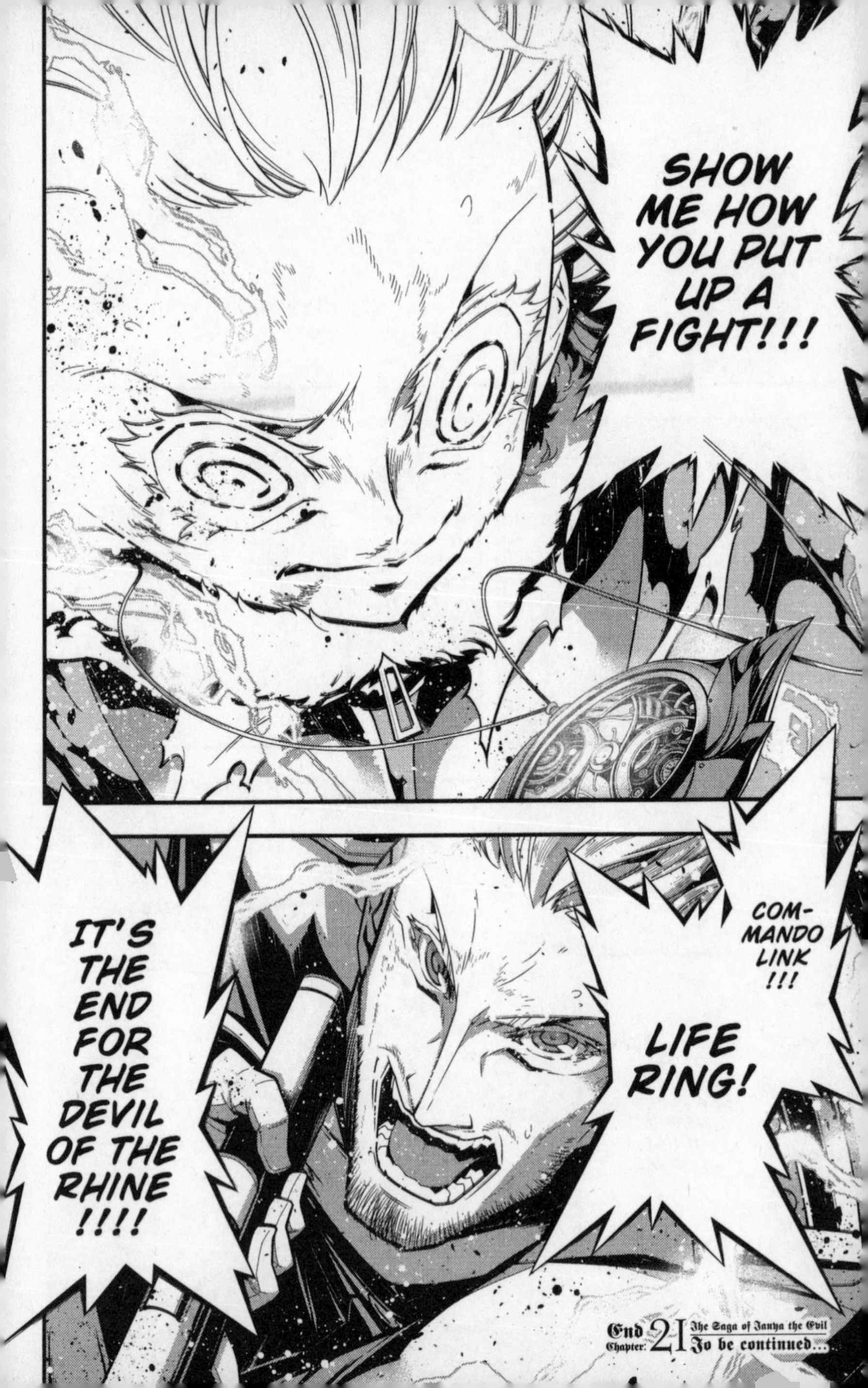
SHOW ME HOW YOU PUT UP A FIGHT!!!
COM-MANDO LINK!!!
LIFE RING!
IT'S THE END FOR THE DEVIL OF THE RHINE!!!!
End Chapter: 21 The Saga of Tanya the Evil To be continued...

The Saga of
Tanya the Evil

07

Original Story: Carlo Zen   Art: Chika Tojo
Character Design: Shinobu Shinotsuki

Special Thanks

Carlo Zen

Shinobu Shinotsuki

Takamaru

KURI

Miira

Yamatatsu

Agatha

Kuuko

Mizuhara Yuuki

THE SAGA OF TANYA THE EVIL 07

ORIGINAL STORY: Carlo Zen

ART: Chika Tojo ❧ CHARACTER DESIGN: Shinobu Shinotsuki

Translation: Emily Balistrieri ❧ Lettering: Rochelle Gancio

YOUJO SENKI Vol. 7
©Chika TOJO 2017
©2013 Carlo ZEN
First published in Japan in 2017 by KADOKAWA CORPORATION, Tokyo.
English translation rights arranged with KADOKAWA CORPORATION, Tokyo
through TUTTLE-MORI AGENCY, INC., Tokyo.

Yen Press
150 West 30th Street, 19th Floor
New York, NY 10001

Visit us at yenpress.com
facebook.com/yenpress
twitter.com/yenpress
yenpress.tumblr.com
instagram.com/yenpress

First Yen Press Edition: July 2019

Yen Press is an imprint of Yen Press, LLC.
The Yen Press name and logo are trademarks of Yen Press, LLC.

Library of Congress Control Number: 2017954161

ISBNs: 978-1-9753-5778-8 (paperback)
978-1-9753-5779-5 (ebook)

10 9 8 7 6 5 4 3 2 1

WOR

Printed in the United States of America